W9-DEA-811

ANATOMY

OF A CRUSADE

1213–1221

THE MIDDLE AGES

a series edited by

EDWARD PETERS

Henry Charles Lea Professor of Medieval History
University of Pennsylvania

ANATOMY

OF A CRUSADE

1213–1221

JAMES M. POWELL

upp

University of Pennsylvania Press

Philadelphia   1986

FRONTISPIECE: Pope Innocent III. Fragment of a
mosaic from the Constantinian Basilica of St. Peter,
Vatican. (Ladner, *Papstbildnisse*, 4:2, 60. Alinari/Art
Resource, New York)

Library of Congress Cataloging-in-Publication Data

Powell, James M.
　Anatomy of a crusade, 1213–1221.

　(The Middle Ages)
　Bibliography: p.
　Includes index.
　1. Crusades—Fifth, 1218–1221.　I. Title.
II. Series.
D165.P68　1986　　　940.1'84　　　86-11403
ISBN 0-8122-8025-3 (Alk. paper)

John's Book

CONTENTS

APPENDIXES

LIST OF FIGURES
AND TABLES

MAPS AND FIGURES

TABLES

ACKNOWLEDGMENTS

Support for research on this topic came from Syracuse University, which granted me leave in spring 1980, as well as from the Graduate School of the university, the Senate Research Fund, the Appleby-Mosher Fund of the Maxwell School, and the American Philosophical Society. Inter-Nationes provided a valuable opportunity for research in Germany. I would also like to express special thanks to Dean Guthrie Birkhead of the Maxwell School for his continued interest in my work.

My enormous debt to libraries also begins at Syracuse. Mrs. Dorcas MacDonald and her staff were successful in the great majority of cases in getting hard-to-find volumes on interlibrary loan. Meod Milac, Associate Director for Collection Development, and Marcella Stark, Bibliographer, were able to add numerous works to our crusade collection. Mrs. Molly Fuller cheerfully helped to make them more immediately accessible. Professor Giles Constable kindly permitted me to use the facilities at Dumbarton Oaks. Among foreign libraries and archives consulted, I wish especially to thank the staffs of the Archivio Segreto Vaticano, Sala di Referenza in the Biblioteca Nazionale in Florence, of the Gennadion Library at the American Academy in Athens, of the Staatsbibliothek in Munich, and of the École française d'archéologie and the Franciscan Institute of Oriental Studies in Cairo. In Bologna, Florence, Lucca, and Palermo, the archivists were most generous of their time and considerate of my needs. In particular, I would like to thank Monsignor Ghilarducci of the Archivio arcivescovile in Lucca for his great kindness.

Numerous colleagues and friends have aided this project. David Abulafia, Steven Epstein, Benjamin Kedar, and M. S. Omron furnished valuable information. In addition, Ben was an excellent guide in Jerusalem. Jeremy Johns and H. Houben were most helpful, too. Franco Cardini, Paolo Delogù, Giosuè Musca (the Director of the Centro di Studi normanno-svevi at the Università di Bari), and Cataldo Roccaro (of the Officina di Studi Medievali in Palermo) were kind enough to invite me to give papers based on this research. James John came through in a number of emergencies. Kenneth Pennington and Donald Queller read the entire manuscript at different stages in its development and made important contributions to its improvement. Mrs. Jane Frost typed the manuscript. Michael Markowski assisted with the computer study and the bibliography. Finally, my wife and children have continued the support I have received from them for many years.

ABBREVIATIONS

The following list includes only those citations in the notes and appendixes that differ from the listing in the bibliography.

AAL	Archivio arcivescovile. Lucca.
Ann. Dunst.	*Annales Prioratus de Dunstaplia.*
AOL	*Archives de l'orient latin.*
Arc. Poitou	*Archives historiques de Poitou.*
ASBRG	Archivio di Stato. Bologna. Registro Grosso.
ASF	Archivio di Stato. Florence.
ASL	Archivio di Stato. Lucca.
B	Röhricht, Reinhold. *Beiträge zur Geschichte der Kreuzzüge.* vol. 2 only.
BEOC	Bibliothêque de l'école de chartes.
Beyer	*Urkundenbuch zur Geschichte der mittelrheinischen Territorien.*
BF	Böhmer, Johann F. *Acta Imperii selecta.*
Blanc.	Delley de Blancmesnil, Alphonse Leon de. *Notice sur quelques anciens titres.*
Book of Fees	Great Britain. Exchequer. *Liber Feodorum.*
Brequigny	*Table chronologique des diplomes. chartes, titres et actes . . .*

BSSS	*Biblioteca della società storica subalpina.*
Calendar	*The Letters of Innocent III concerning England and Wales.*
Cart. Cockersand	Cockersand Abbey. *The Chartulary.*
Cart. Solesmes	*Cartulaire des abbayes de St. Pierre de la Couture et de St. Pierre de Solesmes.*
Cart. Talmond	Talmont. France (Vendée). Abbaye de Talmont. *Cartulaire de l'abbaye de Talmond.*
CDOT	*Codex Diplomaticus Ordinis sanctae Mariae Teutonicorum.*
Cholet	*Cartulaire de l'abbaye de St. Étienne de Baigne.*
Cod. Salem.	*Codex Diplomaticus Salemitanus.*
Cod. Wang.	*Codex Wangianus.*
Coggeshall	Radulphus de Coggeshall. *Chronicon Anglicanum.*
Coventry	Walter of Coventry. *Memoriale.*
CPO	*Le carte della prevostura d'Oulx.*
D	Röhricht, Reinhold. *Die Deutschen im Heiligen Lande.*
DCV	*Documenti del commercio veneziano nei secoli XI–XIII.*
DHGE	*Dictionnaire d'histoire et de géographie ecclésiastique.*
Döbner *UB*	*Urkundenbuch der Stadt Hildesheim.*
DSI	*Documenti di storia italiana.*
DTC	*Dictionaire de theologie catholique.*
Ennen	*Quellen zur Geschichte der Stadt Köln.*
Eracles	*L'Estoire d'Eracles empereur.*
Ernoul	*Chronique d'Ernoul et de Bernard le trésorier.*
Fejér	*Codex Diplomaticus Hungariae.*
FK	Röhricht, Reinhold. *Studien zur Geschichte des fünften Kreuzzuges.*
FRA	Fontes Rerum Austriacarum.
Goerz	*Mittelrheinische Regesten.*
H-B	Huillard-Bréholles, Jean L. A. *Historia Diplomatica Friderici secundi.* . . .
Haupt, Neidhart	Neidhart von Reuenthal.
Hennes	*CDOT*

Horoy	Honorius III. *Opera Omnia.*
Hugo	*Sacrae Antiquitatis Monumenta.*
Jac.	Jacobus de Vitriaco. *Lettres.*
Janicke	*Urkundenbuch des Hochstifts Hildesheim.*
Just. Eyre (Glouc.)	Great Britain. Curia Regis. *Rolls of the Justices in Eyre . . . Gloucestershire.*
Just. Eyre (Linc.)	Great Britain. Curia Regis. *Rolls of the Justices in Eyre . . . Lincolnshire.*
Just. Eyre (Yorks.)	Great Britain. Curia Regis. *Rolls of the Justices in Eyre . . . Yorkshire.*
Klempin, *UB*	*Pommersches Urkundenbuch.*
Lahrkamp	Lahrkamp, Helmut. "Mittelalterliche Jerusalemfahrten. . . ."
Lay.	*Layettes du trésor des chartes.*
Levi	*Registri dei Cardinali Ugolino d'Ostia e Ottaviano degli Ubaldini.*
LFDP	*Liber Focorum Districtus Pistorie.*
LfTK	*Lexikon für Theologie und Kirche.*
Mahille	*Cartulaire de Marmoutier pour le Dunois.*
Meiller	*Regesta Archiepiscoporum Salisburgensium.*
MGH Ep.	*Monumenta Germaniae Historica. Epistolae.*
MGHSS	*Monumenta Germaniae Historica. Scriptores in folio.*
Mon. Boic.	*Monumenta Boica.*
Morice	*Mémoires pour servir de preuves à l'histoire ecclésiastique et civile de Bretagne.*
Mulv.	*Regesta Archiepiscopatus Magdeburgensis.*
Ol.	Oliverus Scholasticus. *Die Schriften. . . .*
Pat. Rolls	Great Britain. Public Record Office. *Patent Rolls of the Reign of Henry III.*
PL	*Patrologia Latina.* J. P. Migne, ed.
Pott.	Potthast, A. *Regesta Pontificum Romanorum.*
Pr.	Pressutti, P. *Regesta Honorii Papae III.*

QFAIB	*Quellen und Forschungen aus italienischen Archiven und Bibliotheken.*
Reg. Boic.	Lang, Karl Heinrich. *Regesta, sive Rerum Boicarum Autographa.*
Reg. Markgraf. Baden	*Regesten der Markgrafen von Baden und Hachberg.*
Rg V	*Regestum Volaterranum.*
RHC Occ.	*Recueil des historiens de croisades. Occidentaux.*
RHC Or.	*Recueil des historiens de croisades. Orientale.*
RHGF	*Recueil des historiens de Gaule et de France.*
RISS	*Rerum Italicarum Scriptores.* New Edition.
RLC	Great Britain. Record Commission. *Rotuli literrarum clausarum.*
Roberts	Great Britain. Public Record Office. *Calendarium genealogicum.*
Rodenberg	*MGH Epistolae Selectae Saeculi XIII.*
ROL	*Revue de l'orient latin.*
RS	Rolls Series.
Sassovivo	*Le carte dell'abbazia di Santa Croce di Sassovivo.*
Sav.	Savioli, L. V. *Annali Bolognese.*
Schles. UB	*Schlesisches Urkundenbuch.*
Seibertz	*Urkundenbuch zur Landes und Rechtsgeschichte des Herzogthums Westfalen.*
Shirley	*Royal and other Historical Letters illustrative of the Reign of Henry III.*
Sied.	Siedschlag, Beatrice. *English Participation in the Crusades, 1150–1220.*
Somerset Pleas	Great Britain. Curia Regis. *Somersetshire Pleas.*
SS	Röhricht, Reinhold. *Quinti Belli Sacri Scriptores.*
Strehlke	*Tabulae Ordinis Theutonici.*
T	Röhricht, Reinhold. *Testimonia minora . . .*
UB Bern	Zeerleder, Karl. *Urkunden für die Geschichte der Stadt Bern.*

UB Diessen	Schlögl, Waldemar. *Die Traditionen und Urkunden des Stifts Diessen.*
UB Frauen	*Urkundenbuch des Unser Lieben Frauen . . .*
UB Meck.	*Mecklenburgisches Urkundenbuch.*
UB Sud-Oldenburg	Ruthning, Gustav. *Urkundenbuch von Sud-Oldenburg.*
Wauters	*Table chronologique des chartes et diplomes . . . Belgique.*
Wendover	Roger of Wendover. *Flores Historiarum.*
Wirt. UB	*Wirtembergisches Urkundenbuch.*
ZGO	*Zeitschrift für die Geschichte des Oberrheins.*
Zahn	*Urkundenbuch des Herzogtums Steiermark.*

INTRODUCTION

The Fifth Crusade had its beginnings in 1213, when Pope Innocent III announced his intention to summon a council of the church to meet in 1215 to discuss reform of the church and the promotion of the crusade. It ended in Egypt in 1221 on the Nile road between Damietta and al-Manṣūrah with the surrender of a major part of the crusader army to the forces of the sultan, al-Kāmil. Its failure marked the last time that a medieval pope would succeed in mounting a major expedition for the liberation of the Holy Land. This crusade involved more extensive planning and a greater commitment than any of its predecessors. Preachers carried its message to virtually all parts of Europe, from Scandinavia to Sicily, from Ireland to Poland. Its ranks were filled with men—and women—of myriad tongues. The greatest charismatic of the age, Francis of Assisi, visited the crusader camp. Through long periods of frustration and intense suffering, the crusader army persevered. In desperation over the threat it posed, the sultan offered several times to exchange Jerusalem for the conquered city of Damietta, the "key to Egypt," but the crusaders refused. Finally, with victory seemingly in their grasp, they lost everything. Yet another disaster had been added to the heavy burden of failure that already weighed on the crusade movement and its supporters because of the meagre results of the Second and Third crusades and the turning of the Fourth Crusade from its goal in the East to the conquest of Constantinople and much of the Byzantine Empire.

Despite the intense interest among modern scholars in the history of the crusade, there has been no previous monograph dedicated completely to the Fifth Crusade, if we except the lengthy essay published by Hermann Hoogeweg a century ago.[1] Shortly before Hoogeweg's work appeared, that indefatigable harvester of crusade sources, Reinhold Röhricht, had begun to collect materials relating to this expedition, which he published in three separate volumes between 1879 and 1891.[2] The major beneficiaries of this industry have been the authors of the numerous general histories of the crusades, especially those who have included lengthier discussions of the Fifth Crusade in their multivolume studies.[3] The most detailed treatment in English is that written by Thomas C. Van Cleve for Kenneth Setton's *History of the Crusades*.[4] Among shorter histories, the best account is that found in Hans Eberhard Mayer's excellent synthesis *The Crusades*. There have been, however, numerous books and articles devoted to particular aspects of this crusade or individuals among its leaders. Helmut Roscher's *Papst Innocenz III und die Kreuzzüge* is a pathbreaking study of the development of that pope's idea of crusade and of the manner in which he worked to carry it out so long as he lived. Since Innocent died in 1216, however, Roscher has little to say about the implementation of the crusade by his successor, Pope Honorius III. Among crusade leaders, the cardinal legate, Pelagius, has attracted continuing attention and controversy.[5] Other studies have dealt with John of Brienne, the king of Jerusalem; James of Vitry, the distinguished crusade preacher and bishop of Acre; and Robert Courçon, the papal legate who preached the crusade in France.[6] There is a considerable literature devoted to Francis of Assisi's visit to the East.[7] The Fifth Crusade has also attracted the attention of genealogists and historians interested in crusade participation.[8] Special studies on canon law, preaching, and finance have contributed to our understanding of its place within the broader movement, as do those general works dealing with the developing ideology of the crusade in the twelfth and thirteenth centuries.[9]

The absence of a specific history of this crusade has been due not as much to a lack of interest as to the absorption of scholars with these other approaches. Recently, however, there has been a renewed concern with individual crusades, and this, combined with other trends in recent research, has demonstrated the need for a study of the Fifth Crusade by highlighting its importance in the history of the crusade movement in the late twelfth and early thirteenth centuries.[10]

The dominant interpretations of the Fifth Crusade have hitherto focussed on military history, emphasizing personality conflicts and decrying the lack of effective leadership that led to the defeat of the crusader army.[11] The leadership question, in both its political and military aspects, has exercised a continuing attraction for those interested in this crusade. As a consequence, most accounts have spent relatively little time on the background and preparation of the crusade. To a considerable degree, this approach reflects the attitudes found in contemporary chronicles and narratives that have provided the chief foundation for general histories of the crusades. From the time of Hoogeweg to the present, the figure of Cardinal Pelagius has remained central to these discussions. Although studies by Hassler, Donovan, and Mansilla have attempted to present Pelagius in a more favorable light, Mayer has not hesitated to lay a large part of the blame for the defeat of the crusaders at his door.[12] Likewise, the failure of Emperor Frederick II to fulfill his crusade vow has encouraged some historians to stress the tensions between the empire and papacy. For Van Cleve, papal-imperial conflict formed an ideological basis for Frederick's postponements of his vow to go on crusade and his quarrel with Pope Gregory IX after Frederick's failure to depart in 1227.[13] Steven Runciman has been critical of the abilities of John of Brienne to provide the leadership needed by the crusader army at Damietta.[14] Even Roscher, who did not discuss the Fifth Crusade in any detail, concluded that it failed because of the national rivalries of the participants and the conflict between Pelagius and other leaders of the crusade.[15]

On a related question, opinion has been more divided. Van Cleve and Mayer have argued that Innocent III deliberately excluded the crowned heads of Europe from this crusade in order to keep it an exclusively papal enterprise.[16] Mayer maintained that Innocent was "most unpleasantly surprised when the young Hohenstaufen, Frederick II, took the cross in 1215."[17] Van Cleve regarded Frederick's action as a "declaration of independence from the papacy."[18] But Hans Martin Schaller suggested in 1957 that papal agents at Frederick's court both knew and approved of his assumption of the cross.[19] More recently, Roscher not only accepted Schaller's position, but argued that Innocent had tried to ensure the participation of King John of England in the crusade as well.[20] He stressed, however, that this crusade was a papal initiative and, to a large extent, a papal responsibility. The views of Mayer and Roscher have moved beyond this question, taking into account changes that had occurred in the papal office, especially under the forceful leadership of Innocent III. While it is true that the crusade, since its inception, had been the affair of the popes, no previous pope had marshalled the resources of his office and of the whole church so vigorously in its behalf. Mayer has suggested that Innocent was at least partially motivated by a desire to use the crusade to realize "his hierarchical ideas."[21] But he also recognized that this pope was sensitive to popular support for the crusade movement. A growing body of literature on the evolution of the idea of crusade in the eleventh and twelfth centuries had already tied its development to an emergent lay spirituality, which aspired to the monastic ideal of "imitatio Christi" and its pursuit in the gospel-inspired *vita apostolica,* with emphasis on evangelical poverty.[22] The most original contributions of Mayer and Roscher have been in identifying the continuing influence of these ideas on the crusade, and especially in delineating Innocent III's own debt to them in the formulation of his ideas. The import of this research has shifted interest from the military history of the crusade toward the study of the society from which the movement sprang.

The present study is an attempt to carry this approach still further and at the same time to explore a number of problems that have not yet received the attention they deserve. In short, it builds on previous work on organization, preaching, and finance and develops previously neglected evidence concerning the recruitment and composition of the crusader army. This research provides the background and framework for a detailed narrative that places this crusade in the context of the movement as a whole. If there is any overriding theme, it is founded on an effort to seek a better understanding of the motives behind the crusade, the commitments made by so many in its behalf, and the reasons for its failure through an investigation of its relation to western European society in the late twelfth and early thirteenth centuries.

Although we now have a good idea of Innocent's strong commitment and careful planning for the Fifth Crusade, much of the implementation of his program remains in shadow. Yet this aspect of his plan may well represent a more original and significant contribution to the crusade movement than his ideological formulations. While he certainly possessed an almost intuitive grasp of the connections between his program and the spiritual currents that enveloped the religious movements of his age, his great genius was as an innovative executor of a broadly conceived vision of the crusade. In some areas, such as the selection of crusade procurators, he drew on the administrative experience of the Roman curia.[23] But the full significance of the roles of crusade legates, commissioners, and preachers has yet to be explored. Above all, previous assumptions regarding the relationship between preaching and recruitment have led to a neglect of the latter topic, which is so important for an understanding of such fundamental questions as the degree of popular interest in the crusade, the composition of the crusader army, and the effects of the recruitment effort on the outcome of the crusade. Through a number of case studies, I have tried to show that the recruitment process was much more complex than previously believed. Moreover, I have made a special effort to trace the relationship between the papal peace program, enacted to promote the crusade, and recruitment.

Techniques developed by social historians and others have enabled historians to pursue questions regarding the behavior of social groups in greater depth and precision than was previously possible. Through a computer-assisted analysis of information about origins, status, arrivals, and death or return of more than eight hundred individuals known to have taken vows to go on the Fifth Crusade, it has been possible to study the composition of the crusader army in somewhat greater detail, to see where its components originated, in what kind of groups they were organized, and how these functioned within the crusade host.[24] A study of arrivals and, to a limited degree, of departures has shed light on the manpower problem that confronted crusade leaders. An examination of mortality rates has added another dimension to research on this question. As a result of these studies, it has been possible to recast the leadership question, which has been central in the explanation of the outcome of this crusade, by placing it against the background of the decision-making process and the options that were available to the leaders at various stages in the crusade.

It is no longer possible to view the Fifth Crusade merely in light of a lack of effective military leadership or as an indicator of the failure of the spiritual and temporal authorities within medieval society to work together in behalf of the crusade. Rather, we have to consider the capacity of western Europe to carry out the ambitious papal program developed between 1213 and 1215. Further, we are confronted with the reality that the papal plan for this crusade had implications that went well beyond its military goals. The linkages between the reform program of the papacy and the crusade, which had become increasingly more explicit during the twelfth century, now achieved a unity so intimate that failure of the crusade could affect the capacity of the papacy to provide effective leadership for the reform of the church. The future of the crusade movement was itself at risk. To write the history of the Fifth Crusade, therefore, is a task that goes well beyond the story of the disastrous defeat of the crusader army at Damietta. It involves an effort to examine the nature of the commitment of western European society to the crusade. The results of that examination indicate that the crusade was a victim of the increasing concentration of many western secular leaders on domestic priorities rather than on the universalism of the papal agenda for Latin Christendom.

As earlier writers have long recognized, it is possible to understand the origins of the Fifth Crusade only by studying its relationship to the two previous crusades that occurred during Innocent's reign. One was the Fourth Crusade, which he summoned in 1198; the other was the spontaneous outburst known as the Children's Crusade. The former was one of the major disappointments of the pope's pontificate; the latter showed the depth of popular frustration over the failure of the highest leaders of medieval society to liberate the Holy Places from the hands of the Moslems. The loss of Jerusalem to Saladin in 1187 and the meagre result of the Third Crusade, led by Frederick Barbarossa, Philip Augustus, and Richard the Lion-Hearted, at first shocked Europeans and then disappointed their hopes for the recapture of Jerusalem. The Third Crusade accomplished little more than to place the crusade more firmly on the agenda of Latin Europe.

Nevertheless, it was not until 1198, early in the pontificate of Innocent III, that planning began for a new crusade. From the start, Innocent, at thirty-seven the youngest medieval pope, took a more active role in promoting the new crusade than had Gregory VIII, the pope at the time of the loss of Jerusalem to Saladin, or Clement III, who succeeded him in 1187. It soon became apparent that the secular rulers of the West would not participate in the new crusade. The succession to the imperial crown remained unsettled after the death of Henry VI in 1197, and England and France were at war. In 1199, Richard the Lion-Hearted died, and his brother John carried on that struggle. During the Third Crusade, Richard and other secular rulers had enacted taxes or otherwise assumed chief responsibility for the cost of the crusade. Since there was no likelihood of their participation, Innocent in 1199 proclaimed a tax of a fortieth on ecclesiastical incomes for one year. The preaching of the crusade met with its greatest response in France and Italy. The nobility of Champagne, many with a family tradition of participation in the crusade, were especially prominent, at least until the death of their count.[25] The most famous crusade preacher was Fulk of Neuilly, a parish priest who had studied at Paris, where he had imbibed many of the ideas of such reform-minded supporters of the crusade as Peter of Blois and Peter the Chanter. For him, "the true chosen ones" to achieve victory in the crusade through divine favor were the poor. The rich, led by the kings, had failed. This open appeal to those who advocated reform based on the evangelical virtues reflected their attitude that the future of the crusade depended more on moral preparation and divine favor than upon the power and wealth of secular rulers. It was a message with which the Paris-educated Innocent III could not help but be familiar.

The leaders of the crusade were optimistic, and they entered into a treaty with the Venetians for transport that reflected their estimate of the numbers who would flock to the cross. Donald Queller has compellingly described the problems confronting the crusaders from this point.[26] True to their agreement, the Venetians built ships and readied transport for the expected crusaders. But the projections of the leaders proved much too ambitious, and they found themselves unable to meet the payments required of them. Drawn into a web of intrigue and commitments, they first joined the Venetians in an attack on the Dalmatian port of Zara, to which the Venetians had laid claim. Successful in this endeavor, they were persuaded to aid Alexius IV, son of the deposed Byzantine emperor, in his bid to gain the throne of Constantinople. In return, he promised substantial aid for the crusade. The campaign to install Alexius in Constantinople was a success, but the results were disappointing. He was unable to deliver on most of his promises. The unhappy crusaders laid siege to the city and captured it in 1204. To the frustration of those who had already been disappointed by the meagre results of the Third Crusade was added this further failure. Few of the participants in this crusade journeyed on to the Holy Land. Moreover, a legacy of conflict between the Latin West and the Greek East received further stimulus from this event. Finally, the effort involved in trying to maintain the Latin conquests in Greece drained support from the crusade movement.

It was not merely the pope and the leadership of the church, or even the secular rulers, who felt the major impact of the diversion of the Fourth Crusade. These leaders were able to rationalize about the advantages, real or supposed, that sprang from the conquest of Constantinople. It was among the masses that disappointment was greatest. The failure of yet another crusade served to reinforce the view that Christians had not sufficiently prepared themselves to win God's support in their fight against the Moslems. Very likely, considerable dissatisfaction simmered after the failure of the Fourth Crusade. Whether this delayed reaction or some other trigger touched off the popular movements of the year 1212 is impossible to say. Already in the immediate aftermath of Pope Urban II's summons of the First Crusade in 1095 the so-called Peasants' Crusade had revealed the potential of the crusade idea to inflame the popular imagination, especially of those people already caught up in the early poverty movement. By the late twelfth and early thirteenth centuries, such currents were, if anything, broader and deeper. The potential for a mass response was great. Recently, Peter Raedts, in his revisionist study of the Children's Crusade, has argued that dissatisfaction with the failure of the rich and powerful to achieve the liberation of the Holy Land was a significant factor in its origination.[27]

The Children's Crusade has long evoked images of misguided enthusiasm and tragic consequences. For Paul Alphandéry, it was a pilgrimage of innocents.[28] Like the biblical Innocents, these too were led to betrayal, slavery, and slaughter. The works of Miccoli and Raedts, however, have questioned the traditional depiction of this movement as a children's crusade. Miccoli's reading of the evidence raised the question whether many of the participants were not adults rather than children. Raedts has further argued that the terms *puer* and *pueri* did not refer to children but to the class of dependents, and he has suggested a relationship of this group to the apostolic poverty movement.[29] He has rejected a Marxist view of the movement as a social protest against the rich and powerful based on class in favor of the position that these "poor" were acting from a fundamentally religious motivation. They saw themselves as the elect of God for the liberation of the Holy Land. Theirs was the authentic "imitatio Christi," they believed, and therefore God would surrender the Holy Land to them rather than to the rich and powerful.

The main thrust of these interpretations is that the Children's Crusade was a popular response to the failure of the crusades led by the kings and great magnates of western Europe. If true, this line of thought may help to explain some aspects of Innocent III's approach to the Fifth Crusade. Certainly it suggests a close relationship between the events of 1212 and the announcement of the council and the crusade in the following year. It is therefore valuable, to reexamine the movement in this light.

In the spring of 1212, shortly after Easter, masses of peasants, some members of the lower clergy, and perhaps some of higher station began to leave from the area around Cologne and head southward with the announced intention of liberating Jerusalem. Their numbers swelled as they moved through Trier and Speyer. About this time, a certain Nicholas, a youth but hardly a child, emerged as their leader. All along their path they were greeted with enthusiasm, fed, sheltered, and encouraged by the masses, though some among the clergy were critical of their judgment in thinking that they could succeed where their leaders had failed. They crossed into northern Italy by one of the Alpine passes and came to Piacenza. Apparently Innocent III had learned of their intentions and sent messengers to intercept them. There is no reliable record of what happened, but presumably he tried to discourage the unfit and the too young and to persuade the suitable to await an organized expedition. There is a suggestion of this, at least, in the story that he gave this advice to Nicholas, who later went on the Fifth Crusade in fulfillment of his vow. Of greater significance is the fact that the pope was apparently well informed regarding the nature and intent of this pilgrimage.

Shortly after the German group set out, a group of similar character left from the region around Vendôme and travelled perhaps to Paris or southward toward Marseilles. The account that records the arrival of these pilgrims in Paris says that they were sent back home by the king. Part of the tradition that describes their journey to Marseilles recounts how some found transport only to be shipwrecked. Merchants sold some of the survivors into slavery. Much less is securely known about the French group than about the Germans, and the later accounts already have the ring of legend. But we may be certain that the popular movement in the Rhineland at least had a counterpart in France.

On the eve of Innocent III's announcement of his intention to summon a council to discuss the reform of the church and the liberation of the Holy Land, an atmosphere of failure and frustration gripped the imagination of many among the lower classes. There was a clear need to examine and alter the agenda of the medieval church with respect to the crusade. At stake was the initiative the papacy had forged for itself during the course of the twelfth century. Western Europe was awaiting the response of the pope, and Innocent III grasped fully the need to go beyond the actions of his predecessors, but he was determined to do so only on the basis of a thorough rethinking and a detailed plan. He was not about to commit the church to precipitous action that might well end in yet another failure. It is this fundamental reevaluation of the crusade and the subsequent effort to carry out the resulting program that form the subject of this book.

NOTES

1. The lack of such an account was noted more than forty years ago by John L. LaMonte in "Some Problems in Crusading Historiography." See Hoogeweg, "Der Kreuzzug von Damiette, 1218–1221."

2. Röhricht, *Quinti Belli sacri scriptores minores, Testimonia minora de quinto bello sacro,* and *Studien zur Geschichte des fünften Kreuzzuges.* In the notes, these will be abbreviated as: *SS, T,* and *FK.*

3. The number of general histories of the crusades is legion. A listing of those published to the early 1960s may be found in Hans Eberhard Mayer, *Bibliographie zur Geschichte der Kreuzzüge,* 96–98, and the same author's "Literaturbericht über die Geschichte der Kreuzzüge," esp. 679–84.

4. Van Cleve, "The Fifth Crusade."

5. For a recent discussion of the leadership question, see my article "Honorius III and the Leadership of the Crusade." This article represents a preliminary stage in my research, but it is useful for certain of its arguments and its citation of the literature.

6. Boehm, *Johann von Brienne;* Funk, *Jakob von Vitry;* and Dickson and Dickson, "Cardinal Robert de Courson."

7. For references to the literature on Francis's mission to the East, see my article "Francesco d'Assisi e la Quinta Crociata: Una Missione di Pace."

8. There are numerous studies of crusade participation by German, French, Italian, English, and other crusaders. Those dealing with the Fifth Crusade have been listed in the bibliography. Among the more significant recent studies have been Dieter Rüdebusch, *Der Anteil Niedersachsens an den Kreuzzügen und Heidenfahrten,* and Dieter Wojtecki, *Studien zur Personengeschichte des deutschen Ordens in 13. Jahrhundert.*

9. Special studies may be found in the bibliography, but see especially Étienne Delaruelle, *L'idée de croisade au moyen âge,* which contains the important essays written by this scholar on the ideological development of the idea of crusade.

10. See, for example, Donald Queller, *The Fourth Crusade: The Conquest of Constantinople, 1201–1204,* and William C. Jordan, *Louis IX and the Challenge of the Crusade.*

11. See, for example, Steven Runciman, *A History of the Crusades,* 3:170. See also Mayer, *Crusades,* 218.

12. Mayer, 218; Hassler, *Heerführer der Kurie*, Donovan, *Pelagius*, and Mansilla, "Pelayo Gaitan."

13. Van Cleve, "Crusade of Frederick II."

14. Runciman, *Crusades*, 3:170.

15. Roscher, *Innocenz III*, 167.

16. Van Cleve, "Fifth Crusade," 378; Mayer, *Crusades*, 205–7.

17. Mayer, *Crusades*, 209.

18. Van Cleve, "Crusade of Frederick II," 431.

19. Schaller, "Kanzlei," esp. 257.

20. Roscher, *Innocenz III*, 153–58. For a different view on John's assumption of the vow, see Christopher R. Cheney, *Pope Innocent III and England*, 262–63.

21. Mayer, *Crusades*, 205.

22. Mayer and Roscher have relied on the works of Paul Alphandéry, *La Chrétienté et l'idée de croisade*, and E. Delaruelle, *L'idée de croisade*, as well as the substantial literature on the papacy and the reform movements of the twelfth century.

23. Roscher, *Innocenz III*, 148–52, and Pixton, "Anwerbung."

24. See appendixes 2, 3, and 4. The basis for this research was the list published by Röhricht in his *Studien zur Geschichte des fünften Kreuzzuges*, 79–135, augmented by Beatrice N. Siedschlag, *English Participation in the Crusades, 1150–1220* (hereafter cited as Sied.), and numerous other studies and sources. This process has involved an enormous task of checking and correcting, removing duplications, and searching for verification of doubtful entries. There is no pretense that the list is complete, but every effort has been made to ensure its accuracy.

25. Longnon, *Compagnons de Villehardouin*.

26. Queller, *Fourth Crusade*.

27. Raedts, "Children's Crusade of 1212." Raedts provides a detailed discussion of the primary and secondary literature dealing with this crusade.

28. Alphandéry, *Chrétienté*, 2:115–28.

29. Miccoli, "La crociata dei fanciulli"; Raedts, "Children's Crusade of 1212," 295–300.

PART I

PREPARATIONS
FOR THE
CRUSADE

CHAPTER I

PLANNING FOR THE CRUSADE

In April 1213, Innocent III summoned the Fourth Lateran Council and, in preparation, initiated a two-year period of planning for the reform of the church and the promotion of the crusade. He described the process in this way:

> Because it is not possible to convene the council for two years, we have decided in the meantime, with the help of prudent men, to investigate in the various provinces those matters that demand the attention of the apostolic supervision and to appoint suitable men as procurators of the business of the Holy Land so that, if the sacred council approves, we may personally take up the promotion of this business more effectively.[1]

Those who have written earlier about this crusade have paid little attention to this extraordinarily long period of preparation in advance of the actual summons of the crusade. Historians dealing with the council, on the other hand, have taken note of the enquiry into the state of the church that the pope launched at this time. Innocent perceived the coming council and the decisions to be taken there as the climax of his pontificate.[2] He determined to make the most of this opportunity to engage the leading experts of his time in the task of planning for the reform of the church and promoting the crusade. In this decision he was moved by his own deep concern for the problems that confronted the contemporary church, as well as by his experience with the failure of the Fourth Crusade. A systematic administrator and determined executive, he brought to his

task an intuitive creativity by which he produced approaches that
went well beyond previous endeavors. As a result of his initiative,
the fusion of the ideology of the crusade with the movements of lay
piety that had begun by the middle of the twelfth century achieved
unity in a theology of the crusade.[3]

But his effort was not restricted to the conceptual level alone.
The entire machinery of the crusade—recruitment, preaching, the
vow, the indulgence, finance—were reinterpreted in terms of their
salvific benefits to the entire Christian community, especially the
laity. For the most part, the various elements in this approach were
not new; some had roots that reached to the very beginnings of the
crusade movement. The influence of St. Bernard of Clairvaux was
certainly evident. Other elements had been tried out during the
Third Crusade or by Innocent himself in his planning for the
Fourth Crusade.[4] But never before had there been a papal effort to
integrate all of these elements into a coherent program linking the
crusade to the reform of the church. This is precisely what Innocent
undertook to do in his announcement of the crusade in 1213. It
was the nature of this program that made it essential for him to ini-
tiate his plan for the crusade well in advance of the council. Innocent saw that much that he proposed would be controversial and
that its achievement depended on creating a favorable climate. He
was, in fact, embarked on an experiment.

In *Vineam Domini*, which was addressed to the hierarchy and to
secular princes, Innocent summoned the council and announced
his plans for it. This letter was sent to areas such as Spain, that did
not receive the letters dealing specifically with the crusade.[5] That it
was not sent to King John of England or to Frederick II was simply
due to the fact that the former was still technically excommunicate,
while the status of the latter in Germany and the Kingdom of Sicily
had not yet been clarified.[6] The curia was merely pursuing its usual
cautious course. The letter itself made clear that neither was to be
excluded from its message, which was addressed to all Christian
princes and peoples.

The Innocentian program for the council attacked the major
problems of the contemporary church and society, defined as

> the extirpation of vices and the implanting of virtues, for correcting
> excesses, and reforming customs, eliminating heresies and strengthen-
> ing faith, for quieting discords and establishing peace, for restraining
> oppressions and favoring liberty, for inducing Christian princes and
> peoples to aid and support the Holy Land.[7]

To implement this program, Innocent ordered the appointment of prudent men to carry out investigations in the various provinces of the church and to report back to him. They also played an important part in planning the crusade. Innocent asserted that nothing was as yet final; only the approval of the council would bring matters to that stage. The decision to go the route of the council aimed at securing the broadest possible base of support for the reform of the church and the promotion of the crusade.

Two further letters dealt specifically with the crusade. In keeping with the fact that the crusade was the affair of the laity, *Quia maior* was directed to all the faithful. The second letter, *Pium et Sanctum,* went to those appointed procurators for the business of the crusade. The list of addresses provided at the end of these two letters in the register of Innocent III shows that the papal chancery was following a specific plan of organization that divided Europe into regions for the purpose of promoting the crusade. Only Spain, where the Christians had recently achieved a brilliant victory over the Moslems at Las Navas de Tolosa, and the Latin Empire of Constantinople seem to have been omitted.[8] *Quia maior* functioned to explain Innocent's crusade program to the Christian community as a whole, but the chief means for accomplishing this goal was to be through its incorporation into the preaching of the crusade procurators, for whom it served as a guide. For this reason, *Quia maior* deserves careful consideration, both in terms of its synthesis of the ideology of the crusade movement and its detailed presentation of the preliminary plan for the new crusade.

Innocent touches virtually all of the chords that connected the crusade movement to the religious currents of the age. He was strongly influenced by the ideas of St. Bernard of Clairvaux, who had emphasized the role of the crusade in the salvation of the individual seeking communion with the sufferings of Christ. As Bernard had stressed the *militia Christi,* exemplified in the military orders, as a service to Christ akin to that of the monastic vocation, Innocent invoked the image of feudal service. The crusaders were vassals fulfilling the obligation to Christ their king, who had been ejected from his kingdom. He thereby invoked the force of customary law—the obligation of the vassal to come to the aid of his dispossessed lord—to illustrate the compelling nature of the summons to the crusade.[9] This conception of the vocation of the crusader confirmed the religious character of his service, which Bernard had already seen in the case of the military orders. A further motive for

the crusade lay in the bonds of love that united the crusader with
the Christian communities of the East who suffered under Moslem
rule or to those of their brethren who were prisoners. The crusade
was a just war because it aimed at liberating those Christian lands
which had been seized by the Moslems. Innocent's vision was of a
Christian world restored to the unity that had marked it in the days
of the Later Roman Empire, "even following the time of Gregory
the Great."[10] The crusade was a means of achieving this basic goal
of the papal reform movement. Invoking the 666 years of the beast
of the apocalypse, he saw in the completion of six hundred years
since the rise of Islam a sign that Divine Providence would respond
to the Christian hope for the liberation of the Holy Land.

The dream of a restored Christian unity was essential to the realization of the papal vision of its role within the church. Under Urban II, the summons of the First Crusade sprang in large measure
from his view that cooperation with the Byzantines in the freeing of
Christians under Moslem rule would pave the way for church unity.
The crusade was a means of reestablishing the Christian golden age
that had extended from Constantine to Gregory the Great, and
which had, in part, been overthrown by the Moslem conquests. Innocent's apocalyptic vision flowed directly from his acceptance of
this historical premise. But it also addressed the question of the im-
mediacy of the need for a new crusade. During the preaching of the
Second Crusade, Bernard of Clairvaux had dealt with this issue by
maintaining, on the basis of a passage from Corinthians, that "now
is the acceptable time" for the liberation of the Holy Places. The
failure of that crusade to achieve any tangible results may well have
raised the question of whether it was not presumptuous of Christians to expect victory according to their own timetable, rather than
at the time ordained by Divine Providence. According to one tradition, Joachim of Fiore, the Calabrian Cistercian who was much
concerned with the interpretation of the meaning of history, raised
this very question in his discussions with King Richard of England
at the outset of the Third Crusade.[11] Very probably, Joachim was
attempting to place the crusade within the framework of his divisions of providential history. Such an effort was not unique, since
Bernard of Clairvaux had perceived the crusade in terms of a new
age. Innocent's appeal to apocalyptic vision was both a response to
those who questioned the place of the crusade in eschatological history and an effort to validate the role of Divine Providence regarding the crusade.

Innocent balanced this theoretical rationale for the crusade with an allusion to the perilous condition of the crusaders in the East. His audience was well aware that the Latin Kingdom of Jerusalem consisted only of a remnant centered on the port of Acre and a few northern strongholds. He pointed to the threat posed by the recent Moslem fortifying of Mt. Tabor as a way of bringing home the practical need for a crusade. Why did he not hold up the liberation of Jerusalem as a goal? The answer lies in the fact that he was appealing to the West to mount an operation to save the Latin Kingdom from total extinction. The specter of such a loss dominated his thinking at this time. On the whole, his audience, especially those members of the lay and ecclesiastical aristocracy in the West who were familiar with Eastern affairs, probably shared his concern. On the other hand, the Easterners themselves were more divided. Given the state of the Aiyūbid sultanate during these years—in which al-ʿĀdil, the brother of Saladin, was trying to concentrate power in his own hands and those of his sons—there was little probability that they would launch an attack on Acre. In fact, King John, at the behest of the pope, had agreed to a truce with al-ʿĀdil for five years commencing in 1212. Moreover, al-ʿĀdil had opposed the fortifying of Mt. Tabor by his son, al-Muʿaẓẓam, on the grounds that it would provoke the Christians. We do not know whether Innocent was aware of this fact, but he certainly had a general knowledge of conditions among the Moslem leaders. But none of this information changed the essential fact that fortifying Mt. Tabor demonstrated the vulnerability of the enclave left in Christian hands.[12] Tabor not only dominated the upland plateau region southwest of the Sea of Galilee, but it could also serve as a base for operations against the coastal areas still in Christian hands. Innocent saw it as a potent symbol of the true state of affairs in the East.

The success of the new crusade depended on the ability of western society to prepare both morally and practically. Ultimately, of course, Innocent argued that it was not contingent on the strength and valor of the crusaders but on the will of God, who could, if he wished, liberate the Holy Land without their aid. The crusade was given to Christians as a means whereby they could attain salvation. Therefore, each Christian should prepare for the crusade by making himself pleasing to God through a moral reformation of his life. The crusade was an instrument for the reform of Christian society. Innocent also called for "exchanging dissensions and rivalries among Christians for treaties of peace and friendship."[13] There was nothing new here. Urban II had issued a similar call during the First Crusade. The eleventh century peace movement, which had fostered the Truce of God and the Peace of God, had gained additional support in the effort of the papacy to divert warfare from Europe to the East. The crusade had placed the papacy securely at the head of efforts to promote internal peace and had thus bound an important grass-roots movement to its program for the restoration of Christian unity.

Where Innocent's plan for the crusade differed most from its predecessors was in its broadening of the meaning of participation in the crusade.[14] Innocent specifically instructed the procurators of the crusade to administer the crusade vow to all who were willing, without raising the question of their suitability to serve in the army or in some other useful capacity. Those who were not suitable might redeem their vows for money, the amount dependent on their status. Alphandéry spoke of this as a *levée en masse*.[15] The plenary indulgence accorded crusaders was offered not merely to those who personally fulfilled their vows, but also to those who paid for substitutes. Finally, whoever contributed to the crusade would share in the indulgence according to the quality of his gift. Thus the crusade indulgence was available to all Christians, both men and women. Not all aspects of this extension of the idea of participation were new, but they had never before been developed into a coherent program. Previous writers have noted the obvious financial significance of this effort but have omitted any discussion of its spiritual significance.[16] Yet it represented an extension of the spiritual benefits of the crusade indulgence to virtually all Christians. Even the poorest could now share in the indulgence in proportion to their contribution. The extension of the benefits of the indulgence also meant that almost every Christian might share in the program of moral preparation and penance that had previously been reserved exclusively for actual participants in the crusade. *Quia maior's* extension of the spiritual benefits of the crusade broadened its links with the penitential system of the church and carried that system significantly closer to the goal enunciated at Lateran IV in the requirement for annual confession of sins, since the sacrament of penance was a prerequisite for the reception of the crusade indulgence.[17]

Quia maior aimed at capturing and harnessing mass popular support for the crusade such as had recently been demonstrated in the Children's Crusade and which was also reflected, to a degree, in the vernacular literature of the period. There were substantial practical reasons for such an approach. The diversion of the Fourth Crusade had revealed serious shortcomings in the areas of finance and recruitment. Innocent made every effort to increase the sources of income for the crusade. The redemption of vows of unsuitable crusaders, especially women, was a major innovation that was certain to raise a substantial amount of money. But Innocent realized that it was also controversial. He argued that "support for the Holy Land would be much impeded or delayed, if it were necessary for everyone to be examined before taking the cross," but he was well aware that many would assume the cross who would not be suitable crusaders. He welcomed their participation. He ordered that trunks should be placed in the churches to collect offerings for the crusades. There were to be three keys, one entrusted to an honest priest, one to a layman, and the third to a religious. He eased financial pressures on crusaders—and perhaps also attempted to remove a cause for previous anti-Semitic persecution—by recommending to secular authorities that Jews should be compelled to forego interest on loans owed by crusaders. In order to call attention to the spiritual benefits available to those who would support the crusade, he directed that monthly processions should be held in these churches. During daily masses, special prayers were to be said, asking God to restore the land consecrated by the blood of Christ to his worshippers. His earlier experience had also taught him that he could not rely on voluntary responses alone to produce a sufficient number of crusaders. He sought arrangements whereby kings, princes, lay and ecclesiastical lords, and cities would supply "an agreed number of warriors with necessary expenses for three years." He requested naval support from maritime cities in an apparent attempt to avoid the problems with transport that had embroiled the Fourth Crusade with the Venetians. He also reinstated the ban on military sales to the Moslems. Finally, he revoked the indulgences previously accorded to those who aided the *reconquista* in Spain and the ongoing war against the Albigensian heretics in southern France on the grounds that recent successes on both fronts made them unnecessary, but he hastened to add that he was willing to reassess his position whenever a change might require it.[18] While the program outlined was impressive, it was still not adequate to meet the needs of the crusade. Most important, there was no provision for a crusade tax. Moreover, some provisions were so controversial as to raise serious question about their success. It would seem that Innocent had decided to advance them at this point in order to have sufficient time to deal with any problems that might arise. His decision was justified, at least in the areas of the administration of the vow to unsuitable crusaders, the efforts to secure specific commitments of crusade contingents, and the revocation of the indulgence for those participating in the Albigensian Crusade.

At the same time, Innocent III directed *Pium et Sanctum* to the men whom he had designated as procurators for the crusade. They were his agents in the field, and he took them into his confidence regarding his plan. He provided them with copies of *Vineam Domini, Quia maior,* and other letters related to the council and the crusade so that they would be fully informed regarding his intentions. The procurators were to hold the office of legate for the preaching of the crusade, for the defense of the privileges of crusaders, and for those matters concerned with the crusade outlined in the general letters referred to above. Innocent referred to those selected in formulaic terms as suitable men, indicating that they had been selected because of their qualifications for the task. He reminded them that they should show the faithful that they were bearers of the "stigmata of Jesus Christ" in their hearts by refusing all gifts save food and necessities and by maintaining modest retinues "so that nothing reprehensible may be found by which you may give the slightest offense to the gospel."[19] He ordered them to deposit all money they collected with a religious house and to furnish him with an annual report on the amount collected, as well as on the results of their recruitment efforts. Unfortunately, neither these reports nor any compilation based on them exists today.[20] The model on which Innocent drew for his advice to the procurators of the crusade was based on his experience with the preaching against the Albigensian heretics, where the ostentation of the papal preachers had drawn criticism both from the heretics and from individuals like St. Dominic and Bishop Diego de Osma, who were engaged in that work. His explicit reference to the gospel model shows that he took seriously the widespread influence of the movement of apostolic poverty and was attempting to accommodate the preaching of the crusade to its spirit.

The appointment of crusade procurators reveals a careful process of selection based on an assessment of local conditions, the education of those chosen, and their previous service to the papal curia. Some knew the pope personally, but this was not true of the majority. Although many were bishops and archbishops and others were abbots of Cistercian or Premonstratensian houses, a surprising number seem to have been drawn from an academic background, or at least to have had some training at the Universities of Paris and Oxford. Most of the episcopal appointments were to regions in Italy, Hungary, Poland, Scandinavia, Ireland, and the French Midi. The monastic contingent was preponderant in Germany, alongside a number of academics, while France received as legate Cardinal Robert Courçon, a man with very close ties to the pope and to the University of Paris. In England, where the conflict between the papacy and King John over the succession to the archbishopric of Canterbury was just entering its final phase, selection favored the scholars.

The German commissioners included two bishops, one of whom, the former bishop of Halberstadt, Konrad von Krosik, had participated in the Fourth Crusade, remaining with the crusaders through the conquest of Constantinople and returning via Rome, where he met the pope. During his sojourn in the East, he had visited the Holy Land and there, perhaps, had fulfilled his vow of pilgrimage.[21] Innocent permitted him to resign from his diocese and to retire to the monastery of Sichem, but in 1211 called upon the abbot of Sichem, Florentius, and him to support the cause of the archbishop of Gniezno against Ladislaus, the duke of Poland.[22] The other German bishop, Conrad of Regensburg, was closely identified with the Hohenstaufen cause in Germany. He had served as chancellor for Philip of Swabia and had supported the candidacy of Frederick II against Otto IV in the contest for the imperial throne. After his appointment as crusade procurator he spent considerable time at the court of Frederick.[23] According to the register of Innocent III's letters, neither he nor his associate, Provost Otto of Salzburg, received appointment to a specific region, leaving open the possibility that Innocent intended to make use of Conrad's ties to the court.[24] The papal subdeacon, Nicholas, also played an important role in the events that led up to Frederick II's assumption of the cross in 1215.[25]

Disturbed political conditions in Germany affected the hierarchy, many of whom were deeply involved on one side or the other in the struggle between Frederick and Otto. The archbishops of Mainz and Magdeburg supported Frederick, while Dietrich of Cologne favored Otto IV. It was not until 1216 that Innocent III ordered a new election for Cologne that resulted in the selection of a strong partisan of Frederick in the person of Archbishop Engelbert of Berg, the brother of Count Adolf of Berg.[26] In all probability, these

political problems influenced the selection of many of the crusade
procurators. Most of these men had strong ties to the papacy, but
they were no doubt acceptable to the court of Frederick II. The
most prominent among them was Oliver of Paderborn, scholasticus
of Cologne, who had probably been a student in Paris around
1207, when Innocent had appointed him a judge delegate, and
who had also preached against the Albigensians in southern France
in 1208.[27] The Cistercian abbots, Eberhard of Salem, Peter of
Neuenberg, and Friedrich of Sichem, reflect Innocent's strong reliance on this order for preaching, as does his choice of Abbot
Radner from the Premonstratensian abbey of Rommersdorf, from
which we possess an important letter book containing materials for
the preaching of this crusade.[28] In the selection of these individuals,
the tradition of crusade preaching in both orders was no doubt a
primary factor.

England posed a particular problem, due to the long drawn-out
controversy between King John and the papacy over the appointment of Stephen Langton as archbishop of Canterbury. Since a
large part of the episcopate was involved in this dispute, Innocent's
appointment of proven administrators and men of academic background was probably a recognition of the fact that most of the bishops would be of little aid to the work of the crusade at this time.
Walter, archdeacon of London, was a Paris-trained theologian of
some repute.[29] Master Philip of Oxford almost certainly was university trained, whether at Oxford or Paris. He had acted for the pope
during preparations for the Fourth Crusade.[30] Master John of Kent,
chancellor of London, is a rather shadowy figure, but he may fairly
be suggested to have received university training.[31] Walter and John
died in 1214 and were replaced by Master William of London and
Leo, the dean of Wells. The procurators normally appointed depu-
ties to assist them; one such was Prior Richard of Dunstable.[32]

In most other regions, including Italy, Innocent showed a marked
preference for bishops and archbishops as crusade commissioners.
In almost every instance, those appointed had previously held positions as judges delegate or had been empowered to represent the
pope in some particular dispute. Some were well known in Rome;
some had previous experience in preaching the crusade or had been
supporters of papal policy in their regions.[33] In Hungary, where
King Andrew had already taken the crusade vow, in the French
Midi, which was enmeshed still in the struggle against the Albigensians, and in the more remote regions, where the choice was nar-

row, Innocent apparently selected commissioners with considerable respect for the local hierarchy.[34] Where commissioners were joined together for service in a particular region, there is evidence that they had previously worked together in curial assignments, obviously to the satisfaction of the pope and the curia. Thus, Bishop John of Florence and the archpriest of Pistoia had served together in 1208 in a case involving the Hospitallers of Pisa. Bishop John was quite active on behalf of the curia in Tuscany.[35] Ventura Trissino of Rimini figured several times in papal letters of this period, as did the bishop of Parma.[36] Both Archbishops Bernard of Split and Leonard of Dubrovnik served on papal missions prior to their appointment as commissioners.[37] Archbishop Henry of Gniezno served as the normal channel for papal business in Poland, if the evidence of Innocent's register is accepted. In 1206, on the basis of his resistance to Duke Ladislaus, Innocent called him a "defender of ecclesiastical liberty," a phrase not loosely used in the pope's correspondence.[38] Henry of London, archbishop of Dublin, and the abbot of Mellifont were named commissioners to Ireland. Henry, no doubt, was to recruit among the English and Normans, the abbot among the native Irish. But the Abbey of Mellifont was badly split into English and Irish factions, and the abbot was deposed in 1217.[39] The archbishop of Trondheim was apparently a regular informant of the pope regarding affairs in Norway.[40] The examples could be multiplied, but the evidence is clear that the curia possessed a network of important individuals on whom they drew for the work of the crusade. Study of this group cannot but lead to the conclusion that, by the standards of the early thirteenth century, papal administration was a model of rational procedure and professional selection.

In dealing with France, Innocent was not content to rely only on general letters or the appointment of crusade procurators for various regions within the kingdom. Instead, in a separate series of letters he named Cardinal Robert Courçon as his legate and commended him to King Philip, his son Louis, and Louis's wife, Blanche.[41] Robert was a former professor at the University of Paris and had served as its chancellor in 1207. He was the author of a *summa* of theology with an excellent reputation as a preacher, and he had frequently served the curia in France. He was devoted to the cause of reform within the church. In 1212, Innocent III had promoted him to cardinal priest of St. Stephen in Coelio Monte in order to make use of his zeal and talents in the papal curia. The reasons for the appointment of a cardinal legate are apparent from these letters. French support was essential to the success of the crusade, but the conflict between France and England was a major threat to that participation.[42] Innocent was already on the verge of reaching an agreement with King John of England, but his position in France was weak. His appeal to Blanche, who could be counted on to support the pope out of piety, was aimed especially at influencing Prince Louis, whose involvement in royal affairs was increasing. Robert's commission was, therefore, of greater political moment than that of other crusade commissioners.

The appointment of Pelagius, the cardinal bishop of Albano, as papal legate to the East in September 1214 ought also to be considered in conjunction with the designation of crusade procurators, even though Innocent made no specific mention of the crusade in his case. The chief purpose of this mission was the establishment of peace between the Latin Empire of Constantinople and Theodore Lascaris, the emperor of Nicaea, which was highly desirable for the success of the crusade.[43] Pelagius was also charged with promoting the union of the Greek and Latin churches, as well as dealing with the Latins themselves. This highly controversial mission enjoyed virtually no success, save among the Latin clergy.[44] Mansilla has made a strong case, however, against those who have judged Pelagius too harshly. The legate was a forceful representative of the pope, whose clear aim was to secure Greek participation in the Fourth Lateran Council. While the Greeks were highly critical of Pelagius's efforts, it would be a mistake to take their estimate of his character at face value. In any case, his mission is more important in demonstrating the ecumenical nature of Innocent's plan for the council and the crusade than for any specific results.

Finally, one other figure deserves serious attention. During this same period, a vacancy in the bishopric of Acre made possible the election of a new bishop. The man chosen was James of Vitry, a distinguished preacher and an ardent reformer closely connected to that group of Paris scholars who were held in such high esteem by Innocent III. Unfortunately, we know little of the circumstances of his election.[45] He was not consecrated and did not depart for the East until after Innocent's death. Nevertheless, his first letter from Acre, written in October 1216, describes conditions and attitudes among the native population that suggest that he was directly tackling problems that Innocent III himself had discerned in the East and had written about during the spring of 1213 in a letter to the

Latin patriarch of Jerusalem that is discussed below.[46] He apparently
conducted a successful campaign of preaching and recruitment for
the crusade not only in Acre but also in the northern cities of Tyre,
Sidon, and Beirut.

Innocent also wrote to Nicholas, the Melkite patriarch of Alexandria, to invite his participation in the upcoming council.[47] He
sought his support for the crusade and asked him to give words of
encouragement to the Frankish captives in Egypt, whose spiritual
care was apparently in the hands of the Melkite clergy. Rome's relations with the Melkites were closer than those with the Coptic
church of Egypt. This letter is only one in a series of exchanges between Nicholas and the papacy.[48] In fact, Nicholas was Innocent's
chief informant regarding the plight of Christians under Moslem
rule and one of his principal links with the eastern churches. This
relationship survived the debacle of the Fifth Crusade, as we learn
from the patriarch's letter to Pope Honorius III, written in the
summer of 1223. That letter is particularly interesting, since the patriarch clearly acknowledges the universality of the papal office and
his own allegiance to it.[49]

Behind much of his careful planning and his decision to call the
council in preparation for the crusade lay Innocent's realization of
the causes of the failure of the Fourth Crusade. He did not dwell
overly long on its results: the conquest of Constantinople represented for him an opportunity to reunite the Latin and Greek
churches. Of much more importance was the fact that this crusade
had gotten out of hand in the first place. There can be little doubt
that Innocent blamed the Venetians for the diversion of the crusade
from its proper goal. He now reminded them in stern language of
their unfulfilled vow to aid the Holy Land. He recalled that it was
their plan that had resulted in the diversion and that they had taken
the crusade vow freely, and they were not free to repudiate that vow.
Therefore, they must prepare for the crusade so that they might redeem themselves both in the eyes of God and man.[50]

The final letters in this series were directed to Patriarch Albert
of Jerusalem and the sultan of Egypt, Saladin's brother, al-ʿĀdil,
known to the Latins as Saphadin.[51] The letter to the patriarch
shows us that Innocent intended his letters to serve as the basis for
the preaching of the crusade and as a response to its critics.[52] He
was concerned about certain detestable gossip emanating from the
Holy Land that might prove injurious to the crusade, as noted
above in the discussion of the election of James of Vitry to the see of

Acre. He also enclosed a letter to al-ʿĀdil, explaining to the patriarch that he did not expect this letter to have any concrete effect, but that it was necessary to put the crusade into the hands of God. Just as he had told the prospective crusaders that God had no need of their arms to free the Holy Land, so he addressed a demand to the sultan in God's name for its return. He hereby affirmed both the legal basis of the crusade as a just war and the theology of the crusade, as a means of salvation offered to Christians by God. He made no appeal for the conversion of the sultan, nor did he mention the differences between Christianity and Islam. Instead, he emphasized their common acceptance of the sovereignty of God. Saladin's conquest of Jerusalem was permitted by God not because Saladin was strong, "but on account of the Christian people in provoking the wrath of God."[53] For Innocent, the internal conversion of Christians would pave the way for the divine mercy to free the Holy Places. But he did not wish to tempt God by vain demands. Therefore, he asked the sultan for their return. Once this was accomplished and Christian captives were also released, there would be peace between Moslems and Christians.

Beyond its theological meaning and its significance in demonstrating the justice of the crusade, this letter also served to lay a foundation for future negotiations.[54] Innocent had some knowledge of the internal problems that confronted al-ʿĀdil. He suggested, for example, that control of the Holy Land presented some difficulties to the sultan. Although this letter had no immediate effect, it may well have planted in the mind of the sultan the idea that an agreement was possible and thus inspired his continual efforts to end the crusade on a negotiated basis once the invasion of Egypt had begun. Innocent emerges from this letter not as an intransigent supporter of holy war, but as a leader attempting to keep his options open for a favorable peace settlement.

Innocent had a fairly definite idea about the timetable to be followed in the period after the council. At his behest, King John of Jerusalem had arranged a truce with al-ʿĀdil that was not due to expire until July 1217. He had, therefore, allowed a period of four years for the preparation of the crusade prior to its scheduled departure. But even though John had obtained a truce, he continued to press for a new crusade.[55] Very likely, this pressure triggered Innocent's preparations in the spring of 1213, which took into account the truce that had been arranged. But Innocent had another reason for moving so quickly in response to John's request. At this time

Europe was deeply disturbed by wars and conflicts at every level. Frederick of Sicily, with the support of the pope, was struggling to wrest the imperial throne from Otto IV. France and England were at odds. Numerous local conflicts ruptured the peace of almost every region. The appointment of his legates and crusade procurators enabled Innocent to begin an intensive effort to resolve some of these problems in advance of the meeting of the council. But it also meant that those still unresolved could be submitted to the council for solution. This period also provided an opportunity for the pope and his representatives to experiment with approaches for uniting peace negotiations with recruitment for the crusade.

On July 27, 1214, the forces of Philip Augustus of France overwhelmed the army of Emperor Otto IV at Bouvines, and the alliances of the combatants reflected the tangled state of European politics at this time. Philip was allied to Frederick II of Hohenstaufen, whose candidacy for the German throne was supported by Innocent III. Otto had as his chief ally his uncle, King John of England, who was fighting to retain his possessions in France. The interests of all of the major powers of Europe were represented at Bouvines and were affected by the victory of Philip II, but this battle, once celebrated as one of the decisive battles of world history, did more to perpetuate the causes of conflict than to resolve them. Though the advantage passed to France and its Hohenstaufen ally, the war against King John continued, now waged in conjunction with his rebellious barons, while a defeated Otto was still able to impede the final victory of Frederick II. Confronted with a timetable for the settlement of these disputes, Innocent employed not only his agents in the field but also the Lateran Council. Innocent's efforts to ensure broad attendance at the council are best understood as a reflection of his belief in the importance of the council for the success of his programs for the reform of the church and the crusade.

The route from the crusade plan outlined in *Quia maior* to the crusade statutes promulgated in *Ad liberandam* at the Fourth Lateran Council was neither direct nor free from pitfalls. Innocent had deliberately reserved some aspects of his crusade plan, especially the enactment of a crusade tax on the clergy, for action by the council. But, as he had stressed, his entire approach was tentative and subject to modification. Before discussing the ways in which his earlier plan was modified at its incorporation into *Ad liberandam,* it is necessary to examine in some detail the reception of this plan. This can best be done through a study of the legation of Cardinal Robert Courçon in France between 1213 and 1215. His mission illustrates both the direction of Innocent's initiatives and the problems they encountered. It also shows how essential elements of Innocent's plan survived to become the basis for the program implemented under his successor, Honorius III.

NOTES

1. *PL*, 216:823–25.

2. Neither Mayer (*Crusades*, 205–6) nor Roscher (*Innocenz III*, 140–69) discusses the significance of this long period of preparation, especially in its aspect as a time for enquiry and experimentation. The best account of these questions is found in Raymonde Foreville, *Latran I, II, III et Latran IV*, 248–50.

3. Roscher does not use the term "theology of the crusade." However, Delaruelle applied it to the ideas of St. Bernard of Clairvaux in his essay "L'idée de croisade chez St. Bernard" in *L'idée de croisade au moyen âge* (p. 163). The Bernardian inspiration of Innocent's crusade ideology is quite clear, but, as is shown below, he has moved well beyond the great Cistercian. That Roscher does not fully explore this aspect of Innocent's thought is evident from his remark that the pope was "in erster Linie Politiker und nicht Jurist" (p. 267). The recent study by Wilhelm Imkamp, *Das Kirchenbild Innocenz' III*, begins to remedy the neglect of Innocent as theologian. For a further development of this theme, see Jonathan Riley-Smith, "The Crusade as an Act of Love."

4. See Delaruelle, *L'idée de croisade*, 158–62; Roscher, *Innocenz III*, 268–70; Foreville, *Latran*, 228–30.

5. *PL*, 216:823–25; Roscher, *Innocenz III*, 142.

6. Roscher, *Innocenz III*, 153–54; see also Warren, *King John*, 209–10.

7. *PL*, 216:824.

8. Ibid., 817–23.

9. Roscher, *Innocenz III*, 143.

10. *PL*, 216:818. Migne has a misprint. The text should read *Gregorii* at this point. See RV 8, 140v, 23.

11. Manrique, *Cisterciencium*, 3:222–23, 233–34. See also Siberry, *Criticism of Crusading*, 201–4.

12. Mayer's statement (*Crusades*, 206) that the fortification of Mt. Tabor was "not itself important" is misleading. Certainly, in light of the internal problems faced by the Moslems, it is a correct conclusion, but it does not fully represent the realities confronting the pope and the Kingdom of Acre.

13. *PL*, 216:818.

14. Roscher notes the precedents in Innocent's summons of the Fourth Crusade in 1198; *Innocenz III*, 144.

15. Alphandéry, *Chrétienté*, 2:152.

16. See, for example, Roscher's comments on commutation of vows (*Innocenz III*, 166–67) and those of Mayer (*Crusades*, 208–9). The pur-

pose of this discussion is not to deny the fiscal implications of Innocent's decisions, but to place them within the context of his theological goals.

17. This point has already been noticed by Foreville; *Latran*, 247.

18. *PL*, 216:820. The text in Migne contains a misprint, which alters the sense of the letter at this point. Innocent reassured those participating in and supporting the Spanish and Albigensian crusades with the statement: "et si forte requireret, nos ingruenti necessitati prospicere curaremus." However, the Migne text (*PL*, 216:820) has "non . . . curaremus."

19. *PL*, 216:822–23.

20. The existence of such reports is attested in a letter of Abbot Gervase of Prémontré to Archbishop Simon of Tyre, written in the fall of 1217. Hugo, 1:34–35.

21. Pixton, "Anwerbung," esp. 168; *PL*, 216:822. For mention of another German preacher, Theobald, see *Regesta Regni Hierosolymitani*, 2:58.

22. *PL*, 216:238.

23. Pixton, "Anwerbung," 172, 179; Van Cleve, *Frederick II*, 87; H.-B., 1:2:389 (June 20, 1215), 447 (March 1216).

24. *PL*, 216:823.

25. Schaller, "Kanzlei," 249–50; *PL*, 216:236–38, 410; H.-B., 1:2:525–26; see also Pixton, "Anwerbung," 181.

26. H.-B., 1:1:271 and n. 1; Rüdebusch, *Anteil Niedersachsens*, p. 50; Hauck, *Kirchengeschichte Deutschlands*, 4:775, n. 1; Pixton, "Anwerbung," 170.

27. Pixton, "Anwerbung," 170.

28. Kempf, "Das Rommersdorfer Briefbuch"; Pixton, "Anwerbung," 176.

29. Andrea, "Walter, Archdeacon of London," esp. 143; Jacobus de Vitriaco, *Historia Occidentalis*, 102–3, 298–99.

30. Roscher, *Innocenz III*, 81.

31. Andrea, "Walter, Archdeacon of London," 147; Cheney, *Innocent III*, 263; *The Letters of Pope Innocent III Concerning England and Wales*, 110, 662; 118, 711 (hereafter cited as *Calendar*).

32. Cheney, *Innocent III*, 263.

33. See, for example, my article "Crusading by Royal Command: Monarchy and Crusade in the Kingdom of Sicily (1187–1230)," esp. 142.

34. *PL*, 216:757.

35. *PL*, 215:583–84. For association with the archpriest of Pistoia, see RV, 8:142r.

36. *PL*, 216:603; RV, 8:95v.

37. *PL*, 215:820–21, 1424–25.

38. Ibid., 1066.

39. *Calendar*, 154, 935; 176, 1065. See also Otway-Ruthven, *History of Medieval Ireland*, 136.

40. *PL*, 215:812–13; 216:436, 1251.

41. *PL*, 216:827–28.

42. Baldwin, *Masters, Princes, and Merchants*, 1:19–25; Dickson and Dickson, "Cardinal Robert de Courson," esp. 75–82.

43. Mansilla, "Pelayo Gaitan," 30.

44. Maleczek, *Papst und Kardinalskolleg*, 167–68.

45. Funk, *Jakob von Vitry*, 37; Ernoul, 410.

46. Jacobus de Vitriaco, *Lettres de Jacques de Vitry*, 86–90 (hereafter cited as Jac.).

47. *PL*, 216:828–30; DHGE, 2:357; Foreville, *Latran*, 247.

48. Roscher, *Innocenz III*, 137–38, 143.

49. Rodenberg, 1:161–62.

50. *PL*, 216:830. For a recent defense of the Venetian position, see Queller, *Fourth Crusade*, 9–18, and Donald Queller and Irene Katele, "Attitudes toward the Venetians in the Fourth Crusade: the Western Sources."

51. *PL*, 216:831–32.

52. Ibid., 830–31.

53. Ibid., 831.

54. Roscher, *Innocenz III*, 287. Evidence to support this view is found in the summary of another letter written by Innocent to al-ʿĀdil shortly after the Lateran Council. He asks that *nuntii* should be chosen to carry apostolic letters to the sultan, "and, if they can they should enter into a peace with him" if he would be willing to restore the Holy Land to the Christians; Theiner, *Vetera monumenta slavorum*, 1:64. Innocent was fully prepared to pursue negotiations all the way up to the beginning of the crusade. Under these circumstances, the later efforts of the sultan to secure a truce in return for the return of Jerusalem appear quite understandable. In this regard, it is worth noting that Patriarch Aymar had informed Innocent as early as 1199 of the possibility that Jerusalem might be obtained by negotiation; Bongars, *Gesta Dei per Francos*, 1125–29.

55. John explained his reasons to Abbot Gervase in 1217. He believed that the truce was unstable and feared a Moslem attack. Hugo, 1:36.

CHAPTER II

THE TESTING GROUND

The first major testing ground for the crusade program of Innocent III lay in France in the period between 1213 and the opening of the Fourth Lateran Council in 1215. As we have seen, Innocent placed considerable emphasis on the support of the French monarchy to ensure the success of the crusade, but the situation in that country was far from favorable. Not only was it divided by the Albigensian Crusade, but large segments of the northern French aristocracy were embroiled in a conflict over the succession to the county of Champagne and the impending war against King John of England and Emperor Otto IV. The appointment of Robert Courçon as legate balanced that of Cardinal Nicholas of Tusculum, who was sent to England in October 1213 to negotiate with King John about the conditions for raising the interdict that had been imposed by Innocent because of the King's refusal to accept the appointment of Cardinal Stephen Langton as archbishop of Canterbury. Although Robert's legation was primarily concerned with the crusade, his powers were not defined so narrowly as to exclude these questions. Nor could they be, for without a successful resolution of these conflicts the work of the crusade would be impeded. Therefore, the legations of Robert and Nicholas were not separate, but were part of a two-pronged papal effort aimed at restoring peace in France and England and thereby promoting the crusade. Moreover, in the work of Robert we get a first glimpse of the way in which recruitment for the crusade was integrated into the papal peace program. Although there is considerable uncertainty regarding details, the assumption of the cross by leading nobles from opposing groups demonstrates the close relationship between the two programs. The enrollment of prominent nobles in the crusade made it possible for the legates to exert pressure on them in the cause of peace. Obviously, such tactics, if carried too far, could arouse opposition from those who saw them as intrusions into the secular sphere. The legation of Robert Courçon revealed both the potential and the risk in this approach.

Robert Courçon, cardinal priest of St. Stephen, was one of the more important intellectuals of the late twelfth and early thirteenth centuries. English by birth, he was closely associated with the schools of Paris, where Innocent III himself had studied. Robert was a member of the circle of Peter the Chanter at Paris, a group of masters who had profound concern for the moral transformation of both clergy and laity.[1] Like so many appointed to be crusade procurators by Innocent III, Robert had participated in numerous cases as a papal judge delegate, in the course of which he became acquainted with some of the leading figures among the French clergy and aristocracy. Innocent made him a cardinal in 1212. Robert was already well known to the pope, both for his commitment to the reform of the church and his effectiveness as a judge.

Nevertheless, the legation of Robert Courçon has proved controversial both to his contemporaries and to modern scholars.[2] There has been a general tendency to view it as a failure and as damaging to the crusade. Some have maintained that it ended in Robert's recall in disgrace.[3] On the surface, at least, it would seem that Innocent III simply picked the wrong man for the job and came to regret it. But the reality is much more complex. There can be no question that Robert's legation aroused considerable opposition and that the pope had to intervene when the efforts of the legate threatened negative results. Robert was not afraid to use his legatine authority to the fullest and on one occasion this brought him into direct conflict with the pope. But whatever errors of judgment he made, he loyally and vigorously pursued the policies laid down by Innocent himself. In particular, the pope could not have asked for a more meticulous servant with respect to the crusade. A letter of Pope Honorius III, written immediately following his accession to the papal throne, demonstrates that most of the leading members of the French crusade contingent were recruited under the direction of

Robert Courçon.[4] Subsequent correspondence shows that strong ties continued to exist between the cardinal and the French crusaders long after the end of his legation in 1215.[5] These facts suggest that, whatever shortcomings Robert had, the effectiveness of his legation cannot be judged by a simple yardstick of success or failure.

Robert Courçon's work was preparatory to the Fourth Lateran Council. It involved the reform of the church, the establishment of peace, and the promotion of the crusade. These three areas were, in fact, closely related to one another. Both the reform of the church and the papal pacification program were of vital importance to the ultimate success of the crusade: the first by preparing the Christian community to be a worthy receptacle of divine favor, and the second by removing a serious impediment to the recruitment of crusaders. But Robert's reform efforts evoked opposition from at least some clergy as an intrusion into their affairs. His efforts to promote peace were partly at the root of complaints made by the aristocracy and the king. Finally, some could not understand why crusade preachers would administer the crusade vow to so many persons who would be useless in combat. The chroniclers of the age viewed all of these initiatives with suspicion and mistrust, raising against them the traditional charges of greed and dishonesty that were the defense of local men against intruders. William the Breton spoke for a large number of his contemporaries when he wrote:

> Robert Courçon, legate of the Apostolic See, and many with him, were preaching through the whole Gallic kingdom. And they signed many indiscriminately with the cross, children, old men, women, the lame, the blind, the deaf, lepers: thereby impeding the work of the cross rather than aiding the work of the Holy Land. Moreover, in their sermons, by which they seemed to want to please the crowd more than was necessary, they defamed the clergy, saying disgraceful things and lying about their life to the people, and so they sowed the seeds of scandal and schism between the clergy and the people. For these reasons, and on account of certain other complaints, both the king and the entire clergy appealed to the Apostolic See against the legate.[6]

When the legate journeyed to Limoges, he enquired into the fitness of the abbot of St. Martial. The local chronicler, Bernard Itier, responded by accusing him of simony.[7] At Laon, the chronicle maintained that he attacked "the dignity of prelates and the customs of important churches."[8]

Historians have generally taken these charges at face value, or at most discounted them as exaggeration, but they have failed to emphasize the myopic quality of the charges, which often showed little concern for the great issues that engaged popes and kings. Nevertheless, the complaints of these chronicles are real, whatever the limitations of their authors. The views they represent are the local perspective on the major issues of the day. They provide a valid insight into the difficulties faced by Robert Courçon, regardless of how deficient they are in explaining the nature of his problems.

The councils held by the legate, his visitations of religious houses, and his decisions about local officials of the church represented to many an unwanted and unnecessary intrusion into local affairs. What was especially resented was that the legate and his associates denounced clerical abuses in their sermons in order to enlist the support of public opinion for the cause of reform. The series of councils Robert summoned—beginning at Paris in June 1213 and moving to Rouen the following February, thence to Bordeaux, Clermont, and Montpellier, and climaxing in Bourges in May 1215—reiterated concerns that had already been formulated at the Third Lateran Council in 1179 and were preparatory to the decisions to be taken at Lateran IV. The condemnation of usury aroused both royal and baronial opposition,[9] but the chief resistance to the legate among the clergy resulted from his involvement in a number of ongoing disputes within the French church. Of these, the most vitriolic involved the Order of Grandmont, founded by Stephen de Muret and profoundly influenced by the reform currents of the twelfth century.[10]

The divisions between the lay brothers and the clerics on the issue of poverty that split the order had broken out in the 1180s and had been the subject of numerous appeals to and decisions by the popes, including Innocent III, who had rendered a detailed judgment in 1202.[11] The crux of this controversy involved the division of control over the order between the two groups, with the *conversi,* or lay brothers, in charge of temporal affairs. Rome received a continuing stream of complaints from the clerics to the effect that the *conversi* were using their powers to injure them. It was on an appeal from the *conversi* charging the clerics with abuses against poverty that Robert Courçon was drawn into the dispute.[12] He summoned the prior of Grandmont, the head of the order, to appear before him to answer the charges. When that official refused, stating that he was forbidden by the rule of the order to leave his house, Robert suspended him from office. In the meantime, the prior had appealed to the pope, who had assumed jurisdiction in the case, and he succeeded in bringing the thunder of Rome down on the head of Robert Courçon on the grounds that he had intervened in a case that was already before the papal court. Innocent arranged that the questions before Robert should be transferred to the archbishop of Bourges and two other prelates, who had previously served as judges delegate in this case. The pope was clearly under the impression that his legate had deliberately overstepped his bounds. On the other hand, given the delay in responses and the difficulty of communication, it is entirely possible that the prior of Grandmont, a man of great experience in such matters, had succeeded in outflanking the legate by his appeal to Rome and then entrapping him in a fait accompli. Whatever the case, matters could not have gone better for the prior or worse for the legate.

Examples of disputes involving Robert Courçon's legation could easily be multiplied. Baldwin notes that Robert suspended at least ten canons of the cathedral of Laon "for having acquired their prebends by simony."[13] He prohibited the monastery of Montieramey, in the diocese of Troyes, from accepting candidates below eighteen years of age, but Honorius III permitted this practice once more in 1218.[14] At Vendôme he initiated proceedings against simoniacal canons.[15] He condemned clerical rebels against King John at Poitiers, as well as members of the clergy who kept concubines and dressed in too secular a manner, an action repeated by Cardinal Guala, who became legate in England in 1216.[16] He proceeded against violations of clerical dress at Treguier and abuses against chastity at Rouen.[17] Marcel and Christiane Dickson have detailed numerous other examples, mostly of a routine sort, in which Robert's legatine office involved him in the affairs of local churches and monasteries.[18] Many of these cases were not controversial, but the investigation of the fitness of the abbot of St. Martial at Limoges did arouse resentment, as the chronicle of Bernard Itier testifies.[19] Still, even granting the ineptitude of the legate in his handling of the Grandmont affair, the reaction of the French prelates in May 1215 at Bourges, where their opposition broke into the open, seems to have been triggered at least as much by concerns expressed by Philip Augustus that the legate had exceeded his mandate by interfering in matters touching the interests of the crown as by complaints about his reform activities.

Robert Courçon's mission involved two issues in which the French monarchy and aristocracy were vitally interested: the Anglo-French conflict and the succession to the county of Champagne.

His correspondence with King John from 1213 to 1215 indicates that he worked to end the war between England and France and to secure Anglo-French support for the crusade. Robert was also charged to enquire into the grounds of consanguinity between Phillipine of Champagne and Erard of Brienne in order to prevent their marriage, by which Erard aimed to strengthen his claim to the county against Blanche and her son Theobald.[20]

Some time before May 1214 Philip Augustus wrote to Innocent III raising a number of issues on which he differed from the legate. This letter has unfortunately been lost, but it is possible to reconstruct the major lines of Philip's argument from Innocent's reply and other sources. Innocent's letter to Philip dealt specifically with the question of the legate's jurisdiction over usury, but it is clear that this was not the only or necessarily the main issue raised by the king. Innocent informed Philip that the other questions he had raised would be taken up in the forthcoming council.[21] The pope defended the actions of the legate with respect to usury, but he obviously was seeking to avoid other more controversial problems. Their nature may be surmised from a letter of Odo of Burgundy to the king and from a temporary negotiated settlement reached by the legate and the representatives of the king on Philip's orders.

As early as June 1213, prior to Robert's arrival in France, Philip had sent Innocent III's letter concerning the crusade (probably *Quia maior*) to his council for examination to see if its provisions infringed upon royal rights. The response of Odo of Burgundy to the king has been preserved. The provisions singled out for special attention by Odo were those by which the persons and goods of crusaders were taken under the protection of the church until the crusaders' return or death and those relating to crusaders' debts and the papal prohibition of usury by the Jews. Regarding these questions, Odo wrote: "It does not seem just or reasonable or licit for the Lord Pope or others to establish something in your kingdom, without the agreement of yourself and your advisers, whereby you and your barons and your subjects should lose the service and the due justices of their men."[22] The advice was hardly exceptional, but was almost certainly the basis for Philip's objections to the pope. Philip's letter was, therefore, directed against *Quia maior* rather than the legate, except to the degree that he was the zealous agent of the pope in carrying out its provisions.

In response to the pope, Philip ordered the bishops of Paris and Senlis, together with the legate, to enquire into the manner in which the church traditionally regulated the rights of crusaders in France in order to establish a norm until the issues could be determined at the council.[23] This enquiry shows that the king was concerned with an even broader range of problems than those revealed in the letter of Odo of Burgundy. The questions dealt with included the obligation of crusaders to pay taxes to the crown before their departure on crusade, their service in feudal and royal armies in this same period, and the jurisdiction of secular and ecclesiastical courts over crimes committed by crusaders. These were very sensitive areas for the king at a time when he and his principal advisers were preparing for war against King John and his ally, Emperor Otto IV. The pope was confronted with a difficult situation, in which Philip's support of the imperial candidacy of Frederick of Sicily against Otto, which he favored, could be jeopardized by conflicts over papal crusade policy. Nevertheless, rather than give up that policy, he temporized. Philip took advantage of the pope's decision to reach a temporary agreement with the legate that would give him a free hand with the French crusaders during the critical period leading up to the Battle of Bouvines in July 1214.

This analysis sheds new light on the interpretation of the sources concerning the recruitment of French crusaders during the legation of Robert Courçon. Thomas C. Van Cleve, for example, echoed the charges levelled by the chroniclers against the recruitment policies of Robert's legation, but his statement that they were most successful "among the masses, the unfortunate, and the weak," deals only with that innovation of the Innocentian crusade program that disturbed the accepted view of the suitable crusader.[24] However, as noted earlier, the letter of Pope Honorius III dated August 7, 1216, provides a substantial list of crusaders from the leading ranks of the French aristocracy, who could only have been recruited during the legation of Robert Courçon.[25] A detailed discussion of these individuals throws additional light on the connections between Robert's involvement in peace negotiations and his recruitment of leaders for the crusade.

The key figure mentioned by Honorius was Odo, duke of Burgundy, one of the major advisers and supporters of Philip Augustus of France. He commanded the rear guard of the French army at Bouvines. Other major supporters of Philip addressed by Honorius included Milo, count of Bar; Henry, duke of Brabant, the son-in-law of the king; Drogo de Merlo, the constable of France; Simon of Joinville, seneschal of Champagne; and Hugh de Lusignan, count

of La Marche.[26] Hervé de Donzy, count of Nevers, was allied to
King John but had also taken the vow from Robert Courçon.[27] In
the aftermath of Bouvines, Robert worked to bring about a reconciliation between the count and the king, acting at the behest of
King John. Following the death of Odo of Burgundy in 1218,
Hugh of La Marche and Hervé of Nevers emerged as the leaders of
the French crusaders.[28]

Evidence that so many important royal supporters had taken the
crusade vow from Robert Courçon, with the possibility that they
had done so before the Battle of Bouvines, suggests a reason for
Philip's concern about the mission of the legate. If Robert had used
their crusader status to impede their participation in Philip's army,
he would have deprived the king of some of his most important
commanders, not to mention the many lesser vassals who would
have withheld their services. A further reason for Philip's reserva-
tions about the mission of the legate arose from the fact that Robert
had entered into direct contact with King John to promote peace
and to obtain joint Anglo-French participation in the crusade as
early as September 1213.[29] This evidence confirms the direction in
which the legate was working. He was committed to a juncture of
the peace program with the recruitment effort. Such a policy imper-
illed the aims of Philip Augustus. Under the circumstances, it is not
surprising that these efforts produced something of a crisis. Perhaps
in this instance, too, Robert had moved beyond the point that Innocent himself would have desired. After all, the pope shared with
Philip a desire to defeat Otto IV and establish Frederick II on the
German throne. Innocent had no choice but to recommend compromise to his legate in the interest of these broader designs.

With the agreement reached between Robert and the bishops of
Paris and Senlis, the way was open for the continuance of his legation in France into the fall of 1215, when he departed for Rome to
participate in the Fourth Lateran Council. In the months following
the Battle of Bouvines, King John used the offices of the legate to
carry on negotiations with the French court.[30] Robert played a significant role in the peace arranged by the two kings in the fall of
1214. In December 1214 he participated in a council at Montpellier. He may have spent the early part of 1215 in Flanders working
in conjunction with Oliver of Paderborn, the crusade procurator for
that part of Germany. It was in May 1215 that Robert summoned a
council to meet in Bourges. Once again he ran into controversy, this
time with the French hierarchy. The seriousness of this dispute may

be judged from the fact that the bishops appealed to Rome and that Robert was unable to proceed with the council. The loss of the register of Innocent III for this period, however, has left us with only the notice of an agreement between the pope and the church of France on the subject of the acts of Robert of Courçon.[31] The full nature of this problem can only be explained, as we shall see below, by events at the council. What is certain is that it did not impede the continuance of Robert's work. It is to the period following this dispute that his important work in reforming the statutes of the University of Paris belongs. Likewise, he received notice of the excommunication of Erard of Brienne, who was continuing to lay claim to the county of Champagne.[32] Robert was still busy on that front. We know that Milo de St. Florentin and other supporters of Erard took crusade vows at some point as part of an effort to force a settlement of his conflict with Blanche. Despite this pressure, Erard remained recalcitrant and never himself took the vow. But his case illustrates in a specific way the attempt by the legate to employ recruitment as an instrument to secure peace.[33] Robert returned to Rome for the celebration of the Fourth Lateran Council, where his views exercised considerable influence.[34] There is no substantial evidence from this period or from the pontificate of Honorius III that he had returned in disgrace or that the substance of his work was repudiated by the papacy.[35] Rather, his mission provided an experiential base for the decisions regarding the crusade reached at the Fourth Lateran Council.

The council—which met between November 11 and 30, 1215—was the largest and most comprehensive assembly of the ecclesiastical hierarchy ever held in the Middle Ages. Innocent's effort to secure attendance resulted in the presence of about four hundred archbishops and bishops, eight hundred abbots, and numerous theologians and heads of chapters and religious communities. Its ecumenical character was established by the attendance of the primate of the Maronites and Deacon Peter, representing the Melkite archbishop of Alexandria. The Latin patriarchs of Jerusalem, Antioch, and Constantinople were present with many of their suffragans. Almost all of the archbishops and bishops appointed as crusade procurators were present, save for the archbishop of Lund.[36] In his opening sermon, Innocent used the image of the Pasch to establish the relationship between the crusade and reform. Innocent interpreted the Pasch in terms of a corporeal passage for the liberation of the Holy Land, a spiritual passage to achieve reform, and an eternal passage to glory. There was, moreover, a special urgency in his words. He seemed unsure that he would live to see the consummation of his plans for the crusade. His theme—reflected in his choice of a quote from the Gospel of Luke (20:13), "I have desired with a great desire to eat this pasch with you before I suffer"—took on a more personal tone later in the sermon when he said, "I do not refuse, such being the will of God, to drink the chalice of the passion, if . . . it is handed to me." Further on, he became even more specific: "Certainly, I would prefer to remain in the chair until the achievement of this enterprise."[37] The work of the council was more than the culmination of his plans; it was the culmination of his life.

The tendency among modern scholars to compartmentalize the various aspects of the council's work into doctrinal, political, ecclesiastical, and crusade categories obscures, to some extent, their interrelationships, their existence as part of a total fabric. Decisions made in one area had definite ramifications in others. Thus, several political issues taken up at the council had particular relevance to the crusade. The most important of these were the conflict between King John and the English barons, which also involved Prince Louis of France, that between Otto IV and Frederick II over the imperial throne, and, less clearly but still at least indirectly related, the matter of the Albigensian Crusade and the status of Raymond, count of Toulouse, and Raymond Roger, count of Foix.[38] Innocent III was already committed to King John, having excommunicated the barons and rejected the Magna Carta.[39] He had also supported the candidacy of Frederick II. Finally, he was the prime mover in the Albigensian Crusade. In all of these matters, the promotion of peace as a prerequisite for the success of the crusade was never far from his mind. On none of these fronts had his previous efforts been fully successful; it was for this reason that they were brought before the council.

The actions taken at the council regarding England were an extension of the efforts undertaken by Innocent's legates. In September 1214, following Bouvines, King Philip and King John had exchanged letters of truce arranged through the efforts of Robert Courçon, whose name appears in the witness list of John's letter with the attestation that the truce was sworn in his presence.[40] Despite this success, John's war with his barons, who were increasingly supported by Prince Louis of France, was a serious cause for concern. When King John took the crusade vow on Ash Wednesday in

1215, he took on not merely the status of a vassal of the Holy See but also the protection due a crusader. Innocent judged the actions of the barons to be directed against the interests of the crusade.[41] The baronial war threatened not only King John but also the recruitment program for the crusade. The chief action of the council was the rejection of the appeal of the barons against John and their excommunication. But, as Christopher Cheney has said, there can be "little doubt that the pope was already aware of the negotiations between the English rebels and the French court" aimed at enlisting the support of Prince Louis in their cause.[42] The excommunication was also, therefore, an attempt to forestall this alliance. Innocent made this clear in the letters that he wrote to King Philip and to Prince Louis himself to inform them of the action taken by the council. The pope also acted quickly to appoint Cardinal Guala as his legate to England to replace Nicholas, who had returned to Rome. Despite the failure of the effort of the Council to restrain either the barons or Louis, Innocent continued to work for peace in England.

The conflict over the imperial throne also had direct ramifications on the crusade. Like King John, Frederick II had taken the crusade vow. Although some historians have continued to argue that his action was undertaken without the knowledge of, and even contrary to the will of, the pope, the weight of evidence now strongly supports the view that Innocent not only knew of but had, through his representatives, even worked toward this goal.[43] Of course, there were obvious advantages for Frederick, as for King John, in taking the cross. He obtained the protections of a crusader against his enemies and gained status in the eyes of the church. But the pope also gained. The crusade vow provided a lever that might be used against Frederick should he prove reluctant to depart on crusade. Moreover, his service on the crusade could at least temporarily serve to reduce tensions between the church and the empire.

The relationship between the Albigensian affair and the crusade was twofold. On the one hand, the continuation of the war against heretics in the south of France posed a threat to the recruitment of French crusaders for the East. Innocent had dealt with this problem by suspending the indulgence for the Albigensian Crusade. Nevertheless, the leaders of the war against the heretics continued to view themselves as crusaders. Secondly, Simon de Montfort and his supporters were not willing to permit the counts of Toulouse and Foix to recover the lands they had lost to the crusaders. They were able

to bring considerable pressure to bear on the pope, first to place
these lands in the care of Simon until a decision could be rendered
by the council, and then, at the council itself, to force the pope to
accept the overwhelming vote of the bishops to make this arrangement permanent. In particular, the bishops argued that any effort to dispossess the count of Montfort would harm the crusade
against heresy.[44] But the pope also had to be concerned about the
effect of the continued war and the disruption of the Midi on his
projected expedition to the Holy Land. Although this aspect of the
problem is not dealt with in our sources, it may well have been a
factor inclining the pope toward the restoration of the counts of
Toulouse and Foix. But the decision of the council to support the
claims of Simon de Montfort closed this approach to the pope and
ensured that the Albigensian Crusade would continue to engage
substantial forces.

Behind these political issues lay Innocent's concern for the success of the crusade and his quest for internal peace in Europe,
because these very issues were among the most serious causes of
conflict in Europe at this time. By bringing them before the council, Innocent was attempting to build a broader base of support for
their solution. His efforts were only partially successful. He had
planned to bring all of the contending parties together at the council to resolve their remaining differences and thus to free them to
devote all their energies to the crusade.[45] It seems clear that he was
willing to make some compromises in order to achieve his goal, but
the fathers at the council were in no mood to permit him to barter
away any of the gains that had been made against the Albigensian
heretics or even to listen to proposals from the adherents of Otto
IV. While the final decisions reached in these matters were generally
consistent with Innocent's aims, they did not represent any dramatic breakthroughs toward the settlement of the conflicts. In
France, England, and Germany, the situation after the council remained much as it had been before. The task of resolving the conflicts was once more one of slow and tedious negotiation.

Innocent did succeed in gaining the support of the council for a
detailed plan for the implementation of the crusade that committed
the clergy to a significant role in financing it. This approbation gave
Innocent and his successor a necessary lever to enforce the financial
commitments made by the clergy.[46] The constitution, *Ad liberandam,* appended to the seventy decrees approved at the council ob-

tained the force of law. For the first time since its inception, the crusade possessed a body of legal regulation that incorporated virtually all aspects of its program, as well as spelling out the obligations of various segments of the Christian community to support it. That this legislation had been approved in the council accorded with the most fundamental views of the period regarding use of the machinery of representation and consent to secure a binding commitment of the Christian community.[47]

The parallels and differences between *Ad liberandam* and *Quia maior,* viewed in the light of intervening experience, not only confirm some of what we have learned from the study of the mission of Robert Courçon, but also demonstrate the incomplete and tentative character of the crusade plan outlined in 1213. Of course, much in *Ad liberandam* repeated what had been stated earlier or dealt with the more immediate task of fixing a date for the beginning of the expedition.[48] It fixed that date for June 1217 and announced Innocent's intention of meeting with the leaders of the crusade going by sea in the environs of the ports of Brindisi and Messina in order to arrange for a sound organization of the army. Similarly, he planned to provide a legate for those who would travel by land. *Ad liberandam* specified a broad range of exemptions from taxation for crusaders during the period of their preparation for departure and while they were actually on crusade, and it forbade the collection of interest on their debts. But an agreement reached with the French hierarchy at the council limited the effect of this provision along the lines desired by Philip Augustus. This was the chief import of the reconciliation reached between the bishops and Robert Courçon at the council.[49] The pope again called upon secular rulers to force the Jews to remit interest on crusader debts and enforced this with a prohibition of Christian business with them until they had complied. He also asked rulers to arrange a moratorium on debts to the Jews. He repeated his call for the kings, feudal aristocracy, and communities to provide expenses for a suitable number of combatants in place of those unable to go in person, with the provision of an indulgence according to the quality of their support, specifically referring to his previous encyclical letters, and thus to *Quia maior.*[50] There were also clear precedents for the prohibition of trade in arms with the Moslems and for efforts to ensure the safety of the crusaders from piracy on their journey.

The most important new element in *Ad liberandam* related to financing the crusade. The pope had omitted any reference to a crusade tax from *Quia maior*. Instead, he had ordered the placement of casks for the collection of freewill offerings in the churches. *Ad liberandam* does not specifically mention the latter, though their continued presence and use can be assumed from a statement at the very end confirming a partial indulgence to all who would contribute to the crusade. It details, instead, both the freewill offerings of the pope and the cardinals and the taxes to be paid by the clergy. To set an example, Innocent pledged thirty thousand pounds, in addition to arming and fitting out ships for the Roman crusaders. He also allotted three thousand marks to the crusade that remained from alms given earlier for the support of the Holy Land. At the same time, the council unanimously agreed to a tax of a twentieth on clerical incomes for three years, with a provision that the pope and cardinals would pay a tenth. Innocent had thus succeeded in laying the financial cornerstone of his policy. But a reading of the text suggests that the final result was the product of rather intensive negotiations to ensure that the pope and cardinals would pay a just share. Still, the approval of the council gave force, especially by its inclusion of specific ecclesiastical sanctions, to the collection of the tax and promised thereby that it would be more effective than the tax the pope had enacted on his own authority in 1199.

Innocent's crusade plan of 1213 does not emerge in *Ad liberandam* precisely as it was expressed in *Quia maior*. There is no direct mention of the pope's advice to administer the crusader vow without respect to the suitability of persons as crusaders. While the conciliar constitution contains a provision for the redemption of the vows of such persons, it seems reasonable to suggest that the criticism levelled at the explicit effort to recruit them as crusaders had had an effect. Even more telling is the fact that canon 3 of the council reinstates the crusade vow for those engaged in the war against heretics.[51] Innocent's effort to subordinate the Albigensian Crusade to that in the East was thus repudiated by the council. Is this one of the matters that came out of the conflict between Courçon and the French bishops and which was referred to in the nonextant letter described in an index of the pope's register for his eighteenth year? Very possibly this is the case. Courçon had visited southern France and had been involved with the Albigensian Crusade during his mission. Given the evidence that Innocent's views regarding the crusade differed from those of the French hierarchy, it is at least worth considering that Courçon's problems with the

French bishops, which came to a head at Bourges in May 1215, arose in part from his effort to pursue the pope's policies vis-à-vis the Albigensians. In this connection it is interesting to note that Robert Courçon made contact with Count Henry of Rodez, the only important member of the southern French aristocracy to participate in the Fifth Crusade.[52] Had Innocent been able to develop his approach unimpeded by the council, there would likely have been others. More important, he was forced to make concessions to the French hierarchy and to Philip with respect to the exemptions of crusaders from taxation. It is, therefore, not at all surprising that Honorius III did not again send Robert Courçon to France as legate following Innocent's death and that Robert's popularity remained high among the French crusaders.

Finally, Lateran IV expanded on the peace program briefly mentioned in *Quia maior.* In 1213, Innocent had viewed the peace program in traditional terms; the crusade was a substitution for unjust war and violence in western society. *Ad liberandam* also stresses the necessity of peace to the success of the crusade but goes on to fix precise terms for its enforcement. Peace is to be observed for four years. Bishops are charged with persuading those in conflict to make peace, or at least to conclude truces. The penalties for violation are the strongest available to the council. Those who refused to make peace would be excommunicated and their lands placed under interdict. If they persisted, the bishops were to denounce them to the secular arm as disturbers of the work of the crusade.[53] The experience gained during the period from 1213 to 1215 had made very evident how difficult it was to secure an end to internal violence.

In spite of these changes, the essential program of Innocent III not only emerged intact but was strengthened by the action of the council. Certainly this was the case with both the crusade tax and the peace program. His theology of crusade remained largely intact, though some features no longer figured prominently in *Ad liberandam,* such as the administration of the vow to unsuitable crusaders. But *Ad liberandam* was not to be regarded as a repeal of *Quia maior* or of previous papal letters concerning the crusade, as its text makes clear in referring to the grant of the indulgence to all contributing to the crusade in proportion to their gift.[54] Despite significant setbacks, the program laid down in 1213 could continue. That it did will become evident as we focus on its implementation in studies of preaching, recruitment, and finance in the following chapters.

NOTES

1. There is no dearth of studies of Robert Courçon. The most valuable for this study is that by Marcel and Christiane Dickson, "Le Cardinal Robert de Courson: sa vie." John Baldwin has some interesting material in *Masters, Princes, and Merchants*, 1 : 19–25. See also Joseph Greven, "Frankreich und der fünfte Kreuzzug," and Maleczek, *Papst und Kardinalskolleg*, 175–79.

2. The most insightful statement to date is that found in Mayer: "Despite the success of his preaching there was opposition from the clergy, whom he wished to reform, and from the feudal nobility, whose jurisdiction he wished to limit in the interest of the church. Even the pope had to disavow some of his actions" (*Crusades*, 206). A more traditional, and critical, view is expressed by Van Cleve; "Fifth Crusade," 380–81.

3. This point has been discussed at length by the Dicksons, "Cardinal Robert de Courson," 126–31. I suggest revisions of their analysis of the evidence later in this chapter.

4. Pressutti, 1 : 4, 14.

5. Ibid., 248–49, 1498–99; 260, 1558.

6. *T*, 78–79.

7. Ibid., 337.

8. Baldwin, *Masters, Princes, and Merchants*, 1 : 22–23; *T*, 90–91.

9. Baldwin, *Masters, Princes, and Merchants*, 1 : 23. See Innocent III's letter to Philip Augustus, *PL*, 217 : 229–30; see also Luchaire, *Innocent III*, 4 : 287, and Greven, "Frankreich," 26–33.

10. Becquet, "Grandmont."

11. Ibid., 318–19.

12. Dickson and Dickson, "Robert de Courson," 97–98.

13. Baldwin, *Masters, Princes, and Merchants*, 1 : 23.

14. Pressutti, 1 : 279, 1678.

15. Ibid., 295–96, 1780.

16. Ibid., 515–16, 3154–55.

17. Ibid., 529, 3239.

18. Dickson and Dickson, "Robert de Courson," 90–107.

19. *T*, 337.

20. Dickson and Dickson, "Robert de Courson," 91; Evergates, *Feudal Society*, 47–48.

21. *PL*, 217 : 229–30.

22. Luchaire, 4 : 287; *Layettes du tresor des chartes*, 1 : 282–83, 768. The editor of *Layettes* places this document in June 1205. Luchaire assigns it to the period of the Fifth Crusade. The content of the letter strongly suggests that it was written after the reception of *Quia maior* in France but probably prior to the arrival of the legate, who is not mentioned. The most reasonable date would seem to be in May or June 1213.

23. *PL*, 217 : 239–40.

24. Van Cleve, "Fifth Crusade," 380.

25. Pressutti, 1 : 4, 14.

26. Ibid.

27. Dickson and Dickson, "Robert de Courson," 93; Painter, *Reign of King John*, 228.

28. Pressutti, 1:248, 1498; 260, 1558. *T,* 238.

29. Dickson and Dickson, "Robert de Courson," 92; *RLC,* 1:105.

30. *RLC,* 1:106–8.

31. Theiner, *Vetera monumenta slavorum,* 1:65, 51; Pott., 1:452, 5161. James of Vitry, writing to his friends in the fall of 1216, described the situation faced by the French crusaders some months earlier. He asked Pope Honorius III for letters of protection for these crusaders, but the pope refused because the defense of French crusaders had been entrusted to the French hierarchy. This information suggests that this decision had been reached at the Fourth Lateran Council and represented the resolution of the dispute between Robert Courçon and the bishops. However, James made it clear that the situation of the French crusaders, oppressed almost everywhere by the *taille* and other exactions ("qui fere ubique talliis et aliis exactionibus opprimuntur"), continued to be serious. Obviously, the French hierarchy were themselves pressured by Philip Augustus to oppose the policies of the legate. Honorius, much to the chagrin of James of Vitry, was unwilling to take any steps to alter this arrangement. Jac., 74.

32. Dickson and Dickson, "Robert de Courson," 115.

33. *FK,* 99. Since André d'Espoisse, who followed Erard, was among the forty knights sent to replace Odo of Burgundy following his death in 1218, it seems probable that others of this group had been followers of Erard. However, Raynaldus of Choiseul, mentioned by Röhricht, appears only in Paris, BNL, 17803, #164 and #421, a collection of Courtois charters. He is most likely spurious. Honorius III did not refer to Erard as a crusader when he invoked the penalties of Lateran IV against him. Pressutti, 1:69, 386.

34. Baldwin, *Masters, Princes, and Merchants,* 1:339–43.

35. Knowles, *Evolution of Medieval Thought,* 227. A close examination of the letters in which Honorius III supposedly "revised" the work of Robert Courçon (Dickson and Dickson, "Robert de Courson," 127–29) reveals that most are routine follow-ups aimed at resolving outstanding issues. Precisely the same type of letters, bearing the same tone, deals with the work of Cardinal Guala. See, e.g., Pressutti, 2:9, 3566, and 2:99, 4150, where both cardinals are referred to, and 2:154, 4457. These letters are of little value in determining the relationship between Robert and the pope. The most telling document would seem to be Honorius's letter of July 28, 1218, to the French crusaders (Pressutti, 1:260, 1558), in which he writes: "Ad hec siquidem vobis assidue suggerenda missimus vobis ad petitionem tuam, fili comes Nivernensis, dilectum filium R[obertum] tituli s. Stephani in Celio Monte, presbiterum cardinalem, ut sicut vir potens in opere ac sermone, proponat vobis, secundum datam sibi a Deo prudentiam, verbum Dei cui legationis officium idcirco dare nequivimus, quia dudum antequam ad nos pervenisset dicta petitio, de consilio fratrum nostrorum venerabili fratri nostro Albanensi episcopo, plenam legationem super totum crucesignatorum exercitum dederamus"; RV, 10:1, 1. This letter suggests that the relations between Honorius and Robert may not

have been as strained as some have suggested. Honorius's reason for not using Robert as legate to France in 1216 and later is discussed below.

36. Foreville, *Latran*, 391–95.
37. Roscher, *Innocenz III*, 159; *PL*, 217:674–80.
38. Roscher, *Innocenz III*, 153–58.
39. Cheney, *Innocent III*, 382–86.
40. *Layettes*, 1:405–6, 1083.
41. Cheney, *Innocent III*, 261–63; Kuttner and Garcia, "Fourth Lateran Council," esp. 156–58.
42. Cheney, *Innocent III*, 391.
43. Foreville, *Latran*, 268–69.
44. Ibid., 265–68.
45. Roscher, *Innocenz III*, 156–57.
46. All papal letters regarding the collection of the twentieth for the crusade included the phrase, "sacro concilio approbante." See *Constitutiones concilii quarti Lateranensis una cum commentariis glossatorum*, 7–8.
47. Ibid., 16–17.
48. For *Ad liberandam*, see *Conciliorum Oecumenicorum Decreta*, 267–71.
49. See n. 31, esp. the discussion of the passage from James of Vitry. Honorius III announced his intention of pursuing policies more favorable to France in his letter to Philip of April 21, 1217; Pressutti, 1:92, 524.
50. *Conciliorum Oecumenicorum Decreta*, 268.
51. Ibid., 233.
52. Dickson and Dickson, "Robert de Courson," 102; *Layettes*, 1:404, 1079.
53. *Conciliorum Oecumenicorum Decreta*, 270–71.
54. Ibid., 268.

CHAPTER III

THE VOCATION OF THE CROSS

The task of tracing the direct influence of Innocent III's crusade plan in the sermons of the preachers of the Fifth Crusade is rendered difficult by the nature of the available sources. Alone among the existing collections, the Rommersdorf letter book, which was designed to serve the needs of the abbot of Rommersdorf in his preaching of the crusade, reveals a conscious effort to bring together the letters of Innocent III and the constitution, *Ad liberandam,* for this purpose.[1] On the basis of this source, it is possible to infer the important role that Innocent's ideas played in the formation of crusade sermons. Unfortunately, little direct evidence of the sermons themselves has survived.[2] This situation is not unusual, since we possess none of the crusade sermons of St. Bernard of Clairvaux, whose works exercised an enormous influence on subsequent preachers and on Innocent III himself. We know St. Bernard's ideas only from his letters and treatises. Among the preachers of the early thirteenth century, we have no crusade sermons of Fulk of Neuilly, who certainly helped to shape the preaching of James of Vitry, Robert Courçon, and perhaps also Oliver, scholasticus of Cologne.[3] It is strange that more such sermons have not been preserved. We can only speculate that their specialized character and the fact that they did not fit into the usual sermon cycles of feasts *de temporibus et de sanctis* were chiefly responsible for their loss. Thus the Fifth Crusade is not unique in the paucity of sermon material and is, in fact, somewhat better served than other crusades, most

notably by the *Ordinacio de predicatione S. Crucis, in Anglia* attributed to Philip of Oxford; by the sermons of James of Vitry; and by
various *exempla* and notices of sermons preserved in other sources.[4]

The *Ordinacio* is not a sermon but a guide for the development of
a sermon on the preaching of the cross to the laity. The author says
that he has aimed chiefly at lucidity and directness, in keeping with
the needs of this audience. Two concepts emerge from this treatise.
First, the crusade is an imitation of Christ. This *imitatio* is made
clear in Christ's suffering and death on the cross. Devotion to the
cross is central to this approach. Second, the crusade is a *vocatio,* a
vocation. The crusader is raised to a new state, and although the
nature of this state is not made explicit, it is exalted above the ordinary life of the laity because it is specially sanctified.[5]

The emphasis of the *Ordinacio* is on the Bernardian theme of the
crusade as a means of salvation. The liberation of the Holy Land has
to some degree receded into the background, to be replaced by the
concern of the individual Christian for his soul. The crusade represents the "shortest road" to the imitation of Christ, "so that the
death of temporal life may be like a door and entrance of the kingdom of heaven and unfailing life."[6] The crusade is bound closely to
the whole salvific mystery. There is a total integration of the human
experience of sin and salvation with the crusade: "In the beautiful
wood of paradise death was hidden under the mantle of life, so, on
the contrary, in the deformed and horrible wood life was hidden
under the mantle of death, just as life is concealed, in the case of the
crusaders, under the mantle of a labor, which is like death."[7] Salvation is in Jerusalem, the "*umbilicus* of the earth," but not merely the
city of Jerusalem, but that Jerusalem where "the lamb conquered the
roaring lion on the cross"; it is the cross that cleanses "hearts of
sins."[8] "Christ on the cross inclines himself to offer the kiss of peace
to the sinner, and stretches forth his arms on the cross to embrace
him."[9]

This portrayal of the crucified Christ as the source of divine
mercy and love, drawn from the increasingly popular images of the
suffering redeemer, builds upon one of the major devotional strains
of the second half of the twelfth and the early thirteenth centuries.
There can be no question but that the art of the period served as an
inspiration to the preacher, since he refers to the single nail that
passed through the feet of Christ, a representation that had become
popular in northern European art during this period. It is difficult
to trace earlier connections between the growth of the devotion to

the crucified Christ and the Crusade, but there can be no doubt that such a relationship existed.[10] The integration of the idea of human suffering with that of the suffering Christ represented the devotional expression of a renewed theological emphasis on the humanity of Christ, of a Christ made near to mankind, a Christ to be imitated.[11] The potential for the imitation of Christ that was at the heart of the movement to restore the *vita apostolica* was also at the heart of the crusade movement in the late twelfth and early thirteenth centuries. The crusade was thereby integrated into the spiritual and devotional life of the church. This process is made even clearer when we note the role of Mary as the mediator between Christ and the sinners at the foot of the cross. The full realm of twelfth-century spirituality had become identified with the crusade movement, perceived as an imitation of Christ. "The Lord on the cross describes for us our whole life that we might imitate him, because every action of Christ is our instruction."[12] There is no direct evidence of borrowing from the ideas of Innocent III in this approach, though the consistency with his views is evident. Perhaps the *Ordinacio,* as an example of the main currents of crusade ideology in the early thirteenth century, might better be regarded as typical of the sources from which the pope himself drew his inspiration.

The crusade was also integrated into the moral teaching of the church.[13] The service of the crucified Christ was not merely military service rendered by knights; in fact, that service was subordinated to the service of Christ that must be rendered through the life of the good Christian. The preacher stresses the need for a previous reformation of life: "Just as water falling on the ground does not return to the vase, so the impenitent sinner does not return to God, from whom he has departed after baptism."[14] Innocent III had made this same point.[15] The conversion to penitence of which he spoke was a moral preparation for the crusade. The point was given a legal expression in the careful manner in which this text formulated the crusade indulgence: "And therefore the Lord Pope justly remits for crusaders the punishment for sins and obligates the universal church in their behalf." The terminology is precise. It is the punishment that is being remitted through the treasury of merit (*universalis ecclesia*). It continues: "They can be cleansed through their own contrition, confession, labor, through prayer and alms-giving, which are done by all Christians on behalf of the pilgrims to the Holy Land."[16] Thus the whole work of the crusade has been integrated into the penitential system of the church, not as a substitute for, but as a kind of heroic culmination of that system for the laity.

The preacher viewed the crusade in terms of a "vocacio hominum ad crucem."[17] The idea of vocation was rich in connotation.[18] God called man to his service. That summons referred particularly to the priestly and religious vocation, but not exclusively so.[19] Its application to the crusade carried with it the same sense of the urgency of responding to the call of God to the religious life that we find in St. Bernard.[20] This section of the *Ordinacio* attempts to illustrate the importance of responding to the call of God to accept the cross: "Therefore, do not despair of Christ, but keeping firm to your faith in Christ and your desire of coming to him, rise up by the washing in his blood, which he has shed for us, and follow him on the cross."[21] Innocent III had put it in stronger terms: "those who are not willing to pay him the service that is his due at the time of his greatest need will merit a just sentence of damnation at the last judgment."[22] The preacher chose to emphasize the positive response to the summons. For example, he spoke of James of Avesnes. His companions wished to retreat from battle because their friends were dying all around them, but James said: "I will go forth more willingly and let no man hold me back."[23] The terms are explicit: "The Lord calls you through his apostles and prophets and us preachers so that, by taking up his cross, you may have that [eternal glory] for which you were made."[24] The Lord offers this eternal peace to those who seek it, "provided that contrition and confession precede." And refusal to respond to the call meets with a similar response to that which Innocent III had forecast: "What will you say on the last day when the Lord asks: 'Why weren't you willing to follow me, when I commanded you?' Beware, lest he say to you, 'Amen, Amen, I say to you, I do not know you' [Matt. 25:12] and lest he say to you, 'Go, ye cursed, into eternal fire.'" (Luke 13:25–27)[25] Just as Innocent had used the term *debita servitudo*, the preacher speaks of *servus obediens*. The idea of *vocatio* removed the crusade from the realm of the voluntary. Those who have received the summons of the Lord have an obligation to respond to the crusade, or else they will imperil their souls.

If we see in the *Ordinacio* some similarity to the ideas of Innocent III as expressed in *Quia maior*, we may well wonder whether such was generally the case with the crusade sermons delivered by the preachers of the Fifth Crusade. Though we possess no sermons of Oliver, the scholasticus of Cologne, he does tell us enough about his preaching to suggest that he followed similar themes.[26] More valuable is the evidence from the sermons of James of Vitry, who preached the crusade and then journeyed to the East with the crusaders. Among his numerous sermons are two of particular interest to us, since they are addressed "Ad crucesignatos." They were not written or delivered during the preaching for the Fifth Crusade, but they confirm in significant ways our analysis of the *Ordinacio*.

In *Soli autem gementes,* James asks about those "who hear that the Holy Land is trampled underfoot by the enemies of Christ, and are not moved to sorrow, or do not seem to care?" He speaks in Bernardian terms of the crusade as a test of the loyalty of Christ's vassals. He develops this point in much the same way that Innocent III did in *Quia maior,* by comparing Christ to a feudal lord. He speaks of crusaders as those "who today he has caused to be summoned to aid him in battle." But James draws back from the implications of this statement to say that the crusaders were not bound to Christ by the feudal law, but that he offered them such great rewards in the remission of their sins "quantum ad poenam et culpam" and also eternal life, that they ought willingly to run to his aid.[27] Thus, in this short piece he managed to dwell on the reward for crusade service while hinting at the vocation of the crusader.

In *Precepit nobis Dominus,* these ideas are more explicit. This sermon also opens with theme of the cross as the key to salvation. James argues that the crusade stands as an outward sign of the internal acceptance of the cross in the hearts of the crusaders. It thus has the character of a sacramental. Like the *Ordinacio,* James of Vitry's sermon is closely tied to contemporary devotion to the crucifix, given concrete form in the image of the loving embrace of the crucified Christ. The cross is a moral symbol signifying the rejection of earthly vanities. For crusaders, the salvific action of the cross is dependent on true contrition and confession, and it is on the basis of this conversion that they are considered to be martyrs, "free at the same time from venial and mortal sins, from every penance inflicted on them, absolved from the penalty of sin in this world, from the pain of purgatory in the next, secure from the torments of Hell, crowned with glory and honor in eternal beatitude."[28] Moreover, their wives and relatives share in this benefit to the degree that they share in the financial and other burdens of the crusade. James here provides an explanation for the extension of the crusade indulgence to those who support the crusade, as expressed in the writings of Innocent III and the constitution *Ad liberandam.* James sees this extension in terms of the meaning of the "plena et integra indulgentia" granted to the crusaders by the pope from the power of the keys. This indulgence is not merited, any more than the laborers in the vineyard merited the reward they received, according to the gospel parable.

James uses an *exemplum,* the story of the testing of Gobaud, the son of the emperor Charles, to illustrate how those who did not obey the command of the Lord would not receive a reward. Charles asked his son to take and eat part of an apple that he held in his hand, but the young man refused. Then Charles offered the apple to his brothers, Louis and Lothar, and each in turn accepted it. Charles rewarded them with kingdoms, but when Gobaud saw this and changed his mind, the emperor told him that his response had come too late. Clearly, there would be no reward.[29] The summons of the Lord was not to be left to the will of those who would either accept or reject it. The urgency of this summons is made clear by James in his citation of the Bernardian theme: "Behold, now is the acceptable time, behold now is the day of salvation." Finally, James, too, stressed that the crusader is responding to a heavenly vocation through obedience. The idea of the compelling nature of the crusade vocation had thus become a significant feature in the crusade preaching of the early thirteenth century.[30]

The evidence of the sermons shows that by the early thirteenth century the crusade had been integrated into the spiritual and devotional life of the church along lines strikingly consistent with the movement for the return to the apostolic life. The crusade was recognized as an imitation of Christ. The stress placed upon the necessity for conversion as a prerequisite to participation in the external work of the crusade had come to dominate the sermons. If there were still promises that the Holy Places would be liberated, this liberation was subordinated to the quest for the heavenly Jerusalem. It was this internalization of the crusade movement that gave meaning to the idea of the crusade as a vocation, one that commanded obedience from those summoned in a manner analogous to the priestly and religious vocation. The crusade had become a tool of conversion as well as a pathway to salvation.

The emphasis on vocation and obligation must be read against the background of Innocent's effort to substitute service in the crusade for internal conflict. Vocation has a sacred character; Christ summons the crusader. The rationale that Bernard of Clairvaux had applied to the crusading orders, particularly the Templars, was now extended to the knightly class as a whole, with the aim of transforming society. Implicit in the Innocentian program for the crusade was a vision of Christian society united in fulfillment of the divine plan. The hierocratic significance of that program cannot be ignored. Its achievement under the leadership of the papacy would have led to the submission of all disputes that might have disturbed the internal peace of Europe to ecclesiastical supervision and judgment, while placing the secular leadership at the head of the crusade. But it is apparent that neither Innocent nor the crusade preachers had in mind an appeal aimed only at the knightly class. The conception of a *Ritterfrömmigkeit* is simply too narrow to encompass the broad streams of lay piety to which they were attempting to appeal.[31] As we have seen, Alphandéry's *levée en masse* was actually a molding of the crusade into an instrument for the reform of all segments of Christian society.[32] All would contribute according to their means, and all would share proportionately in the rewards. But we must be careful not to impute more to the Innocentian program for the crusade than the evidence permits. If the potential for a hierocratic interpretation exists, there is no evidence that its application went beyond the immediate needs of the crusade. Whatever conclusions might follow logically from the Innocentian program and its implementation under Honorius III, there is no evidence that either pope was prepared to draw them. Indeed, it was only the existence of broad-based support for the crusade that could explain the appeal of this kind of program in the first place. The evidence of the sermons supports this view. They assume the existence of substantial popular support for the crusade as the means of ensuring that even the reluctant will fulfill their vows. The positive value attached to the crusade enables preachers to develop the idea of vocation, which raises the crusader to the level of a religious, a monk. This notion was further developed in the conception of crusade as an imitation of Christ. These links with both monastic and popular piety were the foundation on which Innocent built his conception of crusade and from which he drew his vision of the relationship between crusade and reform.

What was new in all of this was not so much the ingredients, most of which had been around for a long time, but their integration into a coherent program. Roscher was quite right in perceiving the way in which the crusade took on a new priority under Innocent III.[33] The sermons that we have analyzed suggest that Innocent was responding and giving direction to a broadly based view that gave the crusade a more central role in the life of the church than previous popes had envisioned. Innocent III seems to have been particularly sensitive to this potential. In broadening the base of participation beyond that of direct combatants by ensuring that all who supported the crusade movement could share in the indulgence, he had opened the movement to the masses, providing an outlet for their devotion and tying them more closely to the official effort of the church. What was occurring was a forging of bonds between the institutional church and the popular modes of religious expression that had captured the minds and hearts of many in this period. If the conflicts aroused in France during the legation of Robert Courçon show how difficult it was to translate this approach into a practical program, a letter written by Gervase of Prémontré to Innocent III shows that there was a mounting popular response that fully justified the initiative taken by the pope.[34] But it is not enough to measure that response in the vague terms possible through an examination of the chronicles and annals of the time. Their concern is entirely with the numbers taking the cross. The success of Robert Courçon, of Oliver Scholasticus of Cologne, of James of Vitry, and of numerous others lay not only in calling forth large numbers to take the cross, but also in the degree to which their message evoked a response in their hearers. Was the message of *imitatio,* conversion, and vocation accepted and acted upon by those who heard their words? No analysis of the chronicles can provide an adequate answer to this question.

The crusade preachers were mediators between the clerical elite and the laity. As members of the former group, they expressed views that were certainly formed within that group, especially in their understanding of the Innocentian theology of crusade. In the process of communicating these ideas, however, they faced the need to appeal to the understanding and experience of their audience. The traditional vehicle for this translation of abstract concepts into concrete teachings was the *exemplum,* defined as "an account or story, a fable or parable, a morality or a description, employed to support a doctrinal, religious, or moral explanation."[35] Crusade preachers were masters of the *exemplum,* and many of these have been preserved in collections such as those of James of Vitry or Caesar of Heisterbach.[36] The importance of the *exemplum* to this study lies not merely in any incidental historical information that we might thereby gain, but from the insight it furnishes into the mentality of the preachers and their understanding of their audience.

The *exemplum* provides one of the few means available for grasping some aspects of popular values. In the absence of sufficient data to test the statements found in our sources about the popular response to the preaching, the *exemplum* enables us to examine more concretely the basis on which the preachers appealed to their lay audience and to evaluate, although in a limited way, the message they were attempting to communicate. It also gives us a somewhat better idea of the manner in which that message was understood by the audience.

In the early thirteenth century, the crusade had developed deep roots in almost every part of Europe. Despite the impression of an episodic character that the study of successive military campaigns has given us, it had become a permanent aspect of medieval society that was especially manifested in the crusading orders—the Hospitallers, the Templars, and the recently founded Teutonic Order. Heavily composed of members of the knightly class and supported by kings, the feudal aristocracy, and the citizens of the urban communes, the orders' numbers and wealth provide an important index of the degree to which the crusade had gained an important place within the outlook of the aristocracy. While it is possible that many of those who found their place among the ranks of the crusading orders were younger sons who found service in the crusade more in keeping with their station than membership in the clergy, the bonds thus created served to draw their families more directly into the crusade movement. The founding of the Teutonic Knights in the early 1190s and their rapid expansion under their distinguished grand master, Hermann of Salza, testifies to the increasing popularity of the crusade among German knighthood.[37] There is, moreover, considerable evidence in the sources that the preaching of such men as Oliver Scholasticus met with enthusiastic response, even if we allow for some exaggeration.[38] Yet some historians have suggested that commitment to the crusade was already waning and that criticism was on the rise.[39] What was the real state of affairs? There are certainly prominent examples of crusaders who avoided or postponed their obligation. Is it possible to understand better the reasons for their reluctance? An examination of *exempla* does shed some light on the efforts of crusade preachers to address these kinds of concerns for their audience.

One of their goals was to establish an image of the ideal crusader. As we have already seen, the *Ordinacio* described James of Avesnes, who, faced with insurmountable odds in battle against the Saracens, responded to his companions who counselled retreat: "I will advance the more willingly and no man will hold me back." What makes this story interesting is that James, who fought in the Third Crusade, had a son in the Fourth Crusade. Moreover, a Walter of Avesnes participated in the Fifth Crusade. At least part of this crusade tradition of the Avesnes family could have been known to the audience, reinforcing the image of selfless generosity illustrated in the *exemplum*. In another story, an unnamed knight was captured by the Moslems and hung on a wall. The Christians were hurling rocks against it to break it down, but they stopped when they saw their comrade suspended there. He called on them to keep up the siege. They did, and the rocks broke the gibbet on which he was hanging and freed him. This *exemplum* concludes by advising the audience to have trust in Christ.[40] Still another recounts the tale of a knight who was wounded four times in battle. The physicians said that his wounds were mortal, but he insisted on returning to battle, saying: "My Lord Jesus Christ suffered five wounds for me; I will return to battle and suffer a fifth for him."[41] While the preacher was clearly evoking the conception of the crusader as an imitator of Christ in these *exempla*, he was also drawing on his knowledge of those characteristics that were valued by the knightly class itself. The willingness to take risks, to suffer, and even to die were fundamental to knighthood. These incidents illustrate the degree to which the Bernardian view of knighthood in the service of Christ was brought within the popular grasp. They suggest that the ideals enunciated had already gained a considerable acceptance, that they would, in fact, be received with approval by a large segment of their audience.

Other *exempla* deal specifically with the problem of reluctant crusaders. Caesar of Heisterbach, a Cistercian whose abbey was involved in crusade preaching in the Rhineland and Frisia, has preserved the story of a certain usurer named Godescalcus related to him by his fellow monk Bernard. Godescalcus, a rustic, had assumed the cross but had redeemed his vow with a donation well below what he could afford to pay. He had lied to the one dispensing him about his circumstances. For this reason, the "just Lord, to show how pleasing the labor and expense of the crusaders were" handed him over to Satan. During the night, the devil drew him out of his house and asked him to throw away his cloak, which bore the cross. He did so, and the devil led him through hell to view the punishments of sinners. When Godescalcus returned home, he told his wife about the terrible things he had seen and said that in three days he would die and receive the reward of his perfidy. His wife sent for the priest, who reminded the man that God would forgive him and that he should not despair, but Godescalcus refused to believe him. He died and went to hell.[42] Caesar also reports that Oliver Scholasticus had administered the cross to a certain rich and honest knight whose wife was about to bear a child. But at the onset of labor she grew so ill that her life was despaired of. Oliver, after talking with her husband, went to her and said: "If you will agree to my advice and permit your husband to fight for Christ, you will be freed from this imminent danger without pain." The woman did as Oliver suggested and gave birth "almost without pain."[43] Another story, little more than an allusion, tells how Oliver found that the crusade was being impeded because of the murder of a rich Frisian noble.[44] Examples such as these indicate that very human problems, things that touched the personal lives of crusaders, rather than criticism of the crusade, posed the most significant problems for preachers in securing adherence to the crusade vow. This conclusion suggests that, just as political interests hindered the powerful, local and personal concerns dominated the world of the lowly. The papal peace program was, in a sense, a political counterpart to efforts by preachers to resolve the numerous personal problems that hindered the crusade. In neither case can we argue that reluctance to participate in the crusade had its roots in a growing dissatisfaction with the crusade movement.

Preachers were also at pains to demonstrate the spiritual value of the crusade not merely to participants, but also to the Moslems. One of the most famous of the *exempla* concerned the appearance in the Frisian sky of two crosses during the preaching of Oliver Scholasticus. This sign made so profound an impression on the crowd that many of them took the cross.[45] There are numerous stories that relate the divine favor shown to crusaders. One of the more unusual is that of Eberwach, an honest servant of the bishop of Utrecht. Accused by envious colleagues and unable to defend himself against their unjust charges, he entered into a pact with the devil to protect himself. He succeeded but was exposed when Oliver came to Utrecht to preach the crusade. The cross was his undoing, and he died impenitent and went to hell. But God took pity on this man, who for so long had been honest, and offered him another chance. He who had sinned through the cross could make satisfaction through it. He returned to life and took the cross and

served his bishop on crusade, providing for all an example of penitence. Returning home to his wife, he "was touched with a sacred
fire." He died, and "even to this day, there is in his body, the heat of
fire without pain."[46] Such was the miraculous character of the crusader cross, a benefit that extended also to the Moslems. During the
captivity of the bishop-elect of Beauvais after the battle of August
29, 1219, a woman from Cairo approached him with her son, who
was ill and near death. She had dreamed that if the bishop baptized
him, he would recover. In the morning, she and her relatives
brought the boy to the bishop for baptism and he was immediately
cured.[47] There is in these stories some sense of the expectations of
the crusaders. The crusade was translated into terms that directly
touched their lives. Its potency was confirmed by divine signs and
miracles. Whether cast in terms of fear or hope, their efficacy spoke
of widely shared values.

But did these *exempla* correspond in any way to the real experience of crusaders? At least some of them had a genuine historical
context. But the important point is not whether they were histori-
cally true, but whether they reflected the perceived reality that was
experienced by many of the audience who listened to the preachers.
Did they represent shared experiences? Of course, notorious sinners had gone on pilgrimage as penance for their sins for centuries,
and likewise on crusade, but what of ordinary people? Did they
translate the salvific benefit of the crusade into their own lives? The
evidence of this is sparse and not entirely direct, but it would seem
so. There is, for example, a charter of Adelaide, countess of Grei-
fenstein, granting freedom to her slave Geltruda and her children.[48]
The children were named Albert, Berthold, and Geltruda. Adelaide
states that she granted this charter, "in part for the love of God and
for the remission of her soul and those of her ancestors, and in part
for the love of her brothers." Her brothers were named Albert and
Berthold, and in 1221 Berthold went on crusade. In another charter, the parish priest of Pragelato, a certain Stephen, made arrangements with another priest, named Peter, to take responsibility for
the parish while he was on crusade. But his chief concern was the
care of "a certain young man" for whom he had provided.[49] There
are no words about penitence in these charters, but the circumstances certainly bear the construction that the time had come for
these individuals to straighten out some of their twisted ways and
that by going on crusade they were setting forth on a new journey
that differed from the one on which they had been travelling.

It is impossible to say how often and how deeply the crusade touched individual Christians in the way in which the preachers intended. What is more certain is that there was a broad acceptance in the early thirteenth century of the importance of the crusade not only as a distant war for the liberation of the Holy Places, but also as part of the salvific work of the church. This view served as the foundation on which Innocent III built his crusade program, particularly that aspect that dealt with recruitment. The theology of the crusade was founded on the belief that the crusade was a fitting instrument for the moral transformation of the individual Christian and of Christian society as a whole. Nowhere was this more definitely spelled out than in the enunciation of the vocation of the crusader, with all its religious and monastic connotations.

The reluctant crusader was the one who did not respond to the *vocatio Christi,* because he was too immersed in mundane affairs. The preachers aimed their *exempla* at persons of both sexes and various stations of life, clergy and laity, high and low.[50] They defined participation broadly in both spiritual and temporal terms. They assumed the merits of the crusade and merely aimed at making its benefits evident to their audience. There is no indication that they felt the need to defend it against any major opposition, though the emphasis they placed on the theme "Now is the acceptable time" may well have been a response to an effort on the part of some to argue that God would take care of the Moslems and liberate his Holy Places in his own good time. This argument was at least partially tied to currents in contemporary spirituality that stressed an eschatological view of human history. It would probably be a mistake, however, to regard the proponents of this view as opposed to the crusade. Aside from the views expressed by some heretics, there was no real opposition. The reluctant crusader had other, more practical, reasons for avoiding the fulfillment of the crusade vow. It is through a study of recruitment that we can better understand the complex manner in which men became crusaders.

NOTES

1. Kempf, "Rommersdorfer Briefbuch," 521–23.
2. Schneyer, *Geschichte der katholischen Predigt,* 172–73; Lecoy de la Marche, *La chaire française,* 75–76.
3. *PL,* 182:564–68, 921–40; Baldwin, *Masters, Princes, and Merchants,* 1:36.
4. *SS,* 3–26; for other sources, see notes 28 and 36 below.

5. Paulus, "Werkung," esp. 731–32.

6. *SS,* 4.

7. Ibid., 7–8.

8. Ibid., 8.

9. Ibid., 12; but, see Alphandéry, *Chrétienté,* 2:164, where he states that this devotion is not found in Innocent III.

10. Compare, e.g., Peter of Blois, *De Hierosolymitana Peregrinatione, PL,* 207:1058–70.

11. Alphandéry, *Chrétienté,* 2:169.

12. *SS,* 13.

13. Alphandéry, *Chrétienté,* 2:160, notes the influence of ideas about moral reform on the preaching of Fulk de Neuilly.

14. *SS,* 18.

15. *PL,* 216:817.

16. *SS,* 9.

17. Ibid., 18.

18. See L. Sempe, "Vocation," *DTC,* 15:3148–81; Roscher, *Innocenz III,* 273–84.

19. *LfTK,* 2:274–75; Paulus, "Werkung," 731–32.

20. *DTC,* 15:3160–62.

21. *SS,* 25.

22. *PL,* 216:817.

23. *SS,* 20; see Ambroise, *Crusade of Richard the Lion-Heart,* 265–66.

24. *SS,* 21.

25. *PL,* 216:817.

26. Cf., Oliverus Scholasticus, *Schriften:* 285–88; Alphandéry, *Chrétienté,* 2:166.

27. Pitra, *Analecta,* 2:421–22; Greven, "Frankreich," 25–26.

28. Pitra, *Analecta,* 2:426.

29. Ibid., 430.

30. Ibid.

31. Waas, *Geschichte der Kreuzzüge;* Brundage, "Recent Crusade Historiography," esp. 499.

32. Alphandéry, *Chrétienté,* 2:152.

33. Roscher, *Innocenz III,* 142.

34. *RHGF,* 19:604–5. Gervase depicts the enthusiasm of the lesser crusaders. Given the date of this letter, he can only be referring to crusaders who had enlisted as a result of the mission of Robert Courçon.

35. Welter, *L'Exemplum,* 1; Brémond, LeGoff, and Schmitt, *L'Exemplum,* 27–38. On the interpretation of *exempla,* see esp. Ibid., 101.

36. On James of Vitry, see Funk, *Jacob von Vitry,* 176–84; Frenken, Jacobus de Vitriaco, *Exempla Jacob von Vitry;* and Jacobus de Vitriaco, *Exempla or Illustrative Stories.* For Caesar of Heisterbach, see *T,* 162–79, 344–45.

37. For a discussion of the literature and historiographical developments relating to these questions, see Wojtecki, *Studien,* 3–4. For social origins of the knights, see ibid., 78–79. For papal and imperial support of the order in this period, there are two interesting manuscripts in the Archi-

vio di Stato della Catena, Palermo: Ms 6, "Tabulario della Chiesa della Magione," fols. 1–38v; and Ms 7, "Privilegi," fols. 1–26. The charters found there illustrate the high favor that the order enjoyed both from Pope Honorius III and Emperor Frederick II. On the diplomatic role of Hermann von Salza, see H.-B., 1 : 2 : 863.

38. See Caesar of Heisterbach, *T*, 178.

39. Such is the view of Van Cleve, "Fifth Crusade," 384; but it is not shared by Mayer, *Crusades*, 202. See also Throop, *Criticism of the Crusade*, 29–31; and Siberry, *Criticism of Crusading*, 2–3.

40. *SS*, 25. See also Jacobus de Vitriaco, *Exempla or Illustrative Stories*, 39.

41. *SS*, 25.

42. *T*, 162–64.

43. Ibid., 171–72.

44. Ibid., 178.

45. *T*, 176; Ol. chap. 9; Oliverus Scholasticus, *Schriften*, 285–86, 287.

46. *T*, 172–75; see also Jacobus de Vitriaco, *Exempla or Illustrative Stories*, 55–56.

47. *T*, 172.

48. *Codex Wangianus*, 322–33, 143.

49. *Le carte della prevostura d'Oulx*, 250–51, 242.

50. In addition to those cited, other examples are: a Cistercian *conversus* (Jacobus de Vitriaco, *Exempla or Illustrative Stories*, 56), a virgin (*T*, 164–65), sailors (ibid., 166), and common people (ibid., 169–70).

CHAPTER IV

RECRUITMENT FOR THE CRUSADE

The words of the preachers throw light on only one aspect of the making of a crusader. They give us some idea why an individual would leave home and family on a pilgrimage that might easily end in death, but they tell us very little about the actual process of recruitment.[1] A narrow focus on preaching as the means of recruitment has led scholars to emphasize the importance of individual decisions to take the cross. In the case of the Fifth Crusade, however, Innocent III early sought to ensure that both the secular and ecclesiastical leaders of society would provide contingents for the crusade, and this approach was reiterated at the Fourth Lateran Council.[2] In practical terms, it meant that the recruitment effort was directed in a particular way to the elites rather than to the masses. There was certainly nothing new in such an approach, nor did it rule out the assumption of the cross by individuals who might later become part of a larger contingent.

Preaching was important in arousing popular support to set the recruitment process in motion. The account provided by James of Vitry of his preaching at Genoa in September 1216 is interesting in this regard. When Bishop James and his retinue arrived in Genoa, they found that the Genoese were about to go off to battle. In accordance with their custom, the Genoese seized the bishop's horses for the duration of the campaign. James took a certain pleasure in using the opportunity thus afforded to preach the crusade to their wives in their absence. His words found an enthusiastic welcome.

When the Genoese troops returned, they were subjected to pressure from their wives as well as the preachers, and many took the cross. Despite the success of this preaching, however, the Genoese were not yet ready to commit a formal contingent to the crusade. It was only after the successful negotiation of peace with their enemies through the offices of Cardinal Hugolino that this step was taken.[3] A letter of Gervase, abbot of Prémontré, to Pope Innocent III also makes clear that the recruitment efforts in France were impeded by the failure of the leaders of the crusade to undertake the tasks of organizing their contingents.[4]

The success of the recruitment effort depended, therefore, not only on the popularity of the crusade, but also on the effectiveness of the mechanism employed in the recruitment of contingents and on the nature of such contingents. By analyzing this, we can get some idea of the composition and cohesion of the crusade forces, as well as of the problems involved in removing the major obstacle to crusade participation: the violence that afflicted every level of medieval society. An essential element in that mechanism was the papal peace program.

Violence posed particular problems for the church, which was drawn into virtually every conflict because its institutions were integrated into the basic fabric of society. Beyond its abstract commitment to peace and order, practical concerns for the security of ecclesiastical property combined with a sense of its own weakness in defending its rights against temporal authorities and powers to make the reformed papacy a major supporter of the cause of peace. Of course, both popes and local prelates had recourse to violence from time to time, seeking allies among kings and secular lords for this purpose, but the ecclesiastical vision tended to exalt a view of order that would make such risky adventures unnecessary. It is therefore not surprising that the papacy had embraced the peace movements that had developed during the eleventh century and, with the promulgation of the First Crusade by Pope Urban II in 1095, had proposed the crusade as a substitute for internal violence. What was new in the early thirteenth century was the application of the more sophisticated bureaucratic and legal machinery developed within the church during the latter half of the twelfth century to the peace program set in motion by Innocent III in 1213. In particular, the Fourth Lateran Council strengthened the hand of the papacy by placing the full armory of ecclesiastical penalties explicitly at the disposal of those charged with enforcing the peace.[5]

When Innocent III died in the spring of 1216, he had been on his way northward to arrange a peace between Pisa and Genoa in the interest of the crusade. His successor, Honorius III, did not continue this journey, but he communicated his intention to support the crusade to the Pisans.[6] In January 1217, he appointed Cardinal Hugolino of Ostia as legate for the establishment of peace and the promotion of the crusade in northern Italy.[7] This legation was an outgrowth of Lateran IV, but it continued the work the bishops and crusade procurators had begun in 1213. One of the best examples of this earlier work is found in Bologna. In September 1214 at a meeting presided over by Count Rodolfo di Guido di Bergogno, podestà of Bologna, the commune promised Archbishop Ubaldo of Ravenna to pay the expenses to the East of all Bolognese who would take the cross. Since this agreement provides no reasons for this action, these can only be inferred from the circumstances surrounding the event. In all probability, the presence of Ubaldo, who was the metropolitan of the ecclesiastical province to which Bologna belonged, was connected to the recent election of Enrico della Fratta as bishop. Enrico, who was already bishop-elect in November 1213, witnessed this agreement as bishop. The election of Enrico had brought to an end a long struggle between leading elements of the commune and the former bishop, Gerardo Ariosti, who had been forced to resign by Innocent III on the grounds that he was unsuitable for office.[8] Conditions in the city were, therefore, for the moment quite favorable for the kind of agreement reached with Archbishop Ubaldo. But Enrico della Fratta proved himself an energetic defender of ecclesiastical interests and soon came into conflict with the commune. At the same time, the Bolognese were involved in conflicts with various of their neighbors. It was not until 1217 that leaders of the major opposing factions within the city, Bonifacio de' Lambertazzi and Baruffaldino de' Geremei, took the cross with their followers.[9] A fragment containing the oath taken by Bonifacio and his followers in the name of their faction has been preserved.[10] During this same period, Cardinal Hugolino actively worked to bring about peace between Bologna and other cities of the region. Thus, the Bolognese contingent that departed for the crusade in the summer of 1219 contained elements from both of the leading factions in the city. Its departure was the product of a lengthy process of negotiation.

Similar patterns of negotiation characterized the recruitment process in other cities of Tuscany and northern Italy. While disputes between bishops and communes were common, each case presented unique circumstances and somewhat different results. Older views of these disputes as struggles for communal liberty against a feudal episcopacy and its allies have had to give way before the fact that the relationship between the communes and the bishops varied considerably throughout this period.[11] In some places, bishops played an important part in the formation of the earliest communal government. On other occasions, commune and bishop might find common ground in cooperating in a policy of communal expansion aimed at providing security for the interests of both.[12] Neither the supporters of the bishops nor those of the communes represented well-defined economic classes. Nevertheless, grounds for conflict were certainly more abundant than bases for cooperation. Under the leadership of the reformed papacy, the episcopacy of northern Italy aggressively pursued efforts to maintain and enlarge the patrimonies of its churches, including the jurisdictions that accompanied these holdings. These disputes fueled local conflicts and contributed to conflict throughout the region.

The example of Volterra illustrates the manner in which parties to such a conflict involved the crusade in their legal struggles and negotiations. For the Italian historian Gioacchino Volpe, the conflict between Bishop Paganus Pannochieschi, a scion of one of the leading families of the region, and the commune was a classic expression of the communal struggle for freedom from feudal power.[13] Volpe also recognized, however, that Paganus was a staunch defender of episcopal rights from lay incursions.[14] The policies of Paganus involved his supporters and him in protracted conflict with the leadership of the commune. Cardinal Hugolino supported the bishop by excommunicating Ildebrandinus quondam Romei, the podestà of Volterra, in 1217 and worked assiduously to promote a settlement throughout this period.[15] A study of the documents shows that all of those named as crusaders were supporters of the bishop. In every instance, they used their crusader status to pursue legal claims, largely against the commune, before ecclesiastical courts manned by judges delegate appointed by the legate.[16] These cases dragged on into the period following the Fifth Crusade, despite serious efforts to settle the fundamental causes of the conflict in 1217 and 1218.[17] It is evident that they impeded Volterran participation in the crusade, although it is impossible to estimate their overall effect. The case of Volterra illustrates what happened when there was no resolution of a conflict, so that the supporters of only one party committed themselves to the crusade. The necessity to proceed through such involved processes consumed very substantial amounts of time for the legate and his co-workers. Critics of the ineffectiveness of recruitment efforts have not usually recognized how difficult and complex the task faced by the legates really was. But such efforts did not always end in frustration, as the case of Lucca shows.

The legation of Hugolino of Ostia bore early fruit at Lucca in 1217, when he reached an agreement with the commune to provide a contingent of crusaders to be supported by a tax of a fortieth levied by the commune. This letter mentions Guidarus Barleti and Henricus Maczavitelli, *milites* of Lucca, as the first to receive the "vexillum Domini," but many others, "tam milites quam populares," followed their example. The situation at Lucca was rather different from that at Bologna. The leaders of the commune and Bishop Robert seem to have worked together to clarify their respective jurisdictions in the *contado*. The main conflicts were between the *milites* and the *populares,* i.e., between the feudal aristocracy of the countryside and the supporters of the commune.[18] The period immediately preceding the arrival of the legate had been marked by considerable strife. Like the Bolognese, the Luccan crusaders elected joint captains and consuls, Ubaldus and Rumonus.[19] While there is insufficient evidence to reach a definite conclusion as to whether they represented opposing factions, the parallel is suggestive.[20] The success of Cardinal Hugolino in securing the support of the commune was matched by the generosity of the bishop in providing a ship for the transport of the Luccan crusaders.[21] Thus the process of reconciliation got off to a good start at Lucca after a period of successful negotiation.

Bishop Robert of Lucca, an able administrator and strong supporter of reforms in his diocese, also prepared to go on crusade. For this reason, it was important for him to reach agreements aimed at protecting episcopal rights. In an important document relating to the commune of Aquilea, which was under the jurisdiction of the bishop, Robert set forth in detail the reciprocal rights of the commune and of his representative, the viscount, Paganellus de Moriano.[22] This charter provides insight into the tangle of jurisdictional rights that often lay behind the conflicts in the Tuscan communes. At issue were concrete privileges and customs that affected both the ordinary life of the citizens and the proprietary rights and income of the episcopacy. In the early thirteenth century, the Tuscan bishops were often hard pressed to meet the multifarious demands on their income. Yet protection of the episcopal *jura* was extremely difficult and involved them in lengthy litigation.[23] Bishop Robert was successful in conciliating local interests, thereby paving the way for significant Luccan participation in the crusade.

Such participation, however, was not achieved without difficulty. Individual crusaders were often involved in litigation that affected their role in the crusade. The notarial register of Ser Benedetto, preserved for the period 1220–21, provides a valuable record of litigation involving the cathedral chapter and the bishop.[24] There are three cases in which crusaders are identified. Unfortunately, the poor condition of the manuscript makes it virtually impossible to follow them in detail, but we can determine that all of the crusaders were men of some substance, deeply involved in the property disputes on which litigation flourished. The commune, represented by its podestà, was a party in two of the cases, as was Bishop Robert, who had returned from the crusade in the spring of 1220. A third case is actually a continuation of a longstanding dispute over land between Bishop Robert and the abbot of Fucecchio, which is located on the Arno southeast of Lucca but which was actually in the archdiocese of Pisa.

A certain Guido, *crucesignatus,* perhaps the same Guido de Cumuli mentioned in a previous document in this register, asked the archpriest of Lucca, in virtue of his office as judge delegate of Pope Honorius III, to invalidate a decision of the abbot of Fucecchio prohibiting the sale of a certain farm by Guido.[25] The sale may well have been needed to pay his expenses on crusade. From the date of the suit, January 1220, it seems that Guido had not accompanied the Luccan contingent led by Bishop Robert, which had departed in the fall of 1218 and did not return until later in 1220.[26] This dispute is typical of many in which ecclesiastical corporations found themselves involved. The fact that Guido was a crusader apparently had no effect on the abbot, who was intent on protecting his rights. Guido's case serves to illustrate the inadequacy of explanations that focus too exclusively on the communal-episcopal aspect of conflicts rather than on the general issue of disputed jurisdiction as a basis for conflict.

The mere existence of multiple jurisdictions nourished the growth of litigation at Lucca, much as it did elsewhere. In January 1221, following the return of Bishop Robert from the crusade, Dominus Passavanti, the brother of Menabui and uncle of Guidoctus, both of whom were crusaders not yet returned from the East, appealed to

Bishop Robert, *ex parte summi pontificis* (representing the Pope), to
defend him from the podestà of Lucca.[27] It is difficult to determine
on what basis Passavanti brought this suit to an ecclesiastical forum.
Apparently, having crusaders in the family seemed to justify the effort. Very likely he was counting on the support of Bishop Robert,
who was himself having problems with the commune of Lucca that
would soon lead to his exile from the city.[28] In another case involving the commune, Oddo, the father of a crusader named Fralmus,
was trying to block the podestà from removing his case from ecclesiastical jurisdiction. The procurator of Lucca in this case argued
that Fralmus was no longer a crusader, because he had returned
from the East to Messina in Sicily.[29] Cases of this sort were quite
common. The privileges of crusaders opened access to ecclesiastical
courts and thereby increased both the causes and the occasions of
litigation. There was a healthy interest in availing oneself of the op-
portunities so offered. It was this interest which increased the capacity of ecclesiastical courts to resolve disputes that might impede
the crusade. But such conflicts also provided grounds for disputes
between ecclesiastical and secular courts, as the cases brought by
Passavanti and Oddo prove. Their effects might not only impede
the crusade, but also fuel attitudes critical of the church. In the case
of Lucca, however, local participation in the crusade was virtually
ended before a new rash of disputes seems to have broken out. As
Professor Osheim has shown, Lucca was not free of the grounds for
conflict between bishops and communes.[30] We can only conclude
that Robert had enjoyed a better relationship with the commune
than some of his episcopal contemporaries and was willing to reach
agreements, like that with the commune of Aquilea, that would
permit him to go on crusade. It was only after his return from the
East that there was a new outbreak of disputes, culminating in his
expulsion from the city and renewed efforts to restore peace.[31]

Throughout northern Italy, Hugolino of Ostia and his representatives arranged truces and secured support for the crusade. In Pisa,
his preaching of the crusade before the citizens of the commune was
identified in the popular mind with the settlement of outstanding disputes, such as the conclusion of peace between Pisa and
Genoa and that achieved earlier between Pisa and Lucca.[32] Although Roberto Cessi has maintained that Venice played almost no
part in the Fifth Crusade, there is clear evidence that Hugolino, in
working to arrange a five-year truce between the Venetians and Pa-
duans, paved the way for the provision of Venetian ships to trans-

port a large contingent of crusaders to the East.[33] Negotiations
between Pistoia and Bologna also progressed, with the probable result of a sizeable Pistoiese group.[34] But the absence or sparsity of
documentation in most places does not permit detailed discussion.

The picture of popular response or reluctance in joining the
crusade has been widely fostered in the literature and forms the
backdrop to the standard interpretations of the crusade movement
in the late twelfth and early thirteenth centuries. Evidence that recruitment of crusaders in northern Italy resulted, to a substantial
degree, from communal commitments and the conclusion of peace
agreements emphasizes the importance of the leaders that we meet
in the crusade documents, showing that they were often a product
of the peace program itself. Each communal contingent had its separate structure. As Hessel has pointed out, the Bolognese contingent
had an organization that was consistent with this status as a separate
unit, with council, captains, and other officials.[35] The same was true
for that of Lucca, and also for much smaller units, of which we
sometimes know little else but the names of leaders. The corporate
nature of crusade recruitment and participation reflects a society in
which power was generally localized in the hands of powerful individuals or groups who commanded the loyalty of their followers.

A study of the recruitment process in other regions—the empire,
the Kingdom of Sicily, Hungary, and England—provides insight
into other dimensions of the task confronting those who were
preaching the cross. Perhaps the most important contribution of
Hans Martin Schaller has been in his reinterpretation of the relations between Frederick II and the papacy in the period prior to
his coronation in November 1220. He presents a picture of papal-
imperial cooperation based on the presence of the papal subdeacon,
Nicholas, at the imperial court and on Frederick's support of the
peace efforts of Cardinal Hugolino of Ostia in northern Italy. Taken
in conjunction with his discussion of Frederick's close ties with the
Cistercian order, this evidence has created a new context for the discussion of Frederick's own assumption of the cross and the participation of other important members of the German aristocracy in
the crusade.

Examination of witness lists of charters issued by Frederick II at
Aachen around the time of his coronation shows that a substantial
portion of the most important German crusaders were present with
Frederick and took their vows at the same time. These included
both bishops and secular lords. Among the bishops were Otto of
Münster and Egbert of Bamberg. Lay lords included Louis, duke

of Bavaria; Otto, duke of Meran, brother of Archbishop Berthold
of Kolocza; William, count of Jülich; Adolf, count of Berg; Ludwig, count of Loos; Werner, the dapifer of Bolanden; and Henry de
Ulmen.[36] The presence of such an impressive group of future crusaders, combined with the presumption that many of them took
their vows at this time, suggests that Nicholas, the papal subdeacon, and Bishop Conrad of Regensburg—as part of the papal
effort to arrange for peace in Germany following the defeat of Otto
IV at the battle of Bouvines—were following basically the same
procedure that we have already witnessed in France under Robert
Courçon and Simon of Tyre and in northern Italy under Hugolino
of Ostia. What has not previously been noticed is that the intensive
and highly successful recruiting activity of Oliver, scholasticus of
Cologne, was centered precisely in an area where there had been the
strongest and most enduring ties to Otto.[37] Innocent III's selection
of Oliver may have been directed against Archbishop Dietrich of
Cologne, one of Otto's major supporters, who was soon replaced
by Engelbert of Berg, the brother of Count Adolf, a strong supporter of Frederick. The final composition of the Rhenish and
Netherlandish contingents reflected in their leadership noble supporters of both Frederick II and Otto IV.[38] While crucial documentation is lacking that would enable us to study the process of
recruitment in this area in detail, certainly the general picture that
emerges not only confirms our hypothesis, but indicates that the
assumption of the cross by Frederick himself played a direct role in
the shaping of a significant part of the German crusade contingent.
The spirit of cooperation between the empire and the papacy discussed by Schaller very probably was translated into direct support
for the crusade.

A letter of Pope Honorius III dated December 16, 1220, sheds
some additional light on the recruitment process in the lands of the
empire. Writing to various abbots concerning a conflict between
two Frisian provinces, he notes the seriousness of this war "by
which a multitude of crusaders in those regions are being delayed
from aiding the Holy Land." He then asks them to arrange for a
firm peace or truce, if necessary by employing ecclesiastical cen-
sures.[39] There can be little doubt that the process Honorius had in
mind was essentially the same as that which he pursued in his effort
to secure the participation of Frederick himself, in which efforts to
settle outstanding differences were paralleled by continuing pressure to fulfill the crusade vow.

The participation of Leopold VI, duke of Austria, and a large contingent of Germans and Austrians who accompanied him, may also have been partially affected by the efforts to promote a settlement between Frederick and Otto. Leopold had first taken the cross in 1208. He had supported King Andrew of Hungary in his bid for the throne, as well as the candidacy of Philip of Swabia for the German crown, but had recognized Otto IV following Philip's murder. He evidently participated in efforts to reconcile the differences between the two houses and showed a certain vacillation in his support for Frederick II during 1211 and 1212. It was at this time that he took part in the war against the Saracens in Spain. He returned, however, to support Frederick II at the battle of Bouvines. Despite the lack of evidence linking his participation in the crusade to the peace process in Germany and the clear fact that he took the vow in 1208, Leopold's contingent contained individuals, such as the Bishop of Münster, who had opposed Frederick and supported Otto until relatively recently. While their inclusion may have been purely a matter of convenience, it seems more likely to have been a result of the process of pacification in Germany.

Frederick II was not only, after 1212, the German king and emperor-elect, he had also been the king of Sicily since 1198. Innocent III had appointed crusade commissioners within the *Regno,* but we have no trace of their work. The conclusion that these efforts were ineffective is, however, far from evident. For one thing, the commissioners appointed were Archbishop Luca of Cosenza and his fellow Cistercian, the abbot of Sambucina. Schaller has already noted Frederick's spiritual ties to the Cistercian order, and in particular his friendship with Luca di Cosenza.[40] It is also possible that the efforts of the archbishop of Ancona extended into the northern reaches of the kingdom. There were crusader contingents from Salpi, led by its bishop, and from the lands of Monte Cassino.[41] However, critical examination of the evidence regarding crusade participation in the Kingdom of Sicily under William II and from the entire reign of Frederick II, including that relating to his own crusade expedition of 1228, shows that in the Kingdom of Sicily crusading was usually taken up by royal command.[42] The methods generally used in military and naval levies seem to have been employed for the crusade, with the king determining the size and composition of the force desired. Thus, in 1220 Frederick II commanded Matthew Gentile, count of Lesina, to lead a force of seventy knights and six galleys to Damietta.[43] He sent another royal fleet, under Count Henry of Malta and Bishop Walter of Palear, in

1221.[44] These were sent in direct response to papal pleas for assistance and did not represent any effort to form a crusader army in the kingdom. The raising of these contingents is more indicative of the cooperative relationship existing between Frederick and the papacy than it is of any support or lack of support for the crusade movement among the inhabitants of the kingdom.

Recruitment of the English contingents to the Fifth Crusade was bound up with the conflict between King John and his barons, as well as their ally, Prince Louis of France. John himself took the cross on March 5, 1215, in company with Ranulf, earl of Chester.[45] The privileges of a crusader were undoubtedly of advantage to the king at a time when he was engaged in a serious conflict with his barons. The rather cynical view, however, that John took the crusader vow only to place his enemies at a disadvantage overlooks the fact that as a vassal of the pope he already enjoyed considerable papal protection. As Roscher has shown, John's assumption of the cross did strengthen Innocent III's hand in the peace negotiations with the barons, but there is every indication that Innocent was serious about John's participation in the crusade.[46] An examination of the recruitment process itself shows that the pope did make successful efforts to enlist the leaders of both the royal and baronial factions for the crusade. Ranulf, a strong supporter of King John, was among the principal leaders of the contingent that departed for the East in 1218.[47] In 1219 there were also contingents under the leadership of both royal and baronial partisans.[48] In Ranulf's company went his brother-in-law, William d'Aubigny, earl of Arundel; his nephew, John de Lacy, constable of Chester and sheriff of York; and Robert Fitz-Walter. Of these, Robert had been a leading rebel against King John. All of them had participated in the Battle of Lincoln; all departed for the crusade within the year following the royalist victory. Thus, the efforts of the papal legate, Cardinal Guala, on behalf of the young king, Henry III, following the death of John in 1216, followed the now-familiar pattern in joining recruitment to the effort to secure peace.

A study of the linkage between recruitment and the negotiation of truces and the ending of myriad internal conflicts sheds considerable light on the composition of the crusader army and the delays encountered in moving various contingents to the East. In an overwhelming number of cases, the time of departure of various contingents depended on the settlement of conflicts in which the leadership was involved. This fact also places in new light the postponements granted to Emperor Frederick II in the fulfillment of his vow, and in particular explains his relative ease in obtaining such postponements prior to the completion of his negotiations with the papacy over imperial and papal claims in Italy and his imperial coronation in December 1220. It also explains the increasing frustration of the papacy with his failure to depart in 1221. Nevertheless, it also suggests why Frederick, deeply involved in the internal problems of the Kingdom of Sicily, felt justified in seeking continued postponements of his departure. There were, in fact, ample precedents in the protracted negotiations leading up to the departures of other contingents. Frederick's case was exceptional only in degree.

A study of the geographical origins of the leadership of the Fifth Crusade (Figures 4.1 and 4.2) reveals that the persistence of unresolved conflicts, as in southern France, severely limited participation by the lay aristocracy.[49] Conversely, it also reflects the success of the papal peace program during this period, even though that success was often very partial and shortlived. The comparison of lay participation with that of the upper clergy illustrates in a striking way the close geographical concurrence between these two groups. Whether or not all who took vows actually went on crusade, the geographical correspondence of the two groups confirms that Innocent III's conception of clerical participation as a means of supporting the spiritual needs of crusade contingents was adhered to by the upper clergy. There is a substantial regional representation of spiritual leaders for almost all of the crusade contingents that seems proportionate to the probable number of lay participants. Similarly, participation of the lower clergy seems to follow the same geographical lines.[50]

In order to understand more fully the recruitment of crusaders, it is necessary to examine the way in which membership in crusade contingents reflected existing institutional structures, as well as ties of loyalty and obligation. Modern views about the role of individual decision making have tended to overshadow the social realities of medieval society, in which kinship, vassalage, communal membership, or loyalty to a particular individual or group played an important role in shaping individual decisions. The joining of the peace program and the recruitment process meant that many among the leadership of the crusade assumed the cross under certain social pressures. The same was true of many of their followers.[51] Once they had taken the vow, they were subject to ecclesiastical penalties to secure its fulfillment. Thus, membership in a particular group

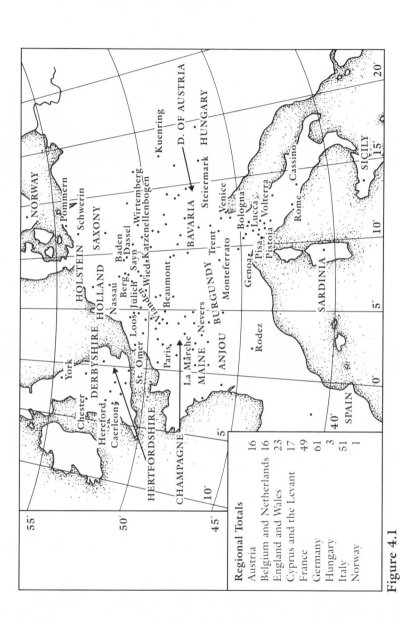

Figure 4.1

Geographical Distribution of Feudal and Urban Aristocracy Participating in Crusade

• Member of feudal aristocracy or participation of urban aristocracy

Regional Totals	
Austria	16
Belgium and Netherlands	16
England and Wales	23
Cyprus and the Levant	17
France	49
Germany	61
Hungary	3
Italy	51
Norway	1

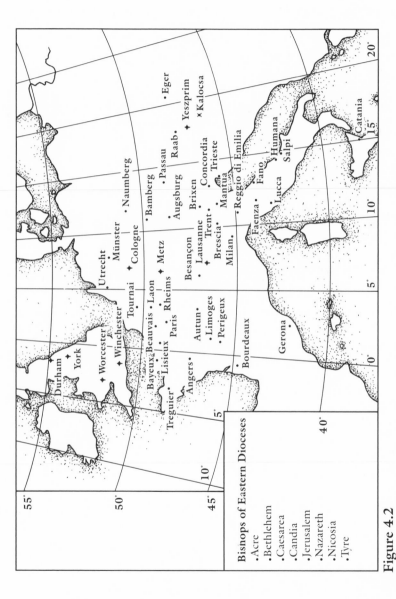

Figure 4.2

Geographical Distribution of Bishops and Archbishops • Fulfilled vow • Did not go on crusade

✖Bertholdus, Archbishop of Kalocsa, went on crusade in 1217; his successor, Ugrinus, took the vow but did not go on crusade.

Bishops of Eastern Dioceses
• Acre
• Bethlehem
• Caesarea
• Candia
• Jerusalem
• Nazareth
• Nicosia
• Tyre

was a significant factor in the decision to go on crusade. Even where a particular leader, or a group such as a commune, may have decided freely, some followers or members may well have felt pressure to participate.

Personal ties of loyalty were of great importance in all parts of Europe, in the more urbanized regions as well as in those that were more apparently feudal. Urban contingents from northern Italy contained many *milites* with strong ties to the rural countryside. Some of these were members of episcopal *familiae,* others had been subsumed into communal organizations, and some retained their feudal status, reflecting the changes that were taking place in northern Italy in this period. The rural-urban distinction between *milites* and *populares* was by no means fixed in this period. The ties of the latter to the land were also strong, regardless of the presence of craftsmen and merchants among them. At places such as Bologna, Lucca, and Volterra, the composition of the total crusade contingent reflected not merely the results of the peace program, but also the realities of these social differences. Although the lack of sources makes the task difficult, it is possible to identify some crusaders as members of episcopal *familiae,* some as members of the feudal aristocracy, and others as *milites* or *pedites* of the commune.[52] The importance of personal ties of loyalty was, of course, very evident among feudal contingents, where service under a particular lord seems to have reflected existing ties of vassalage. Thus, John de Lacy, one of the best-known members of the contingent led by Ranulf, was constable of Chester, sheriff of York, and a nephew and leading vassal of that great baron. Beatrice Siedschlag has identified a number of crusaders who witnessed a charter of John de Lacy at Damietta in 1218, some of whom must have accompanied him on crusade.[53] The preponderance of the Yorkshire element in this group affirms the importance of personal ties among those who took the cross. A group drawn from the followers of Erard of Brienne probably had many bound by similar ties. As we saw earlier, their assumption of the cross was connected to their service with Erard. Finally, the group that accompanied Walter Berthoudus, about whom we will have more to say shortly, illustrates our point quite well. Walter, later lord of Malines, was a vassal of Henry, duke of Brabant, who also took the vow, and was in the company of other vassals of Henry, as well as his own retinue.[54] The structure of groups such as these helps us to see that the crusade host mirrored certain aspects of the society from which it came.

Ties of kinship also played a significant role in recruitment. Longnon has already given considerable attention to them in his discussion of participation in the Fourth Crusade.[55] A charter of Margrave Hermann of Baden, who accompanied Duke Louis of Bavaria on crusade in 1221, provides interesting testimony on the importance of family ties.[56] Hermann's brother, Frederick, had gone on crusade in 1218 and had died. Hermann had earlier promised his brother to carry out whatever offering of their common property he desired to make for the benefit of his soul, and this is precisely what he did in a grant to the Teutonic Knights. But the best support for our argument comes from an analysis of statistical evidence. Among German bishops, for example, I have been able to identify 29 percent with relatives on the crusade (Figure 4.3). The corresponding figure for French bishops is 15 percent. Given the shaky genealogical sources for this period, these figures suggest strongly that family ties with crusaders were a significant factor among episcopal participants. Bishops like Peter of Paris, Otto of Münster, and Eustorgius of Nicosia had brothers on the crusade.[57] Comparison with the feudal aristocracy shows similar results. Twenty-six percent of French, 17 percent of German, and 20 percent of English crusaders had relatives participating in the crusade (Figure 4.4).

Moreover, a study of this latter group lays to rest the idea that the crusade was heavily populated by younger sons seeking their fortunes overseas. Sons and fathers, older and younger brothers went on crusade together. The example of Walter Berthoudus provides significant evidence about the structure of a family group on crusade. Walter travelled to the East in the fall of 1218 and distinguished himself in battle in the defeat suffered by the crusader army opposite Damietta on August 29, 1219.[58] Like so many crusaders, he fell ill during the terrible winter of 1218–19, and he gathered his family and close associates around him in order to make a gift to the Teutonic Knights.[59] These included his brothers, Terri and Gyle, and his sons, Arnoldus and Aegidius, along with Catherine, the wife of Aegidius. There were also two priests and his *famulus,* Basilius, as well as fellow vassals of the duke of Brabant, and others of unknown status. There is no reason to suppose that such a group was unusual in its composition, even in the inclusion of a wife of one of the crusaders.

Such factors as kinship and personal ties of loyalty were important to providing motivation to some crusaders and in giving inter-

Figure 4.3 Family Relationships of Participants (Bishops)

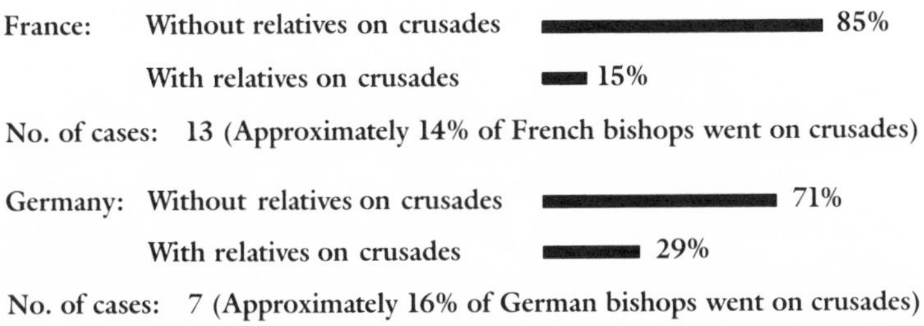

France:	Without relatives on crusades	85%
	With relatives on crusades	15%

No. of cases: 13 (Approximately 14% of French bishops went on crusades)

Germany:	Without relatives on crusades	71%
	With relatives on crusades	29%

No. of cases: 7 (Approximately 16% of German bishops went on crusades)

Figure 4.4 Family Relationships of Participants (Feudal Aristocracy)

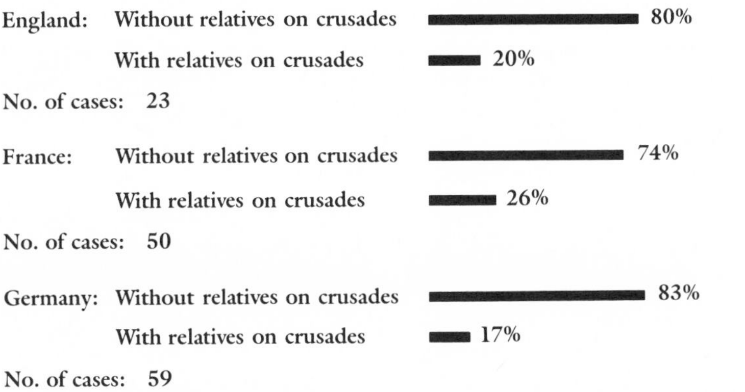

England:	Without relatives on crusades	80%
	With relatives on crusades	20%

No. of cases: 23

France:	Without relatives on crusades	74%
	With relatives on crusades	26%

No. of cases: 50

Germany:	Without relatives on crusades	83%
	With relatives on crusades	17%

No. of cases: 59

nal cohesion to the crusader army. Taken together with the impact of the peace process on the recruitment of many urban and feudal contingents and the support gained from Frederick II, they help account for the presence of a substantial portion of the crusader army as we know it. Does this mean that individual decisions, made out of piety or even greed, were of no importance in the recruitment process? I do not think so. First, one cannot rule out the scope for voluntary decision even within the framework of urban, feudal, or even royal contingents. But, as we saw in the previous chapter, there is ample evidence that many took the cross individually as a result of preaching.[60]

The peace program provided an important mechanism for the recruitment of the secular elite for the crusade. Operating in conjunction with underlying motivations provided by the spiritual and temporal rewards promised the crusaders, the peace program was a significant factor in the implementation of the papal plan to secure commitments of contingents for participation in the crusade. It removed a primary obstacle in the path of those who desired to go to the East. Ideally, from the vantage point of the papacy, it opened the possibility for royal and imperial participation, though that goal was realistically attainable only in the case of Frederick II. But this approach presented difficulties that were to have a major impact on the future of the crusade. The slowness of the peace and recruitment processes meant that, even after the Fourth Lateran Council, many groups would not be ready to depart at the time fixed for the beginning of the crusade. Internal rivalries might also cause problems in contingents that were formed of recently opposed factions. Though the peace program was somewhat successful in dealing with the complexities of societal conflict, it was not adequate as a mechanism for recruitment. Its failure, however, was more the result of the violence that was endemic at every level of medieval society than of any lack of urgency in meeting the needs of the crusade. Moreover, what was true of recruitment was also evident in the papal effort to secure adequate financial support for the crusade.

NOTES

1. On the motivation of crusaders, see Mayer, *Crusades,* 9–40; Van Cleve, "Fifth Crusade," 384. Jonathan Riley-Smith's very interesting recent article, "The Motives of the Earliest Crusaders and the Settlement of Latin Palestine, 1095–1100," provides a valuable introduction to this topic. I have not been able to find any extensive treatment of recruitment for the crusade.

2. *PL,* 216:819. ". . . obsecramus . . . ab archiepiscopis et episcopis, abbatibus et prioribus, et tam cathedralium quam aliarum conventualium ecclesiarum capitulis et clericis universis, nec non civitatibus, villis et oppidis competentem numerum bellatorum cum expensis ad triennium necessariis secundum proprias facultates."

3. Jac., 77.

4. *RHGF,* 19:604–5.

5. For a discussion of later developments, see Heers, *Family Clans in the Middle Ages,* 119–24, in which he discusses formal structures for securing the peace. Important background is found in H. E. J. Cowdrey, "The Peace and the Truce of God."

6. Pressutti, 1:2, 3.

7. Ibid., 49, 272.

8. Hessel, *Storia della città di Bologna,* 195, 208.

9. Heers, *Parties,* 109; Giovanni Gozzadini, *Delle torri gentilizie di Bologna,* 286–90; ASB, Reg. Grosso, fol. 278, 374. Most of the documents in the Registro Grosso (RG) have been printed in L. V. Savioli, *Annali Bolognesi,* 3:2.

10. ASB, Busta strumenti e scritture, 1 (Olim VI, framm. 16); the edition in *FK,* 58, no. 6, is confusing. Hessel omits discussion of the crusade from his section on Bishop Gerardo; *Storia della città di Bologna,* 208. See also Augusto Vasina, "Le crociate nel mondo emiliano-romagnolo," esp. 35–36.

11. Heers, *Parties,* 67–78; Hyde, *Society and Politics,* 106; Waley, *Italian City Republics,* 91–92.

12. See, for example, the relations between Bishop John da Velletri and the Florentine commune; Davidsohn, *Storia di Firenze,* 2:23–87.

13. Volpe, *Lunigiana medievale,* 135; see also his *Toscana medievale,* 174–208.

14. Volpe, *Toscana,* 174.

15. *Regestum Volaterranum,* 124, 349; 125, 350, 353.

16. ASF, Volterra, 92r, 192; *Regestum Volaterranum,* 129, 364; 130, 367; 132, 375; 135, 383; 138, 390; 141, 399; 142, 400.

17. *Regestum Volaterranum,* 138, 380; Volpe, *Toscana,* 208.

18. Pressutti, 1:49, 272; 188, 1120; ASV, RV 9, fol. 221, 900. The Villani Chronicle also mentions that the crusaders were drawn from all factions (chap. 40); see Pasquale Villari, *I primi due secoli della storia di Firenze,* 168.

19. *FK,* 72, 48 (Sav., 3:2, 433, 488).

20. The account of Luccan participation in the Fifth Crusade in A. Pellegrini, "Le crociate in terra santa e la parte che vi ebbero i Lucchesi," mentions a single leader, Lorenzo Sauli (pp. 386 and 389), but there is no evidence in documents from the period that Lorenzo went on crusade, either as a leader or in any other capacity.

21. *T,* 350.

22. Müller, *Documenti,* 91, 59.

23. See Osheim, *Italian Lordship;* Volpe, *Toscana,* 185–86.

24. This register is contained in Lucca, Archivio Arcivescovile, A + 1.

25. Ibid., 114–15.

26. Ibid., 47, shows that Guillelmus was still acting as episcopal vicar in April 1220. See also Ol., chap. 16, p. 187, n. 1.

27. Lucca, Archivio Arcivescovile, A + 1, 138.

28. Pressutti, 2:98, 4143 (Pressutti has an incorrect name for the bishop); ibid., 177–78, 4583.

29. Lucca, Archivio Arcivescovile, A + 1, 158.

30. Osheim, *Italian Lordship,* 74–75.

31. Pressutti, 2:98, 4143.

32. Roncioni, *Istorie Pisane,* 1:478–81; Pressutti, 1:151–52, 896.

33. Cessi, *Storia della repubblica di Venezia,* 214–15; but see Ol., chaps. 49 and 51; see also Syracuse University, Ranke Ms 59, p. 56, which reports on the mission of Cardinal Hugolino to Venice and Ranke Ms 78, where the peace efforts of Cardinal Hugolino figure on pp. 253–60. For Venetian

participation in the transport of Milanese crusaders, see *Documenti del commercio veneziano nei secoli XI –XIII,* 2 : 125 – 26.

34. Hessel, *Storia della città di Bologna,* 84 and 194. There is evidence of Pistoese crusaders in ASF, Olivetani di Pistoia (August 4, 1219), and ASF, Diplomatico (Pistoia), (October 16, 1219, and March 13, 1220).

35. Hessel, *Storia della città di Bologna,* 195.

36. H.-B., 1 : 2 : 401, 405, 407, 408, 410.

37. For example, according to Caesar of Heisterbach, Oliver preached in Brabant, a stronghold of support for Otto, *T,* 164.

38. See, for example, Pressutti, 1 : 226 – 27, 1365 – 66, in which a dispute between Count William of Holland and Count Ludwig of Loos was postponed until their return from the crusade.

39. Rodenberg, 1 : 111, 158.

40. Schaller, "Kanzlei," 250 – 51.

41. Ol., chap. 16; Ryccardus de Sancto Germano, *Chronicon,* 7 : 2 : 80 – 81.

42. See my "Crusading by Royal Command," 144 – 46.

43. *FK,* 81.

44. *FK,* 110; *T,* 239, 245, 254. See David Abulafia, "Count Henry of Malta and His Mediterranean Activities, 1203 – 1230."

45. Sied., 75 – 77.

46. Roscher, *Innocenz III,* 156 – 58.

47. James W. Alexander, *Ranulf of Chester: A Relic of the Conquest,* 77 – 80, provides useful information.

48. For example, Savaric of Mauleon was "a prominent supporter of King John"; Sied., 142. Saher de Quency, a leader of the rebels against John, was also in this contingent; ibid. Many of the twenty-five barons of Magna Carta participated in the crusade; J. C. Holt, *Magna Carta,* 338.

49. Vicomte de Bonald, "Les meridionaux aux croisades," contains little in the way of verifiable information. Only Henry, count of Rodez, and Raymond IV, viscount of Turenne, can be verified from other sources. On a more general note, see Ferdinand Delorme, "Les Espagnols à la bataille de Damiette."

50. I have been able to identify only about seventy-one members of the lower clergy, less than 10 percent of the actual participants in Appendix 2. Since the number is so small and quite unreliable as a sample, I can only suggest this similarity.

51. See, for example, the followers of Erard of Brienne; chap. 2, n. 33.

52. This was certainly true at Volterra. At Lucca, Bishop Robert made Orlanduccione a member of his *familia* after their return from the crusade. Osheim, *Italian Lordship,* 36; Müller, *Documenti,* 438. For members of the feudal aristocracy, see Appendix 2. The terms *milites* and *pedites* are used quite commonly with reference to communal contingents.

53. Sied.: Henry of Tyes and Hugh of Alta Ripa, 139; John of Easton, Jordan de Ranavilla, Martin of Selby, and Philip of Alta Ripa, 140; Robert Grammaticus, 141 – 42; Robert of Kent, steward of John de Lacy, and Roger, porter of Pontefract Abbey, 142.

54. Branden van de Reeth, "Récherches sur la famille de Berthout," esp. 68 – 72; *FK,* 70.

55. Longnon, *Les compagnons de Villehardouin*, 3.
56. *Wirt. UB*, 101–2.
57. See Appendix 2.
58. Ol., chap. 29.
59. *FK*, 70.
60. Jonin, "Le climat de croisade," esp. 280–81; see also Wentzlaff-Eggebert, *Kreuzzugsdichtung des Mittelalters*, 231–33, and Baratier, "Une prédication de la croisade à Marseilles en 1224."

CHAPTER V

FINANCING THE CRUSADE

The question of finance was crucial to the success of the crusade.[1] Already in 1213 the pope had initiated efforts to collect money, and at the Fourth Lateran Council he launched his tax on the clergy. The reasons for these initiatives are not difficult to find. In the late twelfth and early thirteenth centuries, secular rulers were hard put to raise money for their wars. Aside from feudal dues and customs revenues, they depended almost entirely on the incomes from their royal domains, and these were far from sufficient to support extraordinary military activity. In the famous phrase of the time, they were normally expected to "live on their own." And the same was true of the feudal armies that served them. Even the citizens of the nascent communes were expected to support themselves, when possible, in their military service. The resources of government were stretched to the utmost when required to sustain large-scale military operations for more than a few months at a time, and no ruler could support a standing army. Public obligations were grounded on private resources. This reality was reflected in the fundamental structures of society, so any reordering of this military system would entail significant changes in that society. While such changes were definitely in the wind, it was still too early to consider them more than modifications of the basic system, which remained heavily dependent on private resources.

Giles Constable recently underscored the importance of private resources to the crusade movement in the twelfth century.[2] Mort-

gages and loans, chiefly made by religious houses, provided the
ready cash for many members of the feudal aristocracy to leave their
families on this long and hazardous venture.[3] Sales of property were
also common. During periods of preparation for major crusades,
such activity became very intense, sufficient in some regions to
produce a fall in land prices.[4] But most agreements included a provision for the resumption of the crusader's property on his return
or the protection of his heirs in the event of his death. The role
played by religious houses indicates the difficulty involved in raising
large amounts of cash. Such efforts strained the ordinary lending
sources beyond their limits. Even monasteries themselves did not
always possess the ready cash and had to dispose of gold and silver
ornaments and sacred vessels to secure it. And the sums were large.
One loan recorded for Peter the Venerable, abbot of Cluny, just
prior to the Second Crusade, was for four thousand *sous*.[5] Many
involved the mortgage or sale of quite substantial pieces of property, and such exchanges had a significant impact on the transfer of
capital. Crusade expenditures had a stimulating effect on a number
of industries, most notably shipbuilding. Efforts to secure support
for the crusade affected numerous aspects of life, not only for the
feudal aristocracy and the urban upper classes, but also for the rural
peasantry. But this evidence of the deep involvement of twelfth-
century society in the Latin West in the financial support of the
crusades also underlines the inadequacy of contemporary public
fiscal administration, the limited development of sources of taxation, and the generally precarious nature of the economy as a whole.

No more compelling example of the limitations of this approach
to the financing of the crusade can be found than the experience
of the participants in the Fourth Crusade.[6] For a variety of reasons, but chiefly because the numbers taking ship at Venice proved
fewer than anticipated, the crusaders were unable to come up with
enough money to pay the costs of transport. Donald Queller has
documented their strenuous efforts to raise money among themselves.[7] He has made a convincing case that their inability to solve
this problem was chiefly responsible for the diversion of the crusade.
The Venetians demanded crusader help in their attack on Zara as a
condition of providing transport to the East. Thus a crusader army
was employed, against the express command of the pope and under
penalty of excommunication, in an attack on a Christian people,
and this was merely a prelude to the crusader conquest of Constantinople, itself an effort to gain Byzantine support for the

crusade. Ironically, Innocent III had made substantial efforts to provide for the financial support of the Fourth Crusade, including provision of a tax of a fortieth of clerical incomes, but none of this money was available to the crusaders at Venice.[8] In the toughest meaning of the phrase, they were on their own, and as we have seen, the results for the crusade were disastrous.

Thus, in his preparations for the Fifth Crusade, Innocent III could not help but be aware of the importance of adequate finances for the success of the crusade. Yet he was confined within a tradition that limited the potential for innovation. The earliest subsidies to support the crusade, levied not by the church but by royal crusaders, were in the nature of feudal aids.[9] There were, no doubt, many who disbelieved the promise made by Louis VII of France to the Bishop of Le Puy on the occasion of his departure on crusade that "neither we nor any of our successors will exact this [money] further on the basis of custom nor molest the church in this fashion."[10] They would have been right. Louis VII himself enacted a crusade tax of a penny on the pound in 1166, and his rival, the English monarch Henry II, immediately followed suit. These taxes applied to both clerical and lay subjects. The same was true of the taxes levied by Philip Augustus and Henry II in support of the Third Crusade.[11] As Roscher has noted, the papacy was slow to show initiative in these matters.[12] Clement III seems to have commanded a special alms collection from some of the clergy in 1188, but Lunt maintains that this was not a tax.[13] The decision of Innocent III in 1199 to order the clergy to pay a fortieth of their incomes to aid the Holy Land therefore represented a substantial change in papal policy.[14] The implications of this action touched many aspects of Innocent's concerns, representing as it did a rather clear attempt to establish direct papal control over clerical taxation, but it seems to have met with opposition from many local churches and was, perhaps, less than fully successful.[15]

As much as the financial plan that evolved after 1213 owed to these previous experiences, especially Innocent's program for the Fourth Crusade, the pope could not deny that his earlier effort had been a failure. Still, the program that emerged at the Fourth Lateran Council in 1215 did not drastically alter the plan of 1199. Nor was it really possible to do so. In the first place, the fundamental structure of crusade finance could only be modified incrementally, given the resources available even to the papacy. The basic concept that each crusader had to provide for his own needs had proven inadequate, but it remained essentially in place. The decisions taken in *Ad liberandam* in 1215 represented more a fine-tuning of Innocent's earlier plan than a completely new initiative.[16] The most important change was the enactment of this program by the council rather than on the authority of the pope himself, as had been the case in 1199.[17] Whatever the legal force of the earlier decision, there is no question but that political wisdom, combined with the experience of resistance to the tax of 1199, made the approbation of the council important to the success of the 1215 tax. Innocent was able to secure a tax of a twentieth on clerical incomes for three years. He and the cardinals pledged a tenth, and he also agreed to pay thirty thousand pounds and to furnish an armed vessel for the transport of Roman crusaders.[18] The pope also anticipated a substantial income from the redemption of the vows of unsuitable crusaders and from the chests placed in the churches to collect the freewill offerings of the laity.[19] The major changes in his program of 1199 involved a doubling of the tax on incomes and its extension for three years, as well as the emphasis on the collection of money from the redemption of vows. Beyond a doubt, the experience of the Fourth Crusade led to Innocent's increased emphasis on the provision of ships for transport, including his promise of partial indulgence "not only to those who offer their own ships, but also to those who build them for this enterprise."[20] He also offered a partial indulgence to all who donated to the cause of the crusade in accordance with their means, as had been done by popes since the Third Crusade. Finally, in keeping with the character of *Ad liberandam* as a document that reflected the problems faced by the Fourth Crusade, Innocent set the points of assembly for the crusader army at Brindisi on the Apulian coast of Italy and at Messina in Sicily. This decision had the practical effect of enabling crusaders to take ship from numerous ports and to gather prior to their departure to the East. It avoided the problem of straining the resources or putting too much reliance on any one of the major maritime cities. The result was a plan that provided a more adequate financial base for the crusade, one that was more flexible than that of 1199 and that was backed by the Fourth Lateran Council.

The implementation of this program got underway in the last months of Innocent's pontificate but chiefly became the responsibility of his successor, Honorius III. Under Innocent III, it was normal practice that a four-man commission composed of local clergy and two members drawn from the Knights of the Temple and the

Hospital supervised the collection of the twentieth, receiving the funds collected by bishops, abbots, chapters, and others in their respective jurisdictions.[21] This division of responsibility aimed at reassuring local authorities regarding the ultimate use of the funds. Moreover, the popes initially followed a policy of allotting a large portion of the revenue from these sources to meet the needs of local crusaders.[22] At Lucca, much of the twentieth went for the support of poor crusaders.[23] Phylippus Camerarius, captain of the crusaders of Foligno, received the twentieth of the monastery of Santa Croce in Sassovivo for three years, amounting to two hundred *raserias* of grain, to pay for a ship for both the rich and the poor crusaders of Foligno without distinction.[24] The twentieth of Poitiers was assigned to Savaric de Mauleon for a similar purpose, since he incurred a debt of twelve hundred marks with various Sienese merchants in connection with the crusade.[25] Examples of this kind could be multiplied, as Honorius himself made clear in 1220.[26] In the shadow of the Fourth Lateran Council, the papacy endeavored to win as much local support as possible for its crusade tax by demonstrating that it was being used to support local contingents.

As we have seen, Innocent III had attempted to broaden the base of participation in the crusade to include not only the actual crusaders but almost the whole of Christendom. His effort to extend the spiritual benefits of the crusade was tied to his financial program. As we have seen, too, beginning in 1213 he had instructed papal crusade preachers to administer the cross to all without regard to suitability, later permitting those who could not fulfil their vows for good reason to redeem them for a cash donation. Some historians have seen in this provision the seed of abuses that would trouble the medieval church right down to the reformation, laying the responsibility at the feet of Innocent.[27] Innocent merely recognized that this means of involving the masses more deeply in the crusade served both his conception of the crusade and its pressing financial needs. He soon found that the measure aroused considerable criticism, and we hear no more of it in *Ad liberandam*. Yet the redemption of the vows of unsuitable crusaders seems to have provided a substantial source of income for the Fifth Crusade, probably in large measure due to improved methods of enforcement. There is some indication that much of this came from women who had taken the crusade vow and were permitted to redeem it on the grounds of sex alone.[28] On the other hand, the papacy resisted strenuously the efforts of able-bodied crusaders to secure exemp-

tion from their vows, though in some instances it did permit individuals, chiefly because of their poverty, to fulfil them by fighting
the heathen in Prussia.[29] In cases where secular rulers requested that
a particular royal official be allowed to redeem his vow, this was permitted, with the understanding that another would go in his place.[30]
If a crusader died before departure, an effort was made to secure a
replacement of comparable rank.[31] Nevertheless, criticism of reluctant crusaders on the local level was intense, so that there was constant pressure on the papacy to secure compliance.

The papacy was constantly concerned about public opinion and
fearful lest scandal or fraud endanger the crusade. Almost the entire
thrust of its fund-raising efforts was dependent on the cooperation
of local authorities, many of whom were only too willing to believe
the worst about Rome's capability of misusing funds. But there was
another and even more practical reason why the papacy sought to
achieve local confidence. It was seeking the cooperation of secular
authorities at every level in levying taxes for the crusade. Innocent
and the council appealed for this in *Ad liberandam*. In the financial
area, Innocent wanted the two powers, temporal and spiritual, to
act together but independently for the support of the crusade. In
the case of maritime cities, he asked for this support in the form of
ships; from others he asked a tax or subsidy. The effort enjoyed at
least a limited success. We have no way of knowing fully the extent
of the response to Innocent's request for taxes from secular authorities. There was no crusade tax levied in France or England, though
there was a slight compensation for this in the case of France, where
Philip Augustus made a generous donation to the departing crusaders in 1218. For the Holy Roman Empire, although there is
ample evidence that Frederick II furthered the work of the crusade,
there is only a hint that he provided direct financial assistance.[32] We
may presume, however, that those contingents sent at his command
from the Kingdom of Sicily were paid for in part out of the royal
treasury.[33] At Lucca, a tax of a fortieth was levied for the crusade,
and the commune seems to have made a serious effort to collect it.[34]
At Bologna, the agreement reached with the archbishop of Ravenna
specified a substantial contribution to the support of Bolognese
crusaders, and the contract for ships concluded between Milan and
Venice in 1219 probably implies the same.[35] There is, moreover,
considerable evidence of communal support for contingents in
1221.[36] The best-known examples suggest that success in peace negotiations was not only a precondition for success in recruitment,

but also a most important factor in securing major financial support. While our knowledge of this aspect of crusade finance is not sufficient to support broad conclusions, it does provide a rather impressive indication of the financial involvement of secular powers.[37]

There is certainly no evidence of any decrease in the traditional means of support for the crusade in the early thirteenth century. The evidence that survives suggests that such support was broadly distributed among the various social classes and among both participants and nonparticipants. Those about to depart continued to make gifts to secure prayers for themselves and their families. Bequests were not unusual. The register of the Abbey of Montevergine, located south of Naples, records the will of a certain Roger, who left three ounces of gold for the good of his soul to aid the Holy Land.[38] Roger, whose estate was valued at thirty ounces, was a person of some substance, but hardly rich. Three ounces was the price of a good horse. Of course, the wills of those who participated in the crusade were likely to contain legacies for the military orders or for the support of the crusade.

These realities formed the background of the financial plans evolved under Innocent and largely pursued under Honorius III. The consensual basis provided by the Fourth Lateran Council for the levying of the twentieth on the incomes of the clergy signalled a reversal of the policy that Innocent had followed in 1199, when he had promulgated the fortieth on his own authority. Apparently, the effort to secure approval of this tax on a piecemeal basis by local church councils had demonstrated the need to employ the conciliar mechanism in gaining approval of the tax of 1215, and Innocent had been quick to learn the lesson.[39] Innocent and his successor could not help but be mindful of the reluctance of local clergy and laity to permit centralization of fiscal control by the papacy. The papacy demonstrated this sensitivity by employing local officials in the collection of taxes and by designating representatives of both clergy and laity to hold and account for money obtained from the chests in the churches. Moreover, both popes initially followed a policy of allotting a considerable portion of crusade revenues to meet the needs of local crusaders. The question regarding these policies was not, however, the degree to which they conformed to contemporary ideas on the role of government, whether secular or ecclesiastical, but whether they could stand up to the pressures engendered by the needs of the crusade itself. There is evidence that they could not, but there is disagreement. William Lunt has suggested that Hono-

rius III "instituted reforms . . . based on his financial experience as
papal camerarius," whereby tax collection was placed in the hands
of members of his own household. He goes on to say that this
change was influential in establishing papal fiscal policy during the
remainder of the thirteenth century.[40] Recently, Richard Kay has argued, in his study of a tax levied for support of the Albigensian
Crusade in 1221, that this action by Honorius was exceptional and
involved no fundamental change of policy, since he continued to
pursue traditional means of collection as well. Kay thus stressed the
continuity of policy between the pontificates of Innocent and Honorius concluding that they attempted to maintain a balance "between local and central government" in the collection of crusade
taxes and that this balance was decisively disturbed only during the
reign of Gregory IX, who was the initiator of the centralizing trend
that gathered momentum under Innocent IV.[41]

Kay's view has merit, but before agreeing with him completely
we would do well to put the question of a change in papal fiscal
administration into the broader context of the pressures that helped
to shape papal financial decisions during the crusade. This is no
easy task. There is no simple way to demonstrate the difficulties
involved in maintaining a large expedition in the East over a considerable period of time. Previous scholarship has sometimes emphasized the problems involved in collecting and distributing crusade
taxes more than the immense task of sustaining the crusade. We
have tried to show that Innocent III realized the inadequacy of the
measures he had taken in preparing for the Fourth Crusade and
tried to make major improvements, but we cannot really show that
these were either successful or sufficient. Still, some recent research
casts valuable light on the question.

For the crusade of King Louis IX of France, William Jordan has
been able to reconstruct a wealth of detail concerning its finance
and even to suggest some rough estimates regarding revenues and
costs.[42] Since this crusade took place only a generation after the
Fifth Crusade and even shared the same geographical objective, it
seems reasonable to report some of his findings here. Perhaps the
most important is the evidence that he adduces, sparse though it is,
of the strain placed on the French economy by the raising of funds
for the crusades. He shows that royal support for extensive construction by Cistercian houses "came to an end on the eve of the
crusade."[43] Nor did it resume quickly in the period following the
crusade. The same was true of virtually all construction projects in

northern France with which the monarchy was associated.[44] Jordan
also argues that public works projects, other than those connected
with the crusade, were hard hit and that fewer royal administrators
received salaries.[45] It might similarly be pointed out that the pontificates of Innocent III and Honorius III saw few major projects of
reconstruction or renovation undertaken in Rome.[46]

Jordan also shows that Louis relied heavily on income from the
French church to support his crusade. Indeed, crown revenues were
totally inadequate to the task. If his estimates are correct, income
from ecclesiastical taxes paid about two-thirds of the total cost.[47]
Even though Louis applied extraordinary pressure to collect these
taxes, the degree of success he achieved suggests that historians
have underestimated the effectiveness of papal collections for the
Fifth Crusade. What is also suggestive is the fact that Louis secured
the bulk of this income from two separate levies of a tenth on clerical incomes for two years. The tax for the Fifth Crusade, though
not limited to France, consisted of only a twentieth for three years.
It seems reasonable to conclude that the tax levied by the Fourth
Lateran Council was far from excessive. Further, the decision of
Honorius III to permit the use of one-half of the French twentieth
to support the Albigensian Crusade had to have a serious impact on
the total revenue available for the Fifth Crusade, simply because
France was the wealthiest of the European kingdoms.[48] Under these
circumstances, it is not surprising that a lack of sufficient financial
support was a constant complaint of the crusaders. One may seriously doubt whether they had even as much as the army of Louis
IX thirty years later, and that for a campaign that stretched over almost four years, compared to one whose chief campaign lasted less
than two years.

The most important financial document relating to the Fifth
Crusade is a letter of Pope Honorius III to Pelagius dated July 24,
1220.[49] Although much cited, it has been used chiefly for the historical information that it contains rather than for its report on the
financing of the crusade. There are obvious reasons for this, given
the virtual impossibility of resolving problems regarding exchange
rates and the different moneys in which the report lists revenues.
Yet, in spite of these difficulties, it may be possible to reach some
general and tentative conclusions that are worthwhile. The period
covered is only two years, from the departure of the Roman contingent in the summer of 1218 until July 1220. Moreover, an unspecified but significant portion of the income from the twentieth

had already been dispersed for the support of various contingents, and this was generally entrusted to their leaders. There is no way to estimate what percentage of the total income was dispersed in this way. Honorius says that many magnates received the twentieth from their own lands. He admits that it was only rather late that he came to realize that this was not the most effective way of dispersing the twentieth.[50] Not only were the funds tied up until such time as these individuals might decide to depart, but a portion was completely lost. Moreover, there was no way of applying the funds to meet critical needs. Honorius therefore decided to increase his control over both collection and disbursement. He employed papal chaplains and familiars to collect the twentieth, as well as the income from the redemption of vows and other sources. At the same time, he took steps to ensure that money went directly from the source to Pelagius in the East. No doubt this measure considerably increased the power of the legate.

This use of papal collectors was not new and did not signify a permanent change in papal financial administration. The pope continued to rely on the bishops at the same time as he employed papal bureaucrats. To have done otherwise would have been unrealistic and would undoubtedly have provoked a storm of opposition. Honorius was not innovating a more efficient administrative structure but responding to a specific set of problems. The urgent needs of the crusaders forced him to centralize papal collections to this limited degree. Lunt clearly was too prone to emphasize long-term developments and the systematization of administration without giving sufficient heed to the circumstances that produced these changes incrementally and often hesitantly. Honorius was fully cognizant of the fact that he was taking an unusual step in employing papal officials in this way and was at pains to justify it by the nature of the emergency that confronted him. His action illustrates concretely the impact of the crusade on papal administration. If he had any sense of the long-term consequences of this action, it was of the risks involved in an approach that would cause friction between the papacy and the local churches. His commitment to the crusade not only overrode the traditional position of the local churches vis-à-vis the papacy, but also overcame his reluctance to tread this dangerous ground. But Richard Kay has gone too far in trying to argue the exceptional nature of Honorius's use of papal collectors in such a way as to isolate it from developments under Gregory IX. Honorius clearly feared the setting of a precedent, but he also knew that he was setting one. If not the sole, or even the willing, initiator of papal fiscal centralization, he was at least conscious of the direction in which he was moving and of his reasons for doing so. This realization was only one step removed from the development of a policy.[51]

Given the limited character of the pope's report to Pelagius, it is clear that it is of no value in arriving at realistic estimates of the costs and expenditures of the Fifth Crusade, even to the degree that this has been achieved for the crusade of Louis IX.[52] But this does not justify ignoring the figures that have been given or failing to compare them with other data in order to see what they can tell us. Table 5.1 records the destination, source, purpose of transmission, and amount of all sums. Given the ambiguities, it is not possible even to secure clear totals for the various kinds of money listed. However, the total of gold ounces and marks can be expressed as 701,692 marks of silver. There are other figures given as "inter marcas argenti et uncias auri" or as marks sterling that cannot be safely included in this amount. Conservatively, we can account for 775,461 marks. Although this sum is a significant part of the total money listed in the document, it is far from a complete accounting. It is possible to get some idea of the value of this amount of money. A list of knights prepared in 1221 provides useful information regarding the usual subsidy paid to each knight departing for the crusade. It amounted to twenty-five marks.[53] In addition, the same amount was paid for four armed sergeants with horses. The sum of seven hundred thousand marks would have provided subsidies for twenty-four thousand knights, if it were spent for that purpose. There were fewer than three thousand knights in the army that accompanied St. Louis to Egypt in 1248. The total number of troops has been estimated at fifteen thousand. There were about five thousand crossbowmen and between five and six thousand mounted sergeants. The remainder were light-armed infantry.[54] There are good reasons, however, for believing that the army that fought the Fifth Crusade was larger than that of St. Louis, though perhaps not as high as a hundred thousand.[55] Since the bulk of the 775,461 marks went directly to Pelagius and was spent on the army for material, victuals, fortifications, and payments to the troops in one form or another, the legate had to be contributing to the support of a very large army. The best figure that we possess for the size of the army at any one time is that provided by Oliver Scholasticus on the eve of its final march. There were well over ten thousand troops, of whom probably twelve hundred were knights, not including forces left to

Table 5.1. Revenues and Expenditures, 1220

GIVEN TO:	FOR:	SOURCE:	AMOUNT AND TYPE OF MONEY:
Romans	Ships	Papal camera	19,000 marks of silver
Romans	Arms and victuals	Papal camera	5,000 pounds Provençal
Pelagius		Papal camera	1,000 ounces of gold
Pelagius		Papal camera	5,000 ounces of gold
Pelagius		Papal camera	5,000 ounces of gold
Pelagius		20th	612 inter marcas argenti et uncias auri
Pelagius		French 20th	11,600 marks of silver
Pelagius		20th	3,000 marks of silver
Pelagius		20th	160 marks of silver
Jacobus, Marescalcus	Machines	D. of Albano	80 marks of silver
Mag. Matthaeus	Letters to Doge	20th	80 ounces of gold
Duke of Bavaria		Emperor	2,000 marks of silver
Pelagius		Papal camera	3,000 ounces of gold
Pelagius		20th	5,000 ounces of gold
John de Giso and Brother Otto			86 pounds Provençal

Pelagius		English 20th	13,000 marks of silver
Pelagius	Hospitallers, etc.	Hungarian 20th	1,711 marks of silver
Pelagius	Hospitallers, etc.	Hungarian 20th	38 marks of silver
Pelagius		Genoese 20th	1,458 pounds Gen. min.
Pelagius		Spanish 20th	605½ marks of gold
Pelagius		Spanish 20th	25,642 Marabatinos
Pelagius		Spanish 20th	754 Obols Maximutinos
Pelagius		Spanish 20th	353 marks of silver
Pelagius		Spanish 20th	5,100 pounds of monies of Spain
Pelagius		English 20th	5,000 marks of silver
Pelagius		French 20th	6,000 ounces of gold
Cardinal Hugolino	Expenses		100 marks sterling
Cardinal Hugolino	Debts in city		250 pounds Provençal
Bishop of Reggio	Expenses of preaching		40 marks sterling
Cardinal Nicholas	Expenses, trip to Frederick		30 pounds of d. of the Senate
Marquis of Montferrat	Expenses, trip to Frederick		100 ounces of gold
Marquis of Montferrat	Expenses, trip to Frederick		100 pounds of d. of the Senate
Marquis of Montferrat	To be paid at his departure	20th	600 ounces of gold (equals 15,000 marks of silver)
Bishop of Reggio		20th	50 ounces of gold

Source: Rodenberg, 1:89–91, #124.

defend Damietta or those travelling upriver by boat or ship.[56] For reasons that will become apparent later, this number was very likely smaller than the peak number of troops assembled at any one time. Moreover, the Fifth Crusade witnessed numerous arrivals and departures. Periods of service were short. This meant that numbers were larger and costs higher than for Louis's crusade. The manpower implications of this investigation will be the subject of further study throughout the remainder of this book. The immediate question is whether papal financial planning and administration were adequate.

No final answer is possible. The temptation to provide qualitative evaluations of quantitative questions is tantalizing but much too risky. But certain conclusions are reasonable in light of the evidence. Innocent III's dissatisfaction with the financial preparations for the Fourth Crusade resulted in important changes. Not only was the amount of the crusader tax increased, but the sanction obtained from the council tried to assure both political acceptance and legal enforceability. However, the manner of distributing the funds raised problems. Much of the money was going into the hands of local magnates and was therefore not available for the immediate needs of the crusade. Honorius III reluctantly centralized collections and ensured that a greater proportion of the funds would go directly to the legate in the East, but this action did not mean the abandonment of previous policies, nor did it provide an adequate level of support for the conduct of the war. There is no way to confirm the validity of this conclusion, save from statements made by the leaders of the army and the chroniclers. But there is no reason to reject their view that a shortage of money was a serious problem.

What can be argued more convincingly is that Honorius III made significant improvements in the system for collecting and disbursing the funds. Those who have been critical of this aspect of papal administration have perhaps underestimated the obstacles that the pope faced in introducing even the changes that he did, or have failed to follow the possible consequences of his failure to act. Leaving aside the question of adequacy, it seems evident that Honorius III showed himself a careful and capable administrator. He demonstrated here those qualities that had most likely led to his elevation to high office in the papal curia some thirty years earlier as a result of his labors on the *Liber Censuum,* or tax book of the Roman church. He implemented new policies with considerable awareness of the risks they entailed, but he did not hesitate to act when he was convinced of the need.

If the preparations for the Fifth Crusade did not result in dramatic changes in the area of crusade finance, the pressures of the crusade itself did favor the trend toward centralization in papal fiscal administration. Having assumed the initiative in the organization of the crusade, the papacy could not escape the consequences. In the minds of most previous scholars, this relationship could be expressed easily. Innocent III had sought to make this crusade exclusively papal and had of necessity undertaken the full measure of responsibility for it. But we have already seen that there are substantial reasons for refusing to accept this interpretation. There are good reasons for not equating papal initiative with a desire for exclusivity, not least the pope's own efforts to secure significant lay involvement in terms of actual participation and direct financing of the crusade. What we may suggest here is that for Innocent and Honorius the primacy of papal initiative was aimed at securing a more effective papal voice in the crusade, but rather less than the control others have argued to be their goal. They set in motion processes which, if fully successful, might have mobilized Latin Christianity in a total commitment to the crusade. As we have seen, their aim was to exert pressure on the leaders of lay society, building upon a broad involvement in the crusade. Within limits, this effort was successful, but the final result was incomplete. Papal initiative was unable to achieve its goal of total mobilization, especially and most dramatically at the pinnacles of secular society. From this fact arose the particular leadership problem of the Fifth Crusade, with all of its implications not only for the success or failure of the crusade, but also for the straining of relations between ecclesiastical and secular powers.

NOTES

1. The basic studies of papal taxation in this period are Adolf Gottlob, *Die päpstlichen Kreuzzugssteueren des 12. Jahrhunderts,* and William E. Lunt, *Financial Relations of the Papacy with England to 1327.* For the crusades, see Ronald P. Grossman, "The Financing of the Crusades," Giuseppe Martini, "Innocenzo III ed il finanziamento delle crociate," and Siberry, *Criticism of the Crusade,* 111–49.
2. Constable, "Financing of the Crusades."
3. Ibid., 74–76; see also Martini, "Innocenzo III," 309–10.
4. Constable, "Financing of the Crusades," 71–72.

5. Ibid., 73.
6. Queller, "Fourth Crusade," 9–49.
7. Ibid., 46.
8. Ibid., 47–8.
9. Constable, "Financing the Crusades," 66–67; Lunt, *Financial Relations,* 240.
10. Constable, "Financing the Crusades," 68.
11. Ibid., 69–70.
12. Roscher, *Innocenz III,* 75–77.
13. Lunt, *Financial Relations,* 240; but this view has been revised by Roscher, *Innocenz III,* 76.
14. Roscher, *Innocenz III,* 77. Roscher maintains: "Nicht die einzelnen Methoden waren neu, sondern ihre systematische Ausweitung und Anwendung" (ibid.).
15. Martini, "Innocenzo III," 313–14; Lunt, *Financial Relations,* 241–42.
16. Roscher, *Innocenz III,* 145.
17. Martini, "Innocenzo III," 322.
18. *Conciliorum Oecumenicorum Decreta,* 268–69. Note especially the text of *Ad liberandam,* which stresses that the tax on clerical incomes was decided "ex communi concilii approbatione."
19. Lunt, *Financial Relations,* 424–28. In my opinion, Van Cleve has presented too pessimistic a view; "Fifth Crusade," 385–86.
20. Roscher, *Innocenz III,* 145; *Conciliorum Oecumenicorum Decreta,* 268. In the months after the Lateran Council, Innocent wrote to the citizens of Ancona, ordering them to cease levying a tax on departing crusaders and to provide transport for them at a fair price; Theiner, *Vetera monumenta slavorum,* 1 : 69. He also wrote to the consuls of Genoa, asking them to persuade some fellow citizens to rescind an agreement reached with certain papal representatives for the provision of ships to transport crusaders; ibid., 70. It is apparent that he spared no effort to prevent a repetition of the events that had occurred in Venice during the Fourth Crusade.
21. Lunt, *Financial Relations,* 243–44.
22. Van Cleve, "Fifth Crusade," 386; see, e.g., Pressutti, 1 : 290, 1745; and 294, 1770.
23. Pressutti, 1 : 188, 1120. This letter of Honorius III, dated February 26, 1218, details the efforts of the papacy to secure support for Luccan crusaders without sufficient means of their own. The text, based on RV 9, fol. 221, 900, has been edited in Appendix 1.
24. *Le Carte dell'abbazia di Santa Croce in Sassovivo,* 5 : 139–40.
25. Pressutti, 1 : 352–53, 2133, dated July 6, 1219.
26. Rodenberg, 1 : 89, 124.
27. Mayer, *Crusades,* 208.
28. On the importance of redemption of vows, see Rodenberg, 1 : 89, 124, where it is joined to the twentieth as a source of income. On the redemption of the vows of the sick and the poor, see Pressutti, 1 : 63–64, 359; 270, 1619. On the dispensing of women, see Honorius's letter of April 22, 1217, to the archbishop of Tyre; Pressutti, 1 : 93, 529; see also Hugo, 1 : 34–35 and Siberry, *Criticism of Crusading,* 150–55.

29. Pressutti, 1:213, 1290; see also Pressutti, 1:211–12, 1281.

30. Rodenberg, 3:97, 133.

31. The best example is that of Duke Odo of Burgundy. *FK*, 91–92; see also Pressutti, 1:33, 176, in which the citizens of La Rochelle were permitted to send substitutes.

32. Rodenberg, 1:89, 124, mentions money assigned to the duke of Bavaria, which the emperor owed to the pope. See also Pressutti, 1:464–65, 2799, which says that Frederick had promised five thousand marks to the same duke prior to his departure on crusade.

33. Powell, "Crusading by Royal Command," 143–46.

34. ASL Notulario, August 11, 1218, and March 13, 1221.

35. ASB RG, fol. 208; *Documenti del commercio Veneziano*, 2:125–26.

36. Levi, 128–33.

37. For English royal support of crusaders, see Sied., 138, 14; *T*, xxxi, n. 5; xxxii–iii, n. 4.

38. Abbazia di Montevergine, *Regesto delle pergamene* 2:88, 1417. Steven Epstein, in *Wills and Wealth in Medieval Genoa, 1150–1250*, 188, lists fifteen wills for the period 1215–1221 containing legacies for the crusade. Of these, eleven date from the year 1216. James of Vitry, who spent the month of September 1216 in Genoa, comments on the devotion of the Genoese, especially the women, to the crusade; Jac., 76–77. Interestingly enough, ten of the fifteen wills noted were drawn by women. James attributes much of the success of his preaching at Genoa to these women. He notes his awareness that many who took the cross at this time were not suitable crusaders. Obviously, he was following the guidelines which Innocent had laid down in *Quia maior*.

39. Roscher, *Innocenz III*, 162–63; Lunt, *Financial Relations*, 241–42.

40. Lunt, *Financial Relations*, 246–47.

41. Kay, "Albigensian Twentieth of 1221–3."

42. Jordan, *Louis IX*, 65–104.

43. Ibid., 91.

44. Ibid., 92.

45. Ibid., 92–93.

46. Clausen, *Papst Honorius III*, 304, 386–88. See Krautheimer, *Rome*, 203–28.

47. Jordan, *Louis IX*, 81–82.

48. This reversal of policy is evident in Honorius's letters. Pressutti, 1:159–60, 950, contains an appeal to Philip Augustus for support for the leader of the Albigensian Crusade, Simon de Montfort, but not at the expense of the crusade to the East. Eight months later, Honorius granted Philip one-half of the twentieth from France to secure his help for Simon. It was the deterioration of Montfort's position in the Midi that made these efforts necessary. Pressutti, 1:269, 1615. See also Kay, "Albigensian Twentieth," 308–9.

49. Rodenberg, 1:89–91, 124.

50. Ibid., 89.

51. Kay, "Albigensian Twentieth," 314.

52. Jordan, *Louis IX*, 77–82. Gottlob has attempted some estimates for the Fifth Crusade. He cites Matthew Paris for the information that the total of the twentieth for England for three years amounted to 600,000

marks. His estimate of the French twentieth is well below that given in Jordan. *Päpstlichen Kreuzzugssteueren,* 10–11.

53. Levi, 128–31.

54. Jordan, *Louis IX,* 65. Queller notes that far fewer than the expected 4,500 knights arrived in Venice in the summer of 1202; *Fourth Crusade,* 10–11. These numbers are in general accord with those reached by Hans Jahn in *Die Heereszahlen in den Kreuzzügen.*

55. Johannes de Tulbia maintains that in early 1220 there were 100,000 Christians inscribed in the army at Damietta; *SS,* 139. This was the number who received divisions of the loot from the city after its capture. However, this figure, which is not verified in other sources, included noncombatants and, even if accurate, would provide a very inadequate basis for estimating the size of the army at what may well have been the period of its greatest size.

56. Ol., Chap. 57.

CHAPTER VI

THE LEADERSHIP QUESTION

For Sir Steven Runciman, the most important factor behind the ultimate failure of the Fifth Crusade was "the absence of one wise and respected leader."[1] Others have been more specific in attributing the disaster to the pigheadedness of the papal legate, Pelagius.[2] But the result is the same. The interpretation of the Fifth Crusade has come down to the question of the capability, character, and personality of one man, or at most a small group of individuals.[3] This view is consistent with the narrative sources for the crusade, and there is a measure of truth in it that, in the absence of any more broad-based interpretation, strongly recommends its acceptance. So long as the explanation of the failure of the crusade continues to depend on questions of personal leadership and personality, it is inevitable that one of the major figures in the drama, whether pope or legate, emperor or king, will be judged responsible. But such a construction of the leadership question does not give sufficient credit to the realities that produced this problem in the first place.

The Fifth Crusade differs from its predecessors, save for the First Crusade, in the fact that the leadership question remained open well after military operations had begun. In the case of the Second and Third Crusades, the presence of royalty determined the matter. At the beginning of the Fourth Crusade, the barons elected Boniface, marquis of Montferrat.[4] Boniface replaced a troika composed of the counts of Flanders, Champagne, and Blois, but problems over leadership continued to plague the crusaders during their stay in Venice.[5] After the decision to attack Zara, the army began to fragment. When the main body determined to support the imperial claims of Alexius in his bid for the Byzantine throne, a smaller body made its way to the East to fulfil the crusade vow.[6] Though Boniface remained one of the central figures in the crusader army, the Fourth Crusade rapidly degenerated into leadership by committee. In effect, it was the decisions of individual leaders—such as Walter of Brienne, who led the papal army against Markward of Anweiler in the Kingdom of Sicily—that determined the actions of the various contingents. Given the disastrous outcome of what must have been viewed from the papal standpoint as a failure of leadership in 1202, it is impossible to think that Innocent III would not have attempted a better solution for the Fifth Crusade.

Given the dearth of obvious alternatives, it is not surprising that most historians have to some degree supported the notion that Innocent intended this to be a papal crusade. As previously noted, Mayer has gone so far as to argue that European conditions favored the pope's goal, because the kings were all embroiled in conflicts that would keep them from taking on the leadership of the crusade.[7] On the other hand, Schaller and Roscher have shown that, far from preventing royal participation, Innocent attempted to promote it, at least in the case of Frederick II and King John of England.[8] There is no evidence that Innocent made any effort to enlist Philip Augustus, but that is understandable, given papal concern about the Albigensian Crusade and the fact that Philip was a man of advanced years. However, there is evidence of a papal attempt to recruit the heir to the throne, Prince Louis.[9] Moreover, a letter of Honorius III written in March 1220 to encourage Frederick II to fulfill his vow expeditiously invokes the image of royal participation and leadership according to the model of the Third Crusade.[10] The pope called upon Frederick to renew the memory of his grandfather, Frederick Barbarossa, by completing the crusade that he had begun. That this was no passing allusion is indicated by the same pope's letters to Henry III and Philip Augustus in 1223.[11] Roscher has argued that Honorius departed from the policy of his predecessor on this point, but it seems more likely that Innocent III left the question of leadership in abeyance, to be settled at the time of departure.[12] There is no question that he took the initiative in planning the crusade and that he had no intention of making it dependent on the securing of royal participation, but neither can we ignore the evidence that shows how much he desired just that. Honorius's vision of a renewal of the Third Crusade may well reflect the ideas of Innocent III more accurately than historians have earlier believed.

Historians have been too prone to regard the process of recruitment that Innocent set in motion as an accurate reflection of his policy.[13] They have been confused by the nature of that process and, ultimately, by its incompleteness. The previous chapters of this book have tried to show the breadth of Innocent's conception of crusade participation and the precise manner of its implementation. Uniting the papal peace program with the recruitment process was a fundamental means of attracting to the crusade those who already held leadership roles at various levels of society. Thus it was a prime factor in determining the structure of the crusader army. The evidence shows that the greatest success was attained in the settlement of specific conflicts in particular geographical areas, notably in northern Italy, Champagne, the Rhineland-Frisia region, and England. Both the leaders and the major contingents of the crusader army emerged from these regions. We have also seen how the failure to resolve such conflicts was a significant factor in preventing crusade participation. This evidence gives added meaning to the continuing barrage of papal letters addressed to rulers and churchmen in many parts of Europe calling for an end to conflict on the grounds that it was an impediment to the crusade. The absence of Runciman's wise and respected leader was not the result of a specific papal decision or policy, but of the failure of a process that both Innocent and Honorius had opened to the broadest possible participation of the leaders of Latin Europe.

The papal design for the Fifth Crusade contemplated a Europe unified in support of this cause, to which all other conflicts, even the Albigensian and Prussian crusades, were subordinate. Already at the Fourth Lateran Council there were clear signs that this plan was being modified, but whether or not such a vision was ever attainable, it does provide the backdrop against which to view the personalities and behavior of the participants. Further, the recruitment process led to continual arrivals of leaders and contingents during the entire period of the crusade. The command structure of the army was constantly undergoing change, and no doubt this fact increased the need for a strong leader. It also accounts for the constant reiteration in the sources of a concern about the anticipated arrival of Frederick II and, in his continued absence, the problems experienced within the army. Thus the leadership question remains important, but it takes on a rather different meaning than has previously been recognized. The task here and in the remaining chapters of this book is not to diminish the perceived role of important individuals, but to provide a context for a better understanding of the part they played in the crusade.

One obstacle to acceptance of any new interpretation is the attitude most scholars have taken toward Innocent's successor, Honorius III. As has often been the case with those who have followed in the footsteps of the great, his reputation has been overshadowed by that of his predecessor. Seizing on the fact that he was rather elderly and probably suffered from continued poor health, some have labelled him weak and indecisive.[14] Even those impressed by his vigor have found little of note in his character or policies.[15] Such evaluations raise the question of why the cardinals acted so quickly in selecting him as the successor to Innocent.

Prior to his election, Honorius (or Cencius, as he was then named) had been cardinal priest of San Giovanni e Paolo.[16] Educated at the Lateran monastery, he owed his promotion both to the patronage of Pope Celestine III and his own administrative talents, demonstrated in his compilation of the *Liber Censuum Romanae Ecclesiae* (which listed the churches, monasteries, and lands owing dues to the See of Rome) and by his service as *camerarius,* or treasurer, of the Roman church. He had a reputation for deep piety and charity toward the poor, and he seems to have been quite popular with the Romans. Where Innocent III had been outspoken in his statement of papal claims, Honorius hardly alluded to them and seems deliberately to have downplayed the subject, preferring to emphasize the priestly character of his office. Innocent's correspondence is replete with brilliant, if sometimes difficult to interpret, conceptualizations of papal power; the letters of Honorius are the rather conventional products of a first-rate bureaucrat. He certainly did not possess Innocent's brilliance of mind, but he was no unimaginative plodder. He did not hesitate to modify or replace previous policies in the interest of his goals, which were similar to those of Innocent.[17] His depth of feeling and commitment to the cause of reform and the crusade equalled his predecessor's. He seems to have had a good grasp of the whole as well as of details. Far from being indecisive, he proved—especially in his negotiations with Frederick II—quite capable of taking major risks. Finally, a study of his register reveals a promptness in reaction and directness in response that demonstrates the reason for his selection. If, therefore, we reject the view that Honorius was weak and indecisive and argue instead that he acted with a firmness of purpose and fixity of goal worthy of his predecessor, his actions require a new explanation.

In *Ad liberandam,* Innocent and the council had in mind a grand meeting of the crusader army at the Italian ports of Brindisi and Messina, where final deliberations and decisions could be taken under the presidency of the pope. It was there, no doubt, that Innocent expected a military leader to be chosen and a final choice of objective for the crusade to be made. At least the language of the decree suggests that this was the case. The pope was to give his support and advice concerning the "sound organization" of the crusade, and this could only mean that he intended to discuss the leadership question with the crusaders.[18] When Innocent died, he had still made no effort to settle this matter. Moreover, the situation faced by Honorius was quite different from that contemplated at the council. There was an immediate concern, expressed forcefully in a letter Abbot Gervase of Prémontré sent to Honorius soon after his election, lest the death of Innocent cause a postponement of the crusade.[19] The consequences of such a decision were obvious, and Honorius was quick to respond that he planned to move ahead. But, as Gervase pointed out with respect to France and which was equally true of northern Italy and England, few of the leading aristocracy or urban contingents would be ready to depart by the spring of 1217. Only the Germans and Hungarians gave evidence of their readiness to depart on time. Thus the plan for the grand meeting in Messina collapsed and with it the effort to provide a sound organization for the crusade prior to departure.

What is immediately evident is that the Fifth Crusade very quickly developed a rhythm of departures that was not subject to any papal timetable. The role left for the pope was that of a coordinator and at times a clearinghouse for information, rather than a director of operations. But the risk in this impression is that it could be viewed simply as a breakdown in the organization of the crusade, instead of a direct result of the recruitment process. Given the complexity of local negotiations required to set an individual contingent on its path to the East, it was impossible to impose any sort of timetable for departure. Although Innocent III had allowed a generous period for the settlement of conflicts, he bequeathed to his successor a situation in which Innocent's small achievements were outweighed by the large amount of work that remained to be done. Innocent had died at Perugia in July 1216 as he was travelling northward to negotiate peace between Pisa and Genoa. In early 1217, Honorius III entrusted these negotiations, along with the others we have described above, to his legate, Cardinal Hugolino of Ostia.[20] He sent Archbishop Simon of Tyre as *nuntius* to France to carry on the work begun by Robert Courçon.[21] He also turned his attention to Frederick II, opening discussions about the fulfillment of his vow.[22] Throughout this period, Honorius appears as the manager of a myriad of events, endeavoring to move them toward the goal of creating an army for the crusade. By the summer of 1217, prior to the departure of the German-Frisian contingents from the northern European ports, he had apparently reached some agreement with Frederick II to assume command of the crusade.[23] While the timetable planned at the Fourth Lateran Council and the meeting at Messina had fallen by the way, Honorius had grasped the reins of the recruitment process and had moved to provide a "sound organization" for the crusade. In doing so, he had opened the way to Frederick's assumption of the leadership of the crusade. From this point on, whatever other arrangements might be made to meet the needs of the crusade, they were only temporary expedients pending the arrival of Frederick II, who now assumed the character of the real leader of the crusade. After 1217 he came more and more to cooperate with Honorius on important decisions and even to play a decisive role in affairs in the East.

The debate over Frederick's role in the Fifth Crusade has concentrated on two seemingly incontrovertible facts: first, he continually postponed his departure, and second, he and the pope were at odds. Many scholars, whether sympathetic to Frederick or not, have suggested that he manipulated the aged and weak Honorius by dangling his possible participation in the crusade before the pope in order to secure major concessions of a political nature.[24] The problem with this view is that Frederick actively cooperated with the pope on the matter of the crusade throughout the entire period down to 1221. For most of this period, relations between the pope and the emperor-elect were very friendly. Nor was Honorius, as some have thought, naïve. His correspondence with Frederick— and even more so with the imperial chancellor, Bishop Conrad of Metz—shows that he had mastered the techniques of diplomacy and knew quite well how to apply pressure to secure his ends.[25] Honorius was very well informed about the problems that prevented Frederick from leaving Germany and departing on crusade even after the death of Otto IV in 1218. The position of the emperor-elect in Germany continued to be delicate until he succeeded in securing the election of his son Henry as the German king and, above all, until he reached an agreement for the support of the German ecclesiastical princes with the granting of the *Privilegium in favorem Principum Ecclesiasticorum* in the spring of 1220.[26] Probably too much emphasis has been placed upon the difficult negotiations between the emperor and the papal curia prior to his imperial coronation in November 1220. The crux of these problems was the longstanding dispute over the so-called Mathildine lands in Tuscany, bequeathed to the papacy following the death of Countess Matilda in the early twelfth century, as well as controverted claims to other territories in central Italy. Of greater concern was the question of Frederick's plan for the future of the Kingdom of Sicily now that his son was crowned German king. Skeptical historians searching for the roots of later conflicts in this period have not given sufficient credit to the evidence of close cooperation between the imperial and papal representatives in the peace program in northern Italy.[27] Van Cleve has implied that there were doubts on the papal side about Frederick's promise to maintain separate administrations in the Kingdom of Sicily and the empire. There is no evidence of this, nor in fact did Frederick violate this promise. But the chief evidence of close cooperation with the papacy in this period is Frederick's promulgation of imperial legislation against heresy as part of his coronation. Honorius regarded this action as one of the major achievements of his pontificate.[28] Finally, despite the pope's impatience with Frederick's continued postponement of his crusade after his coronation, this era of cooperation continued into 1221, during the second legation of Cardinal Hugolino of Ostia in northern Italy.[29] Frederick also played a more direct role in the conduct of the crusade in this period. There are, therefore, sound reasons for rejecting the usual interpretation of strained relations between the pope and Frederick during the period of the crusade and for accepting the view enunciated by Schaller, which stresses their cooperation.[30]

If we reject the idea that this crusade was to be exclusively papal and its corollary, that there was deeply rooted tension between the pope and the German court, or at least relegate them to a less-significant role, the choice by the crusaders in Acre in 1218 of King John of Jerusalem as the military leader of the crusade and Honorius's appointment of Cardinal Pelagius of Albano as the papal legate to the crusader army require further examination. The election of King John was dictated by the absence of anyone else of sufficient stature to assume the position. John of Brienne had become king of Jerusalem in 1210 as a result of his marriage to Queen Marie, which had the approval of the pope and Philip Augustus of France, who gave him a handsome dowry to assist the Kingdom of Jerusalem. After the death of Marie in 1212, John continued as regent for their daughter Yolande. A member of the noble Briennes of Champagne, with a tradition of participation in the crusades and of loyalty to the papacy, John was a figure of greater substance than some accounts have depicted.[31] His election to the throne of Jerusalem came at one of the lowest points in its history. The conquests made by Saladin in the 1180s had reduced it to a narrow enclave around Acre and a few strongpoints in the vicinity. The territories remaining to the kingdom were insufficient for its needs. The remnant of the Latin Kingdom had become heavily dependent on support from the military orders and from the maritime cities of Italy and the Mediterranean littoral, and it required continued infusions of men and money from the West. Far from improving the position of the kingdom, the Latin conquest of Constantinople in 1204 had drained men and money away from it. Given this precarious position, John had acted early to recommend a new crusade to Innocent and, in the meantime, to arrange a truce with al-ʿĀdil, the brother and successor of Saladin. Had it not been for internal conflicts within the family of Saladin, such a truce would have been unlikely, and the situation of the kingdom even more perilous. As it was, the fortification of Mount Tabor had symbolized the continued weakness of the Latin position.

Circumstances had therefore placed the leadership of the crusader army in the hands of a man whose future hinged on its success or failure. But John was never more than the tactical head of the army. His role in major decisions was always subject to the overall direction of pope and emperor and to the day-to-day limitations imposed by the council of the army. This latter body, with its ever-changing composition, was composed of the leaders of major contingents and others and formed a part of the fundamental command structure of the crusader army. In addition to this group, the presence of the papal legate, Pelagius of Albano, completed the highest level of leadership.

Honorius's appointment of Pelagius has been the subject of considerable study and, as noted earlier, a largely unsettled controversy. It now seems evident that Pelagius was not in any way intended to be the military leader of a papal crusade. That he later came to exercise considerable influence over command decisions was due to the continued absence of the emperor and the actual conditions he faced. But initially his position emerged directly from the process that had brought the crusade together. His function was to preserve peace and unity within the crusader army and to serve its spiritual needs.[32] Later, he was specifically charged with settling conflicts over the division of spoils among crusaders.[33] The reasons for the appointment were not merely those given in *Ad liberandam* but proceeded more from the fact that many leaders of contingents had gone almost directly from the field of battle in Europe, where they had been enemies, to the crusade. Ranulf of Chester and Robert FitzWalter; Hervé of Nevers and Hugh the Brown, count of La Marche; William of Holland and the count of Loos—these and the leaders of other German and northern Italian contingents had been involved in conflict with one another. The appointment of Pelagius was a continuation of the papal program that had resulted in the participation of these rival elements in the crusade. In addition, Pelagius was placed in charge of relations with other Christian bodies in the lands to be freed from the Moslems.[34] The choice of Pelagius for this position was based largely on his previous experience in the east, where he had enjoyed high standing among the Latin clergy, as well as on his experience in negotiations with the Greek church.

Pelagius had served as legate of Innocent III in that region in 1213 and 1214.[35] His work was largely preparatory to the Fourth Lateran Council. The major purpose of his mission was to promote peace between Theodore Lascaris, emperor of Nicaea, and the Latin Empire of Constantinople in order to pave the way for the crusade. However, he had also been involved in negotiations with the leaders of the Greek church, looking toward a possible reunion of the churches. His efforts were not popular with Greek churchmen, whose criticisms of the legate were harsh. Yet, in spite of the charges of arrogance and tactlessness levelled against him, he seems not to have lost his effectiveness as a negotiator.[36] On the face of it, those historians who have accepted the validity of these Greek criticisms without reservation seem to have reacted more strongly than did the Greeks themselves.[37] His mission did bear some fruit in the attendance of Latin and other Eastern bishops at the Lateran Council.[38]

The reexamination of the leadership question cannot stop, however, with a recognition of the inadequacy of previous interpretations concerning the roles of the main figures in the Fifth Crusade. In fact, we have only touched lightly on the aspect of the problem that most immediately affected the course of the crusade. In a fundamental sense, the leadership problem was structural; it was in considerable measure the result of the process whereby the crusader army came into being. As we have already seen, far from being an army made up of individuals grouped into arbitrary or even rationally arranged units, it was composed of contingents that reflected their origins. The crusaders fought under familiar leaders and in units that reflected their usual mode of combat. Smail has touched somewhat on this question, but without regard to its implications.[39] These units had to be integrated into the army in a manner appropriate to their own organization and the type of combat forces they offered, and their commanders formed the council of the army with responsibility for most command decisions under the military commander. This council was a flexible body. References in the sources show that it included the heads of large contingents, other respected members of the aristocracy, clerics of various ranks, and even some ordinary knights.[40] There is no indication that it was a formal body in any sense, yet it clearly exercised broad advisory powers and had great influence. Table 6.1 provides a list of leaders and contingents that are known to have participated in the decision-making process in a significant way at some point during the crusade. This list makes no pretence of being exhaustive and is for illustrative purposes only.

The major conclusions that emerge from a study of this group are derived from its changing composition. The average length of stay for members of the lay aristocracy was just over one year and that for the leading clergy was a bit shorter, this in a crusade that lasted for four years. Stable leadership came chiefly from the legate, King John, the heads of the military orders, and the patriarch of Jerusalem. The men who actually led troops in combat usually stayed the shortest time. It is a notorious fact that King Andrew of Hungary returned home after only a few months in the East. What is less recognized is that departure and death continually thinned the ranks of crusade leaders. Adolf, count of Berg, the head of the Rhenish crusaders, arrived in the spring of 1218 and was dead by August, before he even arrived at Damietta.[41] William, count of Holland, remained for just over a year.[42] Leopold of Austria, who

Table 6.1. Arrival and Departure of Leaders and Contingents

PERSONNEL AND ARRIVAL DATE	DEPARTURE DATE
Fall 1217	
Andrew, king of Hungary	January 1218
Garinus de Monte Acuto, master of Hospitallers	Absent for some periods
Guillelmus de Carnoto, master of Templars	Died 1219
Hermann of Salza, master of Teutonic Knights	Absent for some periods
Hugh, king of Cyprus	Died January 1218
Leopold, duke of Austria	May 1219
Radulfus, patriarch of Jerusalem	Absent for some periods
Spring 1218	
Adolf de Monte, count of Berg	Died August 1218
George, count of Wied	Unknown
William, count of Holland	September 1219
Fall 1218	
Diether von Katzenellenbogen	1220
Hervé, count of Nevers	1220
Hugo Brunus, count of La Marche	August 1219
Peter, bishop of Paris	Died December 1219
Luccan contingent	Fall 1220
Genoese contingent	Unknown
Roman contingent	Unknown
Ranulf, earl of Chester	Summer 1220
William, earl of Arundel	Died 1221
Spring 1219	
No major figures	
Fall 1219	
Bolognese contingent	After 1220
Savaric de Mauleon	Unknown
Spring 1220	
Milanese contingent	After early 1221
Venetian contingent	Unknown
Fall 1220	
Matthew, count of Lesina	1221
Spring 1221	
Louis, duke of Bavaria	1221
Fall 1221	
Henry, count of Malta	1221

had come with Andrew of Hungary, stayed until May 1219, but departed with a large number of Germans and Austrians. Hervé of Nevers stayed for about the average length of time, but incurred the criticism of many when he departed at a time when there was a critical need.[43] Count Diether von Katzenellenbogen arrived in the fall of 1218 and departed in 1220 with a large company. When his ship was attacked and burned by pirates off Cyprus, Oliver was quick to seize on his fate as a valuable lesson for those who would abandon their companions.[44]

The rapid changes in the command structure found their counterpart in the arrivals and departures of the followers. The crusader army was constantly changing size and being reshaped. These factors played a major role in the decision-making process. They were, in part, responsible for many of the disputes that erupted within the army. New arrivals could and did influence military actions by siding with one side or the other among the more experienced leaders.[45] These factors, rather than conflicts of personality, were important to the ultimate outcome of the crusade. This is not to say that personality was a negligible factor, but that it came into play chiefly out of differing assessments of the possibilities open to the crusader army at any given time.

The leadership problem was certainly central to the success or failure of the Fifth Crusade, but it was more complex and more deeply rooted in medieval society than historians have previously realized. The crusaders were not a standing army in the field, awaiting a commander to lead them to victory. They were a force, held together loosely for a relatively brief period of time and constantly affected by the views of those who had gained some experience of the situation and of new arrivals from the West. After the middle of 1220, a very large part of these new arrivals consisted of contingents sent directly by Frederick II, often bearing instructions from him and from the pope. The departure of many earlier crusaders meant that the influence of these new arrivals was increasing. The distant emperor began to assume a more important role in shaping the strategy of the crusade during this period. Thus the leadership question was very much affected by the rhythm of the crusade itself. No decision taken could escape the realities set by the arrival and departure of large or small groups of crusaders. No time for battle could be selected without consideration of the forces available at the moment. The military achievements and failures of the Fifth Crusade must be assessed against this background.

NOTES

1. Runciman, *Crusades*, 3:170.
2. Mayer, *Crusades*, 218.
3. For the literature on Pelagius, see Introduction, n. 12.
4. Queller, *Fourth Crusade*, 22–23.
5. Ibid., 6.
6. Ibid., 75.
7. Mayer, *Crusades*, 206.
8. Roscher, *Innocenz III*, 153–58; Schaller, "Kanzlei," 257.
9. Horoy, 2:369–72, contains a letter of Honorius III to Philip Augustus of April 21, 1217, which states: "Debuerat [Louis], inquam, primitias militiae suae Domino dedicare, ut vires potentiae suae primum exerceret contra inimicos fidei Christiani, ut debellaret gentes quae nobis exprobant gloriam Dominicae passionis, et funiculum haereditatis suae, terram scilicet suo sanguine comparatam, immisericorditer detinent in opprobrium populi Christiani." This letter suggests that Honorius was thinking in terms of a renewal of the Third Crusade, though obviously not with English participation, well before he wrote the letter cited in the next footnote.
10. H.-B., 1:2:692; Powell, "Honorius III," 528–29.
11. Rodenberg, 1:152–55.
12. Roscher, *Innocenz III*, 295–96. His assessment of the evidence is incomplete; he makes no reference to the model of the Third Crusade. While it is impossible to state with certainty that Innocent shared the view of Honorius, the weight of the evidence suggests the likelihood that their ideas were similar.
13. Van Cleve, "Fifth Crusade," 378–84; Mayer, *Crusades*, 208–9.
14. *MGHSS*, 23:379; Clausen, *Papst Honorius III*, 9. The picture that Honorius gives of himself about this time differs from that in the Ursberg chronicle. He writes of himself in relation to his revision of his sermons: "nunc diligentiori studio consummamus, licet dies laboriosos enumeremus nobis et noctes transeamus insompnes" (Powell, "Prefatory Letters," 103).
15. Van Cleve, "Fifth Crusade," 384.
16. See Helene Tillmann, "Ricerche sull'origine dei membri del collegio cardinalizio nel XII secolo," and my article, "Honorius III's *Sermo in Dedicatione Ecclesie Lateranensis* and the Historical-Liturgical Traditions of the Lateran," esp. 197. Tillmann makes a strong case that Honorius was not a member of the distinguished Roman noble family of Savelli.
17. See chapter 5 and my article "The Papacy and the Early Franciscans," esp. 257–61.
18. *Conciliorum Oecumenicorum Decreta*, 267: ". . . disposuimus tunc adesse, quatenus nostro concilio et auxilio exercitus christianus salubriter ordinetur."
19. *RHGF*, 19:618–20.
20. The appointment of Hugolino was announced on January 23, 1217; Pressutti, 1:49–50, 275.
21. The appointment of Archbishop Simon of Tyre was announced on December 5, 1216; ibid., 1:28, 151.

22. Powell, "Honorius III," 523–27.

23. The *Gesta Crucigerorum Rhenanorum* (*SS*, 31) maintains that the German and Frisian crusaders made their decision to assist in the siege of the Alcácer in Portugal in July 1217 with the knowledge that the king of the Romans, i.e., Frederick II, was not yet ready to depart on crusade. This previously unutilized evidence seems to remove all doubt that Frederick's role in the crusade was well known in the spring of 1217, probably at some time after Honorius III contacted him on April 8, 1217. Rodenberg, 1:22, 26. See Van Cleve, "Crusade of Frederick II," 431–32.

24. Van Cleve, "Crusade of Frederick II," 433–36; Mayer, *Crusades,* 222–23.

25. An excellent example is found in Rodenberg, 1:95, 129, where Honorius instructs his subdeacon on the pressures to be applied to Conrad of Metz to force him to surrender the Mathildine lands.

26. Van Cleve, *Frederick II,* 116.

27. Ibid., 128.

28. Pressutti, 1:459, 2766; 463, 2786; Schaller, "Kanzlei," 209–37.

29. Thouzellier, "Legation en Lombardie," esp. 509–10. "Le prélat succède au légat de Frédéric, Conrad de Metz, et, sans en avoir le titre, assume partiellement l'autorité d'une véritable vicaire impérial" (ibid., 509).

30. Schaller, "Kanzlei," 257.

31. Boehm, *Johann von Brienne,* 9–22.

32. RV, 9, 265r, 1173; Powell, "Honorius III," 525–26.

33. Powell, "Honorius III," 530, esp. notes 24 and 25; Horoy, 3: 92, 86.

34. Powell, "Honorius III," 525.

35. Mansilla, "Pelayo Gaitan," 16–31; Gill, *Byzantium and the Papacy,* 40–42; Hoeck and Loenartz, *Nikolaus-Nektarios* 56–61; Setton, *The Papacy and the Levant,* (Memoirs of the American Philosophical Society, Vols. 114, 127, 161, 162) 1:41–42.

36. Gill, *Byzantium and the Papacy,* 41–42.

37. Mayer, *Crusades,* 212; Van Cleve, "Fifth Crusade," 403–4.

38. Mansilla, "Pelayo Gaitan," 25.

39. Smail, *Crusading Warfare,* 98.

40. See, for example, Ol., chaps. 10, 12, 31, 45.

41. *SS,* 40–41.

42. Ibid., 133.

43. Ibid., 127.

44. Ol., chap. 50.

45. The most famous example involves the Duke of Bavaria, who sided with the legate against King John in 1221. But, as we shall see, his reasons for doing so are not clear. Ibid., chap. 54.

PART II

THE CRUSADE

CHAPTER VII

THE FIRST PHASE

The Rhenish and Frisian fleet, some three hundred ships, departed from Vlerdingen in the Netherlands on May 29, 1217. This was the first contingent of the Fifth Crusade to actually get underway. It would not be the first to arrive in the East. The army led by King Andrew of Hungary and Duke Leopold of Austria, which did not set out until the fall of 1217, arrived long in advance of the Rhenish and Frisian contingent, which did not land in Acre until the late spring of 1218. This delay was not a matter of chance, but was premised on the leaders' knowledge of the general state of preparations for the crusade. In most earlier studies, the early departure and slow progress of the Rhenish-Frisian contingent have received little attention, save for the participation of a portion of it in an attack on the Moslem stronghold of al-Qaṣr (Alcácer do Sal) in Portugal. However, there is much more of interest than this in the accounts of their departure, particularly with respect to the organization and discipline of the crusader army.

Having crossed the English Channel to Dartmouth, the assembled crusaders elected Count George of Wied commander of the fleet and chose William, count of Holland, previously selected as leader of the whole army, to take charge of the rear guard. They also established "new laws" for the observance of peace in the army.[1] Following this initial plan of organization, the fleet moved southward along the coast of Brittany, where it joined other units. The constitutions set out at Dartmouth were read again and accepted by the whole army, which "bound itself to observe the same laws."[2]

The peace process, which had begun with the recruitment of the crusaders, so many of whom had recently been in conflict with one another, now achieved a formal legal force binding on all departing crusaders. Very likely, some such ceremony as that held in Dartmouth marked the organization of most if not all crusader contingents.[3] Moreover, the ecclesiastical nature of this legislation, at least in the case of the Rhenish and Frisian crusaders, seems evident from the use of the phrase "ob pacis observanciam" to describe its content in the *Gesta Crucigerorum Rhenanorum* and the reference in the *De Itinere Frisonum* to everything being done properly (*rite*) for the salvation of souls and the peace.[4] These laws laid the groundwork for the role Honorius III assigned to his legate, Cardinal Pelagius of Albano, at his appointment in June 1218. Just as *Ad liberandam* had enabled the papacy, with the approval of the council, to exercise greater control over such areas as clerical taxation and the preservation of the peace, the voluntary acceptance of laws such as these by the crusaders provided a basis for the jurisdiction exercised by the papal legate over the crusader army. As Honorius stated, Pelagius was to precede "the army of the Lord with humility . . . to encourage those in agreement to remain in agreement . . . to recall troublemakers to peace."[5]

The sea route chosen by the crusaders was perilous. There is no way to document fully how many of the ships that left Vlerdingen were lost at sea, but the number must have been substantial. Only a few days out, in the sea off Brittany, a ship from Monheim was wrecked on the rocks, and the fleet had to slow while its men were rescued from the rock onto which they had climbed.[6] Three more ships were wrecked in a storm off the Portuguese coast.[7] Bishop James of Vitry, who had earlier travelled from Genoa to Acre, left a vivid description of the perils of travel on the treacherous waters of the Mediterranean.[8] He described his fear during a storm in which the waters were breaking over his ship, and this was despite the fact that he was travelling on a newly constructed ship and the arrangements on board were well suited to his episcopal rank. There was a room on the upper castle where he could study and eat, and another where he could sleep with his companions. There were also places for his servants, his stores, and his horse. The ship carried wine, meat, and biscuit sufficient for almost three months.[9] Still, the trip was far from comfortable. Contrary winds impeded their progress. They ran into a storm of such magnitude that "fifteen anchors could hardly hold the ship back" as the prow of the vessel rose to the stars and sank into the abyss. During the two days and nights that the storm lasted, many had nothing to eat, and James himself ate nothing cooked, because it was too dangerous to light a fire on the ship. Many on board took the opportunity to confess their sins and prepare for death. But finally the seas calmed and, with dolphins in their wake, they sailed toward Acre. Many travellers to the East were not so fortunate, however, and for them the crusade ended at sea.

The Rhenish and Frisian crusaders came through their early perils, but stopped briefly at the great shrine of Saint James at Compostela, Spain, to obtain the blessing of the Saint, leaving their ships for the short overland journey.[10] On their arrival in Lisbon in late July, they faced their first critical decision. After they had been ashore for a few days, Bishops Severus of Lisbon and Martin of Évora, together with the commanders of the *militia* of Palmela and of the Templars and Hospitallers, came to the crusader camp to ask help against the neighboring Moslems. Lisbon was menaced by the fortress of al-Qaṣr, from which the Moslems were able to launch attacks both by land and sea.[11] While Innocent III had suspended the crusader vow against the Moslems on the Iberian Peninsula, his view had been tempered by the recognition that realities might change. In this instance, it was perhaps the convenient halt of the crusaders that decided the bishops to enlist their aid, despite the fact that Bishop Severus's request for papal support of this project had been rejected by Innocent III at the Fourth Lateran Council.[12] From the first, the counts of Holland and Wied favored the course sought by the bishops, arguing that the season was not good for travel and that they were well in advance of the departure of Frederick II.[13] But the Frisians, with the abbot of Werde taking a leading role, opposed this diversion and decided to continue their journey, alluding to Innocent's refusal.[14]

The mention in the *Gesta Crucigerorum Rhenanorum* of the expected departure of Frederick II in the late spring of 1217 confirms the information found in Honorius III's letter to Frederick dated April 8, 1217, that negotiations regarding Frederick's departure were taking place. But the *Gesta* is more specific in asserting that "the king of the Romans and the Romans, with many German princes, would not set out at this time."[15] Obviously, negotiations between Frederick and the pope had not resulted in a date for Frederick's departure, but it is clear that the Rhenish and Frisian crusaders had set out with an awareness that they were part of a larger crusader army to be commanded by Frederick II.

The counts were correct in maintaining that the spring season was too far advanced to continue the journey, but the fleet could certainly have made Acre with the normal fall sailing. In fact, however, the Frisians, after following the coast of Spain and southern France, finally reached Civitavecchia, where they decided to winter under the protection of the pope and to await the gathering of various Italian contingents from that area. The counts remained behind with 180 ships. Since the Frisians had departed with 80 ships, it would seem that the fleet had lost somewhat more than 10 percent of its total of 300 since leaving Dartmouth. Although historians have often been skeptical of the figures given in the sources, there is a consistency in the enumeration of ships in the *De Itinere* and the *Gesta* that argues for their accuracy.[16] The departure of the Frisians caused a certain bitterness among those who remained behind, with just the tinge of a suggestion that they were evading their duty to their fellows. Indeed, the *Gesta,* which reflects the Rhenish viewpoint, expresses satisfaction in the fact that some of the Frisian ships were driven ashore at al-Qaṣr. While the Frisians defended themselves as being faithful to the purpose of the expedition, the counts and their followers saw themselves as performing a work of charity consistent with that purpose.

After the departure of the Frisian fleet on July 28, the remaining crusaders took up the siege of al-Qaṣr on the thirtieth. The crusaders themselves noted that the fort was located in a very desirable land, one that abounded with fish and wildlife. They no doubt understood the desire of the Portuguese to secure control of such a place. With the arrival of the Bishop of Lisbon and the Brethren of the Sword, the siege commenced in earnest. As with most medieval siege operations, it was rather lengthy and depended for success more on waiting out the besieged and holding off reinforcements than on attempts to breach the walls of the fort. In fact, the situation of the Christians began to look desperate by the beginning of September, when a local emir appeared with a force considerably larger than their own and forced them to take refuge behind their earthworks. At this critical moment, help arrived in the person of Peter of Montague, master of the Templars. The crusaders drew up their forces in battle array with the Templars and the Knights of Palmela, led by their ferocious little commander, in the center. In the mêlée that followed, the Saracens fled—driven from the field, so some maintained, by a miraculous battle line wearing red crosses. Again, however, the crusaders threw themselves against the walls in vain. It was not until October 21 that al-Qaṣr, with its three thousand inhabitants and defenders, fell. It was a glorious but rather costly victory.

Not only had the crusaders suffered heavy casualties in battle, but many found that they were unable to continue their voyage to the East. The Bishop of Lisbon sought and obtained permission from the pope to absolve them of their vows.[17] After wintering in Lisbon, the crusaders resumed their voyage the following March. But it was a smaller fleet than had departed Vlerdingen, even counting the arrival of the Frisians and their Italian contingents, that finally straggled into Acre during late April and May in 1218. There they joined the German and Austrian crusaders, and the remainder of the Hungarian forces of King Andrew, who had arrived in Acre in the preceding September.

King Andrew of Hungary had finally responded to the command of Pope Innocent III to fulfill the crusade vow that had been taken by his father as early as 1195.[18] King Béla III had failed to go on crusade, and his successor, Emeric, who had pledged to go on the Fourth Crusade, was prevented from doing so by the rebellion of Andrew, who had laid claim to the throne. Innocent had attempted to persuade Andrew to fulfill his father's vow at that time. As the peace negotiations between the king and the rebellious duke dragged on, presided over by a papal legate and the archbishop of Mainz, the promise to go on crusade hung in abeyance. The death of King Emeric in 1204 did not end the papal attempt to secure the fulfillment of Béla's vow by Andrew. In January of 1217, Honorius III was able to announce that Andrew planned to depart on crusade at the time fixed by the Fourth Lateran Council.[19] During this same period, Leopold VI of Austria was also making preparations, and the two joined forces, though their contingents remained separate.

The forces Andrew and Leopold gathered were substantial. Andrew concluded a treaty with the Venetians to provide ten large ships to transport himself and his army at a rental of 550 marks each, as well as an unspecified number of smaller ships at lower rates. He also conceded the disputed city of Zara to them.[20] But efforts to estimate the size of the joint forces have been futile. The figure of 15,000 mounted men given by Röhricht is much too large. The same is true of Thomas of Spalato's mention of 10,000 knights. While Thomas himself had doubts about this number, he was greatly impressed by the size of the army, and especially by the fact that there were not sufficient ships available to transport all of Andrew's contingent.[21] Andrew and Leopold recruited participants from a broad area. James Sweeney has found that most of the crusaders in the Hungarian group came from Slavonia and Dalmatia and were longtime supporters of Andrew, as well as being related to him by blood. He noted, however, that "Bishop Egbert of Bamberg and the Margrave Henry of Istria . . . needed a public vehicle to alleviate the lingering suspicions of their complicity in the murder of Philip of Swabia."[22] To this we can add that the forces of Leopold of Austria included both pro- and anti-Hohenstaufen elements, drawn not only from Austria and the Tyrol, but from other parts of Germany as well. Some, like Walter of Avesnes and several bishops, came from France. Leopold was the first to depart; his voyage to Acre took only sixteen days. Andrew arrived at Spalato on August 23, but was unable to depart immediately. He did not arrive in Acre until late September.

The Germans and Hungarians were the vanguard of the Fifth Crusade. It is interesting to speculate how the decision of the Rhenish and Frisian contingents to delay their arrival affected the operation of the crusade at this stage, but the most that one can say with any certainty is that it limited immediate operations in the Holy Land. Although Leopold and Andrew were joined by forces from Antioch, Lebanon, and Cyprus, their meeting with King John of Jerusalem resulted only in a decision to undertake a series of operations in northern Palestine. Historians have been rather critical, or at least uneasy, about this decision, seeing little of long-term value in such an action. In fact, however, it served a number of military objectives, the chief of which was to focus Moslem attention on this region rather than on Egypt, which was the indicated target of the crusade. Secondarily, as we shall see, it served to strengthen the rather tenuous position of the crusader kingdom of Acre. This decision may also have been related to future strategy. Even had all the crusaders who had departed the West in 1217 arrived in Acre by fall, it seems likely that some sort of military sweep in this region would have been necessary merely to keep the Moslems off-balance and to deter them from an all-out attack on Acre. But the point is moot, and the size of the forces available certainly ruled out any immediate invasion of Egypt.

Innocent III had recognized the perilous situation of the crusader kingdom of Acre as early as 1213. The Holy Land (Figure 7.1) consists of a narrow band between the Sea of Galilee and the Jordan River on the east and the Mediterranean on the west. Along the coast there is a plain of varying width, generally broader in the

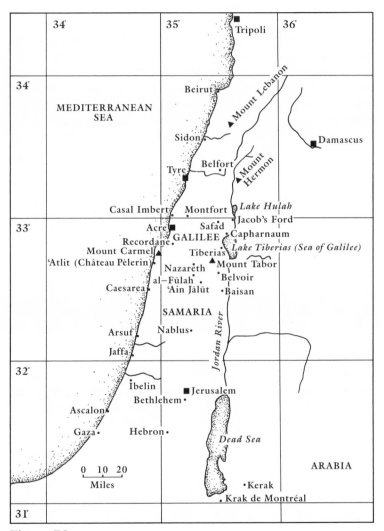

Figure 7.1
The Holy Land (Adapted from Setton, *A History of the Crusades*, vol. 2, p. 520.)

south than in the north, save that Acre commands an extensive plain gradually rising into a pass through the central mountains and offering access to Safad and the Sea of Galilee. It lies on the northern shore of the Bay of Haifa and has one of the best-protected harbors along the whole coastline. To the south, Mount Carmel rises sharply, forming a long ridge that sweeps inland and southward to form a barrier to east–west travel. The interior is a land of rugged hills and mountains, but it offers the possibility of movement along the valleys, and often surprises the traveller with fertile valleys and upland plateaus. To the east lies the Jordan, receiving its waters from the mountains of Lebanon and pausing in the Sea of Galilee, which is surrounded on three sides by high hills and mountains and only opens into a fertile valley to the south, where the Jordan continues its journey to the Dead Sea. Much of this mountainous land was virtually uncontested by the crusaders and the Moslems, since it offered little advantage to either. It was the plain, the upland, and the river valleys over which they fought for control and which they attempted to dominate by their fortifications.

The first operation undertaken by the crusaders was a reconnaissance in force. This action was dictated by conditions in Acre at the time of their arrival. There were severe food shortages due to a drought during the previous two years.[23] Even without that misfortune, Acre would have been hard put to find sufficient foodstuffs to support a large army for any period of time. The *History of the Patriarchs of the Egyptian Church* indicates that this was the purpose behind the first crusader action and describes in some detail the impressment of local Moslems to transport grain. The crusaders carried away all of the wheat from Bethsan "on the heads of the inhabitants of Ghur: a strong lad carried half an *ardab,* he who was less strong a third of an *ardab* . . . until they carried away all the wheat in Bethsan. And if a lad became worn out and set down his load, . . . they killed him."[24] Oliver Scholasticus—who did not himself witness the events at this time, because he did not arrive until April 1218—makes only a cryptic reference to the fact that the crusaders found an abundance of "food and fodder" on this trip.[25]

The crusaders moved from their base at Recordane, south of Acre, to the rich agricultural plateau of al-Fūlah and as far as Fons Tubanie ('Ain aṭ–Ṭubaʿūn). The Moslem forces were gathered in their fortress at Nablus under the command of the son of Sultan al-ʿĀdil, al-Muʿaẓẓam ʿĪsâ, Sharaf-ad-Dīn.[26] As the crusaders moved southward, al-ʿĀdil brought reinforcements to Nablus but showed no inclination to accept his son's recommendation to oppose the crusaders in open battle. Instead, he resorted to a purely defensive tactic. As the crusaders advanced toward Bethsan, showing that they had no intention of attacking Nablus or moving toward Jerusalem, he entered that city ahead of them. With their continued advance, he retreated across the Jordan. Although al-Muʿazzam continued to advocate resistance, al-ʿĀdil refused. It was already apparent that this crusader force had no intention of seeking out the enemy; to risk battle with them would have placed control of the whole north in jeopardy. What was also clear was the fact that in their foraging the crusaders were scouring the region around Mount Tabor, though carefully skirting the important fortress itself. Very likely, they had already laid plans for an attack on the fortress, which was the key to control of the upland plateau region and the route to the Sea of Galilee. At this point, al-ʿĀdil lost nothing by his retreat. The crusaders continued to gather supplies, maintaining a leisurely pace. They crossed the Jordan just south of the Sea of Galilee and followed the eastern shore of the lake northward before turning west and then south again along the western bank. They took time to bathe in the sacred waters of the Jordan and to visit places where Christ had lived and taught, including Capharnaum, before returning to Acre. The whole movement was completed in the month of November 1217. The sources, as is often the case, provide little to tell us how much it accomplished, but severe food shortages apparently ended after the spring of 1218.[27]

The attack on Mount Tabor, the second of these campaigns, was the fulfillment of Innocent III's announced objective for the Fifth Crusade. After only a brief rest, the pilgrims once more departed Acre and made their way southeastward toward the mountain. Tabor is unusual in its isolation, rising from a plateau in a region favorable to agriculture. The mountain is deceptive, seeming to offer the prospect of a more gradual climb than is actually possible, since the final ascent is too steep in most places for any large body of men. The fortress built at the top had seventy-seven towers and housed two thousand troops. If not impregnable, it was almost so. Also, it was in a position to control the southern approaches to the Sea of Galilee, the upland plains from al-Fūlah northward, and the routes from Acre to the interior. Its threat to Acre itself lay in its potential use as a base for raids. Whatever long-term strategy the crusaders would adopt, Moslem control of Tabor posed a serious threat to their plans, and one not easily disposed of. The approaching crusaders were fortunate in meeting a local Moslem youth who agreed to be baptized and who offered to show them the route to the top of the mountain. There was a well-trodden path, and the crusaders, under cover of a cloud that hung about the mountain, were able to ascend it unobserved on December 3. They encountered the castellan and a small force, but drove them back against the gates. Despite the advantage of surprise, however, King John and the other leaders present decided to break off the attack and descend the mountain. Oliver and James of Vitry criticized this decision.[28] Unfortunately, no source provides an adequate explanation, although James mentions their lack of siege machines. The matter did not rest there. A portion of the army resumed the attack two days later, even succeeding in placing a scaling ladder against the walls, but they were soon forced to retreat. Again, the sources do not explain sufficiently the circumstances, but it is evident that there was a substantial difference of view, with King John and Bohemond of Antioch in favor of returning to Acre. What seems likely is that both experienced leaders weighed the probability that a long siege would tie the crusaders down and expose them to attack by the main Moslem force under al-ʿĀdil. In that event, they would not be free to undertake their main objective, the attack on Egypt. Mount Tabor was not worth so great a risk, despite what Innocent had said. And, in fact, the Moslems seem to have come to a similar decision, for they dismantled the fort within about six months and abandoned it.[29] With their major defenses at Nablus and east of the Jordan, Mount Tabor was too exposed. Al-ʿĀdil had never favored its fortification and now had his way.

After the army returned to Acre, a small contingent of venturesome but foolhardy crusaders, five hundred strong, decided to make a sweep northeastward in the direction of Beaufort Castle, through the mountains of Lebanon. It was Christmas time and the weather was cold and damp. This force, which was neither authorized nor sufficient, may well have aimed at establishing a new crusader lordship in the area east of Sidon and Tyre. At least that is the suggestion of Abū-Shāmah, who seems well informed.[30] Apparently, the leader of the expedition was an important Hungarian noble, whom Abū-Shāmah describes as the nephew of King Andrew. But the whole project was ill-considered, and it ended in disaster. The people of the mountains wasted little time in ambushing the crusaders and forcing the survivors to flee. The fierce winds, snows, and cold of the Lebanese mountains took their toll, especially of the poorer crusaders and the animals.

This expedition, described in the sources as the third sortie by the Christians, has long created a negative view of the activity undertaken by the Hungarian and German crusaders in 1217 and early 1218. In addition, the decision of King Andrew of Hungary to depart in January, despite the protests and even the threat of excommunication by the patriarch, has furthered this impression. While it is true that little had been accomplished by arms, this judgment is too critical. King John had kept the crusaders occupied usefully without risking them in pitched battle and, despite numerous defections by the Hungarians, he retained a substantial portion of the arrivals of 1217 intact against the coming of the Rhenish and Frisian crusaders in the spring of 1218. Discounting the disastrous third sortie, these operations had accomplished rather more than has generally been recognized. The Moslem position in the north was weakened, so the crusaders were in a better position to secure needed supplies from this region. Further, they had raised the possibility of an attack on the Moslems of Syria, either by themselves or in cooperation with a Moslem ally. Gottschalk has shown that their later strategy was, in fact, aimed at a two-pronged attack on Syria and Egypt, in which Kai-Kāʾūs, the ruler of Rūm, would march on al-Muʿaẓẓam from the north.[31]

After the disastrous raid into Lebanon, most of the crusaders joined in efforts to strengthen the fortifications in the area around Acre during the late winter and spring of 1218. Part of the army remained in Acre and were castigated by Oliver for their laziness, but two other contingents travelled southward, one to Caesarea and the other to Château Pèlerin ('Atlīt), where they worked to strengthen existing fortifications and build new ones. Both of these forts had usable harbors, though neither was as large or well situated as that of Acre. Caesarea was the key to any future attack on Jerusalem, since it controlled the northern portion of the coastal plain and could serve as a staging area and supply point for crusaders moving south.[32] Château Pèlerin was of primary importance in protecting the land link between Acre and Caesarea at the narrow point where Mount Carmel comes near to the coast and where the coastal road swung west of a promontory and thus could be rather easily cut by a Moslem force. The fortifications at Caesarea were quite extensive, surrounding the town and the cathedral and reaching out to protect the port. At Château Pèlerin, the crusaders attempted to make the place all but impregnable by reinforcing the existing walls and building a tower, called Destroit, that dominated the coastal road. This tower was placed in the hands of the Templars.[33]

The first phase of the Fifth Crusade ended with the arrival of the

Rhenish and Frisian crusaders in Acre in the spring of 1218. Judg-
ments of the crusaders' accomplishments during this period have
generally been harsh. With typical bluntness, Van Cleve maintained
that the "Latin orient had been deceived in its hopes."[34] Runciman
says simply that the Hungarian crusade "achieved nothing."[35]
Sweeney is more favorable, but concludes that "little of permanent value was accomplished by the Hungarians."[36] The winter of
1217 certainly was a season of failures and disappointments, but it
would be a mistake to accept this negative picture without question. Certainly the departure of King Andrew and a large part of
the Hungarian troops in January 1218 was a blow to the crusade. It
signalled the end of any active campaign by the crusaders who had
arrived in the fall of 1217. Yet it is not true that nothing was
accomplished.

The arrival of the forces of Andrew and Leopold so far in advance of the other contingents has led scholars to separate this
phase of the crusade from the campaign against Damietta that began in 1218. Even Gottschalk, who has shown the linkage between
the ambitions of Kai-Kā'ūs to expand his power in the north at the
expense of the heirs of Saladin and the crusader attack on Egypt,
sees no particular significance to the activities of the crusaders during the winter of 1217–18.[37] While it is true that King John and
other leaders were reluctant to become bogged down in any major
campaign and thereby to risk a costly defeat at an early stage in the
crusade, they accomplished a number of limited objectives that
were important to its future. The first, and perhaps most important, was to provide useful activity for the crusaders until larger
forces could arrive. The danger of boredom and the disintegration
of the army was very real, as the sources show. Medieval armies
were ill-suited to camp life. By showing the flag in the region
around the Sea of Galilee, the crusaders not only acquired needed
supplies and satisfied their hunger for booty; but they also demonstrated their ability to move through this strategically important region. Without directly threatening either Jerusalem or Damascus,
they raised the possibility that either might be the target of the
crusade. The brief sieges of the fortress on Mount Tabor helped to
establish its isolation and vulnerability should a major attack be directed against it, and the strengthening of coastal fortifications was
highly desirable, given the plan to attack Egypt. This action reduced the vulnerability of Acre, as would be demonstrated during
the course of the crusade. What part these actions played in estab-

lishing a basis for an agreement with Kai-Kāʾūs to coordinate his attacks in northern Syria with the crusader invasion of Egypt can only be inferred from his military movements against Aiyūbid interests in early 1218.[38]

Far from being an isolated campaign, the so-called Hungarian crusade and the activities of the followers of Leopold of Austria formed a useful preparation for events to come. Already, however, at this early stage, there emerged one of the distinctive problems that confronted the crusade throughout its course. The decisions made in the fall and winter of 1217–18 regarding the employment of the Hungarian and German crusaders were influenced by an estimate of the capabilities of the available manpower and the knowledge that other crusaders were due to arrive in the spring. The rhythm of arrivals and departures that was established at this time limited the ability of the leaders of the crusade to plan for the long term. This factor provided the background for a continuing debate within the army about the conduct of the war.

NOTES

1. *SS,* 29, 59. Lahrkamp, "Mittelalterliche Jerusalemfahrten," esp. 295–96.

2. *SS,* 60.

3. This ceremony was repeated when the Italian contingents joined the Frisians at Corneto in March 1218; ibid., 68–69.

4. Ibid., 29, 59.

5. Powell, "Honorius III," 525, also note 12.

6. *SS,* 29.

7. Ibid., 30.

8. Jac., 76–77.

9. Ibid., 78.

10. *SS,* 30, 60.

11. Ibid., 30, 62.

12. Ibid., 31, 62–63.

13. The summaries from the lost registers of Innocent III, published by Theiner, show that Innocent III had begun to coordinate the plans of the German crusaders for departure in the period immediately following the council; Theiner, *Vetera monumenta slavorum,* 1:64. Honorius III's letter of April 8, 1217, continued this process. For the first time it is clear that Frederick himself was involved in the discussions about the crusade. Rodenberg, 1:22, 26; Pressutti, 1:85, 482. William of Holland and George of Wied seem to have been well informed about the current situation. The *Gesta Crucigerorum Rhenanorum* reports: "Ad hec prefati comites, consilio cum discretis viris habito, discentes etiam a nautis, juramento firmantibus, viam maris ex natura temporis, suos ventos habentem, eis esse preclusam, et presentiam eorum Terre Sancte minus fore utilem, maxime

Romanorum Rex et Romani, cum multis principibus Alemannie hoc tempore non transirent" (*SS*, 31). The reference to both Frederick (Rex Romanorum) and the Romans indicates that the counts knew that Honorius had fallen behind the schedule set at the Fourth Lateran Council.

14. *SS*, 31.

15. Ibid.

16. Ibid., 29. The *Gesta* describes the departure from Vlerdingen, "cum trecentis fere navibus." The *De Itinere Frisonum* speaks of entering the port of Dartmouth and finding the counts of Wied and Holland with 112 ships; ibid., 59. The *Gesta* says that the Frisians left Lisbon to continue their journey to the Holy Land in 80 ships; ibid., 31; see also 36–37.

17. Pressutti, 1:174, 1027.

18. Van Cleve, "Fifth Crusade," 386–87; Sweeney, "Hungary in the Crusades," esp. 478.

19. Pressutti, 1:51, 284.

20. Van Cleve, "Fifth Crusade," 387; *FK*, 24–25.

21. *MGHSS.*, 29:578. The *History of the Patriarchs of the Egyptian Church*, 3:2:214, gives the much more reasonable figure of four thousand knights for the forces of Andrew and Leopold.

22. Sweeney, "Hungary in the Crusades," 478–79.

23. Van Cleve, "Fifth Crusade," 389. The *Annales Ceccanenses*, whose author is well informed concerning events in Rome during this period, reports that due to the shortage a small loaf of bread was selling in Acre for twelve denarii. This source also says that the poor crusaders were sent home. In September alone, sixty-six shiploads returned. It also reports 100,000 dead on the journey. This account, with all its obvious exaggerations, is the kind of story a returned crusader might give out in justification of his decision to come home early. *T*, 237; *MGHSS*, 19:302.

24. *History of the Patriarchs of the Egyptian Church* 3:2:214–15.

25. Ol., chap. 2.

26. See the account in Hans Gottschalk, *Al-Malik al-Kāmil von Egypten und seine Zeit*, 53–57.

27. Van Cleve, "Fifth Crusade," 389.

28. Ol., chap. 3; Jac., 98.

29. Gottschalk, *Al-Kāmil*, 68.

30. Ol., chap. 4; *RHC, Or.*, 5:164–65 (*Livre des Deux Jardins*).

31. Gottschalk, *Al-Kāmil*, 71–76.

32. Ol., chap. 5.

33. Rey, "Excavations at Pilgrims' Castle ('Atlit)," esp. 111.

34. Van Cleve, "Fifth Crusade," 395.

35. Runciman, *Crusades*, 3:149.

36. Sweeney, "Hungary in the Crusades," 479.

37. Gottschalk, *Al-Kāmil*, 53–57, 72.

38. Ibid., 71–76.

CHAPTER VIII

INVASION AND STALEMATE

The arrival of the German and Frisian crusaders in Acre in the spring of 1218 marked a new phase of the Fifth Crusade, with Egypt its objective. Oliver Scholasticus probably gives the most accurate account of this decision when he says that the plan had been decided at the Fourth Lateran Council.[1] We can fill in the subsequent events from other sources. Soon after the new contingents reached Acre, their leaders met with King John, the duke of Austria, the heads of the military orders, and the patriarch of Jerusalem to decide on their next step. The *Gesta Obsidionis Damiate* gives the impression that only then was the decision made to attack Egypt.[2] This account has misled some historians into believing that previously there had been uncertainty regarding the object of the crusade. Van Cleve, for example, has said that "the leaders soon decided to employ the expedition against Egypt rather than in Palestine."[3] However, an analysis of the discussions reported by the so-called Chronicle of Ernoul suggests that attacking Egypt was never in doubt, but that there was a debate whether to make Alexandria or Damietta the specific target of the crusade.[4] Moreover, a speech by King John reported in Ernoul suggests that the real reason for holding this assembly was not to decide between Palestine and Egypt, but to take stock of the troops available and to decide whether these were sufficient for the planned invasion. John supported the view that the number already present and those expected soon made the invasion of Egypt feasible. Oliver Scholasticus "vehemently" agreed.[5] There was, therefore, never a real doubt about the plan to attack Egypt.

It is more difficult to find reasons in the sources for the preference for an attack on Damietta rather than Alexandria, but this decision was not taken on the spur of the moment. The crusaders had long been gathering information about the Damietta region and had considerable knowledge of the terrain that lay between it and Cairo. In all likelihood, Damietta seemed to offer the best line of attack and the one that most safeguarded them in the event they would be forced to retreat. Not only was Damietta a smaller city than Alexandria, but it was somewhat closer to Cairo. It was also more accessible from the crusader ports in the Holy Land. As early as 1169, the Franks, supported by a Byzantine fleet, had laid siege to the city, but they were defeated by Saladin.[6] In 1199, the patriarch of Jerusalem had responded to Innocent III's request for information about conditions in the East and, *inter alia*, had stated that Damietta was "the head and key of all Egypt." He included a description of the fortifications of the city.[7] Thus, the decision to invade Egypt via Damietta resulted from a long-maturing sense of its position in the defense of Egypt as well as its role in the maintenance of Moslem power in Palestine.

On May 24 the crusader fleet sailed southward from Acre to Château Pèlerin in preparation for a landing at Damietta. Most of the ships moved on almost immediately, but the leaders of the army, who had remained in port longer, found themselves caught for a time by adverse winds. Therefore, when the crusaders arrived at the Damietta mouth of the Nile on May 27, 1218, and prepared to disembark, they were without a commander. The matter was serious, since there were necessary decisions to be made, such as selecting a campsite and preparing fortifications. Prior to landing, they elected Count Simon of Saarbrücken, who had travelled to the East in the Rhenish contingent. Fortunately, they met with almost no resistance, and they found a very suitable area for their camp on the west bank of the Nile, occupying the prayerhouse at Saṭ al-Birûg north of Būrah (Figure 8.1).[8] Oliver even noted their good fortune in discovering that the Nile flowed with fresh water at this time, despite the fact that, as they soon discovered, the tides from the sea often made it salty as far as two miles south of Damietta.

The region in which they found themselves has changed considerably over the centuries, though the Damietta branch of the Nile flows in approximately the same course today as it did then.[9] The

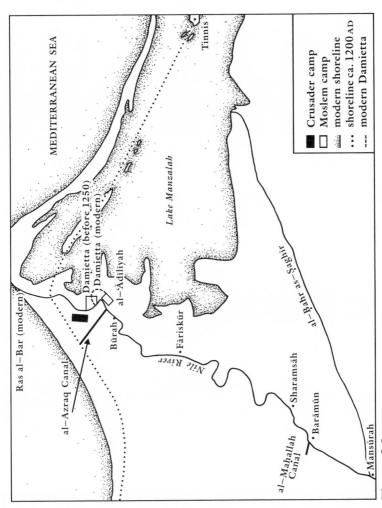

Figure 8.1
The Damietta Region of Egypt

present city on the east bank of the Nile is immediately to the south
of the early-thirteenth-century city, which was destroyed by the
Mamelukes in 1250, after the crusade of King Louis IX. Shortly
thereafter, Sultan Baibars ordered the channel of the river filled
with rocks to prevent the movement of an invading fleet up the
Nile.[10] The modern canal system in the area does not follow the
route of its predecessors, and, more important, centuries of silting
and the action of the sea have altered the shoreline where the Nile
enters the Mediterranean sea.[11] Recent research has shown that the
erection of barrier dams on the Nile has led to substantial alteration
of the process whereby the river deposits silt around Ras al-Bar, but
for centuries the action of river and sea had gradually extended the
land mass at this point.[12] Georges Salmon has stated that the river
added more than a kilometer to the shoreline near its mouth during
the course of the nineteenth century.[13] The presence of dune massifs
several kilometers south of the present shoreline may well indicate
earlier stages in this process of growth, and it suggests that medieval Damietta was several kilometers closer to the sea than at the
present time.[14] Hamaker recognized this fact in 1824 and tried to
indicate the extent of the difference on a map that accompanied his
commentary on the historian al-Makrīzī.[15] A. R. Guest did not deal
with the problem of silting in his article on the delta in the Middle
Ages, and his map shows the modern shoreline. Moreover, his
placement of medieval Damietta is too far north—not very distant,
in fact, from what may have been the mouth of the Nile at that
time.[16] Since the earliest Islamic sources speak of Damietta as lying
at or near the mouth of the Nile in the seventh century, it is probable that during the ensuing five hundred years the process of silting
caused the city to be located no more than three miles upriver.
While complete precision is impossible, some realization of the essential facts is necessary to understand the location from which the
crusaders launched their attack on Damietta.

The city of Damietta, according to the Arab geographer Yaqut,
lay between Lake Manzalah and the Nile. To the north lay the Mediterranean Sea. Across the river was the Gizat Dumyat, the peninsula
of Damietta. Oliver says that the city was surrounded by three
walls, each higher than the other, with a moat between the first and
the second.[17] Supposedly this moat was deep and broad enough to
accommodate vessels. The middle wall had twenty-eight towers.
Oliver was greatly impressed by the abundance of fish, birds, pas-
tures, gardens, and orchards found near the city.[18] But its most

striking feature was the chain that stretched from one tower in the northwest wall of the city across the Nile to another, built on a wooden foundation near the west bank of the river. This chain, which dated to the tenth century or earlier, had been reconstructed during the reign of Saladin. It served to interdict passage to the city or upriver to all but the merchantmen who obtained permission for the voyage, since the channel of the Nile to the west of the chain tower was not deep enough to permit access. During wartime, the chain was further defended by a bridge of boats from the city to the tower. Arabic sources provide various descriptions of this arrangement, indicating that over the centuries there had been a number of changes in it. At one time there had also been a tower on the west bank and a chain from that to the tower in the river, but that was no longer deemed necessary.[19] In all probability, there had been considerable deposit of silt about the tower and in the western channel, so that the tower on the west bank, which was more vulnerable to attack, could be safely abandoned. Thus, the crusaders who landed in May 1218 confronted a strongly fortified city.

The arrival of King John and the other leaders enabled the crusaders to turn from the task of fortifying their camp to the attack on the chain tower, but first they elected a leader in the person of King John.[20] This choice signified that he was the recognized military commander of the forces then in Egypt. The crusaders were merely following their normal procedure for the selection of leaders, as they had, for example, with the election of Simon of Saarbrücken. At this early stage in events, the choice of John recognized not only his military abilities but also his status as a crowned king, the only one present among the crusaders.

The attack on the chain tower immediately illustrated the difficulties faced by the crusaders in conducting a siege of the city. From contemporary descriptions it is evident that the tower rose almost directly from the water and could be attacked only on the north side. The water to the west was too shallow for ships, and the chain obstructed an advance to the east. John, in cooperation with the duke of Austria and the other leaders, first used petraries, or siege engines, to hurl rocks at the tower and its defenders, but with little effect. The tower was well fortified, it contained sufficient food to last for a year, and it was defended by a force of about three hundred men, who were equipped with various military machines. On June 6, al-Kāmil, son of Sultan al-ʿĀdil, arrived in the area from Cairo and set up camp on the right bank of the river a few miles south of the city at a place he called al-ʿĀdilīyah in honor of his father. From this point, he assumed direct command of the defense of the city and the tower.

For almost a month the crusaders made no progress. During this period their efforts were directed chiefly at completing their fortifications and gathering supplies. The biography of the Coptic patriarch John VI describes how both Christian and Moslem women were employed in the grinding of corn for the army. Fishing boats went out and brought in their catches for sale, but the fishermen engaged in price gouging, which led to regulation.[21] The crusaders also built a giant mangonel, which they placed upon the mound of al-Hairah, opposite Damietta, and with which they were able to hurl stones into the center of the city. Oliver relates how the Frisians, in a daring move, crossed the river and rounded up cattle, but the leadership decided that laying siege to the city without first capturing the chain tower would be too dangerous.[22] Around June 23 or 24, the crusaders launched a major attack on the city and the tower, employing seventy or eighty ships. They used siege machines and arrows to try to force the defenders to surrender, but they met with no success. So on July 1, under the leadership of the duke of Austria and the Knights of the Hospital, they began again to attack the tower, using several ships with fortified towers and ladders. At first they were successful, but the knights with their heavy armor put too much strain on one of the masts of the ships and it gave way, hurling them into the water.[23] The Moslems rejoiced at the discomfiture of their enemies, but the Christians were not alone in their losses. While they were attacking the chain tower, another of their ships, manned by Germans and Frisians, anchored in midriver and attacked the city with its *ballistae,* causing heavy losses to the Egyptians in the city and even more to those on the bridge of boats.[24] This ship was beaten back by Greek fire, although the crusaders succeeded in extinguishing the flames and saving the ship. These attacks demonstrated the strength of the Moslem position and made it clear that the Christians could not hope to conquer Damietta without first capturing the tower.

They settled down to a prolonged siege, hurling stones at the tower without significant effect. Oliver states that they had no hope of being able to starve out the defenders, who could be resupplied from Damietta via the bridge of boats.[25] Apparently, they gave some thought to undermining the tower, but the waters of the Nile were too swift and rough to permit them to work. Finally, Oliver, the scholasticus of Cologne, designed a siege machine mounted on two boats that would enable the crusaders to reach the top of the tower. The enterprise was undertaken by the Austrians, Germans, and Frisians, but the actual building was to be by the Frisians, who raised the money to pay for its construction. According to Oliver, who provides the best description, four masts were erected on two ships that had been bound together with beams and stout ropes. At the top of the masts, they built a fort, supported by beams and covered with hides for protection against stones and Greek fire. Projecting from the front of the platform and extending well over thirty feet beyond the prows of the ships, they built a ladder to provide access to the tower. They also erected a bridge that could be used to cross to the lower part of the chain tower. By the time this device was completed, the crusaders had succeeded in partially destroying the bridge of boats that connected the tower to the city. On August 18, with all in readiness, the patriarch of Jerusalem, Ralph of Merencourt, led a procession with a relic of the true cross along the western bank of the river. Men from every country were enlisted in the attack on the tower, though Oliver notes that there were enough Germans and Frisians for the task.[26]

The conditions surrounding the attack were difficult. The Nile had begun to flood on August 18, and water was racing around the tower. Only with extreme difficulty were the crusaders able to drag their fortress into position on the north side of the tower and extend their ladder. While the clergy prayed on the shore and the siege machine was gradually drawn into place, the defenders of Damietta moved petraries into place on the towers of the city nearest the water and began to launch rocks at the fortress-ship. They hurled Greek fire across the river at the boats, and the crusaders had to fight the fires with acidic liquid and gravel. The patriarch lay face down in the dirt before the relic of the cross, and the clergy cried out to heaven for aid. The Moslems on the tower poured oil on the ladder from the ship and set it afire, and when the crusaders rushed forward on the ladder to put out the fire, the moveable bridge at its end began to buckle, and the standard-bearer of the duke of Austria fell into the water. Cheers rose from the Moslems, and the Christian knights cried out at the loss of their comrades in the river. But this disaster proved fortuitous. With the excess weight removed, the ladder was once more raised into position, and the crusaders returned to the attack with swords, pikes, clubs, and flails. With strong pride in his own, Oliver tells of a young man, a knight of

Liège, who was first on the tower and who toppled the Moslem standard-bearer. The battle was not yet won, however, for the Moslems driven from the top of the tower took refuge below and set fire to its upper portion to drive the crusaders away. At this point, using the lower bridge and free of threat from above, the crusaders attacked the door of the tower. Throughout the evening and night of August 24 and into the morning of the following day, under a constant hail of stones from the city, they hammered away in vain. But the defenders now recognized that their situation was hopeless. Some leaped from the tower into the river and swam to the city; others drowned. But about one hundred, a third of the original contingent of defenders, surrendered to Count Feather, as they called the duke of Austria, on condition that their lives would be spared. They chose to entrust their fate to a crusade leader whom they had come to respect for his courage.[27]

To Oliver, the fall of the chain tower was an auspicious victory to be followed up immediately. Instead, the leaders and the army "fell into idleness and laziness according to their custom."[28] James of Vitry was perhaps more realistic, pointing to the difficulty of crossing the river in the teeth of the enemy while it was at flood level.[29] But there was a further factor, as Oliver himself quickly revealed. It was the season of the fall voyage, and the crusader army was about to lose a large part of the German and Frisian contingent. No doubt the leadership was waiting prudently to see what reinforcements would arrive to replace those who were leaving and those who had perished in the siege of the chain tower. They were fortunate, because the ships that arrived in the fall of 1218 brought large numbers of crusaders from England, France, and Italy, led by Ranulf of Chester, William of Derby, Hervé of Nevers, Hugh of La Marche, Marshall James and his Romans, and the papal legate, Pelagius, cardinal bishop of Albano. In the company of the French had come Cardinal Robert Courçon, not as legate, but as spiritual advisor of the French army. Despite the losses and departures, the army that was camped opposite Damietta increased considerably in size as a result of these arrivals.

The arrival of Pelagius has been viewed with particular foreboding by many historians of the Fifth Crusade, but too much attenton has been paid to his personality and too little to his actual function. There is little evidence that he played a leading role in military affairs during the next few months. Of course, he was part of the councils in which important matters were discussed and decided, but he did not emerge immediately as the dominant figure. The evidence cited by Van Cleve to argue that he was merely reflects Pelagius's fidelity to his mandate as legate as set out in his letters of appointment. There was certainly no immediate conflict between the legate and the king of Jerusalem. Besides, Pelagius brought news that Frederick II would soon arrive to assume the leadership of the army.[30] The events of the following months show that disease and weather were more formidable forces in shaping the plans of the crusaders than any conflicts between the personalities of these leaders.

Soon after the capture of the chain tower, sultan al-ʿĀdil died in Syria. One report even connected his demise to the loss of the tower, suggesting that the news of the disaster killed him. There are problems with the chronology, however, that make such an account more a good story than a likely reality. The tower fell on August 25, 1218, and news reached Acre on the twenty-ninth.[31] The sultan died on August 31. While it is certain that he knew of the event from the report of al-Kāmil's ambassador, al-Makrīzī makes clear that the sultan had been ill for at least two or three days before his death.[32] He was, after all, an elderly man. Al-Makrīzī's account thus raises the question of whether news of the fall of the chain tower could have travelled from al-ʿĀdilīyah to Marj aṣ–Ṣuffar in Syria before the sultan's illness began.[33] Most probably, he was already ill when he received the news and died soon after. The account that the loss of the tower had caused his death may exaggerate the connection between the two events.[34]

The death of al-ʿĀdil removed the last vestige of the unity of Saladin's empire, which was now divided among al-ʿĀdil's sons. Al-Kāmil received Egypt. Al-Muʿaẓẓam obtained Syria. Al-Ashraf ruled in Iraq.[35] Al-ʿĀdil's death also injected a new uncertainty into Moslem efforts to resist the crusader invasion of Egypt. Al-Kāmil was dependent for support on the good will of his brothers. On the surface, his position seemed to be very vulnerable, since family rivalries often lay at the root of serious conflicts among the Moslem ruling class. Al-ʿĀdil himself had seized power from his nephews, the sons of Saladin. His sons also began to behave as rivals, but in the immediate situation, the winter season proved favorable to al-Kāmil.

On October 9, the new sultan attempted a surprise attack on the crusader camp. According to the author of the *History of the Patriarchs of the Egyptian Church,* al-Kāmil decided on this action after his spies informed him that many shiploads of crusaders were departing. He obviously wanted to take advantage of the weakness of the remainder.[36] Apparently his own force was fairly large, consisting of about three thousand infantry. It crossed the river by a boat bridge and in galleys, landing near Būrah and moving northward toward the camp of the Roman contingent, which it entered without detection. The signal for the attack was to be the raising of the sultan's standard over one of the towers of Damietta, but the infantry took advantage of the element of surprise to move rapidly against the crusaders. Meeting little effective resistance, they made the mistake of penetrating too deeply into the camp. They were cut off by a small force under the command of King John and thrown into panic. Many were killed. Others fled to the river to find their boats, but drowned as they tried to swim in the swift current. One author describes how the crusaders cut off the heads of the dead and hurled them across the river and into the city, where some were recognized by the defenders.[37] The western accounts state that about a thousand Moslems perished at the river. This seems to be a realistic figure in light of reports from the Moslem camp that total losses were three thousand; the force had been annihilated.[38]

Al-Kāmil's aim had been to prevent the crusaders from crossing the river south of Damietta and encircling the city. On their side, the crusaders were unwilling to risk any action that left their main camp on the west bank of the river exposed. For the time being, they concentrated on repelling attacks by the sultan's troops across the bridge of boats south of the city, and they attempted to destroy the bridge itself. In order to prevent the crusader fleet from moving against the bridge, the sultan had sunk boats in the river to form a barrier, but this ploy was only partially successful. The legate succeeded in sending a ship he had equipped up the river to the bridge, but another ship, outfitted by Bishop James of Vitry, with about two hundred men aboard, had to retreat with losses. James had also sent a smaller boat, a barbot, upriver, but lost it and the twenty men aboard, six of whom were taken captive.[39] On October 26, the Moslems again crossed the bridge in force and moved on the crusaders, striking this time at the camp of the Templars.[40] "But immediately," Johannes de Tulbia tells us, "the Christian army got on their horses and pursued the enemy back to the bridge by which they had come." Crusader losses were much lighter than those of the enemy, but a distinguished Roman named Nicholas was killed by a giant Turk, whom the Sultan believed to be worth a hundred Christian knights. But King John killed the Turk and ended his menace.[41]

To achieve success, the crusaders had to find a better way to get to the upper part of the river, nearer the Moslem camp at al-ʿĀdilī-yah. The walls of Damietta and the ships sunk by the Moslems made the passage southward too risky for any group of ships. They therefore began to enlarge an old canal that connected the river to the Mediterranean. Although this sounds like a formidable task to undertake and complete in one month, the probability is that they merely widened and deepened it in places to permit the passage of their ships. The distance, as we have noted above, was not nearly as great as it is today. Numerous accounts describe the crusader camp as being located in sand. The sandy area extended inland for a considerable distance, but certainly not much more than a couple of miles. Although the sources are silent on this, it is probable that the crusaders not only worked themselves, but also impressed Moslem prisoners and peasants from the area into service. By such means, the canal work was completed by late November. The crusaders had improved their defensive position and were now located on an island, with the sea to the north, the river to the east, and the canal to the south and west of their camp. At the same time, they had gained direct access from the sea to the river south of the city.

But a winter storm struck on November 29, probably from the northwest, forcing the sea up the canal and the river at high tide and sending it over the low-lying shore. The crusaders were only saved from complete disaster by the ramparts they had built for the protection of the camp.[42] Frustration had already set in, however, over their inability to dislodge the Moslems, and they were complaining to the legate and the leaders of the army about the decision to invade Egypt. "Why have you brought us into the land of Egypt to die in this solitude?" they asked. "Wasn't there a cemetery at home? Look at us dying here without fighting and being buried like dogs in the sand." The legate ordered three days of fasting and prayer to find a way out of their problems. While the building of the canal had been a remedy for the frustration brought on by inactivity, the storm aroused new complaints, especially as the crusaders witnessed some of their companions driven with their boats into the hands of the Moslems and killed. "What are we doing here? God is angered at us. We can't advance and we can't retreat, but we stay here almost in despair in the sand."[43] The council of leaders of the army saw no real hope save through divine intervention, and so they turned to the legate, concluding that their sins had visited this disaster on them. They put themselves into his hands to intercede for them with God. Van Cleve sees in this incident an attempt by the legate to seize command of the army, but the crusaders approached the legate as a spiritual guide rather than a military leader.[44] King John and the other leaders of the army said to him: "We have erred, Master, we have acted unjustly, we have done wrong. Intercede for us, holy father, for the sea has broken our dike, and we will all die." There was danger of panic.

Pelagius responded to the fears of the crusaders in a practical way. He told them that the Lord was trying them and they should not be afraid. He told them to go quickly and kill the horses and use their bodies, along with the bodies of the dead they would find in the water, to fill in the break in the rampart made by the sea. He also told them to lay sails from the ships over the rampart to prevent the water from washing away the sand. When the storm continued un-abated on the third day, the crusaders reached the point of panic. They came to the legate again, almost like little children seeking safety at his feet. He stood up and commanded them to go with him to the rampart. He climbed up on it, uncovered his head, raised his cross over the land, and began to preach to the crusaders from the Gospel of Matthew about Christ calming the sea. At this point the sun came out, and immediately the mood changed.[45] The cru-saders set about rescuing their supplies and restoring the camp. In the meantime, the storm had also wreaked havoc on the Moslems at al-ʿĀdilīyah, so they were in no position to take advantage of the plight of the crusaders.[46] Nevertheless, the losses of the crusaders were especially severe. Their camps had been more exposed to the ravages of the sea. Few of their horses remained, and perhaps 20 percent of the army had been lost.[47]

During late fall and winter, pestilence also struck the crusader camp. It especially attacked those who had arrived during the fall passage. If the disease was scurvy, it may well have affected those who, after a month or more at sea, arrived when fresh fruits and vegetables were no longer in abundant supply. The toll was fairly heavy. Among those who died was Robert Courçon, cardinal of St. Stephen, whose death was deeply mourned. However, there is no indication that many of the leaders of the crusade died of the dis-ease, despite the mention of various nobles by James of Vitry.[48] The disease raged well into the winter. It was yet another factor in the weakening of the crusader army in the winter of 1218–19.

Nevertheless, the leadership of the army was functioning adequately. The disputes that arose were settled rather quickly in order to preserve the unity of purpose necessary to carry on the campaign. As Oliver put it: "Differences of opinion produced discord which was quickly settled because of the common need."[49] In general, a spirit of active cooperation marked these months. The problems that confronted the crusaders arose from their sense of isolation during the winter months, in which they received no additional reinforcements, while their losses mounted, due to the attacks of the enemy, the pestilence, and the weather. During this season of tragedy, respect for the legate increased, especially since spiritual guidance appeared to be the one remedy still available to the army. But Pelagius, though playing a more prominent role during the late winter of 1218–19, continued to work within the framework of the collective leadership that prevailed in the army. The sources make it clear that the reason for the failure of the army to move to the attack was the losses it sustained from flood and pestilence.

Morale continued to be low during January 1219, and disasters continued to pile up. A ship of the Templars was cast against the wall of the city by the current and pulled in by grappling hooks. Its defenders fought bravely, even when boarded by overwhelming numbers of the enemy. Finally, it sank and the Templars drowned, taking with them many of the enemy. But there was good news as well. Another ship, laden with Germans and Frisians, attacked the bridge of boats and broke through, opening the passage up the river.[50] The response of the sultan was to begin construction of defenses along the shore in order to prevent the crusaders from crossing the river and following up their victory, and he again sank ships in the Nile to prevent them from moving their fleet into position.[51] Nevertheless, the Christians prepared for the assault. The legate convoked a meeting of the crusaders. He preached to the assembled troops, asking them: "What are we doing here, dearest companions? It is better for us to die in battle than to live like captives in a foreign land." He then commanded everyone to be ready to attack on the feast of the Purification of the Virgin Mary on February 2. Oliver mentions that shortly after this he commanded the ships of the crusaders that were above the vessels sunk by the Moslems to cross the river and attack. While the sources made it clear that Pelagius took the initiative here, there is no evidence that he faced any opposition from any of the other crusade leaders, and in fact the ensuing attack seems to have been a cooperative venture. Perhaps those sources that single out the role of Pelagius at this point do so because his sermon to the troops was the most memorable event leading up to the decision to cross the river and attack the Moslem camp. If this is the case, we may wonder whether Pelagius was not merely acting on behalf of the collective leadership in exhorting the crusaders to a task that had been decided by the whole group.[52] The attack itself did not go well. The duke of Austria breached the fortifications along the riverbank, but a new storm came up and drove the crusaders back with its mixture of rain, hail, and wind. This storm lasted for three days and nights and brought despair to those who found themselves marooned on the riverbank opposite their fellows.[53]

As the storm abated, an apostate crusader called out to those on the bank that the camp of the sultan had been abandoned. Fearing a trick, King John ordered one of his men, Aubert the Carpenter, to investigate. Aubert returned with news that the enemy had fled, but John decided to send a knight by the name of Michel de Viz to spy out the situation. Having examined the sultan's camp, he returned to report that the Moslems had indeed taken flight.[54] The *Gesta Obsidionis Damiate* reports that St. George, together with many knights, had appeared during the previous night in the camp of the pagans and had so frightened them that they left everything. Actually, the good fortune of the crusaders arose from a near disaster for the sultan. Al-Kāmil had heard of a conspiracy against him by one of his richest and most powerful emirs, Ibn-al-Mashṭūb, who had enlisted the support of al-Kāmil's brother, al-Fāʾiz. Al-Kāmil learned of the plot from a soldier, who had been present while it was being discussed, but he had no way of knowing how extensive it was. He fled to Ashmūn. When his army discovered that he had deserted, it fled before its commanders could gain control. Only the timely arrival of al-Muʿaẓẓam from Syria saved the situation. Al-Fāʾiz was arrested and sent to Yemen but died mysteriously on the way; Ibn-al-Mashṭūb was shipped off to Syria. The plot failed, and al-Kāmil was again secure, but the crusaders had taken the opportunity this afforded them to cross the river and occupy al-ʿĀdilīyah.[55] From there they quickly moved to surround the city of Damietta.

Even with this stroke of good fortune, the crusaders were unable to take the city. After describing the repulse of the Templars, who had attempted a surprise attack on the city, Oliver blamed the idleness and laziness of the crusaders for the renewal of enemy attacks.[56] In fact, however, he misread the events. Neither army was prepared to go on the offensive. This was a period of defensive strategy. The success of the crusaders and the threat posed by the conspiracy had created a state of emergency for the sultan during which he was primarily concerned with shoring up the fortifications of Cairo and securing sufficient men and funds to resume the war.[57] The Eastern and Coptic Christian populations of Egypt began to feel the pressure as the sultan forced them to contribute to the public treasury. But during the period that the Sultan was restoring the state of his army, the crusaders enjoyed a respite from attack. This lull probably triggered the idea, advanced by Oliver, that these circumstances provided a good opportunity to take the city. But the army was in dire straits. There was famine. "Such was the misery of the Christians," according to the *Gesta Obsidionis Damiate,* "that, just as a sick man desires health, so the Christians wanted, not I say, to eat, but only to see the grass growing, because there was nothing but sand."[58] The leadership saw the necessity for keeping the army ready. Pelagius and John of Brienne worked together on a program aimed at building a bridge to connect the two crusader camps and to strengthen their fortifications.[59] It was also about this time that the crusaders heard the sad news that al-Muʿaẓẓam had ordered the dismantling of the walls of Jerusalem prior to his arrival in Egypt.[60] King John and the legate, with the other leaders, continued to work on a plan to capture Damietta.[61] Unfortunately, the state of the army hindered serious efforts at direct attack.

Before they could devise a further strategy, the lull came to an end. The crusaders barely had time to dig in when they found themselves surrounded by Moslems. The sultan had moved with his army to Fāriskūr, several miles south of al-ʿĀdilīyah. On March 3 he advanced to the point where the crusaders had crossed the river south of Damietta, but he was repulsed, chiefly by the Germans and Frisians.[62] On the ninth, the Moslem forces again threatened the ramparts, but were driven back. These were mere probes; the main attack came on Palm Sunday, March 31, 1219. The Moslems descended on the crusaders with a fleet of some seventy-one ships and a large army, aiming to dislodge them from their position before Damietta and to relieve the city. The battle was fought hand-to-hand, with the Moslems succeeding in burning part of the bridge connecting the two Christian camps. The duke of Austria was a heroic figure in this battle, which raged through the whole day and into the evening. In the end, the crusader lines held, and the Moslems were forced to retreat.[63]

Early in May, after having fought for a year and a half, Leopold of Austria and many other crusaders decided to return home. After the hard winter, the loss of such a valiant fighter seriously weakened the crusader army. Although some new troops arrived in mid-May, their number was negligible and included no outstanding leader from the West.[64] James of Vitry gives some insight into the difficulties faced by the crusaders when he speaks of the malaise that affected the crusader army after the losses it had suffered. "The majority of our men," he recalled, "were in the grip of despair."[65] The fundamental decisions reached by the leadership of the crusaders in this period were dictated by the resources available for the conduct of the campaign. Johannes de Tulbia sums up their feeling that the army could not move against the encampment of the Moslems, which outnumbered it by a wide margin, without losing the advantage offered by its fortified positions. Its only choice was to concentrate on the beleaguered defenders of Damietta in the hope that they would surrender.[66]

As the hot Egyptian summer commenced, the atmosphere of stalemate and the frustration of immobility pervaded the camp of the crusaders. The two sides had settled down to wait one another out, with periodic probes aimed at ensuring the other's discomfort. The strong defenses of the Christians made it possible for their army to repel the attacks of the Moslems, but their own feeble efforts had no significant effect on the city or the Moslem camp. As July passed, the crusaders reached the point of desperation, and murmurs of discontent were heard widely through the army. Still, the leadership remained committed to a plan of battle aimed at avoiding confrontation with the Moslem army. It was in the ranks that boredom gave rise to criticism of this decision, and agitation for decisive action grew.

Previous accounts have passed too quickly over the reasons for this stalemate and its effect on the army. Their concern has been chiefly with signs of the growing power of Pelagius and the increasing conflict between King John and him, rather than with the humdrum of a war of attrition beset by natural disasters. During the winter and spring of 1218–19, the legate played an increasingly important role, intervening numerous times to shore up the sagging morale of the crusaders. But this was not a period of conflict among the leaders, whose major concern was to occupy the army usefully in order to reduce the complaints of the rank and file against the lack of decisive action without risking defeat by a superior enemy.

Pelagius proved himself the strongest personality among the leaders at Damietta and was able to inspire confidence in his abilities. He acted decisively against the ravages of weather, disease, and boredom. As spring approached, the army might have planned to seize the initiative, had it not been for the departure of Leopold of Austria with a large number of crusaders and the lack of sufficient replacements. Hungry and discouraged, the crusaders faced the long, hot Egyptian summer. For the moment, the course of the war was beyond their control.

NOTES

1. Ol., chap. 10; Kuttner and García, "Fourth Lateran Council," 131.

2. *SS*, 73–74. "Habito quidem consilio, unanimiter omnes statuerunt, cum omni Christianorum exercitu, qui in auxilio Terre Sancte proficiscebantur, in terram Egipti intrare . . ." (ibid.).

3. Van Cleve, "Fifth Crusade," 396. Van Cleve cites James of Vitry to support the view that the decision to invade Egypt was made at this time. While James does discuss the reasons for preferring an invasion of Egypt to a siege of Jerusalem, he does not suggest that there was a debate over the decision. Jac., 102–3.

4. Ernoul raises the point that John and the heads of the Military Orders discussed the relative merits of Alexandria and Damietta as objectives; *T,* 293.

5. Ibid.

6. Mayer, *Crusades,* 124.

7. Bongars, *Gesta,* 1128.

8. *History of the Patriarchs of the Egyptian Church,* 3:2:216.

9. Guest, "Delta," 942. The modern river has been dredged and the water level is therefore different. It was much higher in the thirteenth century. The location of medieval Damietta may be determined from the ruins of the principal mosque, located on the northern edge of the modern city.

10. Salmon, "Mission à Damiette," 84–85.

11. Guest, "Delta," 942–45. I am grateful to Professor M. S. Omran of the University of Alexandria for additional information and drawings of maps from his thesis on the Fifth Crusade.

12. Orlova and Zenkovich, "Nile Delta," esp. 69.

13. Salmon, "Mission à Damiette," 81.

14. Orlova and Zenkovich, "Nile Delta," 69.

15. Al-Makrīzī, *Expeditionibus,* map. Hamaker, who prepared this map, placed Damietta too close to the sea, distorting the relationship between the crusader camp and the city.

16. Guest, "Delta," 941, map. Note location of "Ancient Damietta" as opposed to the modern city.

17. Ol., chap. 38; Jac., 103–4. For Arab descriptions of Damietta, see Salmon, "Mission à Damiette," 76–81.

18. Ol., chap. 32.

19. The best description of the chain tower is found in Gottschalk, *Al-Kāmil*, 60–65.

20. Eracles, *RHC,* Occ., 2:329.

21. *History of the Patriarchs of the Egyptian Church*, 3:2:218.

22. Ol., chap. 11.

23. Ibid.; *History of the Patriarchs of the Egyptian Church*, 4:1:45.

24. Ol., chap. 11.

25. Ibid., chap. 12.

26. Ibid.; see also Jac., 106.

27. Van Cleve, "Fifth Crusade," 401; *History of the Patriarchs of the Egyptian Church*, 3:2:219–20, 4:1:47; see also Ol., chap. 14.

28. Ol., chap. 15.

29. Jac., 107.

30. Van Cleve, "Fifth Crusade," 403. Runciman is, for example, incorrect in maintaining that the passage in Johannes de Tulbia (*SS,* 122–23) portrays the legate acting in opposition to King John; *Crusades,* 3:155. Rather, a certain crusader approached the legate regarding the meaning of a revelation. In the action that followed, Pelagius acted in concert with John and the other crusade leaders.

31. Gottschalk, *Al-Kāmil,* 69.

32. Al-Makrīzī, *Expeditionibus,* 316–17.

33. Ibid.

34. Runciman, *Crusades,* 3:154.

35. Gottschalk, *Al-Kāmil,* 69–70; *History of the Patriarchs of the Egyptian Church,* 3:2:221.

36. *History of the Patriarchs of the Egyptian Church,* 3:2:220.

37. Ibid., 3:2:220; 4:1:51–52.

38. Ibid., 3:2:221.

39. Jac., 114–15.

40. Ol., chap. 18.

41. *SS,* 122.

42. Ol., chap. 19.

43. *SS,* 124.

44. Ibid.; Van Cleve, "Fifth Crusade," 406–7. See the discussion in Siberry, *Criticism of Crusading,* 69–108.

45. *SS,* 124.

46. Ibid., 125; Jac., 116–17; *History of the Patriarchs of the Egyptian Church,* 4:1:52–53.

47. *SS,* 125; Ol., chap. 27.

48. Jac., 105–6.

49. Ol., chap. 31.

50. Ibid., chap. 21.

51. Ibid., chap. 22.

52. *SS,* 125, 83.

53. Ibid., 84.

54. *RHC, Occ.,* 2:335–37; Ol., chap. 22.

55. The quote is from *SS,* 85. The best account is in Gottschalk, *Al-Kāmil,* 76–81; see also Runciman, *Crusades,* 3:157; Van Cleve, "Fifth

Crusade," 408. The *History of the Patriarchs of the Egyptian Church,* 3: 2:223, reports that Ibn-al-Masṭūb was beheaded.

56. Ol., chaps. 22 and 23.

57. *History of the Patriarchs of the Egyptian Church,* 4:1:58–59.

58. *SS,* 87.

59. Ibid., 87; *RHC, Occ.,* 2:337.

60. *RHC, Occ.,* 2:339.

61. *SS,* 87. Van Cleve and Mayer state that al-Kāmil offered a truce to the crusaders during this period; Van Cleve, "Fifth Crusade," 409; Mayer, *Crusades,* 213. This seems highly unlikely. The sultan was busy in Cairo trying to rebuild his army and raise money to continue the war. Moreover, Van Cleve has based his position on a citation from the translation of the *History of the Patriarchs* that appeared in *ROL,* 11 (1908): 254, and a reference to Eracles (*RHC, Occ.,* 2:338–39). However, comparison with the Arabic text shows that the translation in *ROL* is incorrect. See *History of the Patriarchs of the Egyptian Church,* 4:1:64, in which the word "again" in reference to the offer of the truce, does not appear. Further, the account in Eracles cannot refer to this period, because it ascribes actions to the sultan that are at variance with his known activities.

62. Ol., chap. 23.

63. Ibid., chap. 25; Donovan, *Pelagius and the Fifth Crusade,* 55.

64. Ol., chaps. 26 and 27.

65. Jac., 118.

66. *SS,* 128.

CHAPTER IX

THE CONQUEST OF DAMIETTA

The stalemate lasted through the summer and into the fall of 1219. Given the small number of reinforcements that arrived from the West in the spring passage of 1219, the army could do little but maintain its defenses and await the arrival of the fall passage. The crusaders had already learned that Frederick II had postponed his arrival in Damietta until March 1220.[1] Negotiations over his coronation as emperor were proceeding slowly, despite the fact that the death of Otto IV had removed the possibility of opposition from that quarter. With some reluctance, the pope had agreed to this postponement, though it meant that the expected imperial army could not arrive in Damietta before another year had passed.[2] Under these circumstances, the crusaders again had to tailor their initiatives to the limitations imposed by available forces.

There were serious difficulties in laying siege to the city, but the leaders agreed that this approach offered their only viable choice, given the superiority of the sultan's army at Fāriskūr. Fortunately, they were united in this plan and its implementation. The legate provided "copious funds" to those participating in the attack on the city and "the King and others produced ropes and anchors in abundance," while the Pisans, Genoese, and Venetians attacked from their ships.[3] The defenders of the city used Greek fire to repel the attackers, and they reinforced the walls with palisades and wooden towers. The crusaders failed, and not surprisingly, for failure was the usual result in medieval sieges.

In late summer, Francis of Assisi arrived in the crusader camp. He came, not to cheer on the discouraged Christian army or to fight the heathen, but on a mission of peace.[4] The sources of the period are sparing of information about this episode. Francis did not journey to Damietta on a whim. He had thought long about relations between Christians and Moslems and had earlier attempted to journey to the East. He was well aware of the risk of martyrdom and, indeed, sought it. A fundamentally charismatic figure rather than a detailed planner, Francis possessed a profound intuitive understanding of the major currents and issues of his time. His visit to Damietta, far from being an event of passing interest, throws substantial light on the tensions and attitudes to be found in the crusader camp at the height of the summer of 1219.

Very likely he arrived in the camp during the latter part of August, at a time when the rank and file of the crusader army felt frustrated over their failure to capture the city and were complaining bitterly about the refusal of their leaders to attack the main Moslem army at Fāriskūr.[5] The *Gesta Obsidionis Damiate* provides a good insight into conditions and attitudes within the camp at this time. The war of attrition was in effect, and there were atrocities on both sides aimed at instilling fear in the other.[6] The pressure on the crusade leaders from the rank and file was increasing, and in response they decided to mount an attack on the enemy force. Immediately, the army began to prepare for battle. Francis foresaw that the coming battle would lead to disaster for the crusaders. Confronted by the enthusiasm of the common troops for the battle, he was reluctant to announce his prophecy, but he was also troubled in conscience. It was only after consulting a companion—probably Brother Illuminatus, who had accompanied him on this voyage—that he decided to preach to the troops regarding the risks of the battle.[7]

The sermon preached by Francis on this occasion, in which he predicted defeat of the Christian army on the following day, evoked considerable opposition. It is even possible that Francis was viewed as opposed to the crusade. At any rate, his prophecy came true. On August 29 the crusaders advanced on the Moslem camp on land and by ship. The Moslems feigned flight and drew the crusaders into an area without fresh water for themselves and their horses during the oppressive Egyptian summer. While their leaders halted to discuss the best course of action, the crusaders scattered in an undisciplined mass. When the Moslems probed the right flank, the

Cypriots, Italians, and others began to flee. There was immediate danger of a rout, averted by the action of the Templars, the Teutonic Knights, and the Hospitallers, supported by King John, the legate, and many of the great feudal leaders of the army.[8] Nevertheless, losses were heavy, including the capture of a number of nobles with the bishop-elect of Beauvais. The crusaders retreated. It was a disaster that fully justified the prediction of Francis. The sultan, sensing the opportunity offered by this victory, sent one of the Christian prisoners to the crusader camp with the offer of a truce.

The truce negotiations offered Francis an opportunity to carry out the remainder of his mission. He approached the legate to request permission to cross over to the Moslem camp. At first Pelagius refused, because he feared that the Moslems would kill Francis and his companion. But, under Francis's continued urging, he gave in. Apparently, the Moslems thought that Francis was a messenger and escorted his companion and him to the sultan. Al-Kāmil asked his visitors whether they had come as messengers or to embrace Islam. Francis asserted that he was a messenger and sought to demonstrate to the sultan the truth of Christianity. Obviously, Francis saw in conversion the means to peace and reconciliation. The sultan responded by calling in his religious advisers. They demanded that the sultan kill Francis and his companion, but he refused and, after offering him gifts and food, sent Francis back to the crusader camp.[9] As Mayer has recognized, Francis's mission was aimed at accomplishing the goal of the crusade through conversion rather than by force of arms.[10] It was the beginning of the long-term commitment of the Franciscan order to missions among the Moslems, and especially to the custody of the Holy Places. But these two incidents, Francis's preaching to the crusaders and his visit to the Moslem camp, viewed together suggest that his message of conversion as an alternative to war was offered not merely to the Moslems but to the Christians as well.[11] Under these circumstances, the prophetic nature of his approach takes on a broader meaning, one that reflects some currents of contemporary criticism of the crusade and that reaffirms the preeminence of conversion as the resolution of conflict. What Francis was attempting was nothing less than an extension of the aims of the western peace movement to the struggle with Islam. This was entirely consistent with the objectives of the papacy.

Despite its outcome, the battle on August 29 demonstrated that the Moslem army was not able to dislodge the crusaders from their positions. Conditions for both armies were miserable. In addition, the Nile flood, on which the country depended for the irrigation of its crops, virtually failed, and the price of grain rose steeply in the cities. The truce negotiations therefore offered a respite to both sides to recover from their losses. Without question, the sultan hoped to attain by treaty what he had failed to achieve in battle.[12] He may have been encouraged in this both by the letters he had received from Innocent III prior to the crusade and by the mission of Francis. He offered to return the city of Jerusalem to the Christians, along with funds for its reconstruction. He also offered the return of major crusader fortresses west of the Jordan. In exchange, he sought the evacuation of the Christian army from Egypt. As al-Kāmil may have foreseen, his offer caused division in the crusader army.[13] King John, along with most of the northern European crusaders and the Teutonic Knights, favored the agreement, while the legate, the clergy, the Templars, the Hospitallers, and the Italians opposed it. The main reason behind the decision to reject the truce was the refusal of the sultan to include the fortresses of Kerak and Krak de Montréal, located east of the Jordan and regarded as essential to the defense of Jerusalem, in the list of those to be returned. The sultan offered instead to pay an annual tribute of fifteen thousand bezants for them. While the military orders believed these forts to be critical to the defense of Jerusalem, from the viewpoint of the Moslems they posed a serious threat to continued communications between Damascus and Cairo. The sultan could hardly surrender them without sundering his ties to Syria. The crusaders were divided on this issue, but could hardly ignore the threat to their control of Jerusalem if the castles remained in Moslem hands.[14]

It is difficult to gauge how deeply this difference divided the crusaders. The fact that it found wide report in the chronicles shows that it was quite important. It is indicative of the role that King John was coming to play that he disagreed with the legate. This incident represents the first substantial evidence of a deterioration in the cooperative relationship between king and legate that had existed to this point. Matters did not arrive at this state without previous developments, but neither should we trace the increasingly important role being played by the legate all the way back to the time of his arrival. Only after February 1219 had the legate begun to play a larger role in the crusade, and even then it was largely consistent with his office and was exercised in conjunction with the other leaders. During the summer, his position assumed more importance as the morale of the army deteriorated and he used his office to preserve its unity. He had become the focus of considerable admiration during this difficult period, but the offer of a truce brought him into conflict with a significant part of the leadership. Since he emerged as the victor, we may conclude that his views were ascendant at this time, but he was hardly in full command.

By late September 1219, peace negotiations had ended and al-Kāmil resumed his attacks on the crusaders.[15] The author of the *Gesta Obsidionis Damiate* has caught the spirit of the crusader camp very vividly at this time. The visions of the crusaders centered on heavenly aid as they dreamed of the bodies of the dead scattered across the sands of Egypt.[16] And at this critical juncture an enormous number of the crusaders, including the leaders of the Roman contingent, along with the Hungarian archbishop of Kolocza and other counts, departed, leaving the remnant of the army terrified.[17] The Moslems rejoiced. Only the timely arrival of Savaric de Mauleon with a considerable force restored the morale of the Christians.[18] It was a bad time. Oliver later said that it was during this period that a certain Arabic book of prophecies that promised the conquest of Damietta came to the attention of the crusaders. Pelliot has argued that Oliver was incorrect, contending that these prophecies appeared only in 1220.[19] If Oliver's usually good memory played a trick on him, it may well have been because the circumstances of the army in the fall of 1219 were not unlike those in the period after the capture of Damietta.

The wearing siege of Damietta continued through October and into the early days of November. The Moslems attempted to use Christian apostates and traitors to burn the bridge connecting the two camps of the crusaders.[20] Shortly afterward, al-Kāmil launched a major attack to drive through the Christian lines and relieve the city. Despite the element of surprise and the stealthiness of their movements through the swampy areas, they were driven back with 262 captured; only 111 Moslems managed to get into the city. The rest fled, and the women of the camp killed them. They were beheaded and their heads thrown into the sultan's camp. The bodies were dumped in front of the fortifications of the city to gain a psychological advantage through terror.[21]

Discipline within the army had deteriorated seriously, yet the leaders knew that the city could not hold out much longer, for its defenders were also in sad straits. The crusaders sent heralds through the camp to announce plans for the city's capture and to set down rules to regulate the army during the final siege and entry into the city. All present were divided into groups and commanded to guard the camp well. If anyone deserted his or her post—for the women were included—a first offense would mean being tied to a horse and dragged through the camp. For a second offense, a knight would lose his horses and armor and be expelled from the army. Infantrymen would lose a hand, as well as all they possessed. If a merchant or a woman maintained a market in the army, he or she could lose both a hand and all their goods. Men and women found without weapons while assigned to guard the tents, unless they were sick or too young, would be excommunicated. If anyone failed to bring the ladders, boats, and ships that they should to the siege, they would lose a hand and their possessions. Anyone who found money or property and appropriated them, or robbed someone, would lose a hand as well as his share. Those in command were ordered to swear to enforce these statutes. After the heralds had announced them, the leaders proclaimed that the army would attack the city. The people agreed.[22]

But before an attack could be launched, during the night of November 5 some Italian crusaders noticed that one of the towers of the city, which had been partially wrecked in previous attacks, seemed no longer to be guarded. They climbed a ladder, secured the tower, and quickly summoned others to their aid. A later tradition would give the credit for being first to a Florentine. It was a bloodless victory over a dying city. The crusaders found the dead strewn in the field between the second and third walls, in the streets, and in the houses, where living and dead shared the same beds, the former too weak to move. Some had bread and water beside them but were unable to eat. Of an estimated population of sixty thousand, about ten thousand survived, but most of them were sick.[23] The booty was everywhere. The city had numerous rich houses, and the crusaders were overwhelmed at the sight of gold and silver vases, precious stones, and jewels. They captured a huge store of foodstuffs, as well as hundreds of asses and mules. While Oliver and the *Gesta Obsidionis Damiate* suggest that the army maintained its discipline, save for a few who stole precious articles for themselves, James of Vitry reacted in horror at the prevalence of looting.[24]

The immediate reaction of the Moslem forces was to probe the crusader lines in the hope of retaking the city. But, finding the opposition well prepared for battle, al-Kāmil decided to retreat from Fāriskūr towards al-Manṣūrah, where the Nile and a canal provided a more secure defense for Cairo itself. This left the crusaders time to consolidate their gains, but also, unfortunately, time to fight over the rich spoils. The main bone of contention was, of course, control of the city itself. Once again, the legate and King John found themselves at loggerheads. In fact, there was little hope of avoiding such a conflict. As commander on the ground, John was prepared to push his claim for control of the city. But the instructions of the legate had given him the responsibility for dealing with the division of conquered lands. What loomed even larger was the absence of the emperor-elect Frederick II, though he was represented by an imperial party present in the camp, very likely acting under his instructions.[25] The ensuing debate, which has generally been described solely in terms of a personal conflict between Pelagius and King John, was more accurately the result of papal instructions to the legate and an attempt by an imperial party to preserve the rights of the absent emperor-elect. Despite mounting differences, the pope and Frederick II continued to cooperate. In no other crusade did an absent leader exercise such a decisive influence on the course of events.

But the existence of the imperial party does not mitigate the effect of the antagonism between the legate and the king over control of the city.[26] Pelagius, who had been generally popular until this time, now found himself unpopular because of his division of the spoils among the army. The crisis that the pope had anticipated at the time of the appointment of the legate and that the leadership had prepared for in the statutes issued just prior to the surrender of the city now broke out. The army rioted against the legate and threatened his life. They demanded their portion of the city. His response, as reported in the chronicle of Johannes de Tulbia, is especially interesting, because he explained that he had not alone been responsible for the division of the spoils.[27] In the meantime, King John, with the support of the Syrian barons and others, applied pressure by arming three galleys and threatening to withdraw from the crusade.[28] The tumult only subsided when, at the legate's behest, a compromise was reached whereby the city was placed in John's hands until the arrival of the emperor and a new and somewhat more substantial division was made of the booty to the benefit of the common soldiers.

With these arrangements, the crisis passed. On November 11, just six days after the conquest of the city, the leaders joined together to report the victory to Pope Honorius III.[29] The order of the names is interesting. After the patriarch of Jerusalem, Ralph of Merencourt, the document names King John and then the archbishops of Bordeaux and Nicosia. Next come the bishops, including Pelagius as bishop of Albano, the masters of the military orders, the great nobles, and finally the consuls of the communes. Does this order suggest dissatisfaction with the role played by Pelagius? Perhaps they wished to underscore the message they were sending the pope, for in this hour of victory they took the occasion to inform the pope of the realities of their situation and to recommend stepped-up efforts to aid the crusade. They reminded him of their desperate need for men and money. They pointed out that many crusaders were planning to depart in the next passage and that this would jeopardize the plan to capture Egypt. They also asked him to compel Frederick II to fulfil his vow and to cease the redemption of vows for others, which they argued was detrimental to their cause. They were also concerned about the expenditure of funds raised by the papacy for the support of the crusade. This letter, which brought forth a vigorous effort by the pope to meet the needs it outlined, presented a united front dedicated to the successful conclusion of the crusade. On the following day, a group of influential French barons led by Simon of Joinville, seneschal of Champagne, wrote the pope to endorse the position taken in the previous letter, but also to give their special support to King John and especially to his needs.[30] These were John's supporters in the conflict over control of the city, most of them men from the part of France where he had originated. Despite their obvious concern over the way in which their old comrade had been treated, they joined in the common front, indicating that the conflict had not taken very long to resolve, though scars from it no doubt remained.[31]

At the moment of victory, shortly after passions over the division of the great booty won at Damietta had threatened to tear them apart, the leaders of the Fifth Crusade informed the pope of the inadequacy of the army for the task that remained. Part of the problem was that from the beginning their objectives had been somewhat vague. The *Gesta Obsidionis Damiate* speaks of the thorough subjection and rule of Egypt.[32] James of Vitry is more precise:

> We planned to proceed to Egypt, which is a fertile land and the richest in the East, from which the Saracens draw the power and wealth that enable them to hold our land, and, after we have captured that land, we can easily recover the whole kingdom of Jerusalem.[33]

But James does not specify whether Egypt was to serve as a base for further military operations to retake the Holy Land or be exchanged. The chronicle of Ernoul sketches out a far more limited plan. Its author envisions that the capture of either Damietta or Alexandria would result in the return of the Kingdom of Jerusalem.[34] Probably the difference in the sources reflects a corresponding difference in the viewpoints of the crusade leaders. Almost certainly, the truce offered by the sultan had been premised on his knowledge that some crusaders were agreeable to an exchange. The rejection of that truce, however, should not be interpreted as a refusal to end the crusade through compromise. The legate and his supporters wanted better terms than the sultan was willing to offer. With the capture of Damietta, they now realized that continuing the war would require much greater resources than they possessed.

Any hope for a resolution of the conflict, whether military or diplomatic, came down to the question of resources and manpower. These were the issues at the heart of the debate over the future of the crusade, and they continued to be the major causes of conflict among the leadership during the remainder of the crusade. Only by understanding them can we penetrate beneath the conflict of personalities centered on Pelagius and King John that has fascinated virtually all who have written on the Fifth Crusade in order to explain the reasons for the disaster that was in preparation. But that is no simple task.

As we have already seen, the financial data allow only the most general conclusions, but we should mention one critical point regarding the financing of the crusade that contributed substantially to the conflict among the leaders. As we have seen, the crusader army was supported to a considerable degree by the resources of the crusaders themselves.[35] But such funds were insufficient for the maintenance of a long military campaign. The chief support for the crusade came from the money raised by the crusade tax of a twentieth on ecclesiastical incomes, as well as from the redemption of vows and from freewill offerings. Thus, the army was completely dependent on the church at this point and would remain so, at least until the arrival of Frederick II. Control of this money rested in the hands of the papal legate.[36] The longer the emperor-elect delayed his arrival at Damietta, the more the army had to look to the legate and to the pope for financial support. Thus, the financial question inexorably contributed to the growth of Pelagius's role in the leadership of the crusade. Control over money gave the legate a degree of authority that distorted his original mission. Of course, it was not the only factor. The absence of Frederick's strong personality was important in shaping the outcome, but this factor has previously received more attention than Pelagius's power over the purse.

With respect to the manpower situation, it is surprising that, in light of the considerable attention paid to the subject in contemporary sources, the arrival and departure of crusaders has received but little attention from modern authors. Van Cleve has noted the manner in which the arrival of reinforcements helped to shape military tactics, but he made no consistent effort to analyze its impact.[37] Earlier, in discussing the leadership question, we made two points that are important here. The period of service of crusade leaders was on the average surprisingly short, about fifteen months, and their departure usually meant the loss of substantial numbers of crusaders, who returned home with them. To this must be added the losses by death due to disease and fighting. These factors make it clear that the only way in which the strength of the crusader army could be maintained was by a continued supply of fresh arrivals from the West. The pattern of arrivals and departures early assumed the character of a rhythm based on the seasonal arrival of fleets from the West that established the basic tempo of the crusade.

We can never hope to establish the size of the army with accuracy, and at any rate, it was constantly fluctuating. Johannes de Tulbia said that there were one hundred thousand in the camp after the capture of Damietta, but this included all noncombatants.[38] It is likely that no more than a third of these were fighting men. A figure of three thousand knights might appear reasonable, save for the fact that Oliver maintains that there were only twelve hundred knights in the force that moved out of Damietta to attack the sultan in July 1221.[39] Since the arrival of Duke Louis of Bavaria had in the meantime brought substantial reinforcements, the figure offered by Johannes de Tulbia obviously provides no useful guide to the size of the effective fighting force. But if it is impossible to gauge accurately the size of the army in numerical terms at different stages during the crusade, this does not mean that it is also impossible to measure changes in its relative size in other terms. A quantitative analysis of arrivals and mortality rates throws interesting light on this question, and it confirms and strengthens what we can learn from other sources.

This analysis is based on a study of more than eight hundred individuals known to have taken vows to go on the Fifth Crusade. Of these, 92 percent made the journey to the East, and we have information about the season and year of arrival for 59 percent of this

group. On the other hand, we can account for the death or safe return of only 31 percent of them. A serious problem is the validity of
the sample. Obviously, it does not represent a cross section of participants in the crusade. Only 3 percent of the total are women or
members of the lower classes. On the other hand, over 22 percent
are members of the clergy. In fact, just over 8 percent are members
of the upper clergy, defined as archbishops, bishops, abbots, and
cardinals. About 16 percent are classified as townsmen or members
of the urban aristocracy. Another 38 percent are identified as members of the knightly classes. Very probably, a high proportion of the
20 percent of unknown status belonged to this group as well but
did not meet the criteria for inclusion, which consisted either of a
definite identification or a context that left no room for doubt
about status. On the basis of this sample, we cannot make gener-
alizations that are valid for all participants in the crusade. The
sample has value only for certain groups. The upper clergy are, as
expected, the best-documented group on the crusade. Very likely,
most who participated are included in our list. After them, we
know most about the feudal aristocracy, especially the counts, earls,
and dukes. We are much less well informed about ordinary knights
and members of urban contingents. In most instances, our knowledge is limited to their participation in the crusade with a particular
contingent.

    The study of arrivals enables us to examine the availability of re-
placements for those crusaders who returned home or died. The
three graphs in Figure 9.1 show the arrival pattern for the entire
sample, for the feudal and urban aristocracy, and for the upper
clergy. What emerges immediately is the concurrence of the evidence presented. As the crusade progressed, there was an overall
decline in the number of replacements. This trend is strikingly illustrated in the graphs for the feudal and urban aristocracy and for the
upper clergy. After the arrivals of 1217 and 1218, which account
for 58 percent of the total sample, it appears highly probable that
the number of replacements declined and continued to decline until
the end of the crusade. The major exception to this trend appears to
be the arrivals in the fall of 1219, that is, in the period just prior to
the capture of Damietta. The spring passage in that year had been
disappointing, and many crusaders had left during the month of
May. The defeat on August 29 had brought significant losses.
Oliver was, therefore, very aware of the importance of the reinforcements that arrived that fall. The "Mighty Warrior" sent Savaric de

Figure 9.1 Arrival Dates of Crusaders in the East

All crusaders

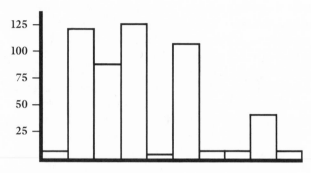

Feudal and urban aristocracy

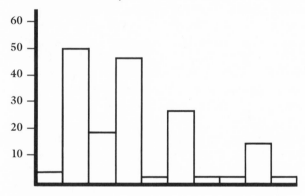

Upper clergy

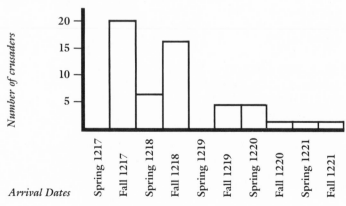

Mauleon over the sea "with armed galleys and very many warriors in this crisis of distress."[40] But the graph showing arrivals of the feudal and urban aristocracy suggests that, important as these reinforcements were, they were well below the numbers that had arrived a year earlier. This same conclusion is reinforced by the graph of arrivals of upper clergy.

The desperate situation for the crusader army continued throughout 1219. As discussed earlier, the departure of Count Diether von Katzenellenbogen in the summer of 1219 aroused considerable concern.[41] In the summer of 1220, Archbishop Henry of Milan arrived with a Venetian fleet and other Italian contingents, but the situation remained serious, as the graph shows. Oliver reports that fewer than one hundred new crusaders arrived in the fall of 1220.[42] The church at Acre undertook an emergency effort to aid the army. The concurrence between the picture presented in the graphs and the situation described in the narrative sources provides proof that the declining number of arrivals was a critical factor in the conduct of the crusade.[43] If any single theme may be said to dominate the narratives of the Fifth Crusade, it is that of arrivals and departures. Oliver sums up his feelings in this passage:

> Meanwhile, the sailors, who were betrayers of Christianity, and with them very many pilgrims, whose love of themselves was greater than their compassion for their brethren, left the soldiers of Christ in the greatest danger; hoisting their sails and leaving port, they afforded dejection to us and courage to the Babylonians [i.e., the Egyptians].[44]

The problems associated with maintaining sufficient troops in the field are further illustrated by the study of the mortality and survival rates in the crusader army (Table 9.1). Death in combat was not the only factor. The pestilence that ravaged the camp in the winter of 1218–19 also took a heavy toll.[45] Narrative sources give an impression of high mortality that is confirmed by statistics for those known to have died in the course of the crusade. Since it has not been possible to determine the cause of death for most crusaders, the figures given include both deaths in combat and those from other factors. Out of the total sample, we have information regarding mortality or survival for 261. Of these, slightly more than one-third died. Given the predominance of clergy and nobility in this sample, a much higher mortality rate for the entire army, which was composed of numerous light-armed infantry more likely to fall in battle and noncombatants little prepared for the onslaught of

Table 9.1. Rates of Mortality and Survival

| | | DIED | | SURVIVED | |
	TOTAL CASES	NUMBER	PERCENT	NUMBER	PERCENT
All crusaders	261	89	34.10	172	65.90
Upper clergy	48	9	18.75	39	81.25
Feudal aristocracy	104	35	33.65	69	66.35
French crusaders	70	25	35.71	45	64.29
German crusaders	64	18	28.13	46	71.88

pestilence, is very possible. The mere suggestion of such high mortality rates raises serious questions about the ability of the West to replace these losses with new arrivals.

Are these figures valid? The group for whom we have the best information in our sample consists of the upper clergy, whose losses are close to 20 percent. There is no evidence that any member of this group died in battle. Given their probable ages and the difficulties of the journey, as well as the susceptibility of Westerners to disease in the East, this percentage should not be surprising. Comparison of the mortality rate of the clergy with that for the feudal aristocracy shows, as we might expect, that the latter group suffered heavier losses, about one-third of its total membership in the course of the crusade. In other words, its mortality rate is almost the same as that for the total sample. Figures for the two largest contingents represented in the sample, the French and the Germans, tend to confirm these results. French losses amounted to 36 percent, while German losses were 28 percent, somewhat less than would be expected. Obviously, a certain amount of caution is needed in interpreting this data, but declining numbers of arrivals and substantial losses through death provide evidence of why, just after a major victory, the leaders of the crusade wrote the pope to inform him of their plight. Though they continued to differ among themselves regarding the effect of the manpower situation on the conduct of the war, they were agreed about their overall needs.

Dissension among the crusaders has been the major theme in the story of the Fifth Crusade. But the explanation of this dissension cannot be left on the level of the personalities of individual leaders. The assessment of resources and manpower provides a measure of the potential for success of the Fifth Crusade that goes beyond that factor. Moreover, behind the actors in the field loomed the pope and the emperor-elect. Pelagius was, of course, the pope's representative at Damietta, but he also had to safeguard the interests of the absent Frederick. King John was the commander in the field, but his role was clearly limited by the pope and the emperor-elect through Pelagius. His disappointment and dissatisfaction with the turn of events after the conquest of Damietta, his concern about the inadequacy of the army, naturally focussed on the legate. There can be no question but that John and his supporters realized that their problem was not so much with the legate as with his master. Hence, the letter written by John's friends to Honorius III took pains to enunciate their position clearly, stressing the manpower problem and commending John's judgment and loyalty.[46] In fact, however, control over the conduct of the war was passing from his hands to those of the legate.

NOTES

1. H.-B., 1 : 2 : 584–86.
2. Ibid., 692.
3. Ol., chap. 28; Van Cleve, ("Fifth Crusade," 412–13) is incorrect in attributing this plan to Pelagius alone, despite the fact that the *Gesta Obsidionis Damiate* (*SS,* 94–95) attributes the entire initiative to the legate. Oliver was much better informed about the manner in which important decisions were made than was the author of the *Gesta,* who normally gives a view from outside the leadership council. Gavigan has suggested that the Italians acted from commercial motives; see Peters, *Christian Society and the Crusades,* 80, n. 1. But the Bolognese charters show that they, at least, had little interest in any long-term commitment in Damietta; *FK,* 72–73.
4. See my article "Francesco d'Assisi e la Quinta Crociata: Una Missione di Pace," in which the major literature is cited. See also Kedar, *Crusade and Mission,* 126–31.
5. Ol., chap. 29; Jac., 120.
6. *SS,* 99–101.
7. *Thomas de Celano, Vita secunda S. Francisci,* 2, 4, 30.
8. Ol., chap. 29.
9. *T,* 302–3; Jac., 132–33.
10. Mayer, *Crusades,* 212.
11. Powell, "Francesco," 74–77.
12. Van Cleve, "Fifth Crusade," 414–15. It is likely that these are the negotiations described in Eracles, *RHC, Occ.,* 2 : 339, since the context seems to fit conditions at this time. See Ol., chap. 29.
13. Van Cleve, "Fifth Crusade," 414–15.
14. Ibid., 415; Eracles, *RHC,* Occ., 2 : 341–42; *History of the Patriarchs of the Egyptian Church,* 4 : 1 : 64.
15. Ol., chap. 30.
16. *SS,* 103–4.
17. Ibid., 104.
18. Ol., chap. 30; but see also Eracles, *RHC, Occ.,* 2 : 343, where arrival dates are confused.
19. Ol., chap. 35; Pelliot, "Deux passages."
20. *SS,* 134.
21. Ibid., 110.
22. Ibid., 111; Van Cleve, "Fifth Crusade," 417–18.
23. *SS,* 113.
24. Ol., chap. 38; *SS,* 114; Jac., 135; Eracles, *RHC, Occ.,* 2 : 346.
25. *SS,* 139. "Tunc Dominus legatus posuit pacem in omnibus, et civitas fuit assignata regi et Alamannis, salvo iussu imperatoris, et promiserunt integram porcionem dare" (ibid.).
26. Eracles, *RHC, Occ.,* 2 : 348.

27. *SS,* 139. "Domine, da nobis porcionem civitatis! Et ipse [legatus] dixit eis: Quicquid habeo, daturus sum vobis, sed nichil alii nolunt vobis dare"; ibid.

28. Ibid., 138–39.

29. *FK,* 43–46.

30. Ibid., 46–48.

31. See Honorius III's letter to the Genoese, July 27, 1220; Rodenberg, 1:91.

32. *SS,* 74.

33. Jac., 102.

34. *T,* 293.

35. See chap. 5.

36. Rodenberg, 1:89–91.

37. Van Cleve, "Fifth Crusade," 405.

38. *SS,* 139.

39. Ol., chap. 57.

40. Ibid., chaps. 26 and 27.

41. Ibid., chap. 50.

42. Ibid., chap. 56.

43. *SS,* 104, 127, 133.

44. Ol., chap. 30.

45. Ibid., chaps. 16 and 31.

46. *FK,* 48–49.

CHAPTER X

THE FAILURE OF THE CRUSADE

The margin between victory and defeat in Egypt was always narrow. The terrible loss suffered by the crusaders on August 29, 1219, was the prelude to the capture of Damietta, but that victory was itself no guarantee of success. On the one hand, the crusaders had gained control of a key port and base of operations that enabled them to dominate the northeastern part of the Nile delta; on the other, they confronted the army of the sultan, which controlled the main route to Cairo. Whatever strategic advantage the crusaders had gained by the conquest of the city depended on their ability to exploit it. Yet they lacked the resources to do this. Instead of capitalizing on their new position, the best they could do was to consolidate their control of the city and the surrounding area by strengthening their fortifications and driving the enemy from nearby outposts. The Frisians donated the siege machine used to capture the chain tower for the common purpose; it was dismantled and the wood used to build a bridge connecting the city to the camp on the opposite bank.[1] They also built earthworks to protect the bridge and put up a watchtower to aid those entering the harbor.

The capture of the city enabled the crusaders to expand their control of the Mediterranean coast. On November 23, a force of about a thousand men moved toward Tinnis, located east of Damietta between Lake Manzalah and the sea. The Moslem garrison fled at their approach. As a result, the crusaders gained control of the rich fishing in the lake, as well as the harbor on the sea. Since adverse winds had from time to time driven their ships into this harbor, where they had been captured, the gain was considerable.[2] Still, the crusaders were in no position to follow up their victory by an attack on the main Moslem force until they received reinforcements from the West.

In the meantime, al-Mu'azzam left Egypt immediately after the fall of Damietta and returned to Syria. He summoned troops from Damascus and ordered the preaching of the *jihad*, then moved rapidly against Caesarea. Despite the fortification of the port in 1218, it fell quickly at the end of November. He next laid siege to Château Pèlerin but was unable to take it.[3] It was also his intention to capture Acre. This was a reversal of the plan employed by the crusaders in 1218, which had called for a joint attack on the Moslems in Syria and Egypt, with Kai-Kā'ūs of Rūm aiding the crusaders in their attack on Syria. That plan had failed because the crusaders were unable to carry out their part of it. Now, al-Mu'azzam's campaign was hampered by threats from fellow Moslems, including the rising power of his brother, al-Ashraf, in the north.[4]

While al-Mu'azzam continued to pressure the remnants of the Kingdom of Jerusalem during the early months of 1220, King John withdrew from the army at Damietta and went to Acre with a substantial following.[5] James of Vitry mentions the departure of many French crusaders at this time. Moreover, the patriarch of Jerusalem and many of the Templars left Damietta in order to counter the attacks against Château Pèlerin and Acre by al-Mu'azzam.[6] It is not surprising that Pelagius was concerned about these withdrawals, especially that of King John. But the immediate reaction of the legate to John's departure is not as obvious as some historians have made it. Oliver says that the king "feigned many reasons for excusing himself" and recounts the story of his claim to the Armenian throne, but he does not mention the reaction of the legate.[7] James of Vitry says only that John "deserted the army."[8] The account in Eracles says that he went off to establish his claim to the throne of Armenia. His wife, Stephanie, was the eldest daughter of the Armenian king, Leo II, who had died in the early summer of 1219, but his wife and their young son died soon after he arrived in Acre.[9] While Eracles makes clear that there was no love lost between Pelagius and John, his narrative does not suggest that the legate opposed the departure. Ernoul reports that John sent some of his knights to Armenia and expressed his intention to go there to make good his claim. But his effort was in vain.[10] Again, there is no mention that Pelagius had been involved in any way in the king's departure. Moreover, John had earlier sought confirmation of his claim to the Armenian throne from Rome, and a papal letter to this effect had been sent on February 2, so in all likelihood Pelagius was apprised of John's intentions well before his departure.[11] The most that can be concluded is that John took advantage of the lull in the fighting after the capture of Damietta to see to his own affairs. But the death of his wife and son quickly removed his main reason for departing. At any rate, it was not expected that he would remain away for long.[12] As the period of his absence lengthened, it is obvious that his reasons for staying in Acre had changed. Possibly concern for the defense of Acre against al-Mu'azzam delayed his return.[13]

All of which is not to say that John's action was popular. Indeed, it was harmful to morale, and as it was prolonged beyond the expected time, it caused increasing confusion within the army.[14] Both Oliver and James of Vitry reflect the views of John's critics. Oliver, in particular, criticized his departure at a time when "kings usually set out to war."[15] Nevertheless, the real blame that attached to John's withdrawal was not that he sought to establish his claim to the Armenian throne, but that he did not immediately return when that cause was lost. Whatever his reasons, whether he was influenced by his anger at Pelagius or by his concern about Moslem activities in the area around Acre—Safad was destroyed about this time by al-Ashraf—his absence and that of the others who left the army at this time made the situation of the crusaders at Damietta desperate.[16] Pelagius went so far as to forbid any further departures, and he kept a careful account of deaths.[17]

At this juncture, a debate broke out between those who believed that the army was ready to fight and those who did not. The summer had brought a substantial number of new arrivals from northern Italy, led by the archbishop of Milan and including ambassadors of Frederick II, who announced his plans for joining the crusaders. In July another imperial contingent, under the command of Count Matthew of Apulia, arrived with eight vessels.[18] Oliver concluded that things were going well for the army. He reported the efforts of the legate to persuade the troops to take to the field. In this he was seconded by the new arrivals but opposed by William, earl of Arundel, and various of the German nobles, who cited John's absence as a reason for their unwillingness to attack.[19] There was also considerable opposition to the legate from those who had wanted to depart in the spring.[20] Oliver reports that some French and German mercenaries who had accepted payment from the legate opposed his efforts.[21] Oliver argued the case for the legate forcefully, maintaining that "the Christians did not lack an abundance of soldiers or attendants. Galleys were in abundance, barbots were prepared, a numerous multitude of archers was present, there was a plentiful supply of provisions."[22] But James of Vitry casts serious doubt on Oliver's objectivity. James was normally in favor of action and was prepared to support the legate, but his view of the situation in the summer of 1220 was in stark contrast to Oliver's. Writing to Pope Honorius III in April 1221 about the period after the arrival of the imperial contingent under the command of Count Matthew, he said: "Our forces, because they were few and could not safely engage the multitude of the Saracens, delayed behind their lines and fortifications in order to protect the city."[23] He goes on to paint a bleak picture of the confusion in the Christian camp, which was compounded by agents in the pay of the sultan. To further complicate the problems confronting the leadership, in the spring of 1221 al-Kāmil offered peace terms that included the return of Jerusalem.[24]

It was apparently at this time that Pelagius ordered a certain book in Arabic with ancient binding and maps, which had been found in the camp, to be translated and read aloud to the army. It purported to contain the words of St. Peter himself to his disciple Clement and predicted the capture by the Christians of a "watery city in Egypt," as well as Alexandria and Damascus. It mentioned two kings, one from the East, the other from the West, who would arrive in Jerusalem in a year when Easter fell on the third of April. Oliver connected this prophecy with the Mongol advance in Persia, and he believed that Genghis Khan, whom he called King David, had freed Christian captives in Bagdad sent there from Egypt by al-Kāmil.[25] James of Vitry was caught up by the same mood and transcribed the Latin text of an *Excerpta de historia gestorum David regis Indorum, qui presbyter Iohannes a vulgo appellatur* in a letter to Honorius III.[26] He also told how some Syrians in the camp showed the crusaders a book with an ancient binding, entitled: *Revelationes beati Petri apostoli a discipulo eius Clemente in uno volumine redacte.*[27] James took these prophecies very seriously, and a substantial number of prophetic works were circulating in the crusader camp. Their significance has been little understood, and, in fact, they raise serious questions that cannot be satisfactorily answered with the available evidence.[28] Even if some of them were actually written very near the time of their discovery, their audience was most receptive to their message. These prophecies contributed directly to the discussion of the future direction of the crusade, which centered around two questions: the ability of the army to move to the offensive and the sultan's offer of peace. Although the debate over these questions reached a new level of intensity during 1220 and early 1221, it had been a standing feature since the first offer of a truce by the sultan. Writers like Oliver and James of Vitry, with their emphasis on the view that victory rested entirely in the hands of the Lord, were very receptive to prophetic interpretations that seemed to reveal the divine plan for the future of the crusade. It would be cynical to regard Pelagius's use of these prophecies as purely manipulative: in an atmosphere that was conducive to prophecy, Pelagius and the other religious leaders among the crusaders were continually attuned to the voice of the supernatural, though this does not mean that they were gullible. Conditioned as they were to the possibility that prophecy might point the way to victory, they retained a certain critical judgment in evaluating these works. They were, according to their lights, responsible leaders, unwilling to pass on to the army anything in which they themselves did not believe. Yet, once satisfied that these prophetic visions were authentic, they gave them stature as authorities in the discussion of the alternatives confronting the crusaders. It is, of course, impossible to assign a precise weight to the influence of these writings, but the manner in which James of Vitry mixes prophecy with fact in his discussion of the aid to be expected from "King David" and his suggestion that the rejection of the peace offer of al-Kāmil was partially due to the way in which the Christian army was exulting "in these rumors" suggest that they were a considerable factor.[29] For James of Vitry, prophecy was an extension of reality. But it was a contingent and indeterminate reality that depended on the interplay of factors in an unknown future.[30]

The year 1220 was indecisive. It brought significant numbers of new recruits, including a Venetian fleet, but it also witnessed the departure of many. A raid against Burlus that netted substantial booty almost ended in disaster. The Venetians retaliated with an attack on Rosetta and Alexandria.[31] Al-Kāmil, on the other hand, was in no position to attack the strongly fortified camps of the crusaders. His brothers were still occupied in Syria and the north, where the Mongols had overthrown the Khwārizmīan shah and advanced into Georgia.[32] Although this posed no immediate threat to the caliph in Bagdad or the Aiyūbid dominions, it was a source of concern for the Moslems, just as it was a reason for hope among the Christians. Al-Mu'azzam continued to operate against the crusaders in Syria. He ordered the further dismantling of the city of Jerusalem, though he spared the major sites in the city, and this caused widespread panic among the remaining population. He also seized Destroit, the tower of the Templars at Château Pèlerin, and destroyed it. He laid siege to the fort but was unable to take it, due to its reinforcement.[33] Meanwhile, at Damietta, Pelagius continued his efforts to persuade the army to move, going so far as to set up a rival camp across the river for those who favored his course of action, but there were few willing to join him.[34] Behind the continuing refusal of the army to venture out to attack the enemy in force lay two factors: the continued absence of King John and the expectation that Frederick II would arrive in Damietta in August 1221.[35]

Whether or not John had papal permission to pursue his claim to the Armenian throne, his departure from Damietta had effectively removed him from the direct control by the legate. Indeed, from the outbreak of discord between the king and the legate after the capture of Damietta, the pope had become directly involved. A letter Honorius sent to the king and the heads of the military orders on February 24, 1220, supported the authority of the legate in the division of the conquered city under the terms of his original commission. It did not, however, as Van Cleve and Donovan state, confer on him new authority in temporal affairs. The reference to *temporalia* in this letter refers specifically to his original commission and his existing authority to arrange the division of newly conquered lands.[36] Papal involvement in the conflicts arising between King John and the other crusader contingents over the division of the city is also shown by Honorius's letter of July 27, 1220, to the podestà and commune of Genoa, which put the future of this matter directly under the control of the apostolic see.[37] Honorius also wrote to John in Acre in August 1220 regarding his departure from the army. He explained that he was not certain why John had left Damietta, suggesting that he may have done so with the good intention of repelling the attack of the Moslems against the crusader forts in Palestine. But he warned him that he should not become involved in other affairs, mentioning the concerns of some that he desired to attack the Kingdom of Armenia. The tone of the letter is pacific, expressing every confidence in John's loyalty to the cause of the crusade, but it also contains the threat of excommunication should he attack the Armenians or any other Christians. Honorius was treading cautiously in an effort to heal the rift between John and Pelagius in order to secure John's participation in the crusade at Damietta once again.[38] If, as is likely, the source of Honorius's information was Pelagius, the legate seems himself to have been uncertain regarding the reasons for John's absence and anxious to secure his return.

The pope continued negotiations with Frederick II preliminary to his imperial coronation and departure for the East. The main stumbling blocks to settlement were the disposition of Frederick's Sicilian crown, which he had renounced in favor of his son Henry prior to his own coronation as German king, and the settlement of conflicting papal and imperial claims in central Italy, especially in the lands bequeathed to the papacy in the early twelfth century by Countess Matilda of Tuscany. Frederick had inherited the imperial policies of his father, Henry VI, and his grandfather, Frederick Barbarossa, and was in no position, even granted his friendly relations with the papacy, to back down on claims that touched the interests of the empire. Indeed, he had the example of Otto IV to point up for him the reality of the pressures on an imperial candidate to maintain these interests despite papal opposition. But Frederick and Honorius both desired to find a settlement for these issues and to promote the business of the crusade, to which they were both committed, if for different reasons. Of course, the issues were difficult. They involved the interests of the communes of northern Italy, the concerns of the south Italians, and the fundamental commitment of the papacy to its independence. The concessions made to Frederick by Honorius III regarding his retention of the Sicilian crown reflected the hope for further cooperation between the empire and the papacy. Suggestions that they were the product of papal weakness or of pressure on the pope to secure Frederick's participation in the crusade fail to take into account the process of negotiation, which was directed not only at a peaceful settlement of longstanding differences, but also at building a solid basis for cooperation in the future.

Of particular importance for an understanding of these papal-imperial negotiations is the letter that Honorius wrote to his representative, the papal subdeacon Raynaldus, with detailed instructions regarding the course to be followed in negotiations with Bishop Conrad of Metz, the imperial chancellor and chief negotiator for Frederick II. Conrad had taken the crusade vow and had bound himself to go on crusade with the emperor in May 1220. Naturally, since the negotiations between Frederick and the papacy had not yet reached a conclusion, he had not done so. Although Frederick had secured a postponement of his journey, the bishop was still technically bound and was subject to the penalty of excommunication for his failure to depart. Honorius advised Raynaldus to appeal to the conscience of the bishop. If Conrad denied that he had a guilty conscience about his failure to depart and claimed that it was due to an impediment, Raynaldus was to advise him to write to the pope and describe the impediment so that Honorius could counsel him. The whole point of this process was to put pressure on the bishop to settle the matter of the Mathildine lands. Honorius asked Raynaldus to let him know the results of this effort immediately.[39] In this letter, Honorius detailed the connection between recruitment for the crusade and the papal peace program. The chancellor was being subjected to the same pressures that had been used by legates and crusade commissioners beginning with the mission of Cardinal Robert Courçon. In the eyes of the pope, even the emperor might be legally subject to this process, based as it was on the voluntary taking of the cross and the canonical penalties for failure to carry out one's obligation.

Honorius continued to keep the pressure on Conrad in his letter of September 4.[40] He also wrote the papal subdeacon Alatrinus, who had been negotiating with Frederick at his court, to bring him abreast of affairs and to enlist his support.[41] Honorius had applied pressure on Conrad because he had good reason to believe that Frederick had sent his chancellor a mandate to turn over the disputed lands. But in writing Alatrinus he revealed his suspicion that the real cause of the delay lay with Frederick, who wanted to use the issue of the Mathildine lands as a basis for further negotiations. During the same month, the pope complained directly to Frederick.[42] Frederick responded in October, assuring the pope of his gratitude for past support and commending his efforts to settle affairs in Lombardy in order to facilitate his journey to Rome for coronation.[43] Many historians have doubted Frederick's sincerity and argued that he was merely leading an aged and rather weak pope down the garden path to disappointment. But the facts do not fully sustain this interpretation, which anyway is largely based on reading backward from the later rift between Frederick and the papacy. There is no question that Frederick employed every diplomatic effort to secure the advantage of the empire, but the ultimate solution was an acceptable compromise that secured for the papacy recognition of its rights over the Mathildine lands and enabled Frederick to maintain his position in the *Regno*.[44] More important, the foundation was laid for cooperation between the empire and the papacy not merely in the matter of the crusade, but also in northern Italy and, of special concern to the church, in the struggle against heresy. Viewed from this vantage point, the negotiations leading up to the imperial coronation of Frederick II in November 1220 were full of promise.

The most direct and tangible effects of this cooperative effort are to be found in the legation of Cardinal Hugolino of Ostia in Lombardy. Christine Thouzellier has shown that Hugolino replaced Conrad of Metz as Frederick's legate in Lombardy, acting at least in part as an imperial vicar.[45] Letter after letter issued from the papal and imperial chanceries in support of the cardinal's mission.[46] Pope and emperor were moved by the desperate situation that confronted the crusaders and the need for mutual support in dealing with the divided communes of northern Italy. The crusade was impeded by the protracted negotiations with Frederick and by the continued absence of King John. As the spring of 1221 approached, this situation changed. Hugolino got his first commitment of new support for the crusade from Siena in March.[47] Once again, the program of pacification and recruitment for the crusade operated hand in hand. At Lucca, for example, Hugolino's intervention was the continuation of a peace effort that had commenced prior to the departure of Bishop Robert and his contingent for the crusade but that had encountered renewed problems after the return of the bishop.[48] Throughout Lombardy and Romagna, Hugolino secured oaths from the communes to preserve peace and to settle both internal and external conflicts. He also secured grants of money and commitments of crusaders from various communes.[49] In two of these charters we find the formula "ad preces domini Honorii summi pontificis et domini Frederici imperatoris," an official recognition of the joint nature of the request made on the communes to furnish money and troops for the crusade.[50] Cardinal Hugolino's legation in Lombardy was part of a significant push to build up the crusader army to be led by Frederick II and to attain victory in Egypt. It also demonstrated the immediate value for both sides of the papal-imperial negotiations leading up to the coronation, as Hugolino worked not merely in the interest of the crusade, but also for a peace in northern Italy that would benefit the empire as well as the recruitment effort. The legateship of Hugolino, the friend of the emperor and the pope, was an example of the new foundation for papal-imperial relations in Italy. Unfortunately, Frederick continued to postpone his departure.[51]

The problem was that events too soon overtook these efforts and deprived them of any significant fruit. The situation in Egypt during the winter and spring of 1220–21, was, as we have seen, devoted to watching and waiting. On January 2, Honorius wrote to Pelagius to urge him to continue to move with caution. He alluded to the preparations underway for strengthening the army and the commitments made by Frederick at his coronation, but he expressed the view that there was still uncertainty about the fulfillment of their plans. In light of this, he suggested that Pelagius should explore the prospects for a temporary agreement with the Moslems, telling him to report back on this quickly if anything developed.[52] In light of Frederick's previous postponements and of Honorius's knowledge of the situation of the army at Damietta, as well as the ongoing effort to recruit a major force to accompany the emperor, the pope was looking for a way to gain time for the crusaders. Without doubt he felt that a truce would enable Pelagius to hold the army together until the arrival of the emperor.[53] There was little likelihood that the Moslems would accept any agreement along the lines that the Pope desired, and in fact their sole interest lay in continuing to press for a peace treaty that would lead to the evacuation of Egypt, but on terms that had proven unacceptable to the crusaders.

The critical point was reached with the arrival of Duke Louis of Bavaria as representative of Frederick II in May.[54] He had been expected since March or April as the harbinger of the new imperial army. Louis, who had taken the cross with Frederick in 1215, was the highest-ranking representative yet sent by Frederick to the East. Moreover, given the absence of King John, he was also the dominant secular leader of the army. It was now for him and Pelagius to survey the situation and to arrive at some decision regarding the immediate future. Of course, that decision had to be accepted by the leadership of the army in the usual way, but the presence of an imperial representative of the stature of Louis overrode the obstacle previously posed by the absence of King John.

Pelagius wanted action. He was concerned about the effects of continued inactivity on his capacity to keep the army together, especially since the season for departures had arrived. The reinforcements brought by the duke of Bavaria represented a necessary condition for any movement of the army. The legate also sent for King John, commanding him to rejoin the army with his forces.[55] What Louis of Bavaria proposed was an attack on the camp of the sultan.[56] His objective was more limited than historians have previously recognized.[57] It did not at first imply a direct move against Cairo. It was, perhaps, a compromise between the growing demand for action by the legate and some segments of the army and the course of action favored by Honorius III and the emperor, both of whom preferred to avoid major confrontations with the enemy until Frederick arrived.

The weeks that followed the decision to launch an attack on the camp of the sultan were filled with moral, spiritual, and material preparations. The sultan had withdrawn the bulk of his forces to al-Manṣūrah, sheltered behind the Damietta and Tanitic arms of the Nile, which there formed the triangular island on which the city of Damietta stood. Duke Louis and the legate wanted to move before the Nile commenced its annual flood early in August, but discussions among the leaders—Oliver speaks of opposition—as well as the time needed for preparations, severely reduced the margin available. It was not until July 6 that the army was ready to depart Damietta. The following day King John returned with a large force to resume his position in the army.

The question that immediately arises is why the duke and the legate continued to press for an attack even though the season was growing late. There is no satisfactory answer. Both Oliver and James of Vitry, however, demonstrate the dismay of the ecclesiastical leaders at the corruption of the crusader army as it remained idle in the city and the camp. Prostitution and drunkenness, gambling and thievery so aroused their concern that Pelagius took special steps to impose a moral code on the camp.[58] Again and again the ecclesiastics inveighed against idleness as the cause of these problems. Also, the energy they had expended in getting the forces moving created a certain inertia that it was difficult to turn off without endangering morale. Nor should we overlook the evidence that Pelagius was confident that the Lord would bring his troops to victory. Finally, however, it is probable that Pelagius and Louis did not see the action as irrevocable. Thus, with the return of King John and the gathering of the army at Fāriskūr, all was in readiness. It was July 17; less than a month remained before the beginning of the Nile flood.

The situation of the Moslems was hardly to be envied. Cairo bordered on panic. The old and new city were evacuated. The *History of the Patriarchs of the Egyptian Church* says: "And these were days, the like of which in fear and hardship and anxiety for all the people, had not been witnessed."[59] Fear was so great that some Moslem leaders were secretly passing bribes to the Christian nobles held captive in the city in order to gain their favor in the event of a crusader victory.[60] Al-Kāmil ordered a general call-up of troops, sending men into the markets to incite the crowds to join their arms to those of the sultan.[61] But even as things looked bleakest, they were beginning to improve. Al-Ashraf and al-Mu'aẓẓam joined forces at Harran and began their march to Egypt to aid their brother. The division of Moslem forces that had persisted throughout 1220 and into 1221 was about to end. Rather than attempting to divide the crusader army by continuing their attacks on Acre and the other crusader forts of Palestine and Syria, they had decided to focus their entire effort on Egypt.

Before the arrival of his brothers, al-Kāmil decided once more to offer peace terms to the crusaders. This was after the return of King John and probably before the army moved from Fāriskūr, since the crusaders were in close contact with the large forces they had left in Damietta. About the same time, the legate received a warning from the queen of Georgia and from members of the Templar and Hospitaller orders in Syria that al-Ashraf and al-Mu'aẓẓam were moving toward Egypt and that there were great risks for the crusaders. Oliver, who had previously supported the position of the legate regarding the acceptance of a treaty, now favored the peace offered by the sultan. Unfortunately, he does not give his reasons, nor does he report the ensuing debate in detail. While he presents King John's argument that the risk of accident might imperil the venture, he merely says that the pope and the emperor had both forbidden acceptance of the peace. In the case of the pope, he is clearly referring to Honorius's letter of January 2, which had asked Pelagius to explore the possibilities of a truce and to refer the matter to him. But Honorius had not forbidden the acceptance of the peace in this letter; rather, he was concerned with securing an advantage that would allow time for the arrival of Frederick. On the other hand, Frederick had forbidden his representatives to accept a peace, since he planned to arrive to take command of the crusader forces. Oliver's report apparently lumped the positions of the pope and the emperor together, probably because he saw little difference between them. Oliver himself had now come to view the future in terms similar to the vision of St. Francis on the eve of the battle of August 29, 1219. He quoted the words of God to Moses in the Book of Numbers: "Go not up or fight, for I am not with you, lest you fall before your enemies."[62] Of course, we do not know when Oliver composed these lines, and they may well reflect hindsight, but his resort to the concept that the time was not ripe for battle provides additional evidence of the role of prophetic vision in shaping the discourse of the ecclesiastical leaders of the crusade. It also suggests that St. Francis's sermon to the crusaders in August 1219 shared in this prophetic vision.

The army that moved south along the Nile from Fāriskūr constituted only a portion of the total army, since a large force had to be left in Damietta for its defense. Nevertheless, if the Moslem estimate of the crusaders remaining in Damietta—about ninety thousand—bears any relationship to the actual numbers, it raises the question whether the army of the legate and Duke Louis represented a full-scale marshalling of resources for the conquest of Egypt or merely a sufficient force to carry the war to the enemy camp.[63] From subsequent statements by Oliver, we know that this army planned to maintain close links with the forces in Damietta and viewed the forces there as reserves.[64] Oliver is very precise about its size. He bases his calculations on reports made by estimators, whose task it was to report the numbers of ready fighters in each category to the leaders on a regular basis. Unfortunately, he does not give a total for the entire army, and his omission of a count of the infantry hampers any attempt to arrive at such a figure. He states that there were twelve hundred knights, as well as Turcopoles and other horsemen. He believed there were about four thousand archers, including twenty-five hundred mercenaries. In addition, there were large numbers of clergy and noncombatants, including women. He speaks of 630 ships of all sizes, implying a considerable force of sailors and fighting men on the water. Since many ships must have been rather small, it is impossible to state the number of fighting men in this segment of the force with any accuracy. Still, it would not seem that the army that set out from Fāriskūr was even half the size estimated for the force that remained in Damietta. Even allowing for a substantial percentage of noncombatants among the latter, one might question whether the crusaders would have left such a disproportionately large group behind if they were planning an all-out offensive.

On July 18, the army reached the area of Sharamsāh, famed for its palace. The Turkish cavalry began to harass the crusaders, staying out of range of the knights and shooting arrows into the infantry columns in the hope of inducing a panic. This forced the Christians to delay and to reply in kind. These tactics had no effect on the crusader force, which was experienced in this kind of warfare and maintained its lines until the Turks withdrew. The Moslems abandoned Sharamsāh, burning the surrounding villages and fields and leaving the palace to the invaders. But their action had only a token impact, because the crusaders had no difficulty in finding sufficient food in the area for their needs. Nevertheless, contact with the enemy raised the question of whether it was wise to continue the advance.[65] It was now July 24.

Apparently it was again King John who advocated withdrawal; the legate opposed it. There were no new reasons advanced to favor one course over the other, but the mass of ordinary crusaders waxed enthusiastic over their "victory" and threatened to kill the king, who had no choice but to advance.[66] The debate consumed several days. Certainly it was near the end of July when the crusader army entered the narrow triangle of land opposite al-Manṣūrah. Beyond Sharamsāh a small stream entered the Nile from the west in the neighborhood of Barāmūn. The crusaders noticed it in passing but concluded that it was of no importance because it seemed too small to support boats of any size. In that error in judgement, as well as in their disregard of the information regarding the arrival of al-Ashraf and al-Muʿaẓẓam in Egypt, the crusader leadership, especially the legate, was guilty of a serious blunder. Pelagius—in his anxiety to promote the crusade, keep the army together, and maintain its morale—had ceased to listen to the advice of King John. At the head of a force inadequate to its task and certainly no match for the combined armies of the sultan and his two brothers, Pelagius moved into a bottleneck created by the Nile and the canal from al-Manṣūrah to Lake Manzalah. Moreover, he did this just as the river began its annual rise.

Misfortune now dogged the crusaders. Al-Kāmil sent ships down the al-Maḥallah canal into the Nile behind the crusader fleet, closing the river to retreat, and sank four ships in the river to impede navigation downstream. At the same time, his brothers' contingents moved to the northeast of the crusaders to cut off their escape. As food supplies dwindled, the leaders of the crusader force began to realize the danger of their situation and to debate the question of withdrawal. Their choices were either to wait for the reinforcements promised by the emperor or to retreat. Oliver numbered himself among those who wanted to wait for relief, relying on the basic strength of their position, which was defended by water on two sides, and the fact that provisions could be made to last for twenty days. But "the opinion of the Bishop of Passau and the Bavarians" to retreat prevailed.[67] We can only wonder that Oliver ascribes such an important voice in this decision, so fateful for the final tragedy, to the bishop of Passau and makes himself the protagonist of an untried but possibly successful alternative. Why did he not here revive the conflict of Pelagius and King John, or even mention the views of the imperial representative, the duke of Bavaria? No matter. The decision was to withdraw.

Shortly after dark on August 26 the army began its retreat. The leaders, "following the judgment of their own will, and not that of reason, set fire to the tents" that were to be left behind.[68] Some of the troops tried to drink the wine they could not carry. It was an army ill-prepared to fight, hampered by wounded and sick as well as by noncombatants, that moved northward along the river. The Nile was at full flood. While in previous years it had been rather low, now it seemed to compensate for its shortages. Many of the common people, who had apparently been the most inclined to drink too much, slept heavily and could not be roused, or wandered off from the army in the dark. Others sought refuge in the ships, overloading them and causing them to sink. The Templars, disciplined as always, formed the rear guard. But the Egyptians harassed the disorganized army and dealt it heavy losses. With the river in flood, it grew harder to maintain close communications between the ships and the army. The ship of the legate got caught in the current and was swept downstream, as was a German ship that found itself under attack from Moslem ships in the river. It caught fire and was destroyed. During the same night, the sultan ordered the sluices opened to flood the fields, forcing the army to find high ground on the road or to wade through the water. The fields turned into a sticky morass that sucked at the hooves of the horses.

The final battle was little more than a series of skirmishes. The Turkish cavalry harassed the flank of the army from the east while black infantry fought the Templars without any great effect. The night of August 27 was made worse because the Moslems opened the floodgates on the small streams entering the Nile, and the water poured over the land and the sleeping crusaders. When the black

troops again attacked, it was only the discipline of the Templars that
saved the huddled groups of crusaders exposed to the enemy.[69]
With dawn came a desire on the part of the leaders to find a peaceful solution through negotiation with the enemy. The army was still
intact. Its position, though weak, posed a serious threat to any
Moslem attempt to seek a final victory. Moreover, the sultan did not
yet know the full extent of the damage inflicted on the crusaders.
But any hope based on this situation was illusory, because a certain
Imbert, who had usually attended the councils held by the legate,
went to the Moslem camp and informed the sultan how bad conditions were.[70] Nevertheless, Pelagius asked King John to undertake
the negotiations. As the titular head of the army, it was his duty.
John sent Guy de Gibelet and others to the camp of the sultan.
There was an immediate suspension of hostilities. From the beginning, al-Kāmil had favored a peaceful settlement, even against his
brother al-Muʿaẓẓam and other leaders. He was not persuaded by
the argument that he should destroy the crusader army that was in
his grasp, because he knew that Damietta was well fortified and
contained numerous troops, and reinforcements were expected there
at any moment. His consistent goal was to secure the withdrawal of
the crusaders from Egypt. The present debacle offered a promising
solution to his problem. Still, it required a show of force by both
sides to persuade the reluctant that a negotiated settlement offered
the best solution. On August 29, 1221, the crusaders at Barāmūn
surrendered to the sultan after agreeing to turn over the city of
Damietta and to depart from Egypt. The treaty included an exchange of all prisoners and a truce of eight years, with the proviso
that this agreement would not be binding on Emperor Frederick II
should he arrive to lead a crusade in person. In the view of Oliver
Scholasticus, who had arrived at the very beginning of the crusade
and who now described its end, the Westerners had made an excellent bargain.[71]

But many of those who had remained in Damietta were not convinced. Even as the crusaders were surrounded, reinforcements sent
by Frederick and commanded by Count Henry of Malta and Walter
of Palear, bishop of Catania, had arrived at Damietta. The masters of the Temple and of the Teutonic order brought news of the
terms of surrender and persuaded those in the city that there was
no point in further resistance. The risk was too great. It would have
meant the loss of the prestigious hostages in the hands of the sultan
and the probable capture of the surrounded army, with but little

prospect of gain. As Oliver noted, there was no remaining leader powerful enough to undertake such a responsibility.[72] Many now left the city. The terms were accepted and preparations made to turn Damietta over to the sultan. The final act was carried out with great propriety. The sultan treated his hostages with the respect befitting their rank and arranged for food for the army, which made its way back to the city. The crusaders boarded their ships and, after making arrangements for the return of hostages and prisoners, sailed to Acre. Al-Kāmil placed Damietta under the command of a governor and returned to Cairo.

With considerable insight, Sir Steven Runciman has recognized how close the crusaders had come to success.[73] Yet it was a success that constantly eluded them. Lacking the forces needed to follow up on their victories, plagued by long delays as they waited for reinforcements, under constant pressure from the departure of large contingents of the army, the leadership found itself faced with increasing odds against victory. More and more, they came to rely on the anticipated arrival of Frederick II to provide the forces necessary for final victory. We cannot fully know the mind of any of the leaders on the eve of the advance up the Nile, save perhaps that of the ever-cautious and consistent King John. But Pelagius and Duke Louis of Bavaria share the responsibility for the decision that impelled the army to its fate. Still, the critical moment really came at Sharamsāh when the common people demanded that the army continue its advance. It was entirely suitable, given the continued problems over leadership, that the costliest decision should have resulted from an act of the popular will.

NOTES

1. Ol., chap. 39.
2. Ibid., chap. 40.
3. Gottschalk, *Al-Kāmil*, 89–90.
4. Ibid., 90–104.
5. Ol., chap. 43; Jac., 135.
6. Jac., 135.
7. Ol., chaps. 43 and 45.
8. Jac., 135.
9. *RHC*, Occ., 2:349.
10. *T*, 300–1.
11. Pressutti, 1:385, 2320.
12. Ol., chap. 43.
13. Rodenberg, 1:95–96.

14. Oliver (chap. 43) says that John planned a speedy return, while Ernoul (*T,* 301) seems to imply that the length of his stay was unexpected.

15. Ol., chap. 43.

16. Mayer, *Crusades,* 215; Van Cleve, "Fifth Crusade," 415; Gottschalk, *Al-Kāmil,* 97.

17. *T,* 301. Van Cleve here follows Ernoul in blaming the cardinal for
leaving the routes from Cyprus and Syria unprotected; "Fifth Crusade,"
421; *T,* 301–2.

18. Ol., chaps. 43 and 44.

19. Ibid., chap. 45.

20. *T,* 301. Ernoul's sympathies appear to lie with those desiring to depart. This account probably reflects attitudes found among the feudal nobility and the knights.

21. Ol., chap. 46.

22. Ibid.

23. Jac., 136.

24. Ibid., 150; *T,* 307.

25. Ol., chap. 56.

26. Jac., 141.

27. Ibid., 152.

28. See Pelliot, "Deux passages," esp. 95–96.

29. Jac., 148–50.

30. Mayer says that Pelagius believed the prophecies; *Crusades,*
216–17.

31. Ol., chaps. 48–51.

32. Gottschalk, *Al-Kāmil,* 106–7.

33. Ol., chap. 53.

34. Ibid., chap. 46.

35. Ibid., chap. 45; Jac., 15.

36. Powell, "Honorius III," 530; Pressutti, 1:388, 2338; Van Cleve,
"Fifth Crusade," 420–21; Donovan, *Pelagius,* 70.

37. Rodenberg, 1:91.

38. Ibid., 95–96.

39. Ibid., 95.

40. Ibid., 99–100.

41. Ibid., 100.

42. Ibid., 101.

43. H.-B., 1:2:863.

44. Rodenberg, 1:107. See a letter of Honorius III confirming feudal
holdings in the lands of Countess Matilda for Azo de Fregnano, December
5, 1220; ibid., 114–16.

45. Thouzellier, "Legation en Lombardie," 509.

46. Levi, 7; Rodenberg, 1:113; Pressutti, 1:519, 3178; also Pressutti,
1:liii, 35, 36, 37. See also Linehan, "Documento español sobre la quinta
cruzada."

47. Levi, 7.

48. Ibid., 10.

49. Ibid., 16–27.

50. Ibid., 7, 11.

51. In June 1221, Honorius wrote Pelagius to inform him that Frederick did not plan to leave until March 1222 because he was short of funds. The pope was disappointed. Rodenberg, 1:122–23.

52. Ibid., 112.

53. There is some confusion among historians concerning the type of truce Honorius was seeking. See, for example, Donovan, *Pelagius*, 82–83. Honorius was not advocating acceptance of the already rejected offers of the return of Jerusalem.

54. Ol., chap. 54.

55. *T,* 307.

56. Ol., chap. 54.

57. Donovan, *Pelagius*, 85–86.

58. See, for example, Ol., chap. 48; Jac., 135.

59. *History of the Patriarchs of the Egyptian Church,* 4:1:75.

60. Ol., chap. 54.

61. *History of the Patriarchs of the Egyptian Church,* 4:1:75.

62. Ol., chap. 71.

63. *History of the Patriarchs of the Egyptian Church,* 4:1:76.

64. Ol., chap. 72.

65. Ibid., chap. 58.

66. Ibid., chap. 73; Van Cleve, "Fifth Crusade," 424.

67. Ol., chap. 73.

68. Ibid., chap. 74.

69. Ibid., chap. 75.

70. Ibid., chap. 76.

71. Ibid., chaps. 79 and 80.

72. Ibid.

73. Runciman, *Crusades,* 3:169.

EPILOGUE AND
CONCLUSIONS

In the immediate aftermath of the defeat at Barāmūn and the surrender of Damietta, the universal concern was to fix the blame for the disaster. Popular opinion was divided. The apologia of Oliver Scholasticus probably represents as well as any the feelings of the clerical leaders of the Fifth Crusade. Carefully adding up the results, he found some positive benefits among the ruins. But he could not bring himself to end even on this mixed note. Instead, he focused on the plans of the pope and the emperor for yet another crusade.[1] The author of this section of the *Éstoire d'Eracles Empereur* placed the blame squarely on the shoulders of the clergy and religious, and this view was widely shared.[2] But the lament written by Richard of San Germano may better sum up the confusion this disaster left in men's minds:

Damietta, bought by such labors and by so much bloodshed,
You formerly obeyed Christian Princes; now you obey their
    enemies.
From you the sound of fame went out: Damietta is not what it was.
In you the faith of Christ flourished where now the son brings
    shame on the maid-servant.
The Ismaelites have brought you down, overturned your altars,
    violated your temples;
As often as they heap up punishments for you, our sins sprout up.
Where now is the honor of the church and the flower of Christian
    knighthood?
Conquered, the legate, the king, and the Duke of Bavaria yielded to
    the poisons of perfidy.

O why did these leaders, guided by bad advice, go forth to battle?
O Damietta, you gave exile to those you favored for almost two
    years.
What mass of evil caused it? It touches all our miseries; it is the
    cause of all our tears.
The whole world and the princes of the world are sharers in this
    pain;
We pray you, O Christ, to help us to vindicate your cause.[3]

In October, Frederick wrote the pope to express his sadness "because
the Lord has glorified the banner of our enemies in our sins." He
promised great zeal in providing aid for the Holy Land.[4] But Honorius poured out his misery in reply. He admitted that everyone
blamed him for the debacle, and he blamed himself for the continual postponements he had granted Frederick. Counting on Frederick had cost the crusade the possibility of obtaining the return of
Jerusalem through acceptance of the peace offered by the sultan and
had brought ignominy to the army. But the pope quickly passed
from recriminations to plans for a new crusade to be led by the emperor. Both men seemed to agree that the best way to escape the
blame attached to the failure of the Fifth Crusade was to commit
themselves anew to the cause.[5]

The stage was set for a new try. The pope and the emperor initiated a series of meetings beginning at Veroli in April 1222 to plan
the new crusade. By 1223 it was evident that Frederick contemplated a much different role for himself than had been anticipated
by the pope. Hermann of Salza, master of the Teutonic Knights and
one of Frederick's closest advisers, proposed that the emperor—
whose wife had died during the previous year—should marry
Yolande, the daughter of John of Brienne and heiress of the crown
of Jerusalem. John was reluctant, but his position was not very
strong, given the enthusiasm of the pope. To allay his fears, he was
apparently given a rather meaningless assurance that he would retain the regency for life. For Frederick, there emerged the possibility of seizing control of the crusade from the papacy and uniting it
to the empire. Public opinion was already convinced of the un-
seemliness of clerical involvement in war, though even after the disaster at Damietta the crusade retained its popularity. What drew
criticism was the too-prominent role of the clergy in its manage-
ment and the feeling that they had bungled it. Frederick sensed an
opportunity. His action could help to establish a proper relationship between the secular and spiritual leadership of the crusade.

He now bound himself to go on crusade in June 1225. But, faced with rebellion among the Moslem population of western Sicily, his plans once more went awry. On March 5, 1224, he wrote Honorius to advise him that under the circumstances he could not leave Sicily. He also reported to him on the difficulties being encountered by preachers of the crusade, who were vilified and ignored. There were charges of negligence, he said, and influential persons were writing letters to him accusing both the church and him of being remiss. Also, John of Brienne had told Frederick that the English and French nobility were not interested in the crusade unless a long-term peace could be arranged between their two kingdoms.[6]

Honorius acted quickly to overcome the obstacles described in Frederick's letter. He worked to make the preaching more effective and to arrange a peace between England and France.[7] At the same time, he had little choice but to grant Frederick another postponement. In order to carry on negotiations aimed at finally securing Frederick's fulfillment of his crusade vow, the pope sent two top papal diplomats to his court: Cardinals Guala and Pelagius.[8] Perhaps the inclusion of Pelagius on this mission was a sign that the pope really meant business, since no one's reputation had suffered more from the failure of the Fifth Crusade than his, and few could have had a greater motivation to expunge that disaster from the record.

The agreement reached between Frederick and the pope at San Germano in July 1225 was very specific. The emperor was to deposit 100,000 ounces of gold with Hermann of Salza, provide a thousand knights for two years for the defense of the Holy Land, and equip 150 ships to transport troops to the East. He pledged to depart by August 15, 1227. Finally, he bound himself to these undertakings under pain of excommunication. This treaty has been the subject of considerable controversy, especially the provision regarding excommunication. Certainly Honorius was at the end of his patience. Moreover, he realized that there was little likelihood of a successful crusade without Frederick's participation. It would seem that the pope was willing to scale down his plan for a crusade to fit what the emperor might be able to provide and in the hope that others would be attracted by his leadership. At San Germano, despite the tension that undoubtedly existed between the emperor and the pope, they had a mutual interest in carrying out the plan for a new crusade in order to rid themselves of the blame for the defeat of the crusaders at Damietta.

Honorius III did not live to see his plan achieved. He died in March 1227. In the meantime, Frederick had proceeded with his marriage to Yolande of Jerusalem and had assumed the title of King of Jerusalem for himself. The way was open for him to establish his own government in the kingdom and to carry out his ideas for its reorganization. Despite his many postponements, there is no reason to doubt Frederick's commitment to the Holy Land. He was conscious of his role as emperor and wanted to make it a meaningful one. In his letter to Honorius in March 1224, he said that he had sworn to marry Yolande in order to make a better contribution to the Holy Land.[9] In light of his subsequent policies, it is certain that he intended to put the government of the kingdom on a stronger political basis. The provision of the treaty of San Germano calling for a thousand knights for two years agreed entirely with Frederick's ideas about the proper way to ensure the future of the Latin Kingdom.

As 1227 approached, Frederick's preparations increased. Unfortunately, there was little likelihood of support from outside his own domains. Louis VIII of France had taken the cross, but to fight the Albigensian heretics in the south of France, and many of the French nobility who likely would have been participants in the crusade to the East joined him. Frederick, always fearful of revolt among the Lombard communes of northern Italy, asked and received the pope's help in maintaining their loyalty. John of Brienne complained to the pope about Frederick's assumption of the crown of Jerusalem after his marriage but got little satisfaction. In the summer of 1227, Frederick's crusader army, composed largely of Germans and his Italian subjects from the Kingdom of Sicily, gathered at Brindisi. The first contingents were ready to sail on August 15, but Frederick and a large force did not actually depart until September 8. Disease had already taken its toll of the departing crusaders, and it struck the ship of the emperor. Louis of Thuringia died, and the emperor himself fell ill. The ship turned back to port at Otranto. The crusader army sailed on without its leader.

The final act of what had begun as the great crusade plan of Innocent III opened with the excommunication of Emperor Frederick II by Pope Gregory IX, the very same Cardinal Hugolino who had played a principal role in the cooperation of empire and papacy under Honorius III. Gregory was unwilling to grant another postponement, no matter how valid the grounds. Committed as he was to the crusade, he decided to use the emperor's embarrassment to force him to settle a whole range of outstanding problems, chiefly involving Frederick's treatment of the church in the Kingdom of Sicily. During his last years, Honorius had become deeply concerned over Frederick's practice of leaving episcopal sees in the kingdom vacant and appropriating their incomes for himself. Although there had been some progress toward a settlement, the issue remained. On his side, Frederick had no desire to negotiate from a weak position. He determined to carry on with his crusade. Success in the East would strengthen his hand. Moreover, his marriage had given him a dynastic interest in the Kingdom of Jerusalem.

But Gregory's excommunication made a crusade impossible. It was at this juncture that al-Kāmil, fearful of the impact Frederick's arrival in the East would have on the Moslem balance of power and particularly on his own ambitions to achieve hegemony over his brothers in Syria and the north, sent an ambassador to Frederick's court to arrange a treaty. We have no knowledge of the terms offered at this time, but Frederick was moved to respond by sending Archbishop Berard of Palermo and Count Thomas of Acerra to the court of the sultan in Nablus to continue the negotiations. These same diplomats also tested the waters by visiting al-Mu'aẓẓam in Damascus. They received no encouragement from that prince, who stood to lose the most by any strengthening of Western power in Palestine. Al-Kāmil, however, responded by resuming his talks with Frederick through his ambassador, Fakhr-ad-Dīn. Frederick was becoming desperate, and well he might have been, for his relations with Pope Gregory IX and with the Lombard communes had reached a low ebb. Gregory's demands reopened questions regarding the government of the Kingdom of Sicily that Frederick had no desire to discuss. Whether or not Frederick's reasons for turning back from his crusade in 1227 were valid, his action had jeopardized the settlement he had reached with the papacy prior to his coronation and had ended many years of fruitful cooperation.

At the end of June 1228, Frederick departed for the East with a fleet composed of forty ships. Although many who had sailed in 1227 had already returned home, the forces under his command remained considerable. They were not, of course, sufficient to mount a full-scale crusade, but they posed a serious threat to the plans of al-Kāmil. Following the Moslem historian Ibn-Wāṣil, Van Cleve, Mayer, and Runciman argue that the death of al-Mu'aẓẓam on November 12, 1227 made al-Kāmil less inclined to continue his talks with the emperor.[10] While there may be some truth in this, it is certain that the sultan was still far from obtaining his objectives in Syria and that he feared the presence of Frederick.[11]

What Frederick wanted was the kind of agreement that al-Kāmil had several times offered to the crusaders at Damietta: the return of Jerusalem, Bethlehem, and various other holy sites, along with the lands of the kingdom on the near side of the Jordan. Al-Kāmil was not willing to offer anything like this. Frederick had already initiated the refortification of Caesarea and Jaffa in order to make his intentions plain to the sultan. The wisdom of these preparations became clear as al-Kāmil continued to hold out. In November, Frederick moved all the forces he could muster—including the Templars and Hospitallers, who overcame their religious scruples to aid the enterprise—southward from Acre to Jaffa, in position to attack the unfortified city of Jerusalem. The sultan had little choice but to come to terms or else abandon his own attempt to conquer Damascus. There could be little question where his chief interest lay. He ceded Jerusalem, Bethlehem, and some other sites on the road from Acre to Jerusalem to Frederick in return for a defensive agreement. On the one hand, this treaty was an embarrassment to al-Kāmil, and it was used against him by his political enemies in Damascus; on the other, it brought Frederick a chiefly symbolic gain.[12] Jerusalem was to remain unfortified, and much of its environs, including its famed Moslem shrines, was to remain in enemy hands. Nevertheless, the emperor had his triumphal entry into the city and assumed the crown of the Latin Kingdom. Then he hastened home to fight the papal forces that had invaded the Kingdom of Sicily during his absence. On this ironic note, it may be said that the Fifth Crusade actually ended in Jerusalem rather than on the road from Damietta to Cairo, but such a view had little appeal to contemporaries and has not found favor with modern writers. Tradition has maintained the separate character of these two crusades, and in doing so has obscured the profound debt Frederick II owed to the plans of Innocent III and Honorius III in obtaining his own treaty with al-Kāmil and the return of Jerusalem. That Frederick himself did not make this mistake is evident from the tenor of his reconciliation with Gregory IX at Ceprano in June 1230.

Viewed from the vantage point of the treaty of 1230, rather than from the defeat in Egypt, the Fifth Crusade reflects the persistence of a strong Western commitment to the crusade. In the past, great stress has been placed on the conflicting interests of the empire and the papacy. The relationship between Frederick II and the popes, especially Honorius III, has been viewed against a backdrop of potential enmities and incipient betrayal. Little attention has been given to their large areas of common interest, particularly in the promotion of a more orderly society, which provided a basis for cooperation. It has been, on the whole, easier to recognize defects and failures in the efforts of these powers to work together than to trace the commonality of concern that bound them together even during the most difficult times.

The picture that emerges from this study of the Fifth Crusade is not just of another military campaign against the Moslem occupiers of the Holy Places but of a vision of a renewed Christian world united in peace to achieve victory against the Moslem usurpers. Troubled by violence at every level, its highest powers, both secular and spiritual, possessed but limited means to maintain order. From its inception, the ideology of the crusade movement had emphasized the substitution of a just war against the enemies of Christianity for the continued violence of Christian against Christian. The Fifth Crusade formulated a program joining the promotion of internal peace to recruitment for the crusade, making use of ecclesiastical sanctions to achieve both ends where necessary. At the same time, the concept of participation in the crusade, as well as in the spiritual benefits accruing to crusaders, was broadened to include potentially every Christian. The crusade as a form of the imitation of Christ was opened up to all Christians, but especially to the laity. The notion of a special vocation for the crusader served to emphasize the spiritual character of this service. The crusade was being forged into an instrument for the moral transformation of society.

Certainly both Innocent and Honorius wanted tangible results from the crusade. They expended enormous effort to plan for the needs of the crusaders. Innocent especially had always before his eyes the memory of the diversion of the Fourth Crusade. He was quite aware of the reasons why those crusaders were unable to meet their obligations to the Venetians, and he attempted to ensure that such an outcome would never happen again. The implementation of the Innocentian program under Honorius III was quite effective. Whatever shortcomings or problems arose, neither pope can really be blamed. The eventual shortages of material and manpower that contributed to the defeat of the crusaders in Egypt in 1221 arose from the distribution of funds to leaders to ensure local support for the papal tax collection and from the insurmountable delays in re-

solving local conflicts in Europe that impeded the crusade. To seek
to apportion blame for these problems is merely to indict European
society for its particularism and its proneness to violence. What is
striking is not that the efforts fell short, but that they achieved the
level of success that they did.

The leadership question does not provide a sufficient explanation
in itself for the disaster at Damietta. The conflict between Pelagius
and King John chiefly emerged after the crusaders' capture of the
city of Damietta. By that time, a lack of sufficient money and manpower to bring the campaign to a successful conclusion overshadowed their differences as a cause of defeat. Their disputes reflected
differing estimates of what was possible with the available resources
and what was necessary to hold the army together until the arrival
of the emperor. Miscalculation and a yielding to the popular clamor
for action put the army in its final jeopardy. The so-called intran-
sigence of the legate has been greatly exaggerated. He was loyal to
the interests of the pope and the emperor while constantly being
buffeted by pressures from various groups within the army. He was,
however, in too exposed a position, especially in light of his ecclesiastical office. His control of funds and his increasing role in military decisions laid him open to the charge that he was responsible
for the final defeat. It was an onus that Frederick II partially escaped
simply through his absence. As the pope himself admitted, the
blame popularly accrued to the church.

If, as many historians have believed, this crusade had been planned
as a purely papal affair, this conclusion would be not merely just but
inevitable. The evidence, however, shows that, while the initiative
and planning of the crusade belonged to the papacy, its conception
broadly involved the appropriate leaders of secular society, especially the emperor. But, where previous crusades had attempted
first to attract kings and princes as leaders, in this instance the effort
was made to build from below. Innocent III assumed that the
popularity of the crusade with the masses would put pressure on
the leaders to lay aside their disputes in the interest of the recovery
of the Holy Places. The existence of such pressure is evident from
the letters of Abbot Gervase of Prémontré. The typical reluctant
crusader was a political leader involved in some kind of dispute that
arose from his interests. Evidence of this pressure from below seems
sufficient to suggest that the main challenge to the crusade perceived by the papacy in the early thirteenth century came not from
the masses but from the lay elite, who were beginning to articulate

a set of rational political objectives for secular society that looked more to internal political development than to the universal goal of a restored Christian unity set by the papacy. The archetypal reluctant crusader was Frederick II himself.

Herein lies the tie between the Fifth Crusade and the so-called crusade of Frederick II. Following the loss of Damietta, Frederick's involvement in the crusade changed. Up to this point, he was to have assumed his position at the head of a Christian army recruited by the church. His role was to be in every sense that of the medieval emperor, the protector of Christendom. He was the realization of a vision of a united Christianity, the perpetuator of the image of Frederick Barbarossa in the Third Crusade. Although Frederick himself often accepted this role rhetorically, it was not the one he forged for himself after 1225. His own crusade was instead founded in part on the dynastic interest arising from his marriage to the heiress of the crown of Jerusalem and in part on his own political vision of an imperial world order. His crusader army was answerable to him, because it was a royal army. Many of his troops were recruited in the usual manner for a royal levy in the Kingdom of Sicily. Service to the king-emperor was service to God. The first steps were being taken toward a secularization of the ideals with which Innocent III and his contemporaries among the clergy had imbued the crusade. The vision of the crusade to which Frederick was committed paralleled that of the popes. It cannot be said that his concern for peace and justice was less strongly held than that of the pope. There can be no doubt of the depth of his religious convictions. But, whereas for Innocent the moral authority of the pope prevailed over any other in establishing the goals of Christendom, for Frederick the coercive power of the emperor was the foundation of all peace and justice. The crusade had entered a new age.[13]

NOTES

1. Ol., chap. 89.

2. Eracles, *RHC, Occ.*, 2 : 352; Mayer, *Crusades*, 218.

3. Ryccardus de Sancto Germano, *Chronica*, 7 : 2 : 98–100; Spreckelmeyer, *Kreuzzugslied*, 257–64.

4. H.-B., 2 : 1 : 206–7.

5. Rodenberg, 1 : 128–30.

6. H.-B., 2 : 1 : 409–13, esp. 412. The text in Huillard-Bréholles is incorrect. See RV, 12, 179r: "Nam predicatores qui predicant verbum crucis in tantum vilipenduntur ab omnibus . . . quod non est qui eos audiat vel intendat. *Immo ascribitur et notatur negligentie cuidam* et sicut a diversis par-

tibus orbis maiorum et potentiorum ad nos littere pervenerunt, videtur eis quod remisse ab ecclesia et a nobis in tanto negotio procedatur." The section in italics has been omitted in Huillard-Bréholles. Also, he has changed "a nobis" to "a vobis." These alterations make the letter accusatory, whereas Frederick is reporting to the pope and sharing the blame. Van Cleve did not understand this context and misinterpreted Frederick's letter to some extent; *Frederick II,* 160–61.

7. For Honorius's efforts to improve the effectiveness of preaching, see Pressutti, 2:336–37, 5480–84; and 338, 5489; Rodenberg, 1:174–75, 181, 195. On his effort to secure peace between France and England, see Pressutti, 2:353, 5575. On his efforts to recruit Henry III and others, see Jane E. Sayers, *Papal Government and England during the Pontificate of Honorius III,* 69, 236–37.

8. Rodenberg, 1:198–99.

9. H.-B., 2:1:410.

10. Van Cleve, "Crusade of Frederick II," 452–54; Mayer, *Crusades,* 227; Runciman, *Crusades,* 3:185–86.

11. See the account in the *History of the Patriarchs of the Egyptian Church,* 4:1:105–9, which in my view gives a more straightforward presentation of the sultan's motives.

12. Moslem accounts of the negotiations present Frederick in a very appealing light, stressing his sympathy with Islam. While there is probably some basis for this, it seems likely that Moslem writers wanted to make the treaty more palatable to their audience. Very likely they exaggerated and took out of context statements and actions of the emperor that cast him in this light. See the interesting remarks in Alois Haas, "Aspekte der Kreuzzüge in Geschichte und Geistesleben des mittelalterlichen Deutschland," esp. 202. Too much reliance has been placed on these accounts by modern writers, who have largely ignored the context in which they were written. For translations of the principal sources, see Gabrieli, *Arab Historians of the Crusades,* 267–75. See also Van Cleve, "Crusade of Frederick II," 453, 456–57, and 461–62; and Runciman, *Crusades,* 3:190. Norman Daniel, in *The Arabs and Medieval Europe,* 162–64, argues that Frederick was no friend of the Arabs.

13. The accuracy of these remarks is amply demonstrated by Jordan. The degree to which Louis IX was indebted to the crusade program outlined above is especially evident in chapter two, "Barons and Princes: The Search for Peace and Allies." It may seem strange to some to see in the work of Louis IX a secularization of the papal program, but there is no inconsistency between his view of the crusade and other aspects of his policies. Also, Mayer's account of the significance of Frederick's coronation is quite valuable; *Crusades,* 229–30.

APPENDIX I

LETTER OF POPE HONORIUS III TO THE BISHOP, THE ARCHPRIEST, AND MASTER UGO OF LUCCA, FEBRUARY 26, 1218

Episcopo, Archipresbitero et Magistro Ugoni Canonico Lucano.

Cum in Lucana civitate venerabilis Frater noster . . . Hostiensis episcopus tunc apostolice sedis legatus crucis negotio institisset quia sicut idem episcopus asserit Guidarus Barleti et Henricus Maczavitelli, milites Lucani, in armis strenui, sanguine generosi, primi inter alios civitatis eiusdem vexillum Domini receperunt, et propter hoc multos tam milites quam populares, concives suos, eorum exemplo ad id et alias etiam ad terre sancte subsidium animarunt . . . abbati de Guamo Lucani diocesis et tibi fili archipresbiter ac Vitali canonico Lucano dedit firmiter in mandatis ut de quadragesima et aliis que a Lucana civitate ad predicte terre obsequium deputantur, auctoritate ipsius eisdem militibus quibus non suppetebant proprie facultates ut exequerentur comode vota sua in certa quantitate pecunie providerent, quod nos etiam postmodum per te, frater episcope, sicut nosti mandavimus exequendam. Verum quia nec impletum fuit nostrum nec episcopi predicti mandatum, iidem milites non sine magnis laboribus et expensis ad sedem apostolicam accesserunt. Nolentes igitur milites ipsos spe sua et huiusmodi pia provisione frustrari, ne forsan contingeret eos retro respicere quasi necessitate coactos destinamus vobis per apostolica scripta, precipiendis mandamus quatenus . . . Sancti Pontiani Lucani et . . . de Catignano, et . . . de Sexto Lucani diocesis abbates et . . . Praepositum Sancti Georgii Lucani ut de suarum ecclesiarum vicesima et . . . Priorem Sancti Fridiani Lucani quod de collecta in truncis elemosina quam habet eisdem militibus usque ad quantitatem in litteris eiusdem Hostiensis episcopi comprehensam providere sine difficultate procurent, ita quod laborare propter hoc iterum non cogantur, efficaciter inducatis eos ad id si necesse fuerit per censuram ecclesiasticam sub apostolica obedientia compellentes. Quod si hoc ad summam non pertingerent pretaxatam, tu, frater episcope, de vicesima quam es ab hospitalibus recepturus super qua tibi scripta nostra direximus quod minus fuerit supplere procures, nullis litteris obstantibus super hoc a sede apostolica impetratis. Quod si non omnis duo vestrum, etc. Dat. Lateran. IIII kl Martii anno secundo.

Source: RV 9, folio 221r–221v, ep. 900; Pressutti, 1:188, 1120. Lateran. February 26, 1218.

A Note on Appendixes
2, 3, and 4

The lists of crusaders in appendixes 2, 3, and 4 consist of those crusaders who are known to have taken vows to go on the Fifth Crusade (i.e., during the period of the crusade) or who are known to have gone, those whose status is doubtful, and those whose names were obtained by Reinhold Röhricht for the crusader list published in his *Studien zur Geschichte des fünften Kreuzzuges,* pp. 79–135, from sources that relied on the so-called Collection Courtois. There is no pretence that these lists are either totally accurate or complete, but great care has been taken to ensure that there is a good evidentiary basis for the inclusion of names on the list of those known to have taken vows. An absence of evidence from charters or narratives supporting the inclusion of a name on appendix 2 has resulted in the creation of the list of doubtful crusaders. Given the substantial evidence that the charters found in the Collection Courtois are forgeries, these names have been eliminated from the list of doubtfuls and are listed separately.[1]

In part, these lists represent a correction of the work undertaken by Röhricht, but they go much further. Appendixes 2 and 3 contain many names not found on the original list composed by him and, as noted, appendix 2 attempts to provide an accurate list of those who took vows or who actually departed on crusade. The sources from which information has been drawn for each name are listed at the end of the entry. In a few instances, where individuals are extremely well known, the reference is to the bibliography at the end of this book. In some cases where there are numerous citations, only those providing new information are listed.

All names listed with an asterisk in appendix 2 are of persons known to have departed for the East. A reference to the date of arrival as unknown or to evidence of return as unknown means only that the information is lacking, as is the case for most of those without an asterisk. "Did not return" means that the person died on crusade. "Did not leave" means that there is evidence to show that this individual did not depart for the East. Many in this category were Italian crusaders recruited by Cardinal Hugolino of Ostia in 1221 and scheduled to depart with Boniface of Montferrat. Titles attached to the names are taken from the sources. If the sources do not provide a title, none is given.

NOTE

1. Bautier, "La collection de chartes de croisade dite 'Collection Courtois'."

APPENDIX II

INDIVIDUALS WHO TOOK
CRUSADE VOWS, 1213–1221

*A. de Malamort. Limoges, France. Arrival: Unknown. Return: Unknown. *FK,* 110; *T,* 337.

Adam de Luci, clericus. Priest. France. Arrival: Unknown. Return: Unknown. *FK,* 109; Paris, AN, S4203, #48.

*Adam of Croxby. Lincolnshire, England. Arrived 1218. Return: Unknown. Sied., 137, #1; *Just. Eyre* (Linc.), 315, #655.

*Adam, filius Gualteri. Belmont, France. Arrived 1218. Returned. *SS,* 90; Jac., 122; *FK,* 79.

Adelogus VI de Kirchberg-Mallersdorf. Germany. Arrival: Unknown. Return: Unknown. *FK,* 106; *D,* 106; *B,* 369.

*Adolfus de Bernsore. Rhineland, Germany. Arrived 1218. Return: Unknown. *FK,* 87; *FK,* 61, #13.

*Adolfus de Dassel, comes. Count. Dassel, Germany. Arrived 1218. Return: Unknown. *FK,* 97; *FK,* 61, #13.

*Adolfus de Stammheim. Rhineland, Germany. Arrived 1218. Return: Unknown. *FK,* 128; *FK,* 61, #13.

*Adolfus, comes de Monte. Count. Berg (Rhineland), Germany. Arrived 1218. Did not return. *FK,* 113; *FK,* 61–2, #13; *SS,* 40; *T,* passim; *D,* 99; Rüdebusch, 50; *Ol.,* 179.

*Adrianus di Matteo Adriani. Bologna, Italy. Arrived 1219. Return: Unknown. *FK,* 79; Sav., 397, #460; Sav., 431–32, #487; Sav., 448, #499.

*Aegidius de Lewes. Penitentiary. Loos, Belgium. Arrived 1218. Returned. *FK,* 79; *T,* 120; *FK,* 41, #5.

Aegidius de Macreta. Modena, Italy. Did not leave. *FK,* 110; Levi, 129, #105.

*Aegidius de Trit, dominus. Lord. Hainault, Belgium. Arrival: Unknown. Return: Unknown. *FK,* 130; *FK,* 66, #30.

*Aegidius Berthoudus. Malines, Belgium. Arrived 1219. Return: Unknown. *FK,* 87; *FK,* 70, #46; Wauters, 3:523, 531; Eracles, 343; *B,* 372; Ol., 215.

*Aegidius, canonicus Atrebatensis. Canon. Arras, France. Arrival: Unknown. Did not return. *FK,* 83; Pr., 2893.

*Aegidius, priest of Sta. Thecla. Priest. Bologna, Italy. Arrived 1219. Return: Unknown. *FK,* 129; *FK,* 68, #40.

*Agnes of Middleton (Quernhow). Yorkshire, England. Arrived 1218. Return: Unknown. Sied., 137, #2; *Just. Eyre* (Yorks.), 384, #1072.

Aimericus Dubois. France. Arrival: Unknown. Return: Unknown. *FK,* 97; *Tables de Fonteneau,* 4:187.

*Alamanus de Costa, comes de Siracusa. Count. Genoa, Italy. Arrived 1219. Returned. *FK,* 129; *T,* 239.

*Alan of Haisthorpe. Yorkshire, England. Arrived 1218. Return: Unknown. Sied., 137, #3; *Just. Eyre* (Yorks.), 353, #972.

*Alardus de S. Antonio: Alart d'Antoine. St. Antoine, France. Arrived 1219. Return: Unknown. *FK,* 81; Eracles, 343.

*Alardus le Flemeng. England. Arrival: Unknown. Did not return. *FK,* 98; Roberts, 1:54–55, 57.

*Albericus, archiepiscopus Rhemensis. Archbishop. Rheims, France. Arrived 1218. Returned. *FK,* 122; Pr., 14, 2028; Ol., 152, 157, 177.

Albericus, dux Lovaniae. Duke. Louvain, Belgium. Arrival: Unknown. Return: Unknown. *RHGF,* 19:605.

Albero de Arnsteine. Germany. Arrival: Unknown. Return: Unknown. *FK,* 82; *FK,* 58, #4.

Albero de Bodemin. Bodensee, Germany. Arrival: Unknown. Return: Unknown. *FK,* 88; *Cod. Salem.,* 1:253.

*Albero de Tunchelstein. Dunkelstein, Austria. Arrived 1217. Return: Unknown. *FK,* 130; *FK,* 59, #7.

*Albero, pincerna de Grimmenstein. Butler. Grimmenstein, Austria. Arrived 1217. Return: Unknown. *FK,* 102; *FK,* 57, #2; *FK,* 63, #17.

*Albert III, de Tyrol, comes. Count. Tyrol, Austria. Arrived 1217. Returned. *B,* 376; *FK,* 131; *D,* 115.

Albert, comes. Count. Holstein, Germany. Did not leave. *B,* 368.

Albertinus de Castro Novo. Reggio nell'Emilia, Italy. Did not leave. *FK,* 93; Levi, 131, #105.

*Albertinus Bolnisii. Bologna, Italy. Arrived 1219. Return: Unknown. Sav., 447, #498.

*Albertus de Antse. Germany. Arrived 1221. Return: Unknown. *Wirt. UB,* 3:124.

*Albertus de Batburk. Rhineland, Germany. Arrived 1218. Return: Unknown. *FK,* 85; *FK,* 64, #24.

*Albertus de Buchele. Germany. Arrived 1217. Return: Unknown. *FK,* 91; *FK,* 62, #13.

*Albertus de Calw, comes. Count. Calw, Germany. Arrived 1221. Returned. *FK,* 92; *Wirt. UB,* 3:148.

*Albertus de Herlaere. Herlin-leSec, France. Arrived 1218. Return: Unknown. *FK,* 103; *FK,* 61, #13.

*Albertus de Hurde. Cologne, Germany. Arrived 1218. Return: Unknown. *FK*, 105; *FK*, 61, #13.

* Albertus de Rafenstein, decanus. Dean. Trent, Italy. Arrived 1217. Returned. *FK*, 130; *Cod. Wang.*, 324; Eubel, 1:525; Winkelmann, 1:535; *D*, 116.

* Albertus de Salzburgensi. Provost. Salzburg, Austria. Arrived 1217. Did not return. Pott., 4727, 7814, 25683; Pr., 539, 2076; *FK*, 87; *FK*, 125; Rodenberg, 1:7–8; Meiller, 528; *T*, 185.

* Albertus de Steusslingen. Steusslingen, Germany. Arrived 1221. Return: Unknown. *FK*, 128; BF, 1309.

* Albertus Cattaneus. Bologna, Italy. Arrived 1219. Return: Unknown. *FK*, 93; *FK*, 73, #52; Sav., 448, #499.

* Albertus IV de Bogen, comes. Count. Bogen, Bavaria, Germany. Arrived 1217. Returned. *FK*, 89; *T*, 184–85; *Mon. Boic.*,12:108.

* Albertus Munsi de Axenellis. Bologna, Italy. Arrived 1219. Return: Unknown. *FK*, 115; *FK*, 58, #6; Sav., 381, #447; Sav. 397, #460; ASB, Busta, 1 (6, fr 16); Gozzadini, 95–96.

* Albertus, frater Henrici de Brenne. Germany. Arrival: Unknown. Return: Unknown. *FK*, 80; Strehlke, 42–43, #52.

* Albertus, electus Concordiensis. Bishop-elect. Concordia, Italy. Arrived 1217. Did not return. Pr., 185, 1897; *FK*, 58, #5.

* Albertus, episcopus. Bishop. Brescia, Italy. Arrived 1220. Returned. Ol., 248; Pr., 1317, 1461, 1573, 3583; *T*, 109; Levi, 19, 20; Eubel, 1:151; *FK*, 91.

Aldebrandino de Picio. Bologna, Italy. Did not leave. *FK*, 120; Levi, 130, #105.

* Aldebrandinus Ariosti. Bologna, Italy. Arrived 1219. Return: Unknown. *FK*, 82; Gozzadini, 90; Sav., 446–47, #497.

Alexander de Archiaco. Archiac, France. Arrival: Unknown. Return: Unknown. *FK*, 82; Cholet, 231–32, #542.

* Alexander de Clescy. Worcestershire, England. Arrival: Unknown. Return: Unknown. Sied., 137, #4; *Just. Eyre* (Linc.), 476–77, #970.

* Alexander de Courçon. England. Arrived 1218. Did not return. Sied., 137, #5; *T*, 64; *FK*, 96.

* Alexander Physicus. Physician. Hungary. Arrived 1217. Return: Unknown. *FK*, 80; *T*, 231.

* Almericus de Osop. Germany. Arrived 1217. Return: Unknown. *FK*, 118; *FK*, 58, #5.

* Amadeus, archiepiscopus Bisuntinus. Archbishop. Besançon, France. Arrival: Unknown. Returned. *FK*, 88; Pr., 14, 381, 1536, 2339, 2450.

* Amalricus de Bouvines. Cysoing, Belgium. Arrival: Unknown. Return: Unknown. *FK*, 90; *FK*, 66, #30.

* Amatus, Priest. Lucca, Italy. Arrived 1218. Return: Unknown. ASL, S. Pon Nov. 13, 1216; ASL, S. Pon June 25, 1216; ASL, S. Pon March 6, 1224; *FK*, 81.

* Amelin de Riort. Anjou, France. Arrival: Unknown. Return: Unknown. *FK*, 117; Eracles, 339.

* Andreas de Essipissia. Espoisses, France. Arrived 1219. Return: Unknown. *FK*, 98; *T*, 93; Eracles, 343; Jac., 122, 130,

150; *SS*, 103–4, 132, 159, 190; Pr., 1734.

* Andreas de Nantolio. Nanteuil, France. Arrived 1218. Returned. *FK*, 116; *T*, 93, 113, 115–16, 130; Jac., 122, 129–30, 150; *SS*, 190; Ol., 216n.

* Andreas de Werkune. Rhineland, Germany. Arrived 1218. Return: Unknown. *FK*, 134; *FK*, 64, #24.

* Andreas von Hohenlohe, Teutonic Knight. Hohenlohe, Germany. Arrived 1221. Returned. *FK*, 104; *Wirt. UB*, 3:92–95, #624–27; Strehlke, 53, #63.

* Andrew of Hungary. King. Hungary. Arrived 1217. Returned. *FK*, 105; see bibliography.

* Andricus, comes de Pingin. Count. Pingin, France. Arrived 1218. Return: Unknown. *FK*, 120; *T*, 112.

* Anonymous. Carter. Lincolnshire, England. Arrival: Unknown. Return: Unknown. Sied., 137, #6.

* Anonymous. Yorkshire, England. Arrival: Unknown. Return: Unknown. Sied., 137, #7; *Just. Eyre* (Yorks.), 74, #178.

Anonymous. Ravenna, Italy. Arrival: Unknown. Return: Unknown. Vasina, "Emilianoromagnolo," 37.

* Anonymous. Hildesheim, Germany. Arrived 1218. Returned. *FK*, 103; Sudendorf Pt. 2, 170–72, #82.

* Anonymous, Babenbergensis decanus. Dean. Bamberg (Bavaria), Germany. Arrival: Unknown. Returned. *FK*, 84; *T*, 345.

* Anonymous, canonicus. Canon. Cysoing, Belgium. Arrival:

Unknown. Return: Unknown. *FK*, 95; *FK*, 66, #30.

* Anonymous, nepos ducis Austriae. Arrived 1217. Did not return. *SS*, 120.

* Anonymous, abbas S. Frontonis. Abbot. Perigord, France. Arrived 1218. Returned. *FK*, 120; Horoy, 2:527–28, #51.

* Anonymous, archiepiscopus Cretensis. Archbishop. Candia, Crete. Arrived 1219. Returned. *FK*, 95; *T*, 109; Ol., 187, 248; Pr., 1919, 1920, 1929, 1950.

* Anonymous, comes de Caerleon. Count. Caerleon, Wales. Arrived 1218. Returned. *FK*, 92; *T*, 60–61.

* Anonymous, comes Glocestriae. Count. Gloucester, England. Arrived 1219. Returned. *FK*, 101; *SS*, 186, 188; Altschul, 54–56.

* Anonymous, episcopus Salpensis. Bishop. Salpi, Italy. Arrived 1218. Return: Unknown. Ol., 187; Eubel, 1:453; *FK*, 125.

* Anonymous, husband of Hawisia. Yorkshire, England. Arrival: Unknown. Return: Unknown. Sied., 137, #8; *Just. Eyre* (Yorks.), 298–99, #823.

* Anonymous, marescalcus Coloniensis. Marshall. Cologne, Germany. Arrived 1218. Return: Unknown. *FK*, 95; *B*, 369; *SS*, 60.

* Anonymous, possessor prebendae. Priest. Meaux, France. Arrival: Unknown. Did not return. *FK*, 111; Pr., 1703.

* Anonymous, Saxon. Siebenburgen, Germany. Arrived 1217. Return: Unknown. *B*, 374.

* Anonymous, Sire de Lupines. Lord. Loupines, France. Ar-

rived 1218. Return: Unknown.
FK, 109; *T*, 112–13.

*Anselmus de Leon, praepositus.
Provost. St. Omer, France.
Arrival: Unknown. Did not return. *FK*, 108; *SS*, 103, 104,
132, 159; Pr. 4013, 4029,
5743.

*Anselmus, episcopus Laudunen-
sis. Bishop. Laon, France. Arrived 1218. Returned. *FK*, 107;
Van Cleve, "Fifth Crusade,"
402–3; Pr., 570, 736, 1271,
1296, 1374, 1388, 2165,
2438, 2500, 2713. etc.

*Ansericus de Coceio. Coucy,
France. Arrived 1218. Return:
Unknown. *FK*, 95; *FK*, 46,
#7; *DSI*, 6:707.

*Ar. dominus de Thoca. Lord.
Talmont, France. Arrival: Un-
known. Returned. *FK*, 129;
Cart. Talmond, 375, #503.

Archembaldus, comes. Count.
Perigord, France. Arrival: Un-
known. Return: Unknown.
FK, 120.

*Archetinus de Faventia. Faenza,
Italy. Arrived 1219. Return:
Unknown. Sav., 442–43,
#493; *FK*, 82; *FK*, 72–73,
#49.

*Ardicius, dominus. Lord. Bo-
logna, Italy. Arrived 1219.
Return: Unknown. *FK*, 82;
FK, 72, #48; Sav., 432–33,
#488.

*Arnaldus Garebertus Gordono.
France. Arrival: Unknown. Return: Unknown. *FK*, 101; *FK*,
74, #54.

*Arnoldus de Gimmenich. Gim-
mich (Cologne), Germany.
Arrived 1218. Return: Un-
known. *FK*, 101; *FK*,
64, #25.

*Arnoldus de Ryminam. Brabant,
Belgium. Arrived 1219. Re-

turn: Unknown. *FK*, 124; *FK*,
70, #46.

*Arnoldus de Wartenberg. Warten-
berg, Germany. Arrived 1217.
Return: Unknown. *FK*, 133;
FK, 59, #7.

*Arnoldus Wilrens. Louvain,
Belgium. Arrived 1218. Return: Unknown. *FK*, 79; *D*,
106–7; Divaeus, 8.

*Arnoldus, filius Walteri Ber-
thoudi. Malines, Belgium.
Arrived 1219. Return: Un-
known. *FK*, 79; *FK*, 70, #46;
CDOT, 2:31, #27; Eracles,
343.

Arrigherus. Volterra, Italy. Did
not leave. *FK*, 133; *Rg V*, 131,
#371; 141, #399; 142,
#400; 142, #401.

*Artuicus de Varmo. Germany. Ar-
rived 1217. Return: Unknown.
FK, 132; *FK*, 58, #5.

*Attamai di quondam Pari. Pis-
toia, Italy. Arrived 1219.
Returned. ASF, Pistoia, July
30, 1219.

*Aubert, homo of King John. Car-
penter. Acre, Palestine. Arrived
1218. Return: Unknown. *FK*,
83; Eracles, 336.

*Audouin (Gaucelin) de Pier-
rebuffiere. Limoges, France.
Arrived 1218. Return: Un-
known. Lecler, 86.

*Aymar de Layron. Marshall of
Hospitallers. France. Arrived
1217. Did not return. Ol.,
217; Eracles, 333.

*Aymarus, quondam dominus
Caesareae. Lord. Caesarea, Pal-
estine. Arrival: Unknown.
Return: Unknown. *FK*, 84;
Eracles, 347.

*Baboneg, comes de Wordicha.
Count. Wordicha, Hungary.
Arrived 1217. Returned. *FK*,
135; Fejer, 3A:244–45.

*Baduinus de Nore. France. Arrival: Unknown. Return: Unknown. *FK*, 117; Pauli, 1:112–13.

*Baldwin de Vere. Oxford, England. Arrived 1218. Did not return. *FK*, 134; Sied., 137, #10; *T*, 65, 334.

*Baldwin of Tyes (Teutonicus). Lincolnshire, England. Arrived 1218. Return: Unknown. Sied., 137, #9; Pontefract Chart., 1:37, #21.

*Balian, lord of Sidon. Dominus. Lord. Sidon, Lebanon. Arrived 1217. Returned. Eracles, 240, 311, 332, 346; *MGHSS*, 32:34.

*Barcellus de Merxadrus. Bologna, Italy. Arrived 1219. Did not return. *FK*, 112; *FK*, 68, #40; Sav., 419–20, #480.

Baro Simeonis. Volterra, Italy. Did not leave. *Rg V*, 130, #367; 131, #371; 133, #378. ASF, Vol. 8, Oct. 1218; 22, Dec. 1224.

*Bartholomaeus, Fürst. Prince. Pommern, Germany. Arrived 1217. Did not return. Klempin *UB*, 2:148, #202; *FK*, 120; *T*, 347; *D*, 111.

*Baruffaldinus Caper. Bologna, Italy. Arrived 1219. Return: Unknown. *FK*, 81; *FK*, 72–73, #48–52; Sav., 433–44, #488; 444, #494; 446–47, #497–98. Gozzadini, 287–89; Heers, *Parties*, 108–9.

Barusonus, filius Mariani. Judge. Siena, Italy. Arrival: Unknown. Return: Unknown. Pr., 2782.

*Basilius, famulus Walteri Berthoudi. Servant. Malines, Belgium. Arrived 1219. Return: Unknown. *FK*, 85; *FK*, 70, #46; *CDOT*, 2:31, #27; Eracles, 343.

*Bastinus Petreius. Louvain, Belgium. Arrived 1218. Return: Unknown. *FK*, 79; *D*, 106–7.

*Benatus, clericus. Priest. Ferrara, Italy. Arrival: Unknown. Did not return. *FK*, 87; *FK*, 72, #49; Sav., 442–43, #493.

*Berarducius Gualterii. Foligno, Italy. Arrival: Unknown. Return: Unknown. *Sassovivo*, 5:139–40.

*Berardus. Sergeant. France. Arrival: Unknown. Return: Unknown. *FK*, 87; *FK*, 74, #54.

Berardus de Gesmele. Osnabrück, Germany. Arrival: Unknown. Return: Unknown. *FK*, 101; Rüdebusch, 51.

*Berlus. France. Arrival: Unknown. Return: Unknown. *FK*, 87; *FK*, 74, #54.

Bernardinus de Villanova. Florence, Italy. Did not leave. *FK*, 133; Levi, 131, #105.

*Bernardinus Villanus. San Gimignano, Italy. Arrival: Unknown. Did not return. Abulafia, "Crocuses and Crusaders," 229–30.

*Bernardonus. Sergeant. France. Arrival: Unknown. Return: Unknown. *FK*, 87; *FK*, 75, #54.

*Bernardus. France. Arrival: Unknown. Return: Unknown. *FK*, 87; *FK*, 74, #54.

*Bernardus d'Euses. France. Arrival: Unknown. Return: Unknown. *FK*, 98; *FK*, 74, #54.

*Bernardus de Turre. Auvergne, France. Arrived 1218. Returned. *FK*, 131; Brequigny, 5:114.

*Bernardus de Valkensteine. Valkenstein, Germany. Arrived 1217. Return: Unknown. *FK*,

132; *FK*, 57, #3; Zahn,
2 : 220–21, #148.

* Bernardus de Villafrancha.
Notary. Villafranca, Spain. Ar-
rival: Unknown. Return:
Unknown. *FK*, 133; *FK*, 75,
#54.

Bernardus, abbas S. Martini. Abbot. Limoges, France. Arrival:
Unknown. Return: Unknown.
FK, 111; *T*, 337; Dickson,
103.

* Bertholdus de Alevelt. Germany.
Arrived 1221. Return: Un-
known. *FK*, 80; BF, 1307.

* Bertholdus de Bogen. Bogen
(Bavaria), Germany. Arrived
1217. Did not return. *FK* 89;
T, 184–85; *Mon. Boic.*,
12 : 108.

* Bertoldus de Eschenlohe,
comes. Count. Garmisch, Germany. Arrived 1217.
Returned. *FK*, 98. *UB Diessen*,
52.

Bertholdus de Michelwinnenden.
Rheinau, Switzerland. Arrival:
Unknown. Return: Unknown.
FK, 112; *D*, 108.

* Bertholdus de Sacro Monte.
Heiligenberg, Germany. Arrived 1221. Return: Unknown.
FK, 125; *Cod. Salem.*, 1 : 155;
BF, 1294, 1297, 1301, 1306–
9; Van Cleve, "Fifth Crusade,"
423.

* Bertholdus de Stege. Germany.
Arrived 1217. Return: Un-
known. *FK*, 128; *FK*, 57, #2.

Bertholdus de Wangen. Trent,
Italy. Arrived 1221. Return:
Unknown. *FK*, 130; *Cod.
Wang.*, 322–23; BF, 1307;
D, 116.

* Bertholdus, archiepiscopus.
Archbishop. Kolocza, Hun-
gary. Arrived 1217. Returned.
FK, 105; Ol., 162, 168, 187;
Pr., 124, 371, 1183, 1186,

1507; *SS*, 133; Van Cleve,
"Fifth Crusade," 387.

Bertholdus, episcopus Lausanen-
sis. Bishop. Lausanne, Switzerland. Did not leave. *FK*, 107;
T, 161; Pr., 2094, 2564.

* Bertholdus, epscopus-electus.
Bishop-elect. Bressanone, Italy.
Arrived 1217. Returned. *FK*,
91; Pr., 1317; Ol., 187n; Eubel, 1 : 147; *Cod. Wang.*,
322–23, #143.

* Bertholdus, senescalcus. Seneschal. Emmerberg, Austria.
Arrived 1217. Returned. *FK*,
97; *FK*, 57, #2; 63, #17.

Bertoldus de Hagilstein. Rhei-
nau, Switzerland. Arrival:
Unknown. Return: Unknown.
FK, 102; *ZGO*, 29, 69.

* Bertrand de Gibelet. Dominus.
Lord. Gibelet, Palestine. Ar-
rived 1217. Return: Unknown.
Eracles, 322.

* Bertrandus. Physician. Acre, Pal-
estine. Arrival: Unknown.
Return: Unknown. *FK*, 88;
FK, 74, #54.

* Bertrandus de Masserebolis.
France. Arrival: Unknown. Return: Unknown. *FK*, 111; *FK*,
74–75, #54.

* Bertrandus de Provincia. Provence, France. Arrival: Unknown. Return: Unknown.
FK, 121; *FK*, 74, #54.

* Bertrandus, notarius. Notary.
France. Arrival: Unknown. Return: Unknown. *FK*, 88; *FK*,
74, #54.

Bochardus de Misnaco. Sens,
France. Arrival: Unknown.
Return: Unknown. *FK*, 113;
Quantin, *Cartulaire*, 1 : 90–
91, #201.

* Bohemond IV, prince of Antioch.
Prince. Antioch, Syria. Arrived
1217. Returned. Van Cleve,
"Fifth Crusade," 392.

*Boidekinus van Larne. Netherlands. Arrived 1219. Return: Unknown. *FK*, 127; Brequigny, 5 : 136.

*Boidinus. Netherlands. Arrived 1219. Return: Unknown. *FK*, 127; Brequigny, 5 : 136.

*Bolnisius Henfangati (Infangati). Bologna, Italy. Arrived 1219. Return: Unknown. *FK*, 105; *FK*, 58, #6; 72, #48. Sav., 381, #447; 433–44, #488.

*Bolnisius, nepos Bonbaronus. Bologna, Italy. Arrived 1219. Return: Unknown. *FK*, 89; *FK*, 68, #40; Sav., 419–20, #480.

*Bolognittus. Bologna, Italy. Arrived 1219. Return: Unknown. *FK*, 89; *FK*, 70, #47; Sav., 391–94, #458; 431–32, #487; 433–34, #488.

Bonacursus de Canusia. Canossa, Italy. Did not leave. *FK*, 93; Levi, 131, #105.

*Bonaguisa de Bonaguisa. Florence, Italy. Arrived 1219. Returned. *FK*, 89; *T*, 263; Hartwig, *Florenz*, 2 : 115; Villani, 5, ch. 40.

*Bonamicus. Notary. Bologna, Italy. Arrived 1219. Return: Unknown. *FK*, 96; *FK*, 70, #47; Sav., 431–32, #487; 433–34, #488.

*Bonbaronus Merxadrus. Bologna, Italy. Arrived 1219. Return: Unknown. *FK*, 112; *FK*, 68, #40; Sav., 419–20, #480.

*Bonifacius Guidonis Guizardi. Bologna, Italy. Arrived 1219. Return: Unknown. *FK*, 89; *FK*, 58, #6; 72, #48; 72, #49; 73, #52. Sav., 381, #447; 385, #451; 385–86, #452; 397, #460; Heers, *Parties*, 108–9.

*Bonromeus Guidonis. Bologna, Italy. Arrived 1219. Return:

Unknown. *FK*, 90; *FK*, 73, #51; Sav., 433, #488; 447, #498. Gozzadini, 170.

*Bridinus de Rode. Germany. Arrived 1219. Return: Unknown. *FK*, 127; Brequigny, 5 : 136.

*Brunicardus de Pastino. Bologna, Italy. Arrived 1219. Return: Unknown. *FK*, 91; *FK*, 72, #58; Sav., 432–33, #488.

*Bruno de Holte. Rhineland, Germany. Arrived 1218. Return: Unknown. *FK*, 104; *FK*, 62, #13.

*Bruno de Stammheim. Rhineland, Germany. Arrived 1218. Return: Unknown. *FK*, 128; *FK*, 61, #13.

*Bruno Lupus. Rhineland, Germany. Arrived 1218. Return: Unknown. *FK*, 109; *FK*, 62, #13.

*Bruno Rufi (Rode). Hildesheim, Germany. Arrived 1218. Return: Unknown. *FK*, 103; Döbner *UB*, 1 : 39, #74; Rüdebusch, 55; Janicke, 663–64.

*Bryanus de Villa (de Insulis). Yorkshire, England. Arrived 1218. Returned. *FK*, 132; Sied., 138, #11; *T*, 60–61, 64; Sayers, 63.

*Burchardus VI, burgravius. Burggraf. Magdeburg, Germany. Arrival: Unknown. Returned. *FK*, 110; *D*, 107. Mulv., 2 : 247, #540; 2 : 281, #610; 2 : 296–97, #643. *UB Frauen*, 89–90.

*Campigliolus de Campiglio. Bologna, Italy. Arrived 1219. Return: Unknown. *FK*, 92; *FK*, 73, #52; Sav., 448, #499.

*Casimirus II, dux Pommeraniae. Duke. Pommern, Germany. Arrived 1217. Did not return. *FK*, 120; Klempin *UB*, 2 : 148, #202; *T*, 347; *D*, 111.

*Catherina Berthoudus. Malines (Mechelen), Belgium. Arrived 1219. Return: Unknown. *FK*, 87; *FK*, 70, #46; Ol., 215; Eracles, 343; *B*, 372.

Cavalcabus. Marquis. Cremona, Italy. Did not leave. *FK*, 93; Levi, 130, #105.

*Christianus, acolytus Ripensis. Acolyte. Ribe, Denmark. Arrival: Unknown. Returned. *FK*, 122; Pr., 2723.

Chunradus de Arnsteine. Arnstein, Germany. Arrival: Unknown. Return: Unknown. *FK*, 82; *FK*, 58, #4.

*Cigolinus Alberti. San Gimignano, Italy. Arrival: Unknown. Returned. Abulafia, "Crocuses and Crusaders," 229–30.

*Claricia, soror Lecilie et Aricie. Coventry, England. Arrival: Unknown. Did not return. *Just. Eyre* (Glouc.), 643–44.

*Clarius de Bazilieri. Bologna, Italy. Arrived 1219. Return: Unknown. *FK*, 86; Gozzadini, 128; Sav., 431–32, #487; 433–34, #488.

Cloz, de familia Ulrici de Bozman. Servant. Weissenau, Germany. Arrival: Unknown. Return: Unknown. *ZGO*, 29, 65; *FK*, 95.

*Cniftlingus, marescalcus. Marshall. Germany. Arrived 1221. Return: Unknown. *FK*, 95; BF, 1307.

*Coco de Osop. Germany. Arrived 1217. Return: Unknown. *FK*, 118; *FK*, 58, #5.

Colard d'Haussegnemont. Champagne, France. Arrival: Unknown. Return: Unknown. *ROL*, 1:369–70.

*Colinus, Anglicus. Priest. England. Arrived 1218. Return: Unknown. *FK*, 95; Jac., 133; Sied., 138, #12.

Cono de Aranone. Aragnon,

Switzerland. Arrival: Unknown. Return: Unknown. *FK*, 81; Blanc., 23–24; *UB Bern*, 1:180, #110.

*Conradus de Blumenau. Blumenau am Furstenfeld, Germany. Arrived 1217. Return: Unknown. *FK*, 88; *FK*, 58, #7; 62, #17.

*Conradus de Condrumberg. Germany. Arrived 1217. Return: Unknown. *FK*, 95; *FK*, 58, #5.

*Conradus de Cuglinbergh. Canon. Wurzburg, Germany. Arrived 1218. Returned. *FK*, 103; Goerz, 2:382, #1395.

*Conradus de Lobenich. Lobenich, Germany. Arrived 1221. Return: Unknown. *FK*, 108; *FK*, 74, #53.

*Conradus de Miresdorf. Meiersdorf, Germany. Arrived 1217. Return: Unknown. *FK*, 112; *FK*, 57, #2.

*Conradus de Pfarr. Ministerial. Salzburg, Austria. Arrival: Unknown. Did not return. *FK*, 120; Meiller, 213, #188; *B*, 373.

*Conradus de Werda. Werde, Germany. Arrived 1221. Return: Unknown. *FK*, 134; D, 117; *Wirt. UB*, 3:124.

*Conradus de Wolre. Wolne, Germany. Arrived 1221. Return: Unknown. *FK*, 135; BF, 1307; D, 118.

*Conradus, comes de Wasserberg. Count. Wasserberg, Austria. Arrived 1217. Return: Unknown. *FK*, 134; *FK*, 58, #4; BF, 956; *Reg. Boic.*, 2:86; *B*, 376.

*Conradus, comes de Werdecke. Count. Werdecke, Germany. Arrived 1221. Return: Unknown. *FK*, 124; BF, 1307.

*Conradus, castellanus Salzburgensis. Castellan. Salzburg,

Austria. Arrived 1217. Returned. *FK*, 125; *Mon. Boic.*, 2 : 195; Meiller, 213, 221; *B*, 374.

Conradus, episcopus Mettensis. Bishop. Metz, Germany. Did not leave. Pr., 2608, 2796, 2803, 3488.

Conradus, pincerna de Winterstellen. Butler. Winterstellen, Germany. Arrival: Unknown. Return: Unknown. *FK*, 134; *D*, 118.

* Conradus, Tergestinus electus. Bishop-elect. Trieste, Italy. Arrived 1217. Returned. Pr., 1186, 3084, 3090; *FK*, 58, #5.

* Constantius de Duacho. Deacon. Acre, Palestine. Arrived 1217. Did not return. Jac., 110.

* Corradinus. Bologna, Italy. Arrived 1219. Return: Unknown. *FK*, 96; *FK*, 68, #40; Sav., 419–20, #480.

D. canonicus Columbrensis. Coimbra, Portugal. Arrival: Unknown. Return: Unknown. *FK*, 95, RV, 9 : 265v, #1180, July 13, 1218; Pr., 792, 1526, 2544.

* Dandus. San Gimignano, Italy. Arrival: Unknown. Returned. Abulafia, "Crocuses and Crusaders," 228–29.

* Deodatus de Castlus. France. Arrival: Unknown. Return: Unknown. *FK*, 93; *FK*, 74, #54.

* Deutacorra d'Albertino del Pino. Bologna, Italy. Arrived 1219. Return: Unknown. *FK*, 120; *FK*, 73, #51; Sav., 447, #498; 448, #499.

* Diepold de Vohburg, comes. Count. Vohburg, Germany. Arrived 1218. Returned. *FK*, 133; *T*, 157; Meiller, 337, #105.

Diepoldus. Prince. Bohemia. Arrival: Unknown. Return: Unknown. *FK*, 97; Pr., 253; Pott., 5421.

* Dietherus de Katzenellenbogen, comes. Count. Rhineland, Germany. Arrived 1218. Returned. *FK*, 106; *T*, 27, 28, 32; Beyer, 3 : 110–11, 253–54.

* Dietmarus de Ahalmsdorf. Ahalmsdorf, Austria. Arrival: Unknown. Returned. *FK*, 79.

* Dietmarus de Lichtenstein. Lichtenstein. Arrived 1217. Return: Unknown. *FK*, 108; *FK*, 57, #2; 63, #17.

* Dionysius, Treasurer of Hungary. Treasurer. Hungary. Arrived 1217. Returned. *FK*, 97; *FK*, 24; Eracles, 325; Van Cleve, "Fifth Crusade," 2 : 392–93; Fejér, 3 : 1 : 458.

* Diopoldus, marchio de Hohingurc. Margrave. Hohenburg, Germany. Arrived 1221. Return: Unknown. *Wirt. UB*, 3 : 124.

Ditericus de Mosen. Mosen, Germany. Did not leave. *FK*, 115; *D*, 108; *Mon. Boic.*, 9 : 482.

Drogo de Merlo, Franciae constabularius. Constable. Loches, France. Arrival: Unknown. Return: Unknown. *FK*, 112; Pr., 14; *Lay.*, 1 #1377, #1378.

* During von Ternberg. Derinberg, Germany. Arrival: Unknown. Did not return. *FK*, 97; *B*, 375.

* Duringus de Styra. Steiermark, Austria. Arrived 1217. Return: Unknown. *FK*, 128; *FK*, 62, #17.

* E. de Reissac. Deacon. France. Arrival: Unknown. Returned. *FK*, 96; RV, 13 : 36v–37r, #205.

* Eberardus de Helfenstein. Count.

Helfenstein, Germany. Arrived 1221. Return: Unknown. *FK*, 103; *D*, 104; BF, 1307–9, 1312; *Wirt. UB*, 3:124.

* Egbertus, episcopus Babenbergensis. Bishop. Bamberg (Bavaria), Germany. Arrived 1217. Returned. *T*, 147–48, 182, 185, 199, 200, 345; *FK*, 84; Ol., 163, 168.

* Egilmar. Provost. Münster, Germany. Arrived 1218. Did not return. Rüdebusch, 58; Lahrkamp, 296.

Egonone, comes de Vraha. Count. Alsace, Germany. Arrival: Unknown. Did not return. Pr., 2653; Lahrkamp, 296.

* Elger de Mendorp. Meindorf, Germany. Arrived 1218. Return: Unknown. *FK*, 112; *FK*, 62, #13.

* Elias Cairel. Provence, France. Arrived 1218. Returned. Throop, 34; Wentzlaff, 232.

* Emericus de Sacy. England. Arrival: Unknown. Did not return. *FK*, 125; Sied., 138, #13; *RLC*, 1:401a.

* Engelbertus de Auersperg. Auersberg, Germany. Arrived 1217. Return: Unknown. *FK*, 83; *FK*, 24.

* Engelbertus de Gorze. Rhineland, Germany. Arrived 1217. Return: Unknown. *FK*, 58, #5; *FK*, 101.

Engelbertus, archiepiscopus. Archbishop. Cologne, Germany. Did not leave. *T*, xlviii.

* Engelhard, episcopus Siciensis. Bishop. Naumberg-Zeitz, Germany. Arrived 1217. Returned. Ol., 163, 168; Pr., 2425, 5582; *FK*, 117.

Engeramus de Nachreta. Modena, Italy. Did not leave. *FK*, 116; Levi, 129, #105.

* Enguerrandus de Boves. Boves, France. Arrived 1219. Returned. *FK*, 90; Strehlke, 45–46, #56–57; Beauville, 3:1–2; Eracles, 343.

* Enjuger de Bohun. Count. Hereford, England. Arrived 1218. Did not return. *FK*, 89; Sied., 138, #14; *T*, 68, 70, 73, 334; *RLC*, 1:383b, 385a, 429a.

* Erhardus de Chacenai. Chassenay, Aube, Bar–sur–Seine, France. Arrived 1218. Returned. *Lay.*, 1:540, #1515; Pott., 5955; *FK*, 43–46, #6; *FK*, 94; Flamare, 424–25.

* Erlandr Thorbergsson. Thorberg, Norway. Arrived 1218. Did not return. *FK*, 129; *T*, 322–23; Riant, 330.

Ernestus de Velseck, comes. Count. Velseck, Germany. Arrival: Unknown. Return: Unknown. *FK*, 132, *D*, 117.

* Ernestus de Wulwede. Rhineland, Germany. Arrived 1218. Return: Unknown. *FK*, 135; *FK*, 64, #24.

Eudes de Ponte. Brittany, France. Arrival: Unknown. Return: Unknown. *FK*, 120; Morice, 1:838.

Eustachius de Maire. France. Arrival: Unknown. Return: Unknown. *FK*, 110; *Tables de Fonteneau*, 190.

* Eustorgius, archiepiscopus. Archbishop. Nicosia, Cyprus. Arrived 1220. Returned. *FK*, 26, 116; Ol., 162, 168, 176; Eracles, 322–23, 397; *T*, 98, 102, 253, 317.

* Evrardus Carnotensis. Chartres, France. Arrived 1218. Returned. Métais, 208.

* Evrardus Oppendorpius. Louvain, Belgium. Arrived 1218. Return: Unknown. *FK*, 79; *D*, 106–7.

* F. de Arkania. Archennes, Belgium. Arrived 1219. Return: Unknown. *FK,* 82; *FK,* 70, #46.

* Faffo de Faffis. Bologna, Italy. Arrived 1219. Return: Unknown. *FK,* 98; *FK,* 72, #48; 73, #52. Sav., 433–44, #488; 448, #499.

Falco de Breaute. Breauté (Seine Inferieure), France. Did not leave. *FK,* 90; *T,* 66.

* Ferri de Betho. Pettau, Germany. Arrived 1217. Returned. *FK,* 88; *FK,* 26; Eracles, 343.

* Figliocarus Vinture Savi. Bologna, Italy. Arrived 1219. Return: Unknown. *FK,* 98; *FK,* 58, #6; 70, #47; 72, #47; 73, #51. Sav., 381, #447; 397, #460; 431–32, #487; 433–34, #488; 447–48, #498; 448, #499.

* Forastus de Vorst. Netherlands. Arrived 1218. Return: Unknown. *FK,* 133; *FK,* 64, #24.

* Fralmus, filius Oddonis. Lucca, Italy. Arrived 1218. Returned. LAA A+1, 160–61; *FK,* 99.

* Francis of Assisi. Assisi, Italy. Arrived 1219. Returned. *FK,* 99; see bibliography.

* Franco de Arkania. Archennes, Belgium. Arrived 1219. Return: Unknown. *FK,* 82; *MGHSS,* 25:229; *FK,* 70, #46.

Frederick II. Emperor. Germany. Did not leave. See bibliography.

* Fredericus de Baden. Baden, Germany. Arrived 1218. Did not return. *Wirt. UB,* 101–2.

Fridericus de Berchtesgaden. Provost. Berchtesgaden, (Bavaria), Germany. Did not leave. Rodenberg 1:6–7, #8; *T,*

185, 199–200; Meiller, 531, #88; *FK,* 87.

* Fridericus de Brehna. Count. Saxony, Germany. Arrived 1221. Did not return. *MGHSS,* 23:199; *B,* 367; *FK,* 90.

* Fridericus de Claromonte. Tuscany, Italy. Arrival: Unknown. Return: Unknown. *FK,* 95; Lami, 3:1648–49.

* Fridericus de Lorike. Lorike (Houtem), Netherlands. Arrived 1218. Return: Unknown. *FK,* 109; *FK,* 64, #24.

* Fridericus de Ponte. Trier, Germany. Arrival: Unknown. Returned. Beyer, 3:215–16, #261; *FK,* 120; Goerz, 369–70, #1349; 407, #1499.

* Fridericus de Stauf, Pincerna. Butler. Staufen (Bavaria), Germany. Arrived 1221. Return: Unknown. *FK,* 128; *D,* 114; *Wirt. UB,* 3:124.

* Fridericus de Vianden. Count. Vianden, Luxembourg. Arrived 1218. Did not return. D, 117; Neyen, 82.

* Fridericus de Wangen. Bishop. Trent, Italy. Arrived 1218. Did not return. *Cod. Wang.,* 321; Eubel 1:525; *FK,* 130.

* Fridericus von Hohenlohe. Teutonic Knight. Hohenlohe, Germany. Arrived 1221. Returned. *FK,* 104; *Wirt. UB,* 3:92–95, #624–27.

Fulconus de Campagnola. Italy. Did not leave. *FK,* 92; Levi, 130, #105.

* Fuscalus. Cesena, Italy. Arrived 1219. Return: Unknown. *FK,* 92; *FK,* 72, #49; Sav., 442–43, #493.

G.   Palencia, Spain. Arrival: Unknown. Return: Unknown. *FK,* 100; RV, 9:145r, #580.

*G.　　　presbyter Nivellensis. Priest. Nivers, Belgium. Arrived 1218. Return: Unknown. *FK*, 117; *FK*, 66, #30.

* Galfridus de Luschi. England. Arrived 1219. Return: Unknown. *FK*, 109; *T*, 65.

Gallus de Campagnola. Italy. Did not leave. *FK*, 92; Levi, 131, #105.

* Galterius de Palearia. Bishop. Catania (Sicily), Italy. Arrived 1221. Returned. *FK*, 93; *T*, 245.

Galterius, abbas St. Amandi Abbot. St. Amand (Valenciennes), France. Arrival: Unknown. Return: Unknown. *FK*, 81; Hugo, 1 : 17–18.

* Galterus de Bethsan. Cyprus. Arrived 1217. Return: Unknown. *T*, 317.

* Galterus, camerarius Franciae. Camerarius. Paris, France. Arrived 1218. Returned. *FK*, 102; *T*, passim; Jac., passim; Ol., 216.

* Galtherus de Avennis, comes. Count. Avesnes, France. Arrived 1217. Returned. *FK*, 84; *FK*, 26; Pr., 14, 281; Eracles, 326; *T*, 91, 98, 100; Ol., 163, 169.

Galvanus. Italy. Did not leave. *FK*, 126; Levi, 132, #105.

* Gamel, son of Gamel. Yorkshire, England. Arrival: Unknown. Return: Unknown. Sied., 138, #15; *Just. Eyre* (Yorks.), 97–98, #234.

* Garinus de Monte Acuto. Master of Hospitallers. Montagu-sur-Champeix, France. Arrived 1218. Returned. Ol., 166n, 279; *T*, 99; Van Cleve, "Fifth Crusade," 389, 413n; Riley-Smith, *Knights of St. John*, 1 : 155–56.

Garnier d'Amance. Champagne, France. Arrival: Unknown. Return: Unknown. *ROL*, 1 : 369.

* Garnier l'Aleman. Germany. Arrived 1217. Returned. Eracles, 322.

Gaufredus de Ivran. Brittany, France. Arrival: Unknown. Return: Unknown. *FK*, 106.

Gaufredus de Sains. Foigny, France. Arrival: Unknown. Return: Unknown. *FK*, 125.

* Gaufredus, filius Aufredi. Mauleon (Poitou), France. Arrived 1218. Return: Unknown. *FK*, 83; *Arc. Poitou*, 1 : 89.

* Gaufridus de Buxeio. Buxeuil, France. Arrived 1218. Return: Unknown. *FK*, 92; *ROL*, 1 : 372, #57.

Gaufridus, episcopus Trecorensis. Bishop. Treguier, France. Arrival: Unknown. Return: Unknown. Pr., 14.

Gautr Jonsson. Mael, Norway. Did not leave. Riant, 330–31.

Gebhardus I, comes de Wernigerota. Count. Heiligenberg, Germany. Arrival: Unknown. Return: Unknown. *FK*, 134; Rüdebusch, 55; Hugo, 1 : 19–20, #14; *D*, 117.

* Gebhardus II de Nassovia, comes. Count. Nassau, Netherlands. Arrived 1218. Returned. *FK*, 116; *T*, 345; Vogel, 207; *B*, 371.

* Geoffrey de Bury. Blois, France. Arrived 1218. Returned. Métais, 209.

* Geoffrey de Chastiller. England. Arrival: Unknown. Return: Unknown. Sied., 138, #17; *Pat. Rolls*, 1 : 151.

Geoffrey de Lucy. Northamptonshire, England. Did not leave. Sied., 138, #19; *Ann. Dunst.*, 55.

*Geoffrey de Say II. Hertford-
shire, England. Arrived 1219.
Return: Unknown. Sied., 138,
#20; *RLC,* 1 : 393a.

*Geoffrey of Houghton. York-
shire, England. Arrival: Unknown. Return: Unknown.
Sied., 138, #18; *Just. Eyre*
(Yorks.), 37–38, #87.

*Geoffrey, son of Norman. York-
shire, England. Arrival:
Unknown. Return: Unknown.
Sied., 138, #16; *Just. Eyre*
(Yorks.), 281–82, #762.

*Georgius, comes de Wied.
Count. Wied, Germany. Ar-
rived 1218. Return: Unknown.
FK, 134; *SS,* 29, 36–37; *T,*
92, 151, 195, 215; *MGHSS,*
24 : 399; *FK,* 43, #6.

*Geraldus de Rocaforti.
Rochefort, France. Arrival:
Unknown. Return: Unknown.
FK, 123; *FK,* 74, #54.

*Geraldus Albertus. France. Ar-
rival: Unknown. Return:
Unknown. *FK,* 80; *FK,*
74–75, #54.

Gerardectus. Pistoia, Italy. Ar-
rival: Unknown. Return:
Unknown. *FK,* 101; ASFOP,
Aug. 4, 1219.

*Gerardus. Sergeant. France. Ar-
rival: Unknown. Return:
Unknown. *FK,* 101; *FK,* 74,
#54.

*Gerardus de Ham. Constable.
Tripoli, Syria. Arrived 1217.
Return: Unknown. Eracles,
322.

Gerardus de Rustigniani. Bolo-
gna, Italy. Arrival: Unknown.
Return: Unknown. *FK,* 124;
FK, 58, #6; Sav., 381, #447;
Gozzadini, 462.

*Gerardus de Upladen. Opladen,
Germany. Arrived 1218. Return: Unknown. *FK,* 132; *FK,*
61, #13.

*Gerardus Carenzone. Lucca, Italy.
Arrived 1218. Return: Un-
known. Sav., 431–32, #487.

*Gerardus Rozus. Bologna, Italy.
Arrived 1219. Return: Un-
known. *FK,* 124; *FK,* 72,
#48; Sav., 433, #488.

*Gerart de Fornivaus. Fournival
(Oise), France. Arrived 1218.
Did not return. *FK,* 99; Era-
cles, 343; Sied., 138, #21.

*Gerbert de Nantolio. Nanteuil,
France. Arrived 1218. Re-
turned. *FK,* 116; *T,* 130.

Gerhardus, filius Adami Claichin.
Furnes, Belgium. Arrival: Un-
known. Return: Unknown.
FK, 101; Wauters, 3 : 494.

*Germundus de Forgis. Forge,
France. Arrived 1218. Did not
return. *FK,* 99; *Arc. Poitou,*
1 : 89.

*Gilbertus de Boi. France. Arrival:
Unknown. Return: Unknown.
FK, 89; *FK,* 74, #54.

*Gilo, Chaplain of Guillelmus
Carnotensi. Priest. Chartres,
France. Arrived 1218. Return:
Unknown. Métais, 208.

Girardus de Camisiano. Count.
Cremona, Italy. Did not leave.
FK, 92; Levi, 131, #105.

Girardus de Fante. Modena, Italy.
Did not leave. *FK,* 98; Levi,
131, #105; Winkelmann,
1 : 114.

Girardus Curtillerius. France.
Arrival: Unknown. Return:
Unknown. *FK,* 96.

*Girbertus de Vecel. France. Ar-
rival: Unknown. Return:
Unknown. *FK,* 132; *FK,* 74,
#54.

*Gislebertus de Sotteghem. Sot-
teghem, Belgium. Arrived
1219. Returned. *FK,* 127;
FK, 70, #46; Eracles, 343;
Brequigny, 5 : 136.

*Godofredus de Arnsberg. Count.

Arnsberg, Germany. Arrived 1218. Returned. *FK*, 82; Pott., 25609; H.-B., 2:806; Seibertz, 2:469–70.

* Godofredus Most. Pisa, Italy. Arrived 1218. Returned. *FK*, 115; Eracles, 333–34, 351.

* Godofredus Neville, senescalcus. Seneschal. England. Arrival: Unknown. Return: Unknown. *FK*, 116; Shirley, 1:30, #24.

* Godofridus de Mendorp. Meindorf, Germany. Arrived 1218. Return: Unknown. *FK*, 112; *FK*, 62, #13.

* Godofridus Radingus. Louvain, Belgium. Arrived 1218. Return: Unknown. *FK*, 79; *D*, 106–7.

Gollo. Volterra, Italy. Arrival: Unknown. Return: Unknown. *Rg V*, 138, #390.

Gospatric White. Yorkshire, England. Arrival: Unknown. Return: Unknown. Sied., 139, #22; Chart. Cockersand, 3:1, 888.

Gosso. Tournai, Belgium. Did not leave. Pr., 2926.

* Gossuinus, episcopus Tornacensis. Bishop. Tournai, Belgium. Arrived 1218. Did not return. *T*, 7; Eubel, 1:489.

Gotefridus. Rheinau, Switzerland. Arrival: Unknown. Return: Unknown. *FK*, 101; *ZGO*, 29, 73.

* Gotefridus II, comes de Sponheim. Count. Sponheim (Coblenz), Germany. Arrived 1218. Returned. *FK*, 127; *D*, 114; Beyer, 3:84, #84.

* Gottfridus, monachus. Monk. Rhineland, Germany. Arrived 1218. Return: Unknown. *FK*, 113; *FK*, 64, #24.

* Gottschalcus de Nitperch. Neuberg (near Hartberg), Germany. Arrived 1217. Return: Unknown. *FK*, 117; *FK*, 63, #17.

Gregorius quondam Gregorii de Sancto Gimignano. San Gimignano, Italy. Arrival: Unknown. Return: Unknown. *Rg V*, 132, #375; 133 #379. ASFVol. Dec. 23, 1218.

* Gremont II. Bethsan, Palestine. Arrived 1217. Return: Unknown. Eracles, 322.

Grimaldus de Monte Silicis. Padua, Italy. Arrival: Unknown. Return: Unknown. *FK*, 115; Pott., 4896, 4898.

Grimoldus de Leiten. Ministerial. Bavaria, Germany. Arrival: Unknown. Return: Unknown. *FK*, 107; *D*, 106; *Mon. Boic.*, 9:482.

* Gualterius de Anomos. France. Arrived 1218. Return: Unknown. *FK*, 81; *FK*, 46, #7.

* Gualterius, filius Milonis. Bar (Marmontier), France. Arrived 1218. Did not return. *FK*, 85; *T*, 93.

* Gualterius, episcopus Eduensis. Bishop. Autun, France. Arrived 1218. Returned. Pr., 1266, 2996, 2997, 3280; *T*, 93, 102; *FK*, 79.

* Guidarus Barleti. Lucca, Italy. Arrival: Unknown. Return: Unknown. RV 9:221, #900; Pr., 1120.

* Guido de Bresse. France. Arrival: Unknown. Did not return. *FK*, 91.

* Guido de Brevenna, comes. Count. Brienne? France. Arrived 1221. Return: Unknown. *FK*, 91; Ol., 257.

Guido de Cumuli. Lucca, Italy. Did not leave. LAA A+1, 114.

* Guido de Palagio. Siena, Italy. Arrived 1218. Returned. *FK*, 118; *T*, 258, 284–85, 350.

*Guido de Pigi. Arcis-sur-Aube, France. Arrived 1218. Return: Unknown. *FK*, 120; *T*, xli.

*Guido de Pollicino. Priest. Bologna, Italy. Arrived 1219. Return: Unknown. *FK*, 102; *FK*, 73, #50; Sav., 446–47, #497.

*Guido de Ronay. France. Arrival: Unknown. Return: Unknown. *FK*, 123; Pauli, 1:290–91.

*Guido de Tilio. Thil-Chatel (Cote d'Or), France. Arrived 1218. Returned. *FK*, 129; *T*, 93.

*Guido Capellus. Priest. Bologna, Italy. Arrived 1219. Return: Unknown. *FK*, 93; *FK*, 58, #6; 73, #50. Sav., 381, #447; 446–47, #497.

*Guido Embriaco, Dominus. Lord. Gibelet, Palestine. Arrived 1217. Return: Unknown. Van Cleve, "Fifth Crusade," 2:412; Eracles, 322.

*Guido Salmoncelli. Bologna, Italy. Arrived 1219. Return: Unknown. *FK*, 125; *FK*, 72, #48; Sav., 433, #488.

Guido Serpui. Italy. Did not leave. *FK*, 126; Levi, 129, #105.

*Guidoctus, filius Passavanti. Lucca, Italy. Arrived 1218. Return: Unknown. LAA, A+1, 138, Jan. 1221.

*Guidonus de Valencia. Valencia, Spain. Arrival: Unknown. Return: Unknown. *FK*, 132; *FK*, 74, #54.

Guidotus Tralignati. Pistoia, Italy. Arrival: Unknown. Return: Unknown. *LFDP*, 202.

*Guillaume de Gibelet, dominus. Gibelet, Palestine. Arrived 1217. Returned. Van Cleve, "Fifth Crusade," 2:426; Eracles, 322, 339.

Guillelmus de Albo Mari. Count.

Albemarle, England. Arrival: Unknown. Return: Unknown. *T*, xxxi, 66.

*Guillelmus de Carnoto. Master of Templars. Chartres, France. Arrived 1218. Did not return. Ol., 188, 210, 255; *T*, 55; Van Cleve, "Fifth Crusade," 2:389. Runciman, 2:159.

*Guillelmus de Elisem. Marshall. Gloucester, England. Arrival: Unknown. Did not return. *FK*, 101; *SS*, xxxv, 190.

*Guillelmus de Floccellariis. Flocelliere, France. Arrived 1218. Return: Unknown. *FK*, 98; *Arc. Poitou*, 1:89.

Guillelmus de Migeio. Miege, France. Arrival: Unknown. Return: Unknown. *FK*, 112; Quantin, 1:88, #196.

Guillelmus de Monteferrato, marchese. Marquis. Monteferrato, Italy. Did not leave. *FK*, 113; Cognasso, *Piemonte*, 527; Levi, 10–11, 101, 128, 140–41, 152–53.

Guillelmus de Rupe Gillebaldi. Guillebaut, France. Arrival: Unknown. Return: Unknown. *FK*, 124.

Guillelmus de Ruppibus, senescalcus. Seneschal. Anjou, France. Arrival: Unknown. Return: Unknown. *FK*, 124; Brequigny, 5:110.

*Guillelmus de Sancto Audemoro. St. Omer, France. Arrived 1218. Did not return. *FK*, 83; Eracles, 343.

*Guillelmus de Tu—— [part of name missing]. St. Omer, France. Arrived 1218. Did not return. *FK*, 130; *SS*, 190.

Guillelmus de Willens. Lausanne, Switzerland. Arrival: Unknown. Return: Unknown. *FK*, 134; *D*, 118.

Guillelmus Alverniae, comes. Count. Auvergne, France. Did not leave. *FK*, 81; Pr., 3696.

* Guillelmus Carnotensis. Chartres, France. Arrived 1218. Returned. Métais, 208.

* Guillelmus II, archiepiscopus Burdigalensis. Archbishop. Bordeaux, France. Arrived 1218. Returned. *FK*, 91; *FK*, 74, #54; Pr., 2151, 2537; Ol., 187.

* Guillelmus Juliacensis, comes. Count. Jülich, Germany. Arrived 1218. Did not return. *FK*, 106; *FK*, 64, #25. Beyer, 3:92.

Guillelmus Penna. Lucca, Italy. Did not leave. ASL SM, Jan. 21, 1208; ASL SM, Aug. 22, 1200; ASL S Pan, Jan., 26, 1220; *FK*, 119.

* Guillelmus Raymundus, Bearnensis. Viscount. Bearn, France. Arrival: Unknown. Returned. *FK*, 86.

Guillelmus, comes Sacri Caesaris. Count. Sancerre, France. Did not leave. Arbois, 102, #122; *FK*, 124.

* Guillelmus, episcopus Andegavensis. Bishop. Angers, France. Arrived 1218. Returned. *FK*, 81; *FK*, 79; *SS*, 90.

* Guillelmus, abbas Gemeticensis. Abbot. Jumièges, France. Arrived 1218. Return: Unknown. *FK*, 101; Pr., 2960.

Guillermus de Fogliano. Reggio nell'Emilia, Italy. Did not leave. *FK*, 99; Levi, 130, #105.

* Guillermus de Haurac. France. Arrival: Unknown. Return: Unknown. *FK*, 102; *FK*, 74, #54.

* Guillermus de Viscanis. France. Arrival: Unknown. Return:

Unknown. *FK*, 133; *FK*, 74, #54.

* Guilleta, wife of Barcellus. Bologna, Italy. Arrived 1219. Return: Unknown. Sav., 419–20, #480.

* Guiot. (Mauleon?) France. Arrived 1218. Return: Unknown. *FK*, 102; *Arc. Poitou*, 1:89.

* Gundacherus de Hausbach. Hausbach (near Glocknitz), Germany. Arrived 1221. Return: Unknown. *FK*, 102; *FK*, 74, #53.

* Gundakarus de Styra. Steiermark, Austria. Arrived 1217. Return: Unknown. *FK*, 128; *FK*, 62, #17.

* Gundakerus de Murberg. Murberg (near Radkersburg), Germany. Arrived 1217. Return: Unknown. *FK*, 116; *FK*, 63, #17.

* Gyle Berthoudus. Malines, Belgium. Arrived 1219. Return: Unknown. *FK*, 87; *FK*, 70, #46; Eracles, 343.

* Gyso de Upladen. Opladen, Germany. Arrived 1218. Return: Unknown. *FK*, 132; *FK*, 61, #13.

H. de Champleto. Champlitte, France. Arrival: Unknown. Return: Unknown. *FK*, 94; Pr., 296; Pott., 5446, 25775.

* H. de Spiegelberc. Spielberg (Knittlefeld), Germany. Arrived 1217. Return: Unknown. *FK*, 127; *FK*, 59, #7.

* Hademarus de Sunnenberch. Sonnenberg, Austria. Arrived 1217. Return: Unknown. *FK*, 129; *FK*, 58, #4.

Hademarus II de Kuenring-Weitra. Kuenring, Austria. Did not leave. *FK*, 107; *FK*, 57–58, #3–4; *T*, 340.

* Hademarus III de Kuenring-Weitra. Kuenring, Austria. Ar-

rived 1217. Return: Unknown.
FK, 107; *FK*, 57–58, #3–4;
T, 340.
* Hademarus, abbas Mellicensis.
Abbot. Melk, Austria. Arrived
1217. Returned. *FK*, 11;
T, 192.
* Haimerus de Toarcio, vice-
scomes. Viscount. Thouars,
France. Arrival: Unknown. Re-
turned. *FK*, 129; *T*, 89.
* Hartwicus, magister coquinae.
Master of Kitchen. Rotenburg,
Germany. Arrived 1221. Re-
turn: Unknown. *FK*, 103; BF,
1307; *D*, 104; *Wirt. UB*,
3:124.
* Hasculf de Suleny. Somerset,
England. Arrival: Unknown.
Return: Unknown. *RLC*
1:410b; *Somerset Pleas*, 1:65,
#302; Sied., 139, #23.
* Hayo de Violgama. Violgama
(Frisia), Netherlands. Arrived
1218. Return: Unknown. *FK*,
103, 108; *T*, 15, 17; *D*, 104;
Ol., 184n, 294; Eracles, 328.
* Heinricus de Elslo. Maastricht,
Netherlands. Arrived 1218.
Return: Unknown. *FK*, 97;
FK, 61, #13.
* Hellinus, abbas de Floreffe Ab-
bot. Floreffe, France. Arrival:
Unknown. Return: Unknown.
FK, 99; *T*, 22, 25.
  Henricus. Rheinau, Switzerland.
Arrival: Unknown. Return:
Unknown. *FK*, 101; *ZGO*,
29, 73.
* Henricus de Bernsore. Rhine-
land, Germany. Arrived 1218.
Return: Unknown. *FK*, 87;
FK, 61, #13.
* Henricus de Buffele, miles.
Knight. Malines, Belgium. Ar-
rived 1219. Return: Unknown.
FK, 91; *FK*, 70, #46; Eracles,
343.
* Henricus de Chemegy. Cham-

pagne, France. Arrived 1218.
Return: Unknown. *FK*, 94;
Arbois, 5:131, #1150.
* Henricus de Fontania. Friuli,
Italy. Arrived 1217. Return:
Unknown. *FK*, 99; *FK*,
63, #17.
* Henricus de Geideggi. Heideck,
Germany. Arrived 1221. Re-
turn: Unknown. *Wirt. UB*,
3:124.
* Henricus de Greifsbach, comes.
Count. Greifsbach, Germany.
Arrived 1221. Return: Un-
known. *FK*, 102; BF, 1309;
Wirt. UB, 3:124.
* Henricus de Hakingen.
Hakingen, Germany. Arrived
1217. Return: Unknown. *FK*,
102; *FK*, 57, #3.
* Henricus de Hernothe. Cologne,
Germany. Arrived 1218. Did
not return. *FK*, 103; *SS*, 40.
  Henricus de Isenburg. Burggraf.
Isenburg, Germany. Arrival:
Unknown. Return: Unknown.
FK, 105. Beyer 3:78, #79;
106–7, #110.
* Henricus de Kuenring-Weitra.
Kuenring, Austria. Arrived
1217. Return: Unknown. *FK*,
107; *FK*, 57–58, #3–4;
T, 340.
  Henricus de Mirkelin. Coblenz,
Germany. Arrival: Unknown.
Return: Unknown. *FK*, 112;
Goerz, 2:341, #1242.
* Henricus de Monte. Berg (Rhine-
land), Germany. Arrived 1218.
Return: Unknown. *FK*, 113;
T, 343; *B*, 366.
* Henricus de Nehusa. Neuss, Ger-
many. Arrived 1218. Return:
Unknown. *FK*, 116; *T*, 220.
  Henricus de Neiffen. Neiffen,
Germany. Did not leave.
Rodenberg 1:97, #133;
Pr., 2638.
* Henricus de Oberndorf.

Oberndorf (near Judenberg), Germany. Arrived 1221. Return: Unknown. *FK*, 117; *FK*, 74, #53; Zahn 2:261, #176.

* Henricus de Okkenheim. Germany. Arrived 1218. Return: Unknown. *FK*, 117; *FK*, 64, #25; *CDOT*, 1:44, #42; 2:7–8, #8; 23–24, #22.

Henricus de Ortenburg, comes. Count. Ortenburg, Germany. Arrival: Unknown. Return: Unknown. *FK*, 118; Meiller, 218, #208–9.

* Henricus de Prunne, Jr. Germany. Arrived 1217. Return: Unknown. *FK*, 57, #3.

* Henricus de Prunne, Sr. Germany. Arrived 1217. Return: Unknown. *FK*, 121; *FK*, 57, #3.

Henricus de Raderei. Rheinau, Switzerland. Arrival: Unknown. Return: Unknown. *FK*, 121; *D*, 111; *ZGO*, 29, 71.

* Henricus de Rodelano. Austria. Arrival: Unknown. Return: Unknown. *FK*, 123; *D*, 112.

* Henricus de Schonrode. Schonrath (Aachen), Germany. Arrived 1218. Return: Unknown. *FK*, 126; *FK*, 61, #13.

* Henricus de Santo Memorio. Champagne, France. Arrived 1218. Return: Unknown. *FK*, 111; Lalore 6:307; *ROL*, 1:371.

* Henricus de Trebancheswinkel. Treibswinkel, Germany. Arrived 1217. Return: Unknown. *FK*, 130; *FK*, 57, #2.

* Henricus de Ulmen. Coblenz, Germany. Arrived 1218. Return: Unknown. *FK*, 131; *T*, 172; *SS*, 52; Ol., 216.

* Henricus de Vileke. Flecke, Germany. Arrived 1218. Return:

Unknown. *FK*, 132; *FK*, 62, #13.

* Henricus de Zebingen. Zebingen, Germany. Arrived 1217. Return: Unknown. *FK*, 135; *FK*, 58, #4.

* Henricus von Hohenlohe. Teutonic Knight. Hohenlohe, Germany. Arrived 1221. Returned. *FK*, 104; Strehlke, 75–78, #98–99; *Wirt. UB*, 95.

* Henricus Bufo. Jülich, Germany. Arrived 1217. Return: Unknown. *FK*, 91; *FK*, 64, #25.

* Henricus Capardus. Lucca, Italy. Arrived 1218. Return: Unknown. *FK*, 93; *FK*, 70, #47; Sav., 431–32, #487.

* Henricus Cornubiensis. Cornwall, England. Arrival: Unknown. Did not return. *FK*, 96; Roberts, 1:78.

* Henricus I, comes de Schwerin. Count. Schwerin (Lower Saxony), Germany. Arrived 1220. Returned. *FK*, 126; Ol., 253; Pr., 4549, 4550, etc.

* Henricus II, abbot of Berg. Abbot. Magdeburg, Germany. Arrived 1217. Returned. *FK*, 87; *T*, 346–47; Mulv. 2:139, #330; 245, #535.

Henricus Longchamp, filius Gosvini. Belgium. Arrival: Unknown. Return: Unknown. *FK*, 108.

* Henricus Maczavitelli. Lucca, Italy. Arrival: Unknown. Return: Unknown. RV 9:221, #900; Pr., 1120.

* Henricus Tokelarius, miles. Knight. Semmering, Germany. Arrival: Unknown. Return: Unknown. *FK*, 129; Zahn, 2:257–58, #175.

* Henricus, capellanus and notarius. Notary. France. Arrived

1218. Returned. *FK,* 103;
FK, 61, #13; Jac., 131.
* Henricus, comes de Malta.
Count. Sicily, Italy. Arrived
1221. Returned, *FK,* 110; *T,*
245; Ol., 277.
* Henricus, comes de Sayn. Count.
Sayn, Germany. Arrived 1218.
Returned. *FK,* 125; *FK,* 64,
#25; Goerz, 2:385, #1408;
399, #1463.
* Henricus, comes Ruthenensis.
Count. Rodez, France. Arrived
1218. Return: Unknown. *FK,*
74, #54; *FK,* 124; Brequigny,
5:121.
* Henricus, frater de Landgheern.
Netherlands. Arrived 1219.
Return: Unknown. *FK,* 127;
Brequigny, 5:136.
* Henricus, nobilis de Bussmanns-
hausen. Dominus. Lord. Buss-
mannshausen, Germany. Ar-
rived 1218. Did not return.
FK, 92; *T,* 156.
* Henricus, archiepiscopus. Arch-
bishop. Milan, Italy. Arrived
1220. Returned. Pr., 2609,
3445; Ol., 248; *DCV,* 2,
125–26; *FK,* 111; *FK,* 70,
#47; *T,* 93, 109; Eubel,
1:347.
Henricus, Brabantis and
Lotharingiae. Duke. Brabant,
Belgium. Did not leave. *FK,*
90; Pr., 3824, 5483, 5484.
* Henricus, canonicus Colonienis.
Canon. Cologne, Germany.
Arrival: Unknown. Returned.
FK, 95; *T,* 344; *B,* 369.
* Henricus, episcopus. Bishop.
Mantua, Italy. Arrived 1218.
Returned. *FK,* 110; Ol.,
187; Pr., 1197, 1217, 2045,
3112, 5631.
* Henricus, marchio de Istria
(Andechs). Margrave. Tyrol,
Austria. Arrived 1217. Re-
turned. *FK,* 105; *FK,* 58, #5;

T, 199, 200. Meiller, 122–23,
#151; *UB Diessen,* 49, 51.
* Henry de Bohun, earl of Here-
ford. Earl. Hereford, England.
Arrived 1219. Did not return.
FK, 103; Sied., 139, #24;
Coggeshall, 188; *T,* 68, 70, 73.
* Henry de Scalar. Essex, England.
Arrival: Unknown. Did not
return. *FK,* 126; Sied.,
139, #27.
* Henry of Tyes (Teutonicus). Lin-
colnshire, England. Arrived
1218. Return: Unknown.
Sied., 139, #29; Pontefract
Chart., 1:37, #21.
* Henry Fitz Count. England. Ar-
rival: Unknown. Did not
return. Sied., 139, #25; *RLC,*
1:515b.
Henry Fitz Regini. Winchelsea,
England. Arrival: Unknown.
Return: Unknown. Sied., 139,
#26; *RLC,* 186b; *FK,* 134.
* Henry Scaudefin. Lincolnshire,
England. Arrived 1218. Re-
turn: Unknown. Sied., 139,
#28; *Just. Eyre* (Linc.),
313–34, #654.
Herbert de Montibus. England.
Arrival: Unknown. Return:
Unknown. *FK,* 115; Sied.,
139, #30; *RLC,* 1:391a.
* Herbertus Torel. Solesmes,
France. Arrived 1218. Return:
Unknown. *FK,* 129; *Cart.
Solesmes,* 199, #271.
* Heribertus, abbas Werdensis.
Abbot. Verden (Saxony), Ger-
many. Arrived 1218. Return:
Unknown. *FK,* 134; *SS,* 31;
B, 377; Rodenberg 1:60–61,
#81; Pr., 1:1723, 1724.
* Hermann von Salza. Master, Teu-
tonic Order. Salza, Germany.
Arrived 1217. Returned. Pr.,
1580, 2338, 2867, 2962,
2963, 2981; *T,* 24, 29–31, 33,

34; *B*, 374; Cohn, *Hermann*, 21–35.

*Hermannus de Alftere. Bonn, Germany. Arrived 1218. Return: Unknown. *FK*, 80; *CDOT*, 2:6–7, #7.

Hermannus de Rudenberg. Westphalia, Germany. Arrival: Unknown. Return: Unknown. *FK*, 124; Seibertz, 1:148.

*Hermannus de Senden. Senden, Germany. Arrived 1218. Return: Unknown. *FK*, 126; *FK*, 64, #24.

Hermannus de Siebrathshausen. Rheinau, Switzerland. Arrival: Unknown. Return: Unknown. *FK*, 126; *ZGO*, 29, 69.

Hermannus de Umendorf. Rheinau, Switzerland. Arrival: Unknown. Return: Unknown. *FK*, 131; D, 116; *ZGO*, 29, 63–64.

*Hermannus, comes de Wartstein. Count. Wartstein, Germany. Arrived 1221. Returned. *FK*, 133; *Cod. Salem.*, 1:174–75.

*Hermannus, advocatus. Advocate. Jülich, Germany. Arrived 1218. Return: Unknown. *FK*, 106; *FK*, 64, #25.

*Hermannus, decanus Coloniensis. Dean. Cologne, Germany. Arrival: Unknown. Returned. *FK*, 95; *T*, 344.

*Hermannus, marchio Badensis. Margrave. Baden, Germany. Arrived 1221. Returned. *FK*, 84; Ol., 257; *T*, 29, 33, 345; *Wirt. UB*, 3:121; *Reg. Markgraf. Baden*, 20–21.

*Hermerus. Cook. Yorkshire, England. Arrived 1218. Return: Unknown. Sied., 139, #31; Pontefract Chart., 1:37, #21.

*Herrandus de Wildonia. Germany. Arrived 1217. Return: Unknown. *FK*, 134; *FK*, 57, #2.

*Hervaeus Ursionis. Vierzon, France. Arrived 1218. Did not return. *FK*, 115; *T*, 55, 93; Ol., 188; *RHGF*, 18:247.

*Hervé of Nevers. Count. Nevers, France. Arrived 1218. Returned. *FK*, 117; Ol., 187, 199n; *T*, 55, 79, 81, 83, 93, 102, 238, 299, 345; *SS*, 79, 122, 131, 158, 178; Pr., 1488, 1543, 1581, 1873, 2119, 2553, 2810, 2818.

*Herveus de Leone. Brittany, France. Arrived 1218. Did not return. *FK*, 108; *T*, 79, 135; Brequigny 5:107.

*Hillinus de Racenghem. Netherlands. Arrived 1219. Return: Unknown. *FK*, 127; Brequigny, 5:136.

*Hroar, relative of king of Norway. Norway. Arrived 1218. Returned. *FK*, 104; *T*, 322; Riant, 330–31.

Hubert de Burgh, bishop of Durham. Durham, England. Did not leave. Lunt, 428.

*Hugh of Alta Ripa. Yorkshire, England. Arrived 1218. Return: Unknown. Sied., 139, #32; Pontefract Chart., 1:37, #21.

Hugh of Sanford. Berkshire, England. Arrival: Unknown. Return: Unknown. Sied., 139, #34; *Pat. Rolls*, 1:147.

*Hugh of Toynton. Lincolnshire, England. Arrived 1218. Did not return. Sied., 139, #35; *Just. Eyre* (Linc.), 146–47, #321.

*Hugh, king of Cyprus. King. Cyprus. Arrived 1217. Returned. Jac., 94, 98–99; Ol., 162, 166n, 168, 289–90.

Hugh, son of Richard. Lincolnshire, England. Arrival: Unknown. Return: Unknown.

Sied., 139, #33; *Just. Eyre* (Linc.), 198–99, #427.

* Hugo (Hugh de la Loge). Champagne, France. Arrival: Unknown. Returned. *ROL,* 1:373.

Hugo de Acelz. Arcelot, France. Arrival: Unknown. Return: Unknown. *FK,* 79; Brequigny, 5:61.

Hugo de Maire. France. Arrival: Unknown. Return: Unknown. *FK,* 110; *Tables de Fonteneau,* 190.

* Hugo de Thorc. Thors (Aube), France. Arrived 1218. Return: Unknown. *FK,* 129; *FK,* 66, #33; *T,* 93.

* Hugo von Puchberg. Puchberg, Austria. Arrived 1217. Return: Unknown. *B,* 373.

* Hugo Brunus, comes Marchiae. Count. La Marche, France. Arrived 1218. Did not return. *FK,* 111; *T,* 55, 81, 93, 238; Pr., 1498, 1543, 1558, 1581; Ol., 187.

Hugo I de Montfort. Bavaria, Germany. Arrival: Unknown. Return: Unknown. *FK,* 115; BF, 951; *D,* 108; *B,* 371.

Hugo Lupus, marquis de Saragna. Marquis. Parma, Italy. Did not leave. *FK,* 109; Levi, 130, #105.

Hugo Lyobardus. Lyons, France. Arrival: Unknown. Return: Unknown. *FK,* 109.

* Hugo Strumo. Rhineland, Germany. Arrived 1218. Return: Unknown. *FK,* 128; *FK,* 64, #24.

* Hugo, miles. Knight. Langres, France. Arrival: Unknown. Return: Unknown. *FK,* 104; Pr., 4653.

Hugo, abbas Sancti Martialis. Abbot. Limoges, France. Did

not leave. *FK,* 111; *T,* 337–38.

Hugolinus. Italy. Did not leave. *FK,* 104; Levi 130, #105.

Hugolinus da Fogliano. Reggio nell'Emilia, Italy. Did not leave. *FK,* 99; Levi, 130, #105.

Hugolinus de Ferraria. Ferrara, Italy. Did not leave. *FK,* 98, Levi, 132, #105.

* Huguetus. France. Arrived 1221. Return: Unknown. *FK,* 104; *FK,* 74, #54.

* I.   diaconus, capellanus. Dean. Upsala, Sweden. Arrival: Unknown. Returned. *FK,* 132; Pr., 5596.

* Ildebrandus, comes Tusciae. Count. Tuscany, Italy. Arrived 1221. Return: Unknown. *FK,* 102; BF, 1307–8, 1312; Winkelmann, 1:59, #62.

* Illuminatus. Franciscan Friar. Italy. Arrived 1219. Returned. *FK,* 105; Roncaglia, *St. Francis,* 27, 64.

* Imbertus. France. Arrival: Unknown. Return: Unknown. Ol., 273.

* Infridus de Hintperg. Hindberg, Germany. Arrived 1217. Return: Unknown. *FK,* 104; *FK,* 57, #3; 58, #4.

* Iohannes Montanus. Louvain, Belgium. Arrived 1218. Return: Unknown. *FK,* 79; *D,* 106–7; Divaeus, 8.

* Iohannes, praepositus Sancti Castoris. Provost. Coblenz, Germany. Arrived 1217. Did not return. Pr., 2135; *FK,* 95.

* Iterius de Tocce, comes. Count. Toucy, France. Arrived 1218. Did not return. *FK,* 130; Ol., 188; *T,* 55, 102.

* J. de Watnes. Lille, Belgium. Arrived 1218. Return: Unknown. *FK,* 134; *FK,* 66, #30.

Jacobinus de Ubertis. Bologna, Italy. Arrived 1219. Return: Unknown. *FK,* 131; Sav., 397, #460.

* Jacobus de Andria, comes marescalus. Count. Rome, Italy. Arrived 1218. Returned. Rodenberg, 1 : 89; *T,* 104, 121, 133, 145, 160, 244; Ol., 187; *FK,* 81.

* Jacobus de Durnai. Marshall. Acre, Palestine. Arrived 1217. Return: Unknown. *FK,* 97; Eracles, 330.

Jacobus de Palude. Reggio nell'Emilia, Italy. Did not leave. *FK,* 118; Levi, 130, #105.

* Jacobus de Ulzano. Notary. Bologna, Italy. Arrived 1219. Return: Unknown. *FK,* 131; *FK,* 68, #40; 72, #48; 73, #50–52. Sav., 419–20, #480; 431–32, #487; 433, #488; 446–47, #497; 447, #498; 448, #499.

* Jacobus de Vitriaco, episcopus. Bishop. Acre, Palestine. Arrived 1216. Returned. See bibliography.

* Jacobus Lieningus. Louvain, Belgium. Arrived 1218. Return: Unknown. *FK,* 79; *D,* 106–7; Divaeus, 8.

* Jacomellus Aderani. Bologna, Italy. Arrived 1219. Return: Unknown. *FK,* 79; *FK,* 73, #50; Sav., 446–47, #497.

* Jacomus de Castro Plumiaco. Priest. Bologna, Italy. Arrived 1219. Return: Unknown. *FK,* 93; *FK,* 70, #47; Sav., 431–32, #487.

* Jacomus de Megliecinis. Bologna, Italy. Arrived 1219. Return: Unknown. *FK,* 111; *FK,* 73, #52; Sav., 448, #499.

* Janellus Praedarius. Magister. Cesena, Italy. Arrived 1219.

Return: Unknown. *FK,* 92; *FK,* 72, #49; Sav., 442–43, #493.

Jaucerandus de Bouzol. Le Puy, France. Arrival: Unknown. Return: Unknown. *FK,* 90.

* Jehan Fuinon. France. Arrival: Unknown. Returned. *FK,* 100; *T,* 112.

* Johannes. Marshall. Tripoli, Syria. Arrived 1217. Return: Unknown. Eracles, 322.

* Johannes d'Ibelin, dominus Beruthi. Lord. Beirut, Lebanon. Arrived 1217. Returned. *T,* 317; Rudt de Collenberg, 127–28.

* Johannes de Aleia. Dominus. Lord. France. Arrival: Unknown. Return: Unknown. *FK,* 80; Brequigny 5 : 131.

* Johannes de Arcis. Arcis-sur-Aube (Champagne), France. Arrived 1218. Return: Unknown. *SS,* 52, 92, 103–4, 128, 132, 153, 190; *FK,* 82; *FK,* 66, #33; Ol., 216; *T,* 4, 93–94, 112–13, 115.

Johannes de Bouilly. Pontigny, France. Arrival: Unknown. Return: Unknown. *FK,* 90; Quantin, 151, #341; Quantin, 429, #1118.

* Johannes de Cameraco, Jr. Priest. Cambrai, Belgium. Arrived 1218. Did not return. *FK,* 105; Jac., 97, 110.

* Johannes de Cameraco, Sr. Priest. Cambrai, Belgium. Arrived 1218. Did not return. *FK,* 92; Jac., 97, 110.

* Johannes de Guzistan. England. Arrival: Unknown. Did not return. *FK,* 102; *RLC,* 1 : 141.

Johannes de Keriti. Brittany, France. Arrival: Unknown. Return: Unknown. *FK,* 106.

* Johannes de Tulbia, presbyter. Priest. Tolve (Basilicata), Italy.

Arrived 1218. Returned. *FK,*
130; *SS,* 119–40.

* Johannes Faber. Cesena, Italy. Arrived 1219. Return: Unknown.
FK, 98; *FK,* 72, #49; Sav.,
442–43, #493.

* Johannes Rubeus de Volta.
Genoa, Italy. Arrived 1219.
Returned. *FK,* 133; *T,* 239.

* Johannes, comes de Sponheim.
Count. Sponheim (Coblenz),
Germany. Arrived 1218. Returned. *FK,* 127; *D,* 114; *T,*
195, 345; Goerz, 2:365.

* Johannes, abbas de Sponheim.
Abbot. Sponheim (Coblenz),
Germany. Arrived 1218. Returned. *FK,* 127; Goerz,
2:365.

* Johannes, episcopus Lemovicen-
sis. Bishop. Limoges, France.
Arrived 1218. Did not return.
FK, 108; *T,* 337–38;
Ol., 177.

* Johannes, Jerosolimitanus rex.
King. Acre, Palestine. Arrived
1217. Returned. See
bibliography.

* Johannina. Arrival: Unknown.
Return: Unknown. *FK,* 105;
FK, 74, #54.

* John de le More. Knight.
Shrewsbury, England. Arrival:
Unknown. Did not return.
Just. Eyre (Glouc.), 521.

* John de Lacy, Sheriff of Chester.
Constable. York, England. Arrived 1218. Returned. Sied.,
140, #38; *FK,* 94; Wendover,
2:135; *T,* 51, 55, 63–65, 69;
Pontefract Chart., 1:37, #21;
Alexander, 2.

* John le Lokier. Coventry, England. Arrival: Unknown. Return: Unknown. *Just. Eyre*
(Glouc.), 299.

* John of Easton. Lincolnshire,
England. Arrived 1218. Return: Unknown. Sied., 140,

#36; Pontefract Chart.,
1:37, #21.

* John of Harcourt. Leicester, England. Arrival: Unknown. Did
not return. *FK,* 102; *T,* xxxix;
Sied., 140, #37.

* John Pascal. Coventry, England.
Arrival: Unknown. Return:
Unknown. *Just. Eyre* (Glouc.),
280–81.

* Jordan de Ranavilla. Yorkshire,
England. Arrived 1218. Return: Unknown. Sied., 140,
#39; Pontefract Chart.,
1:37, #21.

* Jordanus, episcopus Lexoviensis.
Bishop. Lisieux, France. Arrived 1218. Did not return.
FK, 108; *T,* 77, 102; Eubel,
1:304.

* Juhel II de Mayenne. Maine,
France. Arrived 1217. Return:
Unknown. Fourmont, 3:33;
FK, 111.

* Konrad von Boffzen. Paderborn,
Germany. Arrived 1217. Returned. Rüdebusch, 57.

* L. de Denaing. Cysoing,
Belgium. Arrived 1218. Return: Unknown. *FK,* 97; *FK,*
66, #30.

* Lambertus de Scherve.
Leichlingen, Germany. Arrived
1218. Return: Unknown. *FK,*
126; *FK,* 61, #13.

* Lambertus de Vichte. Olden-
burg, Germany. Arrived 1218.
Return: Unknown. *FK,* 132;
Wauters, 3:498.

* Landulfus, judex. Judge. Bologna, Italy. Arrived 1219.
Return: Unknown. *FK,* 107;
FK, 73, #50–52; Sav.,
446–47, #497; 447, #498;
448, #499.

* Laurentius. Hungary. Arrived
1217. Return: Unknown. *FK,*
107; *FK,* 31, n. 17; Fejer,
3a:205–6, 244–49.

* Lecia, mother of William. York-
  shire, England. Arrival:
  Unknown. Return: Unknown.
  Sied., 140, #40; *Just. Eyre*
  (Yorks.), 183, #431.
* Leopold, duke of Austria. Duke.
  Austria. Arrived 1217. Re-
  turned. *FK,* 83; *FK,* 57–58,
  #62–63; *T,* passim; *SS,*
  passim.
Leschek, or Ladislaus, dux
  Poloniae. Duke. Poland. Did
  not leave. *Schles. UB,* 1:116,
  #162; 117, #163; 127, #173;
  128, #174; 151, #205.
  Pr., 3249.
* Leutoldus de Saeven.
  Bressanone, Italy. Arrived
  1221. Return: Unknown. *FK,*
  125; *FK,* 74, #53.
* Leutolfus de Lopeke. Lepik
  (Utrecht), Netherlands. Ar-
  rived 1218. Return: Unknown.
  FK, 109; *FK,* 64, #24.
* Leutpoldus IV de Regensberg.
  Regensberg, Germany. Arrived
  1217. Did not return. *FK,*
  122; Meiller, 221, #223.
* Liupoldus, notarius ducis Aus-
  triae. Notary. Austria. Arrived
  1217. Return: Unknown. *FK,*
  108; *FK,* 57, #2.
* Liutpoldus III, comes de Plage.
  Count. Plaien, Austria. Arrived
  1217. Returned. *FK,* 120; *T,*
  185, 190, 200; *B,* 373.
* Ludovicus de Oettingen, comes.
  Count. Oettingen, Germany.
  Arrived 1217. Return: Un-
  known. *FK,* 117; *T,* 182, 195;
  B, 372.
* Ludovicus Bavariae. Duke. Ba-
  varia, Germany. Arrived 1221.
  Returned. *FK,* 85; Eracles,
  351; Ol., 256–57, 260, 276;
  Pott., 5827.
Ludovicus II, comes de Loos.
  Count. Loos (Liege), Belgium.
  Did not leave. *FK,* 108;

  MGHSS, 16:676; Pott., 2176;
  Pr., 735, 1366.
* Lupoldus de Rotinburg. Roten-
  berg, Germany. Arrived 1221.
  Return: Unknown. *Wirt.
  UB,* 121.
* Mainhardus de Gorze. Count.
  Gorze, Germany. Arrived
  1217. Return: Unknown. *FK,*
  101; *FK,* 58, #5.
Manfredus de Camisiano. Count.
  Cremona, Italy. Did not leave.
  FK, 92; Levi, 131, #105.
* Manfredus, clericus Sancti Mar-
  tini. Priest. Lucca, Italy.
  Arrived 1219. Return: Un-
  known. *FK,* 110; *FK,* 72,
  #48; Sav., 433, #488.
Mangoldus, comes de Nellen-
  burg. Count. Nellenburg,
  Germany. Arrival: Unknown.
  Return: Unknown. *FK,* 116;
  Cod. Salem., 1:152.
* Margerite, niece of King John.
  France. Arrived 1218. Re-
  turned. Eracles, 332.
Maria, wife of Rainerius Flates.
  Foigny, France. Arrival: Un-
  known. Return: Unknown.
  FK, 133.
Marianus, judex. Judge. Sardinia,
  Italy. Did not leave. *FK,* 131;
  Pr., 898, 1674, 2781, 2782;
  Levi, 121–23, #98;
  130, #105.
* Marinus, canonicus. Canon.
  Bologna, Italy. Arrived 1219.
  Return: Unknown. *FK,* 111;
  FK, 73, #50; Sav.,
  446, #497.
* Mariotta, daughter of William.
  Yorkshire, England. Arrival:
  Unknown. Return: Unknown.
  Sied., 140, #41. *Just. Eyre*
  (Yorks.), 297, #818.
* Marquardus de Hintperg. Hind-
  berg, Germany. Arrived 1217.
  Return: Unknown. *FK,* 104;
  FK, 57, #3; 58, #4.

*Marsilius, frater. Hospitaller
Knight. Arrival: Unknown.
Return: Unknown. *FK*, 111;
FK, 75, #54.
*Martin of Selby. Yorkshire, Eng-
land. Arrived 1218. Return:
Unknown. Sied., 140, #42;
Pontefract Chart., 1:37, #21.
*Masilius de Durscheide. Rhine-
land, Germany. Arrived 1218.
Return: Unknown. *FK*, 97;
FK, 61, #13.
Masseus Petri. Foligno, Italy. Ar-
rival: Unknown. Return:
Unknown. *Sassovivo*,
5:139–40.
Mathaeus de Corrigia. Parma,
Italy. Did not leave. *FK*, 96;
Levi, 129–30, #105;
Winkelmann, 1:45.
Matthaeus de Ivran. Brittany,
France. Arrival: Unknown. Re-
turn: Unknown. *FK*, 106.
*Matthaeus, comes Alesinae.
Count. Apulia, Italy. Arrived
1220. Returned. *FK*, 81; *T*,
109, 203; Ol., 249;
Eracles, 354.
*Maurinus, physicus. Physician.
Acre, Palestine. Arrival: Un-
known. Return: Unknown.
FK, 111; *FK*, 74–75, #54.
*Meinhardus de Imzeinsdorf. Im-
zeinsdorf, Germany. Arrived
1217. Return: Unknown. *FK*,
105; *FK*, 58, #4.
*Menabue, frater Passavantis.
Lucca, Italy. Arrived 1218. Re-
turn: Unknown. *FK*, 112;
LAA A+1, 138 (Jan. 1221).
*Michel de Viz. France. Arrival:
Unknown. Return: Unknown.
FK, 133; Eracles, 336.
Miletus, frater Theobaldi de Pru-
vino. France. Arrival:
Unknown. Return: Unknown.
FK, 112.
*Milo de St. Florentin. St. Floren-
tin (Yonne), France. Arrived

1218. Returned. *FK*, 99; *Lay.*,
1:457; Arbois, 4:175.
*Milo, comes de Barro. Count.
Bar (Marmoutier), France. Ar-
rived 1218. Did not return.
FK, 85; Ol., 187–88; *T*,
55, 93.
*Milo, episcopus elect. Bellovacen-
sis. Bishop-elect. Beauvais,
France. Arrived 1218. Re-
turned. Pott., 5819, 5920;
FK, 86; Pr., 1727–28, 1745,
1770, 1795, 2815; *T*, passim;
Ol., 215, 257, 277; *SS*, 51,
102, 104, 132, 159, 190.
*Mirus de Rupe. Angoulême,
France. Arrival: Unknown. Re-
turn: Unknown. *FK*, 124; *FK*,
74, #54.
*Morvanus, vicecomes. Viscount.
Faon, France. Arrival: Un-
known. Did not return. *FK*,
115; *T*, 79.
*Mostar, Turcoman. Arrival: Un-
known. Returned. *FK*, 115;
Eracles, 339.
*Munsarinus. Bologna, Italy. Ar-
rived 1219. Return: Unknown.
FK, 115; *FK*, 73, #51; Sav.,
447, #498.
*N. de Hochstaden, comes.
Count. Hochstadt, Germany.
Arrived 1218. Did not return.
FK, 104; *T*, 156.
*Neidhart de Reuenthal. Poet.
Reuenthal, Austria. Arrived
1217. Returned. *FK*, 122; *B*,
373; *D*, 112; Neidhart, 108;
Hagen, 4:437.
Nicholas de Letres. Notting-
hamshire, England. Arrival:
Unknown. Return: Unknown.
Sied., 140, #44; *Pat. Rolls*,
1:21.
*Nicholas, son of Robert Gubald.
Yorkshire, England. Arrived
1218. Return: Unknown.
Sied., 140, #43; *Just. Eyre*
(Yorks.), 3, #15.

*Nicolaus. Rhineland, Germany. Arrived 1218. Return: Unknown. *FK,* 116; *D,* 109; *B,* 379.

*Nicolaus de Antonia. Rome, Italy. Arrived 1218. Did not return. *SS,* 122, 147; *FK,* 81.

Nicolaus de Sancto Remigio. Canon. Sens, France. Arrival: Unknown. Return: Unknown. *FK,* 122; Lalore, 2:160; *ROL,* 1:371–72.

Nicolaus Niclasson. Denmark. Arrival: Unknown. Return: Unknown. *FK,* 116; Riant, 317.

*Nicolaus, filius Boni. Hungary. Arrived 1217. Returned. *Regesta Regni,* 2:59.

*Nicolaus, episcopus Reginensis. Bishop. Reggio nell'Emilia, Italy. Arrived 1220. Returned. *FK,* 122; *T,* 109; Ol., 187; Rodenberg, 1:88–91, #124.

*O. de Dinant. Priest. Dinant, Belgium. Arrived 1218. Return: Unknown. *FK,* 97; Jac., 131.

*Odo de Castellione. Châtillon, France. Arrived 1218. Returned. *FK,* 93; Jac., 130, 150; Flamare, 423–24.

*Odo de Montbelliardo. Constable. Acre, Palestine. Arrived 1218. Returned. *FK,* 113; Eracles, 333–34; Strehlke, 41, #49, 50; 43–46, #53–56. Eracles, 355.

Odo de Pontchâteau. France. Arrival: Unknown. Return: Unknown. *FK,* 120; Fourmont, 2:47.

Odo Borelli, dominus Curiae Alani. Lord. Courtalain, France. Arrival: Unknown. Return: Unknown. *FK,* 96; Mahille, 211, #228, 229.

Odo III, duke of Burgundy. Duke. Burgundy, France. Did

not leave. *FK,* 91; *T,* 79, 93; Pr., 14, 1498, 2818.

*Odonell, Fitz William d'Aubeny. England. Arrived 1218. Return: Unknown. Sied., 140, #45; *FK,* 117; *T,* 56.

*Ogmundr de Spanheimr. Spanheimr (Hardanger), Norway. Arrived 1218. Returned. Riant, 330–31.

*Oliver, natural son of King John of England. England. Arrived 1218. Did not return. *FK,* 117; *T,* 55, 65; Sied., 140, #46; Ol., 188; Rymer, 1A:124.

*Oliverus, scholasticus Coloniensis. Scholasticus. Cologne, Germany. Arrived 1218. Returned. *FK,* 91; *T,* passim; *SS,* passim; Ol., passim.

Orlandinus de Ferraria. Ferrara, Italy. Did not leave. *FK,* 98; Levi, 132, #105.

Orlandinus Aldeprandini. Lucca, Italy. Did not leave. *FK,* 109; Levi, 132, #105.

*Orlanduccius. Lucca, Italy. Arrived 1218. Returned. *FK,* 109; Müller, 438.

*Ostexanus. Priest. Bologna, Italy. Arrived 1219. Return: Unknown. *FK,* 118; *FK,* 73, #50; Sav., 446–47, #497.

*Otto de Anzenberg. Anzenberg, Germany. Arrived 1217. Return: Unknown. *FK,* 81; *FK,* 58, #4.

*Otto de Cremese. Krems, Austria. Arrived 1217. Return: Unknown. *FK,* 96; *FK,* 59, #7.

Otto de Goldeck. Salzburg, Austria. Arrival: Unknown. Return: Unknown. *FK,* 101.

*Otto de Husperg. Husberg, Germany. Arrived 1221. Return: Unknown. *FK,* 105; *FK,* 74, #53.

*Otto de Walkenstein. Walkenstein, Germany. Arrived 1217. Return: Unknown. *FK*, 135; *FK*, 63, #17.

*Otto de Wasen. Wasen, Austria. Arrived 1217. Return: Unknown. *FK*, 134; *FK*, 63, #17.

Otto von Mere. Mere, Belgium. Arrival: Unknown. Return: Unknown. *D*, 108.

*Otto von Puchberg. Puchberg, Austria. Arrived 1217. Return: Unknown. *B*, 373.

*Otto II, episcopus Trajectensis. Bishop. Utrecht, Belgium. Arrived 1217. Returned. *Ol.*, 163, 168, 290; *T*, 26, 31, 174; *SS*, 36; Pr., 1502, 1868, 1869; *FK*, 130.

*Otto III, comes de Tecklenburg. Count. Tecklenburg (Bentheim), Germany. Arrived 1217. Returned. *FK*, 129; *B*, 375; *UB Sud-Oldenburg*, 32, 41, 44.

*Otto, dux Meraniae. Duke. Meran, Germany. Arrived 1217. Returned. *FK*, 112; *T*, 92, 147, 182, 184; *T*, 199, 200, 345; *Ol.*, 162; *UB Diessen*, 51.

*Otto, episcopus Monasteriensis. Bishop. Münster, Germany. Arrived 1217. Did not return. *FK*, 113; *T*, 26, 31, 345; *B*, 371; *Ol.*, 163, 168, 172, 290; Rüdebusch, 49–51.

*Otto, praepositus. Provost. Regensburg, Germany. Arrived 1221. Returned. *MGHSS*, 9:593; *FK*, 122; *D*, 112; *B*, 373.

*Ottokarus de Walkenstein. Walkenstein, Germany. Arrived 1217. Return: Unknown. *FK*, 135; *FK*, 63, #17.

*Ottonellus de Roffono. Bologna, Italy. Arrived 1219. Return:

Unknown. *FK*, 123; *FK*, 68, #40; Sav., 419–20, #480.

P. de Poy. France. Arrival: Unknown. Return: Unknown. *FK*, 121.

P., subdiaconus. Subdeacon. Metz, Germany. Arrival: Unknown. Return: Unknown. *FK*, 112; Pr., 1327.

*P. nepos Germundi de Forgis. Forge (Poitou), France. Arrived 1218. Return: Unknown. *FK*, 118; *Arc. Poitou*, 1:89.

*P. Bru. Monk. Limoges (St. Martial), France. Arrived 1217. Did not return. *FK*, 91; *T*, 338.

Paganus Buderca. Salerno, Italy. Arrival: Unknown. Return: Unknown. *FK*, 91; Pr., 2043; RV 9:92, #441.

*Pelagius. Cardinal. Rome, Italy. Arrived 1218. Returned. *FK*, 118; see Bibliography.

Pelaus. Italy. Did not leave. *FK*, 104; Levi, 130, #105.

Peter de Letres. Nottinghamshire, England. Arrival: Unknown. Return: Unknown. Sied., 140, #47; *Pat. Rolls*, 1:21.

*Petrobonus de Rodaldis. Bologna, Italy. Arrived 1219. Return: Unknown. *FK*, 123; *FK*, 58, #6; 73, #52. Sav., 431–32, #487; 448, #499.

*Petrus de Castello. Genoa, Italy. Arrived 1218. Returned. *FK*, 93; *T*, 238, 353.

Petrus de D. France. Arrival: Unknown. Return: Unknown. *FK*, 97; *Lay.*, 1:81b.

*Petrus de Glisy. Glisy, France. Arrived 1219. Return: Unknown. *FK*, 101; Eracles, 343; Beauville, 3:1–2.

*Petrus de Merceto. Merzig, Germany. Arrived 1218. Returned. *FK,* 111; Goerz, 2 : 369, #1349; 407, #1499.

* Petrus de Monte Acuto. Master of Templars. Montagu-sur-Champeix, France. Arrival: Unknown. Returned. Ol., 277, 280; Van Cleve, "Fifth Crusade," 2 : 413n; Riley-Smith, *Knights of St. John,* 1 : 156, 168–69.

* Petrus de Peicols. France. Arrival: Unknown. Return: Unknown. *FK,* 118; *FK,* 74, #54.

* Petrus de Walde. Rhineland, Germany. Arrived 1218. Return: Unknown. *FK,* 133; *FK,* 64, #25.

* Petrus Arces. Arques, France. Arrival: Unknown. Return: Unknown. *FK,* 82; *FK,* 44, #54.

* Petrus Aurie. Genoa, Italy. Arrived 1219. Returned. *FK,* 83; *T,* 239.

* Petrus Braidu. France. Arrival: Unknown. Return: Unknown. *FK,* 90; *FK,* 74, #54.

* Petrus Cornutus. Sergeant. France. Arrival: Unknown. Return: Unknown. *FK,* 96; *FK,* 74, #54.

* Petrus de Ubertis. Bologna, Italy. Arrived 1219. Return: Unknown. *FK,* 120; *FK,* 72–73, #48, 50–51; Sav., 397, #460; 433–34, #488; 446–47, #497; 447, #498.

* Petrus Donadeu. France. Arrival: Unknown. Return: Unknown. *FK,* 97; *FK,* 74, #54.

* Petrus Durandus de Amisau. Amisau, France. Arrival: Unknown. Return: Unknown. *FK,* 81; *FK,* 74–75, #54.

* Petrus Hannibal. Rome, Italy. Arrived 1218. Return: Unknown. Jac., 110; Ol., 158; *FK,* 102.

* Petrus Physicus. Physician. Acre, Palestine. Arrival: Unknown.

Return: Unknown. *FK,* 120; *FK,* 74, #54.

* Petrus Ugolinus de Beroarda. Bologna, Italy. Arrived 1219. Return: Unknown. *FK,* 72, #48; Sav., 433, #488.

Petrus, frater Hugonis Lyobardi. Lyons, France. Arrival: Unknown. Return: Unknown. *FK,* 109.

* Petrus, archiepiscopus Caesariensis. Archbishop. Caesarea, Palestine. Arrived 1217. Returned. Van Cleve, "Fifth Crusade," 2 : 389; Pr., 16, 23, 3663, 3687; Eubel, 1 : 153.

* Petrus, episcopus Parisiensis. Bishop. Paris, France. Arrived 1218. Did not return. *FK,* 118; *T,* 79, 93–102; Eubel, 1 : 391; Jac., 116; Ol., 187.

* Petrus, episcopus Jauriensis. Bishop. Raab, Hungary. Arrived 1217. Return: Unknown. *T,* 238; Ol., 162, 168; Pr., 749, 1036.

Petrus, comes Namucensis. Count. Namur, Belgium. Did not leave. Ol., 285; Pr., 2553, 2739.

Petrus, episcopus Wintoniensis. Bishop. Winchester, England. Did not leave. *T,* 58, 66, 70, 78; Pr., passim.

* Philip of Alta Ripa. Yorkshire, England. Arrived 1218. Return: Unknown. Sied., 140–41, #48; *Just. Eyre* (York.), 263–64, #713; 416–17, #1137. Pontefract Chart., 1 : 37, #21.

* Philip of Cromhall. Gloucester, England. Arrival: Unknown. Return: Unknown. *Just. Eyre* (Glouc.), 39.

* Philippus d'Ibelin. Beirut, Lebanon. Arrived 1217. Return: Unknown. *T,* 317.

* Philippus de Albineto. Belvoir,

England. Arrived 1221. Re-
turned. *FK*, 80; *FK*, 50–51;
Pr., 3313.
* Philippus de Planceio. Cham-
pagne, France. Arrived 1218.
Returned. *FK*, 120; *FK*, 46,
#7; Eracles, 341; *DSI*, 6:707;
Lay., 1:515, #1442;
1:540–41, #1515.
* Phylippus, camerarius. Foligno,
Italy. Arrival: Unknown. Re-
turn: Unknown. *Sassovivo*,
5:139–40.
* Pietro Ziani. Doge. Venice, Italy.
Arrived 1220. Returned.
Rodenberg, 1:89; Ol., 253.
* Pontius de Grancejo. Count.
Grancey-sur-Ource, France. Ar-
rived 1218. Did not return.
FK, 101; *T*, 93; Eracles, 343.
* Pontius, drapparius, frater.
Knight Hospitaller. Hungary.
Arrived 1217. Return: Un-
known. *FK*, 121; *FK*,
74, #54.
Poppo de Stierberg. Stierberg,
Germany. Arrival: Unknown.
Return: Unknown. *FK*, 128;
Mon. Boic., 24:45.
* Poppo XIII de Henneberg,
comes. Count. Henneberg,
Germany. Arrived 1217. Re-
turned. *FK*, 103; *T*, 182, 195;
Hagen, 62–63.
R.   capellanus regis
Hungriae. Priest. Hungary.
Did not leave. *FK*, 121;
Pr., 3933.
R.   clericus. Priest. Toul,
Germany. Arrival: Unknown.
Return: Unknown. *D*, 116;
Pr., 2659; *FK*, 130.
R. de Mosteles. Brittany, France.
Arrival: Unknown. Return:
Unknown. *FK*, 115; Morice,
1:827; Fourmont 2:130–31.
* R.   clericus Monasteriensis.
Münster, Germany. Arrival:
Unknown. Return: Unknown.

FK, 113; *Neues Archiv*,
2:613–14.
* Radulfus de Belmont. Viscount.
Beaumont, France. Arrived
1218. Returned. *FK*, 86;
Pott., 5409; Jac., 122, 150;
Ol., 216; *Lay.*, 1:438, #1197;
Flamare, 424.
* Radulfus de Bondeburg, mag-
ister. France. Arrived 1218.
Did not return. *T*, 64; *FK*, 89.
* Radulfus de Hundirsingin. Hun-
dersingen, Germany. Arrived
1221. Return: Unknown.
Wirt. UB, 3:124.
Radulfus de Moric. Poitou,
France. Arrival: Unknown. Re-
turn: Unknown. *FK*, 115; *Arc.
Poitou*, 2:196, #46.
Radulfus de Toucheto. France.
Arrival: Unknown. Return:
Unknown. *FK*, 129; Bre-
quigny, 5:418.
Radulfus de Tübingen, comes.
Count. Tübingen, Germany.
Did not leave. *FK*, 130; D,
116; *MGHSS*, 24:674.
Radulfus, comes Suessionensis.
Count. Soissons, France. Ar-
rival: Unknown. Return:
Unknown. *FK*, 128; Pr., 14;
Van Cleve, "Fifth
Crusade," 313.
* Radulfus, Jerosolimitanus patri-
archa. Patriarch. Acre,
Palestine. Arrived 1217. Re-
turned. See bibliography.
* Rainaldinus Moldinarius (Bar-
banus). Barber. Bologna, Italy.
Arrived 1219. Return: Un-
known. *FK*, 110; *FK*, 68,
#40; Sav., 419–20, #480.
Rainerius di quondam Gislieri.
Pistoia, Italy. Arrival: Un-
known. Return: Unknown.
ASF, Pistoia, July 28, 1219.
Rainerius Flates de Vorges.
Foigny, France. Arrival: Un-

known. Return: Unknown. *FK*, 133.

* Rainerius Leodiensis. Liège, Belgium. Arrived 1218. Return: Unknown. *FK*, 122; *T*, 329.

* Ralf le Frankelein. Franklin. Gloucester, England. Arrival: Unknown. Return: Unknown. *Just. Eyre* (Glouc.), 28.

* Ranulf, episcopus Petragoricensis. Bishop. Perigord, France. Arrival: Unknown. Returned. *FK*, 120; Pr., 14, 265, 2457, 3449.

* Ranulf, earl of Chester. Earl. Chester, England. Arrived 1218. Returned. Sied., 141, 49; *T*, passim; Ol., 187n, 207–8, 215, 223; *FK*, 93; Alexander, passim.

* Rapotus de Lapide. Halberstadt, Germany. Arrived 1221. Return: Unknown. *FK*, 107; *FK*, 74, #53.

* Raymundus de Arnoldo. France. Arrival: Unknown. Return: Unknown. *FK*, 82; *FK*, 74, #54.

* Raymundus IV, vicecomes Turennae. Viscount. Tourenne, France. Arrived 1219. Returned. *FK*, 130; Brequigny, 5 : 122; Lecler, 88.

* Raymundus, archiepiscopus Gerundinus. Archbishop. Gerona, Spain. Arrived 1218. Did not return. *FK*, 101; Pr., 644; Ol., 176n, 187; Eubel, 1 : 261.

* Raynerius. Cesena, Italy. Arrived 1219. Return: Unknown. *FK*, 92; *FK*, 72, #49; Sav., 442–43, #493.

Recuperus de Lucardo. Florence, Italy. Did not leave. *FK*, 109; Levi, 129, #105.

Reginaldus de Andegavia. Angers, France. Arrival:

Unknown. Return: Unknown. *FK*, 81; *BEOC*, 4 (1859): 254–55.

* Reginaldus de Ponte. Brittany, France. Arrived 1218. Returned. *FK*, 120; Ol., 215n; Pott., 6080.

* Regnerius, episcopus Bethelemitanus. Bishop. Acre, Palestine. Arrived 1217. Returned. Ol., 176, 190; *T*, 238; Pr., 1580, 3203, 3213, 3689.

* Reinaldus de Barbachon, magister. Acre, Palestine. Arrived 1217. Did not return. Jac., 110–11.

Reinardus de Aquis. Cologne, Germany. Arrival: Unknown. Return: Unknown. *FK*, 81.

* Reinbotus de Batburk. Rhineland, Germany. Arrived 1218. Return: Unknown. *FK*, 85; *FK*, 64, #24.

* Reinerus. Germany. Arrived 1221. Return: Unknown. *FK*, 121; *FK*, 74, #53.

* Reinerus de Rotheim. Rotheim, Germany. Arrived 1218. Return: Unknown. *FK*, 124; *FK*, 64, #25.

Reinhard. Aachen, Germany. Arrival: Unknown. Return: Unknown. *D*, 97; Ennen, 2 : 74, #61.

* Reinprecht de Murekke. Mureck (near Leibnitz), Germany. Arrived 1217. Return: Unknown. *FK*, 116; *FK*, 57, #2; 59, #7; 63, #17.

* Remboldus de Bernsore. Rhineland, Germany. Arrived 1218. Return: Unknown. *FK*, 87; *FK*, 61, #13.

* Remboldus de Hursbeke. Rhineland, Germany. Arrived 1218. Return: Unknown. *FK*, 105; *FK*, 61, #13.

* Renaldus, senescalcus Cypri. Seneschal. Cyprus. Arrived

1217. Return: Unknown. *FK,*
128. Pauli, 1 : 112–13, #106.

Renatus III de Dampetra. Dam-
pierre, France. Did not leave.
FK, 96; *AOL,* Doc. 189,
2 : 192–97.

Repetto. Ravenna, Italy. Arrival:
Unknown. Return: Unknown.
Vasina, "Emiliano-romagnolo,"
37.

* Ricardus, episcopus. Bishop.
Fano, Italy. Arrived 1219. Returned. *FK,* 98; Pr., 1176,
1888, 4109; Levi, 128, #105;
Eubel, 1 : 254.

Richard de Marisco. Chancellor.
Northumberland, England.
Did not leave. Cheney, *Innocent III,* 261; *Pat. Rolls,* Index,
1 : 660.

Richard de Scakerlunde. Eng-
land. Arrival: Unknown.
Return: Unknown. *FK,* 126;
Sied., 141, #51.

* Richardus de Argentun.
Hertfordshire, England. Ar-
rived 1218. Return: Unknown.
FK, 82; *T,* 333; Sied., 141,
#50; Coventry, 2 : 243.

* Richardus de Jericho. Acre, Palestine. Arrival: Unknown.
Returned. *FK,* 105; *FK,*
48–49, #9.

* Richwinus de Rusche. Her-
scheide, Germany. Arrived
1218. Return: Unknown. *FK,*
124; *FK,* 62, #13.

Ricus Franceschi. Pistoia, Italy.
Arrival: Unknown. Return:
Unknown. *LFDP,* 180.

Rinuccius de Lucardo. Florence,
Italy. Did not leave. *FK,* 109;
Levi, 129, #105.

* Rivolus Faber. Cesena, Italy. Arrived 1219. Return: Unknown.
FK, 98; *FK,* 72, #49; Sav.,
442–43, #493.

* Robert de Vere, earl of Oxford.
Earl. Oxford, England. Arrival:

Unknown. Did not return.
FK, 132; *T,* 334; Sied.,
142, #61.

* Robert of Carlisle. Carlisle, Eng-
land. Arrived 1218. Return:
Unknown. Sied., 141, #54;
Pontefract Chart., 1 : 37, #21.

* Robert of Kent. Steward. Lincolnshire, England. Arrived
1218. Return: Unknown.
Sied., 142, #58; Pontefract
Chart., 1 : 37, #21.

* Robert Courçon. Cardinal.
Derbyshire, England. Arrived
1218. Did not return. *FK,* 96;
Sied., 141, #55; see
Bibliography.

* Robert FitzWalter. England. Arrived 1219. Returned. *FK,*
123; Sied., 141, #56; *T,* 55,
62, 65, 69.

* Robert Grammaticus. Teacher.
Yorkshire, England. Arrived
1218. Return: Unknown.
Sied., 142, #57; Pontefract
Chart., 1 : 37, #21.

* Robert Russell. Yorkshire, England. Arrival: Unknown.
Return: Unknown. Sied., 142,
#59; *Just. Eyre* (Yorks.),
214–15, #539.

* Robert Savage. Nottinghamshire,
England. Arrived 1219. Return: Unknown. *FK,* 125;
Sied., 142, #60; *RLC,*
1 : 397b, 399b.

Robert Westfili. Lincolnshire,
England. Arrival: Unknown.
Return: Unknown. Sied., 142,
#62; *Just. Eyre* (Linc.), 641,
#1428.

Robert William Colee. Lin-
colnshire, England. Arrival:
Unknown. Return: Unknown.
Sied., 142, #63; *Just. Eyre*
(Linc.), 641, #1428.

* Robert, abbot of York. Abbot.
York, England. Arrival: Unknown. Return: Unknown.

Sied., 141, #52; *Pat. Rolls,*
1:161.

* Robert, son of Colus. Yorkshire,
England. Arrived 1219. Return: Unknown. Sied., 141,
#53; *Just. Eyre* (Yorks.),
354–55, 979.

* Robertus de Bello Monte.
France. Arrival: Unknown.
Did not return. *FK,* 87;
Ol., 252.

* Robertus de Pachi. France. Arrived 1218. Did not return.
FK, 118; *SS,* 150, 190.

Robertus de Vallibus. England.
Did not leave. *Pat. Rolls,*
1:124, 235, 320, 369, 374,
441, 519.

* Robertus, archiepiscopus
Nazaren. Archbishop. Acre,
Palestine. Arrived 1217. Re-
turn: Unknown. Van Cleve,
"Fifth Crusade," 389; Pr.,
1070, 4831; Eubel, 1:358.

* Robertus, episcopus Bajocensis.
Bishop. Bayeux, France. Arrived 1217. Returned. Ol.,
163, 168; Pr., 14, 621, 3454,
3578; *FK,* 85.

* Robertus, episcopus Lucanus.
Bishop. Lucca, Italy. Arrived
1218. Returned. LAA A + 1,
93, Nov. 1220; 40, Oct. 1220.
Müller, 91, #59, p. 438; Pr.,
138, 1086, 1120, 1546, 2064,
2213, 2421, 2851, 3131,
4143, 4583; *FK,* 109.

Robertus, episcopus Veszpri-
miensis. Bishop. Veszprimia,
Hungary. Did not leave. *FK,*
105; Pr., 2533.

* Robertus, medicus. Physician.
Lucca, Italy. Arrived 1218. Return: Unknown. Sav.,
432–33, #488; 447–48,
#448; 442–43, #493;
433–34, #489.

Rochillus de Demmin. Dean.
Mecklenburg, Germany. Ar-

rival: Unknown. Return:
Unknown. *FK,* 97; *UB Meck,*
1:270, #285.

* Roger 'Medicus.' Physician. Yorkshire, England. Arrived 1218.
Return: Unknown. Sied., 142,
#65; Pontefract Chart.,
1:37, #21.

* Roger de Vere. Oxford, England.
Arrival: Unknown. Did not return. *T,* 334; Sied., 142, #68.

Roger Millirs. Dorset, England.
Arrival: Unknown. Return:
Unknown. Sied., 142, #66;
Book of Fees, 1:89; *Pat. Rolls,*
1:147.

* Roger, man of Philip de Alta
Ripa. Yorkshire, England. Ar-
rived 1218. Return: Unknown.
Sied., 142, #64; *Just. Eyre*
(York.), 263–64, #713;
416–17, #1137. Pontefract
Chart., 1:37, #21.

* Roger, porter of Pontefract.
Monk. Pontefract Abbey, Eng-
land. Arrived 1218. Return:
Unknown. Sied., 142, #67;
Pontefract Chart., 1:37, #21.

* Rolandinus Bronzola. Bologna,
Italy. Arrived 1219. Return:
Unknown. *FK,* 91; *FK,* 73,
#50; Sav., 446–47, #497.

* Rolandus, episcopus. Bishop.
Faenza, Italy. Arrived 1220.
Did not return. *FK,* 98; Eubel,
1:255; *T,* 109; Ol., 248.

* Rolant de Lucque. Lucca, Italy.
Arrived 1218. Return: Un-
known. *FK,* 109; Eracles, 330.

* Rolland Fitz Simeon. Lin-
colnshire, England. Arrival:
Unknown. Did not return.
FK, 123; Sied., 142 #69.

* Rudolfus de Potendorf. Poten-
dorf, Germany. Arrived 1217.
Return: Unknown. *FK,* 121;
FK, 57–58, #4.

Rudolfus de Ramsberg. Rheinau,
Switzerland. Arrival: Un-

known. Return: Unknown.
FK, 121; *ZGO,* 29, 72–73.
Rudolfus de Rapperswyl.
Switzerland. Arrival: Un-
known. Return: Unknown.
FK, 121.
* Rumone. Lucca, Italy. Arrived
1218. Return: Unknown. Sav.,
431–32, #487; 433–34,
#488.
* S. de Fursac. Monk. Limoges,
France. Arrived 1217. Re-
turned. *FK,* 100; *T,* 338.
* Saer de Quency, earl of Win-
chester. Earl. Winchester,
England. Arrived 1219. Did
not return. *FK,* 134; Sied.,
142, #70; *T,* 55, 65, 68–70,
73; Alexander, 2.
* Salatinus. Cesena, Italy. Arrived
1219. Return: Unknown.
FK, 92; *FK,* 72, #49; Sav.,
442–43, #493.
* Sanguignus, episcopus. Bishop.
Umana, Italy. Arrived 1218.
Returned. *FK,* 131; Gams,
665; Ol., 187.
* Santius Ortic. France. Arrival:
Unknown. Return: Unknown.
FK, 118; *FK,* 74, #54.
* Savaric de Malleon. Mauleon
(Poitou), France. Arrived
1219. Returned. *FK,* 110;
Sied., 142–43, #71; *Arc.
Poitou,* 6, 31–32, #27; Ol.,
219; Shirley, 1:89, #164.
Sebrandus Chabot. Fonteneau,
France. Arrival: Unknown. Re-
turn: Unknown. *FK,* 94;
Tables de Fonteneau, 191; Four-
mont, 3:242.
Sigefridus. Italy. Did not leave.
FK, 126; Levi, 132, #105.
Sigfridus II, dominus de Runkel.
Lord. Seligenstadt, Germany.
Arrival: Unknown. Return:
Unknown. *FK,* 124; *B,* 374;
D, 112.
* Sigfridus, episcopus Augustensis.
Bishop. Augsburg, Germany.

Arrived 1219. Returned. *T,*
157; Ol., 187n; Pr., 3425,
5724.
* Sigmus de Monte. Berg (Rhine-
land), Germany. Arrived 1218.
Did not return. *FK,* 113;
SS, 133.
Sigtragg, canonicus. Canon.
Linttoeping, Sweden. Did not
leave. *FK,* 108; Svenskt Dipl.
1:180.
* Sigurdus, relative of king of Nor-
way. Norway. Arrived 1218.
Returned. *FK,* 126; *T,*
321–22; Riant, 330–31.
Simon de Bricon. Champagne,
France. Arrival: Unknown. Re-
turn: Unknown. *ROL,* 1:372.
* Simon de Joinville. Seneschal.
Champagne, France. Arrived
1218. Returned. *FK,* 105;
FK, 46, #7; Pr., 14; Pott.,
5325, 5947.
* Simon de Rupeforti. Bar-sur-
Saone, France. Arrived 1218.
Returned. *FK,* 124; *FK,* 66,
#33; Mahille, 219.
* Simon II, comes de Sarroponte.
Count. Saarbrücken, Germany.
Arrived 1218. Returned. *FK,*
125; *T,* 102, 254, 259, 261;
H.-B., 2:760; Ol., 176n,
177, 215.
* Simon Moisant. Lincoln, Eng-
land. Arrived 1218. Return:
Unknown. Sied., 143, #72;
Just. Eyre (Linc.), 42–43,
#106.
* Simon, archiepiscopus Tyrensis.
Archbishop. Tyre, Lebanon.
Arrived 1217. Returned. Van
Cleve, "Fifth Crusade," 389;
Pr., 16, 18, 23 . . . 3687;
Eubel, 1:505.
Siripere de Urxis. Bologna, Italy.
Arrival: Unknown. Return:
Unknown. *FK,* 127; *FK,* 58,
#6; Sav., 397, #460;
Gozzadini, 384.
* Siuredus de Pneuma. Germany.

Arrived 1217. Return: Unknown. *FK,* 120; *FK,* 58, #5.

* Stephanus de Logia. Champagne, France. Arrived 1220. Returned. *FK,* 128; Lalore, 5 : 150–52; *ROL,* 1 : 373, #60.

* Stephanus de Malavilla. Knight Hospitaller. France. Arrival: Unknown. Return: Unknown. *FK,* 109; *FK,* 75, #54.

* Stephanus, comes de Wordicha. Count. Wordicha, Hungary. Arrived 1217. Returned. *FK,* 135; *FK,* 24.

* Stephanus Calca. France. Arrival: Unknown. Return: Unknown. *FK,* 92; *FK,* 74, #54.

Stephanus Lecacorum. Piacenza, Italy. Did not leave. *FK,* 107; Levi, 89, #66; 130, #105.

Stephanus Marchisortis C. of Crotone. Count. Crotone, Italy. Did not leave. *FK,* 96; Eracles, 359; Kamp, 1 : 2, 955; *QFAIB,* 36 : 15.

Stephanus, presbyter Pratigelati. Priest. Oulx (Piedmont), Italy. Arrival: Unknown. Return: Unknown. *CPO,* 250–51, #242.

* Suikerus de Lintlo. Lintlar (Berg), Germany. Arrived 1218. Return: Unknown. *FK,* 108; *FK,* 61, #13.

* Swederus de Dingede. Münster, Germany. Arrived 1218. Returned. *FK,* 97; *FK,* 61, #13; H.-B., 2 : 806.

Sylvester, episcopus Wigorniae. Bishop. Worcester, England. Did not leave. *RS,* 36 : 4; *Pat. Rolls,* 1 : 144–45.

* Terri Berthoudus. Malines, Belgium. Arrived 1219. Return: Unknown. *FK,* 87; Eracles, 343; *FK,* 70, #46.

Th. de Rupeforti, Dominus. Lord. Bar-sur-Saone, France. Arrival: Unknown. Return: Unknown. *FK,* 124; Pr., 1972.

Theobald, Clericus of Helena von Luneburg. Priest. Braunschweig, Germany. Arrival: Unknown. Return: Unknown. *B,* 375; Rüdebusch, 54.

* Theobaldus de Roche. France. Arrival: Unknown. Return: Unknown. *FK,* 123; Brequigny, 5 : 131.

Theobaldus, presbyter de Dimonte. Priest. France. Arrival: Unknown. Return: Unknown. *FK,* 97; Quantin, 85–86, #190.

* Theodoricus de Coselar. Jülich, Germany. Arrived 1218. Return: Unknown. *FK,* 96; *FK,* 61, #13.

Theodoricus Theutonicus e Cornubia. Cornwall, England. Arrival: Unknown. Return: Unknown. *FK,* 129; *T,* xxxiii; *RLC* 1 : 457b.

* Thietmarus. Hildesheim, Germany. Arrived 1218. Returned. *FK,* 129; *D,* 115; Röhricht, *Bibliotheca geographica,* 47–48.

Thomas de Saxolo. Modena, Italy. Did not leave. *FK,* 125; Levi, 131, #105.

* Thomas the Despencer. Despencer. Yorkshire, England. Arrival: Unknown. Return: Unknown. Sied., 143, #74; *Just. Eyre* (Yorks.), 275, #740.

* Thomas Esturmy. Worcestershire, England. Arrival: Unknown. Return: Unknown. Sied., 143, #75; Book of Fees, 1 : 140; *Pat. Rolls,* 1 : 158.

* Thomas Monachus. Monk. St. Albans, England. Arrived 1218. Returned; *T,* 58, 70.

* Thomas Noviensis, magister. Magister. Noyen, France. Arrived 1218. Did not return. *FK,* 129; *T,* 64, 69; Jac., 110; Ol., 172; Sied., 143, #73.

*Thomas, episcopus Agriensis.
Bishop. Erlau (Eger), Hun-
gary. Arrived 1217. Returned.
Pott., 6338, 6526, 6845; FK,
79; FK, 24, 31; SS, 104–33;
Ol., 162, 168, 187.

*Tiburtinus Rainerii Spiularia.
Bologna, Italy. Arrived 1219.
Return: Unknown. FK, 128;
FK, 68, #40; Sav., 419–20,
#480.

Tirisendus de Canusia. Canossa,
Italy. Did not leave. FK, 93;
Levi, 131, #105.

*Ubaldinus Pascipovere. Bologna,
Italy. Arrived 1219. Return:
Unknown. FK, 73, #51; Sav.,
447, #498.

*Ubaldus. Lucca, Italy. Arrived
1218. Return: Unknown. Sav.,
431–32, #487; 433–34,
#488.

*Ubertellus de Corvaria. Bologna,
Italy. Arrived 1219. Return:
Unknown. FK, 96; FK, 68,
#40; Sav., 419–20, #480.

*Ubertinus de Pastino. Bologna,
Italy. Arrived 1219. Return:
Unknown. FK, 91.

Ubertus de Panzano. Modena,
Italy. Did not leave. FK, 118;
Levi, 129, #105.

*Ubertus Armanni. Bologna, Italy.
Arrived 1219. Return: Un-
known. FK, 82; FK, 73, #50;
Sav., 446–47, #497.

*Ucherius. Lucca, Italy. Arrived
1218. Return: Unknown. Sav.,
431–32, #487; 433–34,
#488. FK, 131; FK, 72, #48.

*Ugo Medicus. Physician. Lucca,
Italy. Arrived 1219. Return:
Unknown. FK, 111; FK, 70,
#47; Sav., 431–32, #487;
ASBRG, 218r, Oct. 15, 1216;
Waley, 101.

*Ugolinus Atticontis. Bologna,
Italy. Arrived 1219. Returned.
FK, 83; FK, 73, #50; Sav.,

446–47, #497; ASB, 20/956,
March 14, 1223; ASBRG,
90rv, Sept. 8, 1200, etc.

Ugrinus, archiepiscopus Colo-
censis. Archbishop. Kolocza,
Hungary. Did not leave. Pr.,
2533.

*Ulgerus, servus ducis Austria.
Slave. Austria. Arrived 1217.
Return: Unknown. FK,
131; D, 116; Kurz, Pt. 2,
531–32, #58.

*Ulricus de Beca. Pechau, Ger-
many. Arrived 1217. Re-
turned. FK, 86; FK, 63, #17;
Zahn, 2:225–26, #153, 157;
Meiller, 123, #154.

*Ulricus de Eppan. Count. Bozen,
Austria. Arrived 1217. Return:
Unknown. FK, 98. Cod.
Wang., 310–11, #136; FK,
63, #17.

*Ulricus de Friberc. Carinthia,
Austria. Arrived 1221. Return:
Unknown. FK, 100; FK,
74, #53.

*Ulricus de Gumpoldeskirchen.
Gumpoldeskirchen, Austria.
Arrived 1221. Return: Un-
known. FK, 102; FK, 74, #53.

*Ulricus de Murberg. Murberg
(near Radkersburg), Germany.
Arrived 1217. Return: Un-
known. FK, 116; FK, 63, #17.

*Ulricus de Stubenberg. Steier-
mark, Austria. Arrived 1217.
Did not return. FK, 128; FK,
58, #7; 62, #17.

*Ulricus II, episcopus Patavinus.
Bishop. Passau, Germany.
Arrived 1221. Returned.
FK, 118; Eubel, 1:392; T,
153–55, 159, 193, 199, 334,
346, 354; Pr., 117, 766, 775,
2168, 2462, 2501, 3227; Ol.,
257, 270.

*Ulricus, plebanus de Uischa.
Tischau, Austria. Arrived
1217. Return: Unknown. FK,
131; FK, 57, #2.

*Ulricus, marescalcus de Valkensteine. Marshall. Falkenstein, Austria. Arrived 1217. Return: Unknown. *FK*, 132; *FK*, 57, #3; 63, #17.

*Ulvinus de Chetse. Germany. Arrived 1221. Return: Unknown. *FK*, 94; *FK*, 74, #53.

*Ulvinus de Stubenberg. Steiermark, Austria. Arrived 1221. Return: Unknown. *FK*, 128; *FK*, 74, #53.

*Urias von Martinsberg. Abbot. Martinsberg, Hungary. Arrived 1217. Return: Unknown. *FK*, 111; *FK*, 24.

*Vallete, wife of Jordanus de Cuzol. France. Arrived 1218. Return: Unknown. *FK*, 132.

W. de Marolio. Bordeaux, France. Arrival: Unknown. Return: Unknown. *FK*, 111; Pr., 1576.

*W. Chapda. Monk. Limoges, France. Arrived 1218. Return: Unknown. *FK*, 94; *T*, 338.

*W.   clericus Monasteriensis. Priest. Münster, Germany. Arrival: Unknown. Return: Unknown. *FK*, 113; *Neues Archiv*, 2:613–14.

*W. de Arkania. Archennes, Belgium. Arrived 1219. Return: Unknown. *FK*, 82; *FK*, 70, #46.

W.   canonicus Dolensis. Canon. Dols, France. Arrival: Unknown. Return: Unknown. *FK*, 97; RV, 9:171, #715.

*Walter de Imrode. Rhineland, Germany. Arrived 1218. Return: Unknown. *FK*, 105; *FK*, 64, #25.

Walter de Letres. Nottinghamshire, England. Arrival: Unknown. Return: Unknown. Sied., 143, #76; *Pat. Rolls*, 1:21.

*Walter Berthoudus. Malines, Belgium. Arrived 1219. Returned. *FK*, 87; *FK*, 70, #46; Eracles, 343; Ol., 215; Wauters, 4:549.

*Walter Caesar. Louvain, Belgium. Arrived 1218. Return: Unknown. *FK*, 79; D, 106–7; Divaeus, 8.

*Walterus Bertoldus de Spenimbergo. Spelimberg, Austria. Arrival: Unknown. Return: Unknown. *FK*, 127; D, 113.

*Walterus Tornacensis. Archdeacon. Acre, Palestine. Arrived 1217. Did not return. *FK*, 30; Jac., 110.

Walterus, archiepiscopus Eboracensis. Archbishop. York, England. Did not leave. *FK*, 97; *RLC*, 1:510a.

*Walther the Chaplain. Priest. Gloucester, England. Arrival: Unknown. Returned. *Just. Eyre* (Glouc.), 80.

*Werenboldus de Werkune. Rhineland, Germany. Arrived 1218. Return: Unknown. *FK*, 134; *FK*, 64, #24.

*Werner, Germany. Arrived 1217. Returned. *B*, 2:377.

*Wernerus de Bolanden. Dapifer. Steward. Pfalz, Germany. Arrived 1221. Returned. *FK*, 89; Pott., 6414, 6415; Pr., 2796; Goerz, 2:403.

*Wezilo, abbas Gottwicensis. Abbot. Gottweih, Austria. Arrived 1217. Return: Unknown. *FK*, 101.

*Wichardus de Linnefe. Rattingen, Germany. Arrived 1218. Return: Unknown. *FK*, 108; *FK*, 61, #13.

*Willelmus. Middlesex, England. Arrival: Unknown. Return: Unknown. Bracton, *Note Books*, 2:53.

*Willelmus de Belmont. Priest. Beaumont (Hainaut), France. Arrived 1219. Return: Un-

known. *FK,* 86; *FK,* 70, #46;
Eracles, 343.
* Willermus, capellanus de Cal-
munte. Priest. Chaumont
(Brabant), Belgium. Arrived
1219. Return: Unknown. *FK,*
92; *FK,* 70, #46; Eracles, 343.
William "le tanur." Yorkshire,
England. Arrival: Unknown.
Return: Unknown. Sied.,
143, #77; *Just. Eyre* (Yorks.),
24, #50.
* William d'Aubeny, earl of
Arundel. Earl. Arundel, Eng-
land. Arrived 1218. Did not
return. *T,* 55, 57, 62–63,
65–66, 69–70; *FK,* 83; Sied.,
143, #80; Ol., 249;
Alexander, 2.
* William de Cresek. Wiltshire,
England. Arrival: Unknown.
Did not return. *FK,* 96; Sied.,
143, #81; *T,* xxxiii; *RLC,*
1:413a.
* William of Foxcote. Serf. England. Arrival: Unknown. Re-
turn: Unknown. *Just. Eyre*
(Glouc.), 59–60.
* William of Harcourt. England.
Arrived 1218. Return: Un-
known. *FK,* 102; *T,* 55, 62,
64, 69; Sied., 144, #83.
* William of Huntingfield. Eng-
land. Arrived 1219. Did
not return. *FK,* 105; Sied.,
144, #84.
* William of Somervilla. Yorkshire,
England. Arrived 1218.
Return: Unknown. Sied.,
144, #86; Pontefract Chart.,
1:37, #21.
* William of Southwell. Yorkshire,
England. Arrived 1218. Re-
turn: Unknown. Sied., 144,
#87; Pontefract Chart., 1:37.
* William Ferrers, earl of Derby.
Earl. Derbyshire, England. Ar-
rived 1218. Return: Unknown.
FK, 98; Sied., 143, #82; *T,*

51, 60, 62–63; *FK,* 40–41,
#4; Alexander, 2.
* William Longspee, earl of Salis-
bury. Earl. Salisbury, England.
Arrived 1218. Returned. *FK,*
125; *FK,* 43, #6; *T,* 51; *SS,*
51, 201; Pr., 2307, 3827.
* William, count of Holland.
Count. Holland, Netherlands.
Arrived 1218. Returned. *FK,*
104; Pott., 5502–3; Pr.,
452–53, 456–57, 605, 670,
1027, 1359, 1364–66; Ol.,
173, 215.
* William, brother of Gilbert.
Coventry, England. Arrival:
Unknown. Did not return.
Just. Eyre (Glouc.), 275.
William, son of Maud. Lin-
colnshire, England. Arrival:
Unknown. Return: Unknown.
Sied., 143, #78; *Just. Eyre*
(Linc.), 108, #248.
* William, son of Robert Peper.
Yorkshire, England. Arrival:
Unknown. Return: Unknown.
Sied., 143, #79.
* Winandus de Gurcenich. Rhine-
land, Germany. Arrived 1218.
Return: Unknown. *FK,* 102;
FK, 64, #25.
* Winemarus Vrambalch. Rhine-
land, Germany. Arrived 1218.
Return: Unknown. *FK,* 133;
FK, 64, #25.
* Wolferus de Romberch. Vorau,
Austria. Arrived 1217. Return:
Unknown. *FK,* 123; *FK,*
63, #17.
* Zaccaria Rolandini di Galiana.
Bologna, Italy. Arrived 1219.
Return: Unknown. *FK,* 100;
FK, 73, #50; Sav., 446–47,
#497.
* Zagno de Castro Episcopo. Bo-
logna, Italy. Arrived 1219.
Return: Unknown. *FK,* 93;
FK, 68, #40; Sav., 419–20,
#480.

APPENDIX III

INDIVIDUALS WHOSE
PARTICIPATION IS IN DOUBT

Alanus de Basset. Basset, France.
FK, 85; *T*, xxxi.

Alberto Mazzoli. Bologna, Italy.
FK, 111; Ghirardacci 1:121.

Albertus di Alberti, comes.
Count. Tuscany, Italy. *FK*, 80;
T, 263.

Albertus Solario de Gavone. Asti,
Italy. *FK*, 127; *T*, 286.

Albertus, archiepiscopus. Archbishop. Magdeburg, Germany.
FK, 112.

Aldobrandinus de Corbizzi. Florence, Italy. *FK*, 95; *T*, 264.

Alfonsus de Coxano. Asti, Italy.
FK, 96; *T*, 286.

Andreas Ritius. Asti, Italy. *FK*,
123; *T*, 287.

Angelo della Tuada. Bologna,
Italy. Ghirardacci, 1:121.

Anonymous, abbas de Valle
Josaphat. Abbot. Calabria,
Italy. *FK*, 132; Kamp, 1:2,
818–19; Pr., 2245.

Anonymous, Frisian.
Netherlands. *FK*, 100;
T, 168–69.

Anonymous, marchio d'Este,
Marquis. Ferrara, Italy. *FK*,
98; *T*, 263.

Anonymous, Ritter. Germany.
B, 374.

Anonymous, decanus Trecensis.
Deacon. Troyes, France. *FK*,
130; RV, 12:198v, 23.

Anselmus de Justingen, marescalcus. Marshall. Germany.
FK, 106; BF, 1341;
Winkelmann, 1:51, 91, 146;
151, 159.

Arardo Bonandrei. Bologna,
Italy. Ghirardacci, 1:120.

Arca Noe (sic). *FK*, 117.

Arduino Benacci. Bologna, Italy.
Ghirardacci, 1:121.

Arnoldus, comes Clevensis.
Count. *FK*, 95; *T*, 345–46;
B, 369.

Artemisio Artemisi. Bologna,
Italy. Ghirardacci, 1:121.

Aymo de Praellis, miles. Knight.
Ainay, France. *FK*, 121;
Vachez, 117–18.

Azzolino de Azzolino Cospi. Bologna, Italy. Ghirardacci,
1:121.

Baldwinus de Bentheim, comes.
Bentheim, Germany. *FK*, 87.

Bartholomeo Tuschi. Bologna,
Italy. Ghirardacci, 1:121.

Jacobus de Ancisia. Asti, Italy.
FK, 81; *T*, 287.
Jacobus Palsaveno. Asti, Italy.
FK, 118; *T*, 287.
Jean de St. Martin. France.
Roger, *Noblesse*, 232.
Johannes de Agia. Agia, France.
FK, 79.
Johannes de Bouffle. Malines,
Belgium. *FK*, 90.
Johannes de Savary. Baugerais,
France. *FK*, 125.
Johannes de Tor. France. *FK*,
129; *T*, xlvi.
Johannes Forestarius. England.
FK, 99; *T*, xxxi.
Jordanenus. Salis, France. *FK*,
105; *FK*, 74, #54.
Juhel Serent. France. *FK*, 126;
Fourmont, 2:62.
Kuno de Tulpeto. Germany. *FK*,
136; *B*, 376.
Lambertus de Lamberti. Flor-
ence, Italy. *FK*, 107; *T*, 263.
Lanfrancus de Rubeis. Genoa,
Italy. *FK*, 124; *T*, 238.
Lazarus Barleta. Asti, Italy. *FK*,
85; *T*, 287.
Leonardus Bulla. Asti, Italy. *FK*,
91; *T*, 287.
Lorenzo Sauli. Lucca, Italy.
Pellegrini, 386.
Ludovicus Isnardus. Asti, Italy.
FK, 105; *T*, 287.
Lugarisio Lambertacci. Bologna,
Italy. Ghirardacci, 1:121.
Maffeus Ubaldino. Florence,
Italy: *FK*, 131; *T*, 263.
Mahelin de Lameth. France.
Roger, 104–5.
Marco de Vignali. Asti, Italy. *FK*,
132; *T*, 287.
Micheluccio Mussolini. Bologna,
Italy. Ghirardacci, 1:121.
Monsino Sabbatini. Bologna,
Italy. Ghirardacci, 1:121.
Nicolaus de Fontaines. France.
Roger, 229.

Nicolaus de Molis. Surrey, Eng-
land. *FK*, 113; *RLC*, 1:582a.
Nicolaus de Sopron, comes.
Count. Germany. *FK*, 127;
Pr., 4170.
Nicolo Baccilieri. Bologna, Italy.
Ghirardacci, 1:121.
Nicolo Feliciano. Bologna, Italy.
Ghirardacci, 1:120;
Alberti, xx.
Nicolo Rodaldi. Bologna, Italy.
Ghirardacci, 1:121.
Odoninus Rotarius. Asti, Italy.
FK, 123; *T*, 287.
Opizione de Canedoli. Bologna,
Italy. Ghirardacci, 1:121.
Orlando Foscarari. Bologna,
Italy. Ghirardacci, 1:120.
Osteano de Piantavigne. Bolo-
gna, Italy. *FK*, 120.
Otho Carnevelli. Bologna, Italy.
Ghirardacci, 1:121.
Othone Othonelli. Bologna,
Italy. Ghirardacci, 1:121.
Paolo Ligapasseri. Bologna, Italy.
Ghirardacci, 1:121.
Paulus Aemilius de Turchis. Asti,
Italy. *FK*, 130; *T*, 287.
Philippe d'Agneaux. France. *FK*,
79; Blanc., 242.
Phillipus Novellus. Asti, Italy.
FK, 117; *T*, 287.
Pierbello Canetoli. Bologna,
Italy. Ghirardacci, 1:121.
Pietro dell Gasparina. Bologna,
Italy. Ghirardacci, 1:121.
Pietro Alberto Mazzoli. Bologna,
Italy. Ghirardacci, 1:121.
Prencivale Gozzadini. Bologna,
Italy. Ghirardacci, 1:121.
Primirano Sabbatini. Bologna,
Italy. Ghirardacci, 1:121.
Rambertus di Bologna. Bologna,
Italy. *FK*, 89; *T*, 265.
Ran. di Benedetto de Vernaccio.
Pisa, Italy. *FK*, 132; *T*, lxix.
Raymundus de Malacastello.
France. *FK*, 110; *FK*,
74, #54.

Rinaldo Scossaprede. Bologna,
Italy. Ghirardacci, 1 : 121.

Robertus de Floure. France.
FK, 99.

Robertus de Nereford. England.
FK, 116; *T*, xxxi.

Rodaldo Asinelli. Bologna, Italy.
Ghirardacci, 1 : 121.

Rosa Salimbeni. Bologna, Italy.
Ghirardacci, 1 : 121.

Rutilio Ubaldini. Bologna, Italy.
Ghirardacci, 1 : 121.

Salimbene Foscarari. Bologna,
Italy. Ghirardacci, 1 : 120.

Seceh, filius Conradi. Germany.
FK, 126.

Sigerius Visconti. Pisa, Italy. *FK*,
133; *T*, 283.

Sigerus, sacerdos. France. *FK*,
126.

Simon de Montfort. France. *FK*,
115; *RHGF*, 18, 247; *T*, 78.

Solario de Vignali. Asti, Italy.
FK, 132; *T*, 287.

Syrius. Siena, Italy. *FK*, 129;
T, 350.

Tebalduccio Malpigli. Bologna,
Italy. Ghirardacci, 1 : 121.

Testa Rodaldi. Bologna, Italy.
Ghirardacci, 1 : 121.

Thaddeus de Burgomari. Italy.
FK, 91; *T*, 287.

Theobaldus IV de Campania.
Count. Champagne, France.
FK, 92; Pr., 386, 4332; *Lay.*,
1 : 516.

Theodoricus de Isenburg. Wied,
Germany. *FK*, 105; Beyer,
3 : 80–82.

Tilardus. Netherlands. *FK*, 129;
T, 11.

Tolomeo del Gesso. Bologna,
Italy. Ghirardacci, 1 : 121.

Tomaso Plastelli. Bologna, Italy.
Ghirardacci, 1 : 120.

Ubaldus de Tosinghi. Florence,
Italy. *FK*, 130; *T*, 264.

Ugo Fugnani. Bologna, Italy.
Ghirardacci, 1 : 121.

Ugolino de Salomone. Podestà.
Siena, Italy. *FK*, 131; Maconi,
Raccolta, 1, ch 11.

Ugolino di Ugolino Albergati.
Bologna, Italy. Ghirardacci,
1 : 121.

Ugolino Foletti. Bologna, Italy.
Ghirardacci, 1 : 120.

Venturino Bianchi. Bologna,
Italy. Ghirardacci, 1 : 121.

Verdiano de Infangato. Florence,
Italy. *FK*, 105; *T*, 264.

Walter von der Vogelweide. Poet.
Germany. *FK*, 133; *D*, 117.

Wirnt de Grafenberg. Poet.
Grafenberg, Germany.
FK, 101.

Wolfraudus de Nellenburg,
comes. Count. Nellenburg,
Germany. *FK*, 116; *Wirt. UB*,
3 : 103, #631.

APPENDIX IV

COLLECTION COURTOIS

A. de Bellomonte. France. *FK,*
  86; BNL, 17803, #190.
Agapitus de Gazolo. France. *FK,*
  69.
Aicardus Baldenus. France. *FK,*
  85; BNL, 17803, #356.
Anselme d'Alenes. France. *FK,*
  80.
Anselme Ferraudi. France. BNL,
  17803, #362.
Anselmus de Flaicaco. France.
  BNL, 17803, #369.
Anselmus Arbaldus. France. *FK,*
  82; BNL, 17803, #355.
Archembaldus de Murat. France.
  Roger, *Noblesse,* 232.
Archembaldus Barboniensis.
  France. *FK,* 89; BNL, 17803,
  #436.
Archembaldus Menratus. France.
  BNL, 17803, #436.
Arnaldus de Noerio. France.
  BNL, 17803, #129.
Balduinus de Merode. Julich,
  Germany. Roger, *Noblesse,* 231.
Balduinus de Romevilla. France.
  BNL, 17803, #366.
Balduinus de Wiquet. France.
  Roger, *Noblesse,* 235.

Balduinus Neuchini. France.
  BNL, 17803, #321.
Bartholomaeus de Naduche.
  France. Blanc., 445, 486.
Bartholomaeus, decanus. France.
  FK, 83; BNL, 17803, #321.
Benedictus Gracianus. France.
  BNL, 17803, #55.
Berengarius Vincentius. France.
  BNL, 17803, #202, 358.
Bernard de la Lande. France.
  Roger, *Noblesse,* 230.
Bernardus de Bera. France. *FK,*
  87; BNL, 17803, #355.
Bernardus de Stagno. France.
  BNL, 17803, #374.
Bernardus Memisius. France.
  BNL, 17803, #363.
Bernardus Morerius. France.
  BNL, 17803, #54, 354.
Bertonus Scarella. Genoa, Italy.
  BNL, 17803, #314, 343, 389.
Bertrandus de Bourbourg.
  France. Roger, *Noblesse,* 226.
Bertrandus Altrichi. France. *FK,*
  81; BNL, 17803, #374.
Bertrandus Locceis. France.
  BNL, 17803, #59, 260.

Girardus de Claellis. France.
BNL, 17803, #369.
Gobertus de Merceio. Mercey,
France. BNL, 17803, #189,
303.
Gossellus de Hamel. France.
BNL, 17803, #389.
Gosuin de Franqueville.
Netherlands. Roger, *Noblesse*,
229.
Gosvin de Heule. France. Roger,
Noblesse, 104.
Gosvinus, clericus Leodiensis.
Priest. Liège, Belgium. Roger,
Noblesse, 104–5.
Gualterius Guelezin. France.
BNL, 17803, #328.
Gualterus de Lingnea. Hainault,
France. BNL, 17803, #343.
Gualterus de Lucheux. Picardie,
France. Roger, *Noblesse*, 230.
Guattinus, clericus. Priest.
France. BNL, 17803, #328.
Guibertus de Vaiguero. France.
BNL, 17803, #364.
Guido de Altoclocque. France.
FK, 80; BNL, 17803, #321.
Guido de Bosco. France. BNL,
17803, #165.
Guido de Meladuno. Melun,
France. BNL, 17803, #348.
Guido de Vernolio. France. BNL,
17803, #371.
Guillaume d'Arles. France. *FK*,
82; Roger, 226.
Guillaume d'Halluin. France.
Roger, *Noblesse*, 230.
Guillaume de Halud. France.
Roger, *Noblesse*, 104–5.
Guillaume de Hostequerque.
Flanders, Netherlands. Roger,
Noblesse, 230.
Guillaume de Malinguen. France.
Roger, *Noblesse*, 232.
Guillaume de Vieges. France.
Roger, *Noblesse*, 232.
Guillaume Bras de Fer. France.
Roger, *Noblesse*, 227.

Guillelmus de la Warde. France.
BNL, 17803, #343.
Guillelmus de Brya. France.
BNL, 17803, #372.
Guillelmus de Campotocando.
France. BNL, 17803, #402.
Guillelmus de Faiaco. France.
BNL, 17803, #353.
Guillelmus de Freavilla. France.
BNL, 17803, #59, 423.
Guillelmus de Grasse. Provence,
France. BNL, 17803, #362.
Guillelmus de Herbovilla. France.
BNL, 17803, #59, 423.
Guillelmus de Hometo. Con-
stable. Normandy, France.
BNL, 17803, #59, 423.
Guillelmus de Novocastro.
France. BNL, 17803, #357.
Guillelmus de Proseio. France.
BNL, 17803, #58, 205, 392.
Guillelmus de Roseriis. France.
BNL, 17803, #371.
Guillelmus de Tocheto. Toucy,
France. BNL, 17803, #59,
423.
Guillelmus Areletanus. France.
FK, 82; BNL, 17803, #359.
Guillelmus Matthani. France.
BNL, 17803, #59, 423.
Guillelmus Ramisaltus. France.
BNL, 17803, #357.
Guiotus de Toussat. France.
BNL, 17803, #370.
Henri d'Asche. France. *FK*, 83;
Roger, *Noblesse*, 226.
Henricus de Mamesgart. France.
BNL, 17803, #365.
Henricus de Mehalio. France.
BNL, 17803, #348.
Henricus de Newkerke. Ger-
many. Blanc., 438.
Henricus de Sonnature. France.
BNL, 17803, #366.
Henricus de Vendolio. France.
BNL, 17803, #58, 205, 392.
Henricus de Ver. England. BNL,
17803, #368.

Henricus Noef. France. BNL,
17803, #367.
Henricus, abbas de Rassons.
Abbot. France. BNL, 17803,
#353.
Herveus de Aguzandra. France.
FK, 79; BNL, 17803, #203.
Hugo de Bar. France. *FK,* 85;
BNL, 17803, #347.
Hugo de Dona. France. Roger,
Noblesse, 229.
Hugo de Essatis. France. BNL,
17803, #348.
Hugo de Gusnone. France. BNL,
17803, #402.
Hugo de Mailmineyo. France.
BNL, 17803, #128.
Hugo de Monfiguet. France.
Roger, *Noblesse,* 232.
Hugo de S. Salvatore. France.
BNL, 17803, #348.
Hugo Montisfortis. France.
BNL, 17803, #55, 360.
Hugue d'Antoing. France. *FK,*
81; Roger, 226.
Hurto Pas de Fer. France. BNL,
17803, #367.
Jacobus de Clapa. Genoa, Italy.
BNL, 17803, #328.
Jacobus Aspriani. Genoa, Italy.
FK, 83; BNL, 17803, #402.
Jean de Cussy. France. Roger,
Noblesse, 229.
Jean de Custine. France. Roger,
Noblesse, 229.
Jean de Dernen. France. Roger,
Noblesse, 229.
Joannes de Dion. France. Roger,
Noblesse, 229, 333–34.
Jocelinus de Hynul. France. BNL,
17803, #364.
Johannes de Bonoloco. France.
FK, 89; BNL, 17803, #436.
Johannes de Hautmont. France.
BNL, 17803, #353.
Johannes de Morogia. France.
BNL, 17803, #366.
Johannes de Sonneteria. France.
BNL, 17803, #373.

Johannes de Villeriis. France.
BNL, 17803, #58, 205, 392.
Johannes Buro. Genoa, Italy.
BNL, 17803, #203.
Johannes Droarz. France. BNL,
17803, #372.
Justus Andriolus. Genoa, Italy.
FK, 81; BNL, 17803, #128.
Lambertus de Anglucio. France.
FK, 81; BNL, 17803, #368.
Luchinus Corsali. Genoa, Italy.
BNL, 17803, #303, 383.
Martinus de Montolieu. France.
BNL, 17803, #55, 360.
Martinus Calvus. Genoa, Italy.
Blanc., 17, 243, 426.
Masuch. Procurator. France.
BNL, 17803, #190.
Michaelus Gallianus. France.
BNL, 17803, #357.
Milo de Bocher. France. *FK,* 88;
BNL, 17803, #165.
Milo de Sales. France. BNL,
17803, #368.
Milo de Vernolio. France. BNL,
17803, #164, 421.
Nicolaus Bessaltus. France. *FK,*
88; BNL, 17803, #374.
Odo de Agia. France. *FK,* 79;
BNL, 17803, #203.
Odo de Rochederrain. France.
Roger, *Noblesse,* 97–98.
Odo de Ronkeroles. France.
Blanc. 450–51.
Pancetus Astaldus. France. *FK,*
83; Roger, *Noblesse,* 226.
Perinus de Sica. France. BNL,
17803, #365.
Perrinus de Claviaco. France.
BNL, 17803, #373.
Petrus de Groc. France. BNL,
17803, #436; *Lay.,* 223b,
291a.
Petrus de Matrone. France. BNL,
17803, #363.
Petrus de Montosul. France.
BNL, 17803, #362.
Petrus de Pontis. France. BNL,
17803, #362.

Petrus de Roceio. France. Roger, *Noblesse,* 236.

Petrus de Spenasso. Espinasse, France. BNL, 17803, #347.

Petrus Barsilionensis. France. *FK,* 85; BNL, 17803, #355.

Petrus Divitisburgi. France. BNL, 17803, #59, 423.

Petrus Gaugiran. France. Roger, *Noblesse,* 230.

Petrus Gugeranus. France. BNL, 17803, #359.

Petrus Leidetus. France. BNL, 17803, #363.

Petrus Pene. France. BNL, 17803, #54, 354.

Philippe de la Woestine. France. Roger, *Noblesse,* 231.

Philippe de Grimberghe. Flanders, Netherlands. Roger, *Noblesse,* 230.

Philippe de Nantolio. Nanteuil, France. Roger, *Noblesse,* 232.

Placel de Berghes. France. *FK,* 87; Roger, *Noblesse,* 226.

Radulfus de Alimonte. France. *FK,* 80; BNL, 17803, #189, 303.

Radulfus de Bosco. France. BNL, 17803, #128.

Radulfus de Marolio. France. BNL, 17803, #58, 205, 392.

Radulfus Bengeiaci. France. *FK,* 87; BNL, 17803, #164, 421.

Raimundus de Auris. France. *FK,* 83; BNL, 17803, #360.

Raimundus Aigardus. France. *FK,* 80; BNL, 17803, #203, 358.

Raimundus Guascan. France. BNL, 17803, #357.

Raimundus Lowetus. France. BNL, 17803, #356.

Rasse de Gavre. France. Roger, *Noblesse,* 230.

Raynaldus de Beffreio. France. *FK,* 86; BNL, 17803, #164, 421.

Renardus de Ba——io. France.

FK, 84; BNL, 17803, #189, 303.

Renatus de Choisello. Choiseul, France. BNL, 17803, #164, 421.

Rigaud Elavat. France. *FK,* 88; Roger, *Noblesse,* 226.

Robert de Grimonville. France. Roger, *Noblesse,* 230.

Robert de Royville. France. Roger, *Noblesse,* 232.

Robertus de Boeriis. France. *FK,* 88; BNL, 17803, #348.

Robertus de Esnaville. France. BNL, 17803, #60, 317.

Robertus de Hedovilla. France. BNL, 17803, #58, 205, 392.

Robertus de Herriceio. France. BNL, 17803, #402.

Robertus de Hervileio. France. BNL, 17803, #58, 205, 392.

Robertus de Maulde. France. Roger, *Noblesse,* 231.

Robertus de Pontisvilla. France. BNL, 17803, #54, 423.

Robertus de Pratellis. France. BNL, 17803, #59, 423.

Robertus de Quesneto. France. BNL, 17803, #383.

Robertus de Vic. France. Roger, *Noblesse,* 235.

Robertus de Vitreio. France. BNL, 17803, #436.

Rolandus de Jaranta. France. BNL, 17803, #347.

Rolandus Guauttaz. France. BNL, 17803, #356.

Rollandus de Aqueriis. France. *FK,* 81; BNL, 17803, #362.

Rufus de Varagna. France. BNL, 17803, #129.

S. Izembertus. Procurator. France. BNL, 17803, #190.

Safic de Gazolo. France. *FK,* 69.

Salvagius Bioni. Genoa, Italy. *FK,* 88; BNL, 17803, #125, 165, 204, 349.

Salvagius Brioni. France. BNL, 17803, #164, 421.

Simon de Breville. France. Roger,
Noblesse, 227.
Simon Arnulfus. France. *FK,* 82;
BNL, 17803, #24, 125, 349.
Simon Calitus. France. BNL,
17803, #356.
Stephanus de S. Albano. France.
FK, 80; BNL, 17803, #347.
Stephanus Bernalt. France. *FK,*
87; BNL, 17803, #128.
Thad. de Gazolo. France. BNL,
17803, #193.
Theodoricus de Hamayde.
France. Roger, *Noblesse,* 231.

Thomas de Bosreyo. France.
BNL, 17803, #364.
Ugo Scarella. Genoa, Italy. BNL,
17803, #328.
Ulricus de Verreriis. France.
BNL, 17803, #365.
W. de Beffreio. France. *FK,* 86;
BNL, 17803, #164, 421.
Willelmus Fadranus. France.
BNL, 17803, #374.
Willelmus Garnerius. France.
BNL, 17803, #362.
Willelmus Porcellus. BNL,
17803, #363, 374.

BIBLIOGRAPHY

Manuscripts

Bologna. Archivio di Stato. (ASB)
    Busta strumenti e scritture
    Demanio S. Petri, 21/208, no. 20
    Registro Grosso (RG)
Florence. Archivio di Stato. (ASF)
    Diplomatico
        Olivetani di Pistoia
        Pistoia
        Volterra
Lucca. Archivio arcivescovile.
    A + 1
Lucca. Archivio di Stato. (ASL)
    Notulario
    San Pancrazio
    San Ponziano
Paris. Bibliothèque Nationale. Lat. 17803. (Paris. BNL)
Palermo. Archivio di Stato (della Catena)
    Ms 6, Tabulario della Chiesa della Magione
    Ms 7, Privilegi
Syracuse University. Ranke Manuscripts.
    Ms 59 "Cronica della città di Venezia sin all'anno MCCCCXLI"
    Ms 78 "Cronicae Venetorum serenissimi Andrea Dandulo"
Vatican. Archivio Segreto.
    Registers (RV)
        Innocent III (1198–1216) RV 4-8
        Honorius III (1216–1227) RV 9-13
        Gregory IX (1227–1241) RV 14-19.

Primary Sources

NARRATIVES

Abulfeda. *Géographie d'Aboulfida*. Trans. M. Reinaud. 3 vols. Paris, 1848.
Abu Shamah. *Livre des deux jardins. RHC, Or.*, 5.
Aegidius Aureae Vallis. *Gesta pontificum Leodiensium. T,* 10.
Albericus Trium-Fontium. *Chronica. RHGF,* 18.
———. *Chronicon. T,* 92–96.
Albertus Stadensis. *Chronicon. T,* 179.
Albicius, Bartholomaeus. *Liber Conformitatum S. Francisci cum Christo. T,* 267–69.
Ambroise. *The Crusade of Richard the Lion-Heart.* New York, 1941.
Ampzing, Samuel. *Beschrijving e end lof der Stad Haerlem in Holland. T,* 41–48.
Añales Toledanos I. T, 211.
Andreas Dandulus. *Chronicon Venetum. T,* 261–62.
Annales Ceccanenses. T, 238.
Annales Claustroneoburgenses. T, 152–55.
Annales de Waverleia. RS, Annales Monastici, 2.
Annales de Wigornia. RS, 36:4.
Annales Garstensis. MGHSS, 9.
Annales Marbacenses. T, 181–82.
Annales Mellicenses. T, 192–93.
Annales Prioratus de Dunstaplia. RS, Annales Monastici, 3.
Annales S. Rudberti Salisburgenses. T, 184–86.
Annales Schefflarienses minores. T, 183.
Annali Genovesi di Caffaro e de' suoi Continuatori. 4 vols. Rome, 1890–1929.
Anonyme, Prisonnier au Chatelet. *Chronique de France et des croisades. T,* 131–34.
Anonymous Laudunensis. *Chronicon. T,* 90–91.
Auctarium Mortui Maris ad Sigebertum Gemblacensem. T, 91–92.
Balduinus Ninoviensis. *Chronicon. T,* 12.
Bayrische Chronik. T, 198–201.
Bernardus Iterius. *Chronicon S. Martialis. T,* 81, 337–38.
Biondo, Flavio. *Historiarum Decades. T,* 274–80.
S. Bonaventura. *Vita s. Francisci. T,* 249–51.
Bongars, J. *Gesta Dei per Francos.* Hannover, 1611.
Brut j Tywysogion. T, 60–62.
Burchardus Biberacensis. *Chronicon. T,* 155–58; 339–40.
Caesarius Heisterbacensis. *Dialogus miraculorum. T,* 162–75.
———. *Homiliae. T,* 175–79.
———. *Octo libri miraculorum. T,* 344–45.
Chronica comitum et principum de Clivis et Marca Gelriae, Juliae, et Montium. T, 345–46.
Chronica de Mailros. T, 67, 336.
Chronica Fratris Salimbene de Adam, ordinus minorum. MGHSS, 32.
Chronica regiae Coloniensis. T, 145–47, 147–52, 160–61.
Chronica Tornacensis. T, 40.

Le croniche de Viterbo. T, 247.
Chronicon Britannicum. T, 135.
Chronicon de Dieulacres. T, 335.
Chronicon Montis Sereni. MGHSS, 23.
Chronicon Petroburgense. T, 63.
Chronicon Rothomagense. T, 129.
Chronicon S. Medardi Suessionensis. T, 127.
Chronicon Sanpetrinum. T, 191.
Chronicon Tolosani canonici Faventini. Vol. 6 of *Documenti di Storia Italiana.* Florence, 1876.
Chronicon Turonensis. T, 86–90.
Chronicon viconiense. MGHSS, 24; *T,* 18–20.
Chronique d'Ernoul et des Bernard le trésorier. Ed. L. de Mas Latrie. Paris, 1871.
Chronique rimée de Floreffe. T, 25.
Chroniques de France. T, 130–31.
Chronographi Senenses. T, 284–85.
Cipolla, Carlo. "Una narrazione bobbiese sulla presa di Damietta nel 1219." *Archivio Storico Italiano* 31 (1904): 5–14.
Clausson, Pehr. *Norske Kongers Chronica. T,* 323.
Cono, Prepositus Lausannensis. *Notae. T,* 161.
De Itinere Frisonum. SS, 59–70.
Delisle, Leopold. "Fragments de l'histoire de Gonesse." *BEOC* 20 (1859): 247–77.
Edmundus Dynterus. *Chronica Ducum Lotharingiae. T,* 25–26.
Emo. *Chronicon. MGHSS,* 23.
L'Éstoire d'Éracles empereur. RHC, Oc., 2.
Fragmentum de captione Damiatae. SS, 169–202.
Gabrieli, Francesco. *Arab Historians of the Crusades.* Berkeley, Calif., 1969.
Georgii Acropolitae annales. Vol. 29 of *Scriptorum Historiae Byzantinae.* Ed. J. Bekker. Bonn, 1836.
Gervase of Canterbury. *Gesta Regum. RS,* 73:2.
Gesta abbatum Bergensium. T, 346–47.
Gesta abbatum Orti S. Mariae. T, 10–11.
Gesta crucigerorum Rhenanorum. SS, 29–56.
Gesta Frisiorum. T, 12–18.
Gesta obsidionis Damiate. SS, 73–115.
Gesta Sanctorum Villanensium. MGHSS, 25.
Gesta Trevirorum continuata. MGHSS, 24.
Guillelmus Andrensis. Annales. T, 330.
———. *Chronicon Andrense. MGHSS,* 24.
Guillelmus Brito. *Historia Philippi Augusti. T,* 78–80.
Hadrianus Junius. *Batavia. T,* 35–36.
Hermannus Altahensis. *Annales. T,* 184.
Herold, Johannes. *Continuatio belli sacri. T,* 201–7.
Histoire des rois d'Engletierre. T, 78.
History of the Patriarchs of the Egyptian Church. Trans. A. Khater and O. H. E. KHS-Burmeister. 4 vols. Cairo, 1943–74.

Ibn al Furat. *Ayyubids, Mamluks and Crusaders*. 2 vols. Cambridge, 1971.
Jacobus de Vitriaco. *Historia Iherusolimitana*. In *Gesta Dei per Francos*. Ed. Jacques Bongars. Hannover, 1611.
―――. *The Historia Occidentalis of Jacques de Vitry*. Ed. John Hinnebusch. Freiburg, 1972.
Jacobus de Voragine. *Chronicon Ianuense. T,* 251.
Johannes A. Leidis. *Chronicon Belgicum. T,* 36–37.
Johannes de Beka. *Historia veterum episcoporum ultraiactensium. T,* 21.
Johannes de Garlandia. *De triumphis ecclesie. T,* 59.
Johannes de Tulbia. *De Domino Iohanne Rege Ierusalem. SS,* 119–40.
Johannes de Ypra. *Chronicon S. Bertini. T,* 23–24.
Johannes Mariana. *De rebus Hispaniae. T,* 214–15.
Die Jüngere Hochmeisterchronik. T, 26–34.
Klerk, Ian. *Kronijk van Holland. T,* 21–22.
Liber duelli Christiani in obsidione Damiate. SS, 143–66.
Liber fundationis monasterii Zwetlensis. T, 340–44.
Lucas Tudensis. *Chronicon mundi. T,* 212–13.
Magnum Chronicon Belgicum. T, 35.
al-Makrīzī. *Expeditionibus, a Graecis Francisque adversus Dimyatham ab A.C. 708 ad 1221 susceptis*. Ed. Henricus Hamaker. Amsterdam, 1823.
―――. *Histoire d'Égypte*. Trans. E. Blochet. Paris, 1908.
Malespina, Rigordano. *Istoria Fiorentina. RISS,* 8.
Marangone, Bernardo. *Croniche di Pisa. T,* 270–72.
Marcus. *Chronicon de Gestis Hungarorum. T,* 232–33.
Matthew of Westminster. *Flores Historiarum. T,* 69–70.
Matthew Paris. *Chronica Majora*. 7 vols. *RS,* 57.
―――. *Historia minor Anglorum. T,* 54–59.
Le Ménestrel de Reims. T, 110–18.
Meyer, Paul. "La prise de Damiette en 1219: Relation inédite en Provençal." *BEOC* 38 (1877): 497–571.
Monachus Patavinus. *De rebus Insubium. T,* 248–49.
Mousket, Philippe. *Chronique rimée. T,* 6–9.
Neidhart von Reuenthal. *Neidharts lieder*. Ed. Moriz Haupt. Leipzig, 1923.
Nicole le Huen. *Voyages, guerres, croisées et expeditions faites en la terre sainte. T,* 136–37.
Österreichische Reimchronik. T, 187–90.
Oliverus Scholasticus. *Die Schriften des kölner Domscholasters, späteren Bischofs von Paderborn und Kardinal-Bischofs von S. Sabina*. Ed. Hermann Hoogeweg. Tübingen, 1894.
Paulus Puteolanus. *Satyrica. T,* 259–61.
Peters, Edward. *Christian Society and the Crusades, 1198–1229*. Philadelphia, 1971.
Petrus de Harenthal. *Catalogus abbatum Floreffensium. T,* 22–23.
Pierre d'Esrey. *Faits et gestes du preux Godefroi de Bouillon. T,* 137–41.
Ptolomey of Lucca. *Die Annalen des Tholomaeus von Lucca. MGHSS, Rerum Germanicarum*, n.s., vol. 8. Berlin, 1955.
Pugliola, Bartolomeo. *Chronica di Bologna. T,* 265–66.
Radulphus de Coggeshall. *Chronicon Anglicanum. RS,* 66.

Reinaud, Joseph. *Estraits des historiens arabes, relatifs aux guerres des croisades, ouvrages formant, d'après les écrivains musulmans, un récit suivi des guerres saintes.* New ed. Paris, 1829.

———. "Histoire de la sixième croisade et de la pris de Damiate, d'après les écrivains arabes." *Journal Asiatique* 8 (1826): 18–40.

Reinerius. *Annales. MGHSS*, 16.

Reinerius Leodiensis. *Chronica. T,* 329–30.

Renerius Snoius. *Rerum Batavorum libri XIII. T,* 38.

Robertus Abolant. *Chronologia Autissiodorensis. T,* 81–86.

Robertus Autissiodorenesis. *Historia episcoporum Autissiodorensium. RHGF,* 18.

Robertus de Monte. *Cronica. T,* 77.

Röhricht, Reinhold. *Quinti belli sacri scriptores minores.* Geneva, 1879.

———. *Testimonia minora de quinto bello sacro.* Geneva, 1882.

Roger of Wendover. *Flores historiarum. RS,* 84.

Rogerius de Hoveden. *Cronica. T,* 52.

Ruy de Piña. *Chronico do muito alto. T,* 215–25.

Ryccardus de Sancto Germano. *Chronica. RISS,* new series, 7:2.

Sächsische Weltchronik. T, 180–81.

Saga Hakonar Konungs Hakonarsonar. T, 321–22.

Sanuto, Marino. *Liber secretorum fidelium crucis super Terrae Sanctae recuperatione . . . Gesta Dei per Francos.* Ed. J. Bongars. Hannover, 1611.

Sercambi, Giovanni. *Storia di Lucca. T,* 349–50.

Sigebertus Gemblacensis. *Continuatio Bergensis. MGHSS,* 6.

Sigismundus Tizius. *Chronicon. T,* 350.

Stephanus de Borbone. *Sermo. T,* 118–19.

Thomas Cantipratensis. *Bonum universale de Apibus. T,* 119–26.

Thomas de Celano. *Vita prima S. Francisci. T,* 246–47.

———. *Vita secunda S. Francisci.* Quaracchi, 1923.

Thomas Spalato. *Ex Thomae historia pontificium Salonitanorum et Spalatinorum. MGHSS,* 29.

Trithemius, Johannes. *Chronicon Hirsaugiense. T,* 195–96.

Trivet, Nicholas. *Chronicon. T,* 67–68.

Turzanus, Franciscus. *De rebus memorabilibus Astensium. T,* 286–88.

Villani, Giovanni. *Cronica.* Florence, 1844.

Vincentius Bellovacensis. *Memoriale. T,* 96–97.

———. *Speculum historiale. T,* 97–110.

Vita Sancti Engeberti. T, 159–60.

Wachtendorp, Caspar. *Oude Hollandsche Geschiednissen of te corte Rym Kronyck. T,* 39–40.

Walter of Coventry. *Memoriale.* 2 vols. *RS,* 58.

Walterus, Praepositus Marchtalensis. *Historia Monasterii Marchtalensis. MGHSS,* 24.

Waltherus de Hemingburgh. *Chronicon. T,* 70.

Watt, Ioachim von. *Chronik der Aebte des Klosters St.-Gallen. T,* 196–98.

Wilhelmus Egmundanus. *Chronicon. T,* 20.

DOCUMENTS

Abbazia di Montevergine. *Regesto delle pergamene.* vol. 2 only. Rome, 1957.

Archives historiques de Poitou. 3 vols. Poitiers, 1872.

Armorial Général de France. Ed. Charles d'Hozier. 2 vols. Dijon, 1875–76.

Beauville, Victor de. *Receuil des documents inédits concernant la Picardie.* 5 vols. Paris, 1860–82.

Böhmer, Johann F. *Acta Imperii Selecta.* 1870. Reprint. Aalen, 1967.

Bracton, Henry de. *Bracton's Note Books.* 3 vols. 1887. Reprint. Littleton, Col., 1983.

Le carte della prevostura d'Oulx. BSSS, 45. Pinerolo, 1908.

Le carte dell'abbazia di Santa Croce di Sassovivo. 7 vols. Florence, 1973.

Cartulaire de l'abbaye de St. Étienne de Baigne. Ed. Paul F. Cholet. Angoulême, 1867.

Cartulaire de l'église du S. Sepulchre. Paris, 1849.

• *Cartulaire de Marmoutier pour le Dunois.* Ed. Louis Émile Mahille. Paris, 1874.

Cartulaire des abbayes de St. Pierre de la Couture et de St. Pierre de Solesmes. Le Mans, 1881.

Catalogue of the Records of the Order of St. John of Jerusalem in the Royal Malta Library. Comp. A. Zammit Gambarretta et al. Malta, 1964–.

Il Chartarium Bertonense ed altri documenti del comune di Tortona (943–1346). BSSS, 31. Pinerolo, 1909.

"Chartes de départ et de rétour des comtes de Dampierre-en-Astenois." *Archives de l'Orient Latin,* Documents. 2 (1884): 184–207.

Cockersand Abbey. *The Chartulary of Cockersand Abbey of the Premonstratensian Order.* 3 vols. Manchester, 1898–1909.

Codex Diplomaticus Hungariae. Ed. György Fejér. 11 vols. Buda, 1829–44.

Codex diplomaticus ordinis sanctae Mariae Teutonicorum. Ed. J. H. Hennes. 2 vols. Mainz, 1845–61.

Codex diplomaticus Salemitanus: Urkundenbuch der Cisterzienserabtei Salem. Ed. F. von Weech. 3 vols. Karlsruhe, 1883–95.

Codex Wangianus: Urkundenbuch des Hochstiftes Trent. Fontes Rerum Austriacarum, Part 2, 5. Vienna, 1852.

Codice Diplomatico Barese. 19 vols. Bari, 1897–1971.

Codice Diplomatico Brindisino (492–1299). Ed. G. M. Monti. 2 vols. Trani, 1940–64.

Conciliorum Oecumenicorum Decreta. Ed. Joseph Alberigo et al. 3d ed. Bologna, 1973.

Constitutiones concilii quarti Lateranensis una cum commentariis glossatorum. Ed. Antonio García y García. Vatican City, 1981.

Delaville le Roulx, Joseph. *Cartulaire général de l'ordre des hospitaliers de S. Jean de Jerusalem.* 4 vols. Munich, 1980.

Delisle, Leopold V. *Catalogue des actes de Philippe-Auguste. Paris, 1856.*

Demandt, Karl. *Regesten der Grafen von Katzenelnbogen.* Wiesbaden, 1953.

Divaeus, Petrus. *Opera varia.* Louvain, 1757.

Dobenecker, Otto. *Regesta diplomatica necnon epistolaria historiae Thurigiae.* Jena, 1896.

Documenti del commercio veneziano nei secoli XI–XIII. Ed. R. Morozzo della Rocca and A. Lombardo. Rome, 1940.

Documenti di storia italiana. 17 vols. Florence, 1867–1956.

Ennen, Leonhard. *Quellen zur Geschichte der Stadt Köln.* 6 vols. Cologne, 1860–79.

Epistolae selectae saeculi XIII. Ed. Carl Rodenberg. 3 vols. *MGH. Ep.* Saeculi XIII.

Fourmont, Hyacinthe D. de. *L'Ouest aux Croisades.* 3 vols. Nantes, 1864–67.

Great Britain. Curia Regis. *Rolls of the Justices in Eyre . . . Gloucestershire.* London, 1940.

Great Britain. Curia Regis. *Rolls of the Justices in Eyre . . . Lincolnshire, 1218–19.* London, 1934.

Great Britain. Curia Regis. *Rolls of the Justices in Eyre . . . Yorkshire.* London, 1937.

Great Britain. Curia Regis. *Somersetshire Pleas (Civil and Criminal) from the Rolls of the Itinerant Justices.* 2 vols. London, 1897–19--.

Great Britain. Exchequer. *Liber Feodorum. The Book of Fees.* 3 vols. London, 1920–31.

Great Britain. Public Record Office. *Calendarium genealogicum.* Ed. Charles Roberts. 2 vols. London, 1865.

Great Britain. Public Record Office. *Patent Rolls of the Reign of Henry III.* 6 vols. London, 1901–13. Vol. 1 only.

Great Britain. Record Commission. *Rotuli litterarum clausarum.* 2 vols. London, 1833–44.

Guidi, P., and O. Parenti. *Regesta del capitolo di Lucca.* 4 vols. Rome, 1937.

Hampe, Karl. *Die Aktenstücke zum Frieden von S. Germano.* Berlin, 1926.

Hertel, Gustav. *Urkundenbuch der Stadt Magdeburg.* 3 vols. 1892–96. Reprint. Aalen, 1975–78.

Holtzmann, Walther. "Papst, Kaiser, und Normannenurkunden aus Unteritalien." *QFAIB* 36 (1956): 1–85.

Honorius III. *Opera omnia.* Ed. C. A. Horoy. 5 vols. Paris, 1879–82.

Huillard-Bréholles, Jean L. A. *Historia Diplomatica Frederici Secundi.* 6 vols. Paris, 1852–61.

Innocent III. *Opera Omnia. PL,* 214–17.

Jacobus de Vitriaco. *Die exempla des Jacob von Vitry.* Ed. Goswin Frenken. Munich, 1914.

———. *The Exempla, or Illustrative Stories from the Sermones Vulgares of Jacques de Vitry.* Ed. T. F. Crane, London, 1880.

———. *Lettres de Jacques de Vitry.* Ed. R. B. C. Huygens. Leiden, 1960.

———. *Medieval Sermon Stories.* Philadelphia, 1901.

Kohler, Charles. "Chartes de l'abbaye de Notre Dame de la Vallée de Josaphat en Terre Sainte." *ROL* 7 (1899): 108–222.

Krühne, Max. *Urkundenbuch der Klöster der Grafschaft Mansfeld.* Halle, 1888.

Lalore, Charles. *Collection des principaux cartulaires du diocèse de Troyes.* 7 vols. Paris, 1875–90.

Lang, Karl Heinrich. *Regesta, sive rerum Boicarum autographa.* 14 vols. Munich, 1822–54.

Layettes du trésor des chartes. 5 vols. Paris, 1863–1909.

The Letters of Pope Innocent III Concerning England and Wales. Ed. C. R. Cheney. Oxford, 1967.

Liber focorum districtus Pistorii. Rome, 1956.

Maconi, Giuseppe. *Raccolta de documenti storici.* Livorno, 1876.

Martène, Edmond. *Collectio nova veterum scriptorum et monumentorum moralium, historicorum, dogmaticorum, etc.* Rothomagi, 1700.

Mecklenburgisches Urkundenbuch. 25 vols. Schwerin, 1863.

Mitis, Oskar. *Urkundenbuch zur Geschichte der Babenberger in Österreich.* Vienna, 1950.

Mittelrheinische Regesten, oder chronologische Zusammenstellung des Quellen Material für die Geschichte der Territorien der beiden Regierungsbezirke Coblenz und Trier. Ed. Adam Goerz. 4 vols. Cologne, 1876–86.

Mongitore, Antonio. *Monumenta historica sacrae domus mansionis SS. Trinitatis Militaris Ordinis Theutonicorum urbis Panormi.* Palermo, 1721.

Monumenta Boica. 60 vols. Munich, 1763–1912.

Müller, Giuseppe. *Documenti sulle relazioni delle città toscane coll'oriente cristiano e coi turchi.* 1879. Reprint. Rome, 1966.

Oldenburgisches Urkundenbuch. Oldenburg, 1914.

Overmann, Alfred. *Urkundenbuch der Erfurter Stifter und Klöster.* 3 vols. Magdeburg, 1926–34.

Pauli, Sebastiano. *Codice diplomatico del sacro militare ordine gerosolimitano.* 2 vols. Lucca, 1733–37.

Philip of Oxford. "*Ordinacio* de predicacione S. Crucis in Anglia." *SS,* 3–26.

Pitra, Jean Baptiste. *Analecta novissima spicilegii Solesmensis.* 2 vols. Paris, 1885–88.

Pommersches Urkundenbuch. Ed. R. Klempin. 9 vols. Stettin, 1868–1962.

Pontefract Priory. *The Chartulary of St. John of Pontefract.* 2 vols. Leeds, 1899–1902.

Précis de l'histoire d'Egypte par divers historiens et archéologues. Cairo, 1932.

Prophetia Filii Agap. SS, 214–22.

Prophetie de Hannan le Fil Ysaac. SS, 205–13.

La Prophetie le Fil Agap. SS, 223–28.

Quantin, Maximilien. *Recueil de pièces pour faire suite au cartulaire générale de l'Yonne.* Auxerre, 1873.

Quellen der westfälischen Geschichte. Ed. Johann Seibertz. 3 vols. Arnsberg, 1857–69.

Recueil des actes de Philippe Auguste, roi de France. 3 vols. Paris, 1913–66.

Regesta archiepiscopatus Magdeburgensis. Ed. Georg von Mülverstedt. 3 vols. Magdeburg, 1876–86.

Regesta Archiepiscoporum Salisburgensium inde ab anno MCVI usque annum MCCXLVI. Ed. Andreas von Meiller. Vienna, 1866.

Regesta Chartarum Italiae. Rome, 1907–.

Regesta Historica-Diplomatica Ordinis S. Mariae Theutonicorum, 1198–1525. 2 vols. Göttingen, 1948.

Regesta Honorii Papae III. Ed. Petrus Pressutti. 2 vols. 1888. Reprint. Hildesheim, 1978.

Regesta Imperii. Ed. J. F. Böhmer. New ed. Graz, 1950–.

Regesta Pontificum Romanorum. Ed. August Potthast. 2 vols. Berlin, 1874–75.

Regesta Regni Hierosolymitani. Ed. R. Röhricht. 2 vols. New York, 1960.

Die Regesten der Erzbischöfe von Köln im Mittelalter. 4 vols. Bonn, 1901–15.

Regesten der Markgrafen von Baden und Hachberg, 1050–1515. Innsbruck, 1900–.

Regesten zur Geschichte der Markgrafen und Herzoge Österreichs. Ed. Andreas von Meiller. Vienna, 1850.

Les regestes des actes du patriarchat de Constantinople. Istanbul, 1932–.

Die Register Innocenz' III. Ed. O. Hageneder and A. Haidacher. 2 vols. to date. Graz, 1968–79.

Regestum Senense. Ed. Fedor Schneider. Rome, 1901.

Regestum Volaterranum. Ed. Fedor Schneider. Rome, 1907.

Registres de Gregoire IX. Ed. L. Auvray. 4 vols. Paris, 1890–1955.

Registri dei Cardinali Ugolino d'Ostia e Ottaviano degli Ubaldini. Ed. Guido Levi. Rome, 1890.

Royal and other Historical Letters illustrative of the Reign of Henry III. Ed. W. W. Shirley. 2 vols. London, 1862–66.

Rüthning, Gustav. *Urkundenbuch von Süd-Oldenburg.* Oldenburg, 1930.

Rutebeuf. *Onze poèmes concernant la croisade.* Paris, 1946.

Rymer, Thomas. *Foedera, conventiones, litterae et cujuscumque generis acta publica.* 20 vols. London, 1704–35.

Sacrae antiquitatis monumenta, historica, dogmatica, diplomatica. Ed. Karl Ludwig Hugo. Vol. 1. Stivagii, 1725.

Savioli, L. V. *Annali Bolognesi.* 3 vols. in 6. Bassano, 1784–91.

Schlesisches Urkundenbuch. 2 vols. Graz, 1963–77.

Schlögl, Waldemar. *Die Traditionen und Urkunden des Stifts Diessen, 1114–1362.* Munich, 1967.

Siena. Archivio di Stato. *Inventario delle pergamene conservate nel diplomatica dell'anno 736 all'anno 1250.* Siena, 1908.

Sudendorf, Hans F. *Registrum, oder merkwürdige Urkunden für die deutsche Geschichte.* 3 pts. Jena, 1849–54.

Svenskt Diplomtarium. 3 vols. Stockholm, 1875–84.

Table chronologique des chartes et diplomes imprimées concernant l'histoire de la Belgique. Ed. A. Wauters. 11 vols. Brussels, 1866–46.

Table chronologique des chartes et diplomes imprimées concernant l'histoire de la Belgique. Ed. A. Wauters. 11 vols. Brussels, 1866–1946.

Tables de Fonteneau. Poitiers, 1839.

Tabulae Ordinis Theutonici. Ed. E. Strehlke. 1869. Reprint. Toronto, 1975.

Talmont, France (Vendée). Abbaye de Talmont. *Cartulaire de l'abbaye de Talmond.* Poitiers, 1873.

Theiner, Augustin. *Vetera monumenta slavorum meridionalium historiae.* 2 vols. Rome, 1863.

Die Urkunden des Deutsch-Ordens Central-Archives zu Wien. Ed. Eduard von Pettenegg. Prague, 1887.

Urkundenbuch der Stadt Göttingen bis zum Jahre 1400. 2 vols. Hannover, 1863–67.

Urkundenbuch der Stadt Halle, ihrer Stifter und Klöster. Ed. Arthur Bierbach. 2 vols. Halle, 1954–57.

Urkundenbuch der Stadt Hildesheim. 8 vols. Ed. Richard Döbner. Hildesheim, 1881–1901.

Urkundenbuch des Herzogtums Steiermark. Ed. Hans Perchegger and O. Dungern. 3 vols. Graz, 1875–1949.

Urkundenbuch des Hochstifts Hildesheim und seiner Bischöfe. Ed. K. Janicke. 1896. Reprint. Osnabrück, 1965.

Urkundenbuch des Hochstifts Merseburg. Halle, 1899.

Urkundenbuch des Klosters Berge bei Magdeburg. Ed. H. Holstein. Halle, 1879.

Urkundenbuch des Klosters Pforte. Ed. Paul Boehme. Halle, 1893.

Urkundenbuch des Klosters Unser Lieben Frauen zu Magdeburg. Halle, 1878.

Urkundenbuch des Landes ob der Enns. 9 vols. Vienna, 1852–1906.

Urkundenbuch für die Geschichte des Niederrheins oder des Erzstifts Köln. 4 vols. in 5. Düsseldorf, 1840–58.

Urkundenbuch zur Geschichte der Mittelrheinischen Territorien. Ed. H. Beyer. 3 vols. Hildesheim, 1974.

Urkundenbuch zur Landes und Rechtsgeschichte des Herzogthums Westfalen. Ed. Johann Seibertz. 3 vols. Arnsberg, 1839–54.

Veterum Scriptorum Monumenta. Ed. Edmund Martène and Ursinus Durand. 9 vols. 1724. Reprint. New York, 1968.

Winkelmann, Eduard. *Acta imperii inedita saec. 13 et 14.* 2 vols. Innsbruck, 1880–85.

Wirtembergisches Urkundenbuch. 11 vols. Stuttgart, 1849–1913.

Zeerleder, Karl. *Urkunden für die Geschichte der Stadt Bern.* 3 vols. Bern, 1853–54.

Secondary Sources

Abulafia, David. "Count Henry of Malta and His Mediterranean Activities, 1203–1230." In *Medieval Malta: Studies on Malta before the Knights,* ed. Anthony Luttrell, 104–25. London, 1975.

———. "Crocuses and Crusaders: San Gimignano, Pisa, and the Kingdom of Jerusalem." In *Outremer,* ed. B. Z. Kedar, H. E. Mayer, and R. C. Smail, 227–43. Jerusalem, 1982.

———. "Invented Italians in the Courtois Charters." In *Crusade and Settlement,* ed. Peter Edbury, 135–43. Cardiff, 1985.

Ahmad, Hilmy M. "Some Notes on Arabic Historiography during the Zengid and Ayyubid Periods (521/1127–648/1250)." In *Historians of the Middle East,* ed. Bernard Lewis and P. M. Holt, 79–97. London, 1962.

Alberti, Leandro. *Historie di Bologna.* 1531. Reprint. Bologna, 1970.

Alexander, James W. *Ranulf of Chester: A Relic of the Conquest.* Athens, Ga., 1983.

Alphandéry, Paul. *La Chrétienté et l'idée de croisade.* 2 vols. Paris, 1954–59.

Altschul, Michael. *A Baronial Family in Medieval England: The Clares, 1217–1314.* Baltimore, 1965.

Andrea, Alfred J. "Walter, Archdeacon of London, and the 'Historia Occidentalis' of Jacques de Vitry." *Church History* 50 (1981): 141–51.

Arbois de Jubainville, M. H. *Histoire des ducs et des comtes de Champagne.* 5 vols. Paris, 1863.

Arnold, W. "Beruf." In *LfTK* 2:274–75.

Ashtor, E. *A Social and Economic History of the Near East in the Middle Ages.* London, 1976.

Baldwin, John W. *Masters, Princes, and Merchants: The Social Views of Peter the Chanter and His Circle.* 2 vols. Princeton, N.J., 1970.

Baratier, Edouard. "Une prédication de la croisade à Marseilles en 1224." In *Économies et sociétés au moyen âge: Mélanges offerts à Edouard Perroy,* ed. 690–99. Paris, 1973.

Barbour, N. "The Emperor Frederick II, King of Jerusalem and Sicily, and His Relations with the Moslems." In *Orientalia Hispanica: sive studia F. M. Pareja,* ed. J. M. Barral, 1:77–95. Leiden, 1974.

Barthélemy, A. de. "Les pèlerins champenois en Palestine, 1097–1249." *ROL* 1 (1893): 354–80.

Bautier, Robert-Henri. "La collection de chartes de croisade dite 'Collection Courtois.'" Académie des inscriptions et belles-lettres. *Comptes rendus des séances de l'année* (1956): 382–86.

Becquet, Jean. "La première crise de l'ordre de Grandmont." *Bulletin de la société historique et archéologique du Limousin* 87 (1958–60): 283–324.

Bertaux, E. "Les Français d'Outremer en Apulie et en Epire au temps des Hohenstaufen d'Italie." *Revue Historique* 85 (1904): 225–51.

Blake, E. O. "The Formation of the 'Crusade Idea.'" *Journal of Ecclesiastical History* 21 (1970): 11–31.

Blochet, E. "Les relations diplomatiques des Hohenstaufen avec les sultans d'Égypte." *Revue Historique* 80 (1902): 51–64.

Boase, T. S. R. "Recent Developments in Crusading Historiography." *History* 22 (1937): 110–25.

Boehm, L. *Johann von Brienne: König von Jerusalem, Kaiser von Konstantinopel, um 1170–1237.* Dissertation, Heidelberg, 1938.

Bonald, Vicomte de. "Les meridionaux aux croisades." *Revue historique de Toulouse* 14 (1927): 5–22.

Brand, Charles M. "The Fourth Crusade: Some Recent Interpretations." *Medievalia et Humanistica* 12 (1984): 33–45.

Branden van de Reeth, Felix. "Recherches sur la famille de Berthout." *Mémoires couronnés et mémoires des savants étrangers publiés par l'académie royale des sciences et belles-lettres de Bruxelles.* 17:2 (1843–44).

Brem, Ernst. *Papst Gregor IX bis zum Beginn seines Pontifikats.* Heidelberg, 1911.

Brémond, Claude, Jacques LeGoff, and Jean-Claude Schmitt. *L'Exemplum.* Turnhout, 1982.

Briggs, Martin S. *Muhammadan Architecture in Egypt and Palestine.* Oxford, 1924.

Brundage, James A. *Medieval Canon Law and the Crusader.* Madison, Wis., 1969.

———. "Recent Crusade Historiography: Some Observations and Suggestions." *Catholic Historical Review* 49 (1963–64): 493–507.

Buchthal, Hugo. "The Beginnings of Book Illumination in Norman Sicily." *Papers of the British School at Rome* 24 (1956): 78–85.

———. "A school of Miniature Painting in Norman Sicily." In *Late Classical and Medieval Studies in Honor of A. M. Friend, Jr.,* ed. Kurt Weitzmann, 312–39. Princeton, N.J., 1955.

Burdach, Konrad. "Der Kampf Walthers von der Vogelweide gegen Innocenz III and das vierte lateranische Konzil." *Zeitschrift für Kirchengeschichte* 55 (1936): 445–522.

Cahen, Claude. *La Syrie du Nord à l'époque des croisades et la principauté franque d'Antioche.* Paris, 1940.

Cannuyer, C. "La date de rédaction de l'Historia Orientalis de Jacques de Vitry (1160/70–1240), évêque d'Acre." *Revue d'Histoire Ecclésiastique* 78 (1983): 65–72.

Cardini, Franco. "Nella presenza del soldan superba: Bernardo, Francesco, Bonaventura e il superamento spirituale dell'idea di crociata." *Studi Francescani* 71 (1974): 199–250.

Cessi, Roberto. *Le colonie medievali italiane in Oriente.* Bologna, 1942.

———. *L'Italia e le crociate in Terra Santa.* Naples, 1941.

———. *Storia della repubblica di Venezia.* Florence, 1981.

Cheney, Christopher R. "Gervase of Prémontré: A Medieval Letter-writer." In *Medieval Texts and Studies,* ed. C. R. Cheney, 242–76. Oxford, 1973.

———. *Pope Innocent III and England.* Stuttgart, 1976.

Clausen, Johannes. *Papst Honorius III* (1216–1227). Bonn, 1895.

Clifford, Rose C. "England as a Papal Fief: The Role of the Legate in the Early Period, 1216–1241." Ph.D. diss., University of California, Los Angeles, 1972.

Cognasso, Francesco. *Il Piemonte nell'età sveva.* Turin, 1968.

———. *Storia delle crociate.* Milan, 1967.

Cohn, Willy. *Hermann von Salza.* 1930. Reprint. Aalen, 1978.

Constable, Giles. "The Financing of the Crusades in the Twelfth Century." In *Outremer,* ed. B. Z. Kedar, H. E. Mayer, and R. C. Smail, 64–88. Jerusalem, 1982.

Cowdrey, H. E. J. "The Genesis of the Crusades: The Springs of Western Ideas of Holy War." In *The Holy War,* ed. Thomas P. Murphy, 9–32. Columbus, O., 1976.

———. "The Peace of God and the Truce of God in the Eleventh Century." *Past and Present* 46 (1970): 42–67.

Creswell, Keppel A. C. *A Bibliography of the Architecture, Arts, and Crafts of Islam to January 1960.* Cairo, 1961.

Daniel, Norman. *The Arabs and Medieval Europe.* London, 1975.

Davidsohn, Robert. *Storia di Firenze.* 8 vols. Florence, 1956–68.

Delaruelle, E. "The Crusading Idea in Cluniac Literature of the Eleventh Century." In *Cluniac Monasticism in the Central Middle Ages,* ed. Noreen Hunt, 191–216. Hamden, Conn., 1971.

———. *L'idée de croisade au moyen âge.* Turin, 1980.

Delley de Blancmesnil, Alphonse Léon de. *Notice sur quelques anciens titres, suivie de considérations sur les salles des croisades au musée de Versailles.* Paris, 1866.

Delorme, Ferdinand. "Les Espagnols à la bataille de Damiette." *Archivum Franciscanum Historicum* 16 (1923): 245–46.

Dickson, Marcel, and Christiane Dickson. "Le Cardinal Robert de Courson: sa vie." *Archives d'histoire doctrinale et litteraire du moyen âge* 9 (1934): 53–142.

Dirks, Jacob. "Herinnerung an den Kruistocht der Friezen en het jaar 1217." *De Vrije Fries* 16 (1883): 51–59.

Donovan, Joseph. *Pelagius and the Fifth Crusade.* Philadelphia, 1950.

Dopsch, Heinz. "Probleme ständischer Wandlung beim Adel Österreichs, der Steiermark und Salzburgs vornehmlich im 13. Jahrhundert." In *Herrschaft und Stand,* ed. by J. Fleckenstein, 207–53. Göttingen, 1977.

Ehrenkreutz, Andrew. *Saladin.* Albany, 1972.

Epstein, Steven. *Wills and Wealth in Medieval Genoa, 1150–1250.* Cambridge, Mass., 1984.

Erbstösser, Martin. *The Crusades.* New York, 1979.

Erdmann, Carl. *The Origin of the Idea of Crusade.* Princeton, N.J., 1977; translation by Walter Goffart of German edition of 1935.

Eubel, Conrad. *Hierarchia Catholica Medii Aevi.* 3 vols. Padua, 1960.

Evergates, Theodore. *Feudal Society in the Bailliage of Troyes under the Counts of Champagne, 1152–1284.* Baltimore, 1975.

Faivre, J. "Alexandrie." *DHGE,* 2 : 290–369.

Falco, Giorgio. "I preliminari della pace di San Germano." *Archivio della R. Società romana di storia patria* 33 (1910): 441–79.

Flamare, H. de. "La cinquième croisade et les chevaliers teutoniqes en Nivernais." *Bulletin de la société nivernaise,* 3d ser., 2 (1886): 413–35.

Fleckenstein, Josef, ed. *Herrschaft und Stand: Untersuchungen zur Sozialgeschichte im 13. Jahrhundert.* Göttingen, 1977.

Fonseca, Cosimo D. *Medioevo canonicale.* Milan, 1970.

Foreville, Raymonde. *Latran I, II, III, et Latran IV.* Paris, 1965.

Fuller, Thomas. *The Historie of the Holy Warre.* 2d ed. 2 vols. Cambridge, 1640.

Funk, Philipp. *Jakob von Vitry.* Leipzig, 1909.

Gabrieli, Francesco. "The Arabic Historiography of the Crusades." In *Historians of the Middle East,* ed. Bernard Lewis and P. M. Holt, 98–107. London, 1962.

———. "Federico II e la cultura musulmana." *Rivista Storica Italiana* 64 (1952): 5–18.

Gams, Pius B. *Series Episcoporum Ecclesiae Catholicae.* Graz, 1957.

Gayet, Albert. *L'itinéraire des expéditions de Jean de Brienne et de Saint Louis en Égypte et les traces qu'elles y ont laissées.* Paris, 1900.

Ghirardacci, Cherubino. *Della historia di Bologna.* 2 vols. Bologna, 1596–1657.

Gill, Joseph. *Byzantium and the Papacy, 1198–1400.* New Brunswick, N.J., 1979.

Golubovich, Giovanni, ed. *Biblioteca bio-bibliografica della terra santa e dell'oriente francescano.* 9 vols. Quarracchi, 1906–27; n.s., 14 vols. Quarracchi, 1921–39; 3d ser., 2 vols. Quarracchi, 1928–48; 4th ser., ed. M. Roncaglia, 2 vols. to date. Cairo, 1954–.

———. "San Francesco e i Francescani in Damietta, 5 Nov. 1219–5 Feb. 1220." *Studi Francescani* 23 (1926): 307–30.

Gottlob, Adolf. *Die päpstlichen Kreuzzugssteueren des 13. Jahrhunderts.* Heiligenstadt, 1892.

———. "Hat Papst Innocenz III sich das Recht zuerkannt, auch die Laien für Kreuzzugszwecke zu besteueren?" *Görres-Gesellschaft zur Pflege der Wissenschaft im katholischen Deutschland* 16 (1895): 312–19.

Gottschalk, Hans L. *Al-Malik al-Kāmil von Egypten und seine Zeit.* Wiesbaden, 1958.

———. "Die Friedens angebote al-Kāmils von Ägypten an die Kreuzfahrer." *Wiener Zeitschrift für Kunde des Morgenlandes* 51 (1948–50): 64–82.

Gozzadini, Giovanni. *Delle torri gentilizie di Bologna.* Bologna, 1875.

Greven, Joseph. "Frankreich und der fünfte Kreuzzug." *Historisches Jahrbuch* 43 (1923): 15–52.

Grossman, Ronald P. "The Financing of the Crusades." Ph.D. diss., University of Chicago, 1966.

Grousset, René. *Histoire des croisades et du royaume franc de Jerusalem.* 3 vols. Paris, 1934–36.

Guerrieri, Giovanni. *I cavalieri templari nel regno di Sicilia.* Trani, 1909.

Guest, A. R. "The Delta in the Middle Ages." *Journal of the Royal Asiatic Society of Great Britain and Ireland* 64 (1912): 941–80.

Gumblat, H. *Ueber einige Urkunden Friedrichs II für den deutschen Orden.* Innsbruck, 1908.

Haas, Alois. "Aspekte der Kreuzzüge in Geschichte und Geistesleben des mittelalterlichen Deutschland." *Archiv für Kulturgeschichte* 46 (1964): 185–202.

Haas, Robert. "Die Kreuzzugsbewegung und die Ritterorden im Erzbistum Köln während des 13. Jahrhunderts." *Zur Geschichte und Kunst im Erzbistum Köln. Festschrift für Wilhelm Neuss.* 89–101. Düsseldorf, 1960.

Hagen, Friedrich von der. *Minnesinger: Deutsche Liederdichter des zwölften, dreizehnten und vierzehnten Jahrhunderts.* 5 vols. Leipzig, 1838–61.

Hallinger, Kassius. "The Spiritual Life of Cluny in the Early Days." In *Cluniac Monasticism in the Central Middle Ages,* ed. Noreen Hunt, 29–55. Hamden, Conn., 1971.

Hartwig, Otto. *Quellen und Forschungen zur ältesten Geschichte der Stadt Florenz.* 2 vols. Marburg, 1875, and Halle, 1880.

Hassler, Otto. *Ein Heerführer der Kurie am Anfang des 13. Jahrhunderts: Pelagius Galvani, Kardinalbischof von Albano.* Diss., Basel, 1902.

Hauck, Albert. *Kirchengeschichte Deutschlands.* 5 vols. Leipzig, 1911–22.

Heers, Jacques. *Family Clans in the Middle Ages.* Amsterdam, 1977.

———. *Parties and Political Life in the Medieval West.* Amsterdam, 1977.

Hehl, Ernst-Dieter. *Kirche und Krieg im 12. Jahrhundert.* Stuttgart, 1980.

Hessel, Alfred. *Storia della città di Bologna, 1116–1280.* Trans. Gina Fasoli. Bologna, 1975.

Heyck, Eduard. *Genua und seine Marine im Zeitalter der Kreuzzüge.* Innsbruck, 1886.

Hoeck, J. M., and R. J. Loenartz. *Nikolaus-Nektarios von Otranto: Abt von Casole.* Ettel, 1965.

Holt, J. C. *Magna Carta.* Cambridge, 1964.

Hoogeweg, Hermann. "Die Kreuzpredigt des Jahres 1224 in Deutschland mit besonderer Rücksicht auf die Erzdiöcese Köln." *Deutsche Zeitschrift für Geschichtswissenschaft* 4 (1890): 54–74.

————. "Der Kreuzzug von Damiette, 1218–1221." *Mitteilungen des Instituts für Österreichische Geschichtsforschung* 8 (1887): 188–218; 9 (1888): 249–88, 414–47.

Huillard-Bréholles, Jean L. A. *Vie et correspondence de Pierre de la Vigne.* Paris, 1865.

Humphreys, R. Stephen. *From Saladin to the Mongols: The Ayyubids of Damascus, 1193–1260.* Albany, 1979.

Hunt, Noreen. *Cluniac Monasticism in the Central Middle Ages.* Hamden, Conn., 1971.

Huygens, R. B. C. "Les passages des lettres de Jacques de Vitry relatifs à Saint François d'Assise et à ses premières disciples." In *Hommage à Léon Hermann,* ed., 446–53. Brussels, 1960.

Hyde, J. K. *Society and Politics in Medieval Italy.* New York, 1973.

Imkamp, Wilhelm. *Das Kirchenbild Innocenz' III.* Stuttgart, 1983.

Jacopozzi, Nazareno. "Dove sia evvenuta la visita di San Francesco d'Assisi al Sultano Malek El-Kamil." In *Congrès international de Géographie,* 5 (1926): 141–56.

Jahn, Hans. *Die Heereszahlen in den Kreuzzügen.* Diss., Berlin, 1907.

Johns, C. N. *A Guide to Atlit.* Jerusalem, 1947.

Jonin, Pierre. "Le climat de croisade des chansons de geste." *Cahiers de civilisation médiévale* 7 (1964): 279–88.

Jordan, William C. *Louis IX and the Challenge of the Crusade.* Princeton, N.J., 1979.

Kamp, Norbert. *Kirche und Monarchie im staufischen Königreich Sizilien.* 4 vols. Munich, 1971–75.

Kay, Richard. "The Albigensian Twentieth of 1221–3: An Early Chapter in the History of Papal Taxation." *Journal of Medieval History* 6 (1980): 307–15.

Kedar, Benjamin Z. *Crusade and Mission.* Princeton, N.J., 1984.

Kedar, B. Z., H. E. Mayer, and R. C. Smail. *Outremer: Studies in the History of the Crusading Kingdom of Jerusalem.* Jerusalem, 1982.

Kempf, Friedrich. "Das rommersdorfer Briefbuch des 13. Jahrhunderts." *Mitteilungen des Österreichischen Institut für Geschichtsforschung, Ergänzungsband* 12 (1933): 502–71.

Knowles, David. *The Evolution of Medieval Thought.* New York, 1962.

Krautheimer, Richard. *Rome: Profile of a City.* Princeton, N.J., 1980.

Krueger, Hilmar C. "Economic Aspects of Expanding Europe." In *Twelfth Century Europe and the Foundations of Modern Society,* ed. Marshall Clagett et al., 59–76. Madison, Wis., 1966.

Kurz, Franz. *Beiträge zur Geschichte des Landes Oesterreich ob der Enns.* 3 pts. Leipzig, 1905–8.

Kuttner, Stephan, and Antonio García y García. "A New Eyewitness Account of the Fourth Lateran Council." *Traditio* 20 (1964): 115–78.

Labib, Subhi Y. *Handelsgeschichte Aegyptens im Spätmittelalter (1171–1517)*. Wiesbaden, 1964.

Lahrkamp, Helmut. "Mittelalterliche Jerusalemfahrten und Orientreisen westfälischer Pilger und Kreuzritter." *Westfälische Zeitschrift* 106 (1956): 269–346.

————. "Nordwestdeutsche Orientreisen und Jerusalemwallfahrten im Spiegel der Pilgerberichte." *Oriens Christianus* 40 (1956): 113–30.

Lami, Giovanni. *Sanctae ecclesiae Florentinae monumenta*. 3 vols. Florence, 1758.

LaMonte, John L. "Some Problems in Crusading Historiography." *Speculum* 15 (1940): 57–75.

Lane-Poole, Stanley. *A History of Egypt*. 1901. Reprint. New York, 1969.

Lanzoni, Francesco. *Cronotassi dei vescovi di Faenza dai primordi à tutto il secolo XIII*. Faenza, 1918.

Lecler, A. "Les Limousins aux croisades." *Bulletin de la société archéologique et historique du Limousin* 47 (1899): 74–89.

Lecoy de la Marche, A. *La chaire française au moyen âge*. 2d ed. Paris, 1886.

Lemmens, P. L. "De sancto Francisco Christum praedicante coram soltano Aegypti." *Archivum Historicum Franciscanum* 19 (1926): 559–78.

Lewis, Bernard, and P. M. Holt. *Historians of the Middle East*. London, 1962.

Linehan, Peter. "Documento español sobre la quinta cruzada." *Hispania Sacra* 20 (1967): 177–82.

Longnon, Jean. *Les compagnons de Villehardouin: Recherches sur les croisés de la quatrième croisade*. Geneva, 1978.

Lopez, R. S. *Storia delle colonie genovesi nel mediterraneo*. Bologna, 1938.

Lunt, William E. *Financial Relations of the Papacy with England to 1327*. Cambridge, Mass., 1939.

McArdle, Frank. *Altopascio*. Cambridge, 1978.

Makhouly, N., and C. N. Johns. *Guide to Acre*. 2d ed. Jerusalem, 1946.

Maleczek, Werner. *Papst und Kardinalskolleg von 1191 bis 1216*. Vienna, 1984.

Mancini, Augusto. *Storia di Lucca*. Lucca, 1975.

Mansilla, Demetrio. "El Cardenal hispaño Pelayo Gaitan (1206–1230)." *Anthologica Annua* 1 (1953): 11–66.

Manrique, Angel. *Cistercensium seu verius ecclesiasticorum annalium*. 4 vols. Farnsborough, England, 1970.

Martini, Giuseppe. "Innocenzo III ed il finanziamento delle crociate." *Archivio della R. deputazione romana di storia patria* 67 (1944): 309–35.

Marullo di Condojanni, Carlo. *La Sicilia ed il sovrano militare ordine di Malta*. Messina, 1953.

Mayer, Hans Eberhard. *Bibliographie zur Geschichte der Kreuzzüge*. 2d ed. Hannover, 1965.

————. "Der Brief Kaiser Friedrich Barbarossas an Saladin vom Jahre 1188." *Deutsches Archiv* 14 (1958): 488–94.

————. *The Crusades*. Trans. John Gillingham. Oxford, 1972.

————. "Literaturbericht über die Geschichte der Kreuzzüge." *Historische Zeitschrift*, Sonderheft 3 (1968): 641–731.

Mémoires pour servir de preuves à l'histoire écclésiastique et civile de Bretagne. Ed. Hyacinthe Morice. 3 vols. Paris, 1742–46.

Métais, Charles. "Croisés chartrains et Dunois." *Bulletin de la société a dunoise* 8 (1894–96): 198–209.

Meyer, Gisela. "Untersuchungen zu Herrschaft und Stand in der Grafschaft Jülich im 13. Jahrhundert." In *Herrschaft und Stand,* ed. J. Fleckenstein, 137–56. Göttingen, 1977.

Miccoli, G. "La crociata dei fanciulli." *Studi Medievali,* 3d ser., 2 (1961): 407–43.

Monti, G. M. *L'espansione mediterranea del mezzogiorno d'Italia e di Sicilia.* Bologna, 1942.

———. *L'Italia e le crociate in terra santa.* Naples, 1940.

Moore, John. "Count Baldwin IX of Flanders, Philip Augustus, and the Papal Power." *Speculum* 37 (1962): 79–89.

———. "Pope Innocent III and His Relations with the French Princes." Ph.D. diss., Johns Hopkins University, 1960.

Morgan, Margaret. *The Chronicle of Ernoul.* London, 1973.

Morris, Wentworth S. "A Crusader's testament." *Speculum* 27 (1952): 197–98.

Murphy, Thomas P. *The Holy War.* Columbus, O., 1976.

Neyen, Auguste. *Histoire de la ville de Vianden et de ses comtes.* Luxembourg, 1851.

Norgate, Kate. *John Lackland.* 1902. Reprint. New York, 1970.

Orlova, G., and V. Zenkovich. "Erosion of the Shores of the Nile Delta." *Geoforum* 18 (1974): 68–72.

Osheim, Duane J. *An Italian Lordship: The Bishopric of Lucca in the Late Middle Ages.* Berkeley, 1977.

Otway-Ruthven, Annette. *A History of Medieval Ireland.* London, 1968.

Painter, Sidney. *The Reign of King John.* Baltimore, 1949.

Paulus, N. "Die Werkung der weltlichen Berufe im Mittelalter." *Historisches Jahrbuch* 32 (1911): 725–55.

Pellegrini, A. "Le crociate in terra santa e la parte che vi ebbero i Lucchesi." *Studi e documenti di storia e diritto* 19 (1898): 379–91.

Pelliot, P. "Deux passages de *La Prophetie de Hanna, fils d'Isaac.*" *Académie des Inscriptions et Belles-Lettres, Mémoires* 44 (1951): 73–96.

Pissard, Hippolyte. *La guerre sainte en pays chrétien.* Paris, 1912.

Pixton, Paul B. "Die Anwerbung des Heeres Christi: Prediger des fünften Kreuzzug in Deutschland." *Deutsches Archiv* 34 (1978): 166–91.

Poggiaspalla, Ferminio. "La chiesa e la partecipazione dei chierici alla guerra nella legislazione conciliare fino alle decretali di Gregorio IX." *Rivista di storia del diritto italiano* 32 (1959): 233–47.

Powell, James M. "Crusading by Royal Command: Monarchy and Crusade in the Kingdom of Sicily." In *Potere, società e popolo tra età normanna ed età sveva* (1187–1230), 131–46. Bari, 1983.

———. "Francesco d'Assisi e la Quinta Crociata: Una Missione di Pace." *Schede Medievali* 4 (1983): 68–77.

———. "Honorius III and the Leadership of the Crusade." *Catholic Historical Review* 63 (1977): 521–36.

———. "Honorius III's 'Sermo in Dedicatione Ecclesie Lateranensis' and the Historical-Liturgical Traditions of the Lateran." *Archivum Historiae Pontificiae* 21 (1983): 195–209.

————. "The Papacy and the Early Franciscans." *Franciscan Studies* 36 (1976): 248–62.

————. "The Prefatory Letters to the Sermons of Pope Honorius III and the Reform of Preaching." *Rivista di storia della chiesa in Italia* 33 (1979): 95–104.

Pratelli, F. *Storia di Poggibonsi.* 2 vols. Poggibonsi, 1929–38.

Prawer, Joshua. *Histoire du royaume latin de Jerusalem.* 2 vols. Paris, 1969–70.

Queller, Donald. *The Fourth Crusade: The Conquest of Constantinople, 1201–1204.* Philadelphia, 1977.

Queller, Donald, and Irene Katele. "Attitudes toward the Venetians in the Fourth Crusade: the Western Sources." *International History Review* 4 (1982): 1–36.

Raedts, Peter. "The Children's Crusade of 1212." *Journal of Medieval History* 3 (1977): 279–333.

Rey, E. G. "Excavations at Pilgrims' Castle ('Atlīt)." *Quarterly of the Department of Antiquities in Palestine* 1 (1932): 111–49.

Riant, Paul. *Expéditions et pèlerinages des scandinaves en terre sainte au temps des croisades.* Paris, 1865.

Riley-Smith, Jonathan. "The Crusade as an Act of Love." *History* 65 (1980): 177–92.

————. *The Knights of St. John in Jerusalem and Cyprus.* Vol. 1. London, 1967.

————. "The Motives of the Earliest Crusaders and the Settlement of Latin Palestine, 1095–1100." *English Historical Review* 98 (1983): 721–36.

Röhricht, Reinhold. *Beiträge zur Geschichte der Kreuzzüge.* 2 vols. Berlin, 1874–78.

————. *Bibliotheca geographica Palestinae.* New ed. Jerusalem, 1963.

————. *Die Deutschen im Heiligen Lande.* Innsbruck, 1894.

————. *Geschichte der Kreuzzüge im Umriss.* Innsbruck, 1898.

————. "Die Kreuzpredigten gegen den Islam." *Zeitschrift für Kirchengeschichte* 6 (1884): 550–72.

————. *Studien zur Geschichte des fünften Kreuzzuges.* 1891. Reprint. Aalen, 1968.

Rösener, Werner. "Ministerialität und niederadelige Ritterschaft im Herrschaftsbereich der Markgrafen von Baden vom 11. bis zum 14. Jahrhundert." In *Herrschaft und Stand,* ed. Josef Fleckenstein, 40–136. Göttingen, 1977.

Roger, Paul. *Bibliothèque historique, monumentale, ecclésiastique et littéraire de la Picardie et de l'Artois.* Amiens, 1844.

————. *La noblesse de France aux croisades.* Paris, 1845.

Roncaglia, Martiniano. *St. Francis of Assisi and the Middle East.* 2d ed. Cairo, 1957.

————. "San Francesco d'Assisi in Oriente." *Studi Francescani* 50 (1953): 97–106.

Roncioni, Raffaello. *Istorie Pisane.* 4 vols. 1844–45. Reprint. Bologna, 1972.

Roscher, Helmut. *Innocenz III und die Kreuzzüge.* Göttingen, 1969.

Rossi, Teofilo, and Ferdinando Rossi. *Storia di Torino.* Turin, 1914.

Rossini, Carlo C. "Il libro dello pseudo-Clemente e la crociata di Damietta." *Rivista degli studi orientali* 9 (1921–23): 32–35.

Rousset, Paul. *Histoire des croisades.* 2d ed. Paris, 1978.

———. *Les origines et les caractères de la première croisade.* Geneva, 1945.

Rudt de Collenberg, W. H. "Les Ibelin aux XIIIe et XIVe siècles." In *Familles de l'Orient latin,* ed. W. H. Rudt de Collenberg. London, 1983.

Rüdebusch, Dieter. *Der Anteil Niedersachsens an den Kreuzzügen und Heidenfahrten.* Hildesheim, 1972.

Runciman, Steven. *A History of the Crusades.* 3 vols. Cambridge, 1966.

Salmon, Georges. "Rapport sur une mission à Damiette." *Bulletin de l'institut français d'archéologie orientale* 2 (1901): 71–89.

Sayers, Jane E. *Papal Government and England during the Pontificate of Honorius III.* Cambridge, 1984.

Schaller, Hans Martin. *Kaiser Friedrich II.* Göttingen, 1964.

———. "Die Kanzlei Kaiser Friedrichs II: Ihr Personal und ihr Sprachstil." *Archiv für Diplomatik* 3 (1957): 207–86.

Schlumberger, Gustav. "Une Prise de possession chrétienne de la ville de Jerusalem en l'an 1229." In *Byzance et croisades,* ed. G. Schlumberger, 337–60. Paris, 1927.

Schneyer, Johann Baptist. *Geschichte der katholischen Predigt.* Freiburg, 1969.

Schwerin, Ursula. *Die Aufrufe des Päpste zur Befreiung des Heiligen Landes.* Berlin, 1937.

Sempe, L. "Vocation." *DTC,* 15:3148–81.

Setton, Kenneth M. *The History of the Crusades.* 5 vols. to date. Madison, Wis., 1969–.

———. *The Papacy and the Levant.* 4 vols. to date. Philadelphia, 1974–.

Siberry, Elizabeth. *Criticism of Crusading, 1095–1274.* Oxford, 1985.

———. "Missionaries and Crusaders, 1095–1274: Opponents or Allies?" In *The Church and War,* Studies in Church History, 20:103–10. Oxford, 1983.

Siedschlag, Beatrice N. *English Participation in the Crusades, 1150–1220.* Ph.D. diss., Privately published, Menasha, Wis., 1939.

Slessarev, V. *Prester John: The Letter and the Legend.* Minneapolis, 1959.

Smail, R. C. *Crusading Warfare (1097–1193).* Cambridge, 1967.

Smet, J.-J. de. "Mémoire sur Baudouin IX, comte de Flandre et de Hainault, et sur les chevaliers belges à la cinquième croisade." *Académie royale des sciences, des lettres, et des beaux arts de Belgique, Brussels, Memoires,* 31 (1856).

Spreckelmeyer, Goswin. *Das Kreuzzugslied des lateinischen Mittelalters.* Munich, 1974.

Sweeney, James R. "Hungary in the Crusades, 1169–1218." *International History Review* 3 (1981): 467–81.

Tangl, Georgine. *Studien zum Register Innocenz III.* Weimar, 1929.

———. *Die Teilnehmer an den allgemeinen Konzilien des Mittelalters.* Cologne, 1969.

Thouzellier, Christine. "La Legation en Lombardie du Cardinal Hugolin (1221): Une épisode de la cinquième croisade." *Revue d'histoire ecclésiastique* 45 (1950): 508–42.

Throop, Palmer. *Criticism of the Crusade.* 1940. Reprint. Philadelphia, 1975.

Tillmann, Helene. "Ricerche sull'origine dei membri del collegio cardinalizio nel XII secolo." *Rivista di storia della chiesa in Italia* 29 (1975): 363–402.

Tronci, Paolo. *Memorie istoriche della città di Pisa.* 1682. Reprint. Bologna, 1967.

Umar Tusun. *La géographie de l'Égypte à l'époque arabe.* Cairo, 1926.

Underhill, Frances A. "Papal Legates to England in the Reign of Henry III (1216–1272)." Ph.D. diss., Indiana University, 1965.

Vachez, Antoine. *Les familles chevaleresque du Lyonnais, Forez, et Beaujolais aux croisades.* Lyon, 1875.

Van Cleve, Thomas C. "The Crusade of Frederick II." In *A History of the Crusades,* ed. Kenneth Setton, 2:429–62. Madison, Wis., 1969.

———. *The Emperor Frederick II of Hohenstaufen.* Oxford, 1972.

———. "The Fifth Crusade." In *A History of the Crusades,* ed. Kenneth Setton, 2:377–428. Madison, Wis., 1969.

Vasina, Augusto. "Le crociate nel mondo emiliano-romagnolo." *Deputazione di storia patria per le province di Romagna, Atti e memorie,* n.s., 23 (1972): 11–44.

———. *Le crociate nel mondo italiano.* Bologna, 1973.

Verbruggen, J. F. *The Art of Warfare in Western Europe during the Middle Ages.* Amsterdam, 1977.

Vergottini, Giovanni de. *Studi sulla legislazione imperiale di Federico II in Italia.* Milan, 1952.

Vicaire, M.-H. *St. Dominic and His Times.* New York, 1964.

"Vie du cardinal Robert de Courson." *Revue historique de l'Ouest* 10 (1894): 352–434.

Villari, Pasquale. *I primi due secoli della storia di Firenze.* Florence, 1905.

Vogel, Christian Daniel. *Beschreibung des Herzogthums Nassau.* Wiesbaden, 1843.

Volpe, Gioacchino. *Lunigiana medievale.* Florence, 1923.

———. *Toscana medievale.* Florence, 1965.

Waas, Adolf. *Geschichte der Kreuzzüge.* 2 vols. Freiburg, 1956.

Waley, Daniel. *Italian City Republics.* New York, 1969.

Warren, W. L. *King John.* Berkeley, 1961.

Welter, J.-Th. *L'Exemplum dans la literature religieuse et didactique du moyen âge.* Paris, 1927.

Wentzlaff-Eggebert, Friedrich-Wilhelm. *Kreuzzugsdichtung des Mittelalters.* Berlin, 1960.

Wojtecki, Dieter. *Studien zur Personengeschichte des deutschen Ordens in 13. Jahrhundert.* Wiesbaden, 1971.

Zarncke, Friedrich. "Zur Sage vom Priester Johannes." *Neues Archiv* 2 (1877): 611–15.

Zur Geschichte und Kunst im Erzbistum Köln: Festschrift für Wilhelm Neuss. Düsseldorf, 1960.

INDEX

THE MIDDLE AGES

Edward Peters, General Editor

Law, Church, and Society: Essays in Honor of Stephan Kuttner. Edited by Robert Somerville and Kenneth Pennington

The Fourth Crusade: The Conquest of Constantinople, 1201–1204. Donald E. Queller

The Magician, the Witch, and the Law. Edward Peters

Daily Life in the World of Charlemagne. Pierre Riché. Translated, with an Introduction, by Jo Ann McNamara

Repression of Heresy in Medieval Germany. Richard Kieckhefer

The Royal Forests of Medieval England. Charles R. Young

Popes, Lawyers, and Infidels: The Church and the Non-Christian World, 1250–1550. James Muldoon

Heresy and Authority in Medieval Europe. Edited, with an Introduction, by Edward Peters

Women in Frankish Society: Marriage and the Cloister, 500 to 900. Suzanne Fonay Wemple

The English Parliament in the Middle Ages. Edited by R. G. Davies and J. H. Denton

Rhinoceros Bound: Cluny in the Tenth Century. Edited, with an Introduction, by Edward Peters

On the Threshold of Exact Science: Selected Writings of Anneliese Maier on Late Medieval Natural Philosophy. Edited and translated by Steven D. Sargent

Miracles and the Medieval Mind: Theory, Record, and Event, 1000–1215. Benedicta Ward

The Chronicles of Theophanes: An English Translation of anni mundi *6095–6305 (A.D. 602–813)*. Translated, with an Introduction, by Harry Turtledove

The English Medieval Landscape. Edited by Leonard Cantor

Dante's Italy and Other Essays. Charles T. Davis

Maurice's Strategikon: Handbook of Byzantine Military Strategy. Translated by George T. Dennis

The Republic of St. Peter: The Birth of the Papal State, 680–825. Thomas F. X. Noble

Pope and Bishops: The Papal Monarchy in the Twelfth and Thirteenth Centuries. Kenneth Pennington

The Origins of Courtliness: Civilizing Trends and the Formation of Courtly Ideals, 939–1210. C. Stephen Jaeger

The Conversion of Western Europe, 350–750. Edited by J. N. Hillgarth

From Servitude to Freedom: Manumission in the Sénonais in the Thirteenth Century. William Chester Jordan

Ransoming Captives in Crusader Spain: The Order of Merced on the Christian-Islamic Frontier. James William Brodman

Aristocracy in Provence: The Rhône Basin at the Dawn of the Carolingian Age. Patrick J. Geary

Meister Eckhart: Thought and Language. Frank Tobin

Dino Campagni's Chronicle of Florence. Translated, with an Introduction, by Daniel Bornstein

Anatomy of a Crusade, 1213–1221. James M. Powell

The First Crusade and the Idea of Crusading. Jonathan Riley-Smith